BUILDING A V...
FOR THE TES...
FOREIGI...

The Test of English as a Foreign Language™ (TOEFL®) is among the most important tests used around the world, to assess English language proficiency for academic admissions and placement decisions, and to guide English language instruction. This landmark volume provides a detailed description and analysis of Educational Testing Service's research and development efforts to develop a major revision of the TOEFL. The result is a book that serves as a case study of test design drawing upon theory in the complex domain of English language proficiency while attempting to meet standards of educational measurement.

Building a Validity Argument for the Test of English as a Foreign Language™ is distinctive in its attempt to develop a coherent story of the rationale for a test or its revision, explain the research and development process, and provide the results of the validation process. Through its treatment of one test, it expands on and tests principles and approaches to educational measurement, providing an in-depth, integrated perspective on the overall process of test revision. Moreover, because the conceptual foundation and history are presented alongside the empirical studies and validity argument, these sometimes disparate areas are presented in a way that demonstrates their connections—an approach that represents a departure from, or extension of, conventional materials on test revision.

This volume is particularly relevant for professionals and graduate students in educational measurement, applied linguistics, and second language acquisition as well as anyone interested in assessment issues.

ESL & APPLIED LINGUISTICS PROFESSIONAL SERIES

Eli Hinkel, Series Editor

Visit www.routledge.com for additional information on titles in the ESL & Applied Linguistics Professional Series

BUILDING A VALIDITY ARGUMENT FOR THE TEST OF ENGLISH AS A FOREIGN LANGUAGE™

Edited by

Carol A. Chapelle
Iowa State University, USA

Mary K. Enright
Educational Testing Service, Princeton, USA

Joan M. Jamieson
Northern Arizona University, USA

Routledge
Taylor & Francis Group

NEW YORK AND LONDON

First published 2008
by Routledge
270 Madison Ave, New York, NY 10016

Simultaneously published in the UK
by Routledge
2 Park Square, Milton Park, Abingdon, Oxon OX14 4RN

Routledge is an imprint of the Taylor & Francis Group, an informa business

Typeset in Sabon by EvS Communication Networx, Inc.
Printed and bound in the United States of America on acid-free paper by Walsworth Publishing Company, Marceline, MO

Library of Congress Cataloging-in-Publication Data

Building a Validity argument for the Test of English as a Foreign Language™ / edited by Carol A. Chapelle, Mary K. Enright, Joan M. Jamieson.
p. cm. -- (ESL & applied linguistics professional series)
Includes bibliographical references and index.
ISBN 978-0-8058-5455-8 (alk. paper) -- ISBN 978-0-8058-5456-5 (pbk. : alk. paper)
1. Test of English as a Foreign Language--Validity. 2. English language--Study and teaching--Foreign speakers. 3. English language--Ability testing. I. Chapelle, Carol A., 1955- II. Enright, Mary. III. Jamieson, Joan.
PE1128.A2.B768 2008
428.0076--dc22
2007023704

British Library Cataloguing in Publication Data
A catalogue record for this book is available from the British Library

ISBN 10: 0-8058-5455-X (hbk)
ISBN 10: 0-8058-5456-8 (pbk)
ISBN 10: 0-203-93789-9 (ebk)

ISBN 13: 978-0-8058-5455-8 (hbk)
ISBN 13: 978-0-8058-5456-5 (pbk)
ISBN 13: 978-0-203-93789-1 (ebk)

For
Jim and Annie
David, Chris, and Kate
Rita, George, and Nora

Contents

Preface

The three of us met sometime during the 1990s at the many meetings that were held as part of what was then called the TOEFL 2000 project at Educational Testing Service in the United States. The project entailed discussion and research studies aimed at the ultimate development of a new Test of English as a Foreign Language™ (TOEFL®) and validation of its use for admissions decisions at English-medium universities. Because of the high-stakes decisions involved, development and validation of the new TOEFL proceeded according to accepted professional practices, as outlined in the *Standards for Educational and Psychological Testing* (American Educational Research Association, American Psychological Association, & National Council on Measurement in Education, 1999) and the *ETS Standards for Quality and Fairness* (Educational Testing Service, 2002). These sources provide a basis for conceptualizing test design and validation in view of the intended interpretation and use of the test. On the surface, the two anchors—interpretation and use—appear to provide guidance for specifying the necessary test tasks and planning validation research. However, the project team found it extremely difficult to design tasks and plan research for the complex domain of academic English language ability. Moreover, specifying the interpretation and use in the terms available to test developers throughout the 1990s did not point to a clear means of synthesizing research into a validity argument.

Synthesizing the products from the TOEFL research and development efforts into a validity argument was the challenge we faced when we embarked on this book project. By 2002, when the TOEFL 2000 teams had completed their work, a wealth of knowledge and research results pertaining to the new TOEFL had been produced. But how could this work be represented in a way that argued for the validity of TOEFL interpretation and use? The guidelines all advocated gathering a lot of evidence pertaining to validity, but they did not clearly express what should be done with it once gathered. We spent considerable time over the past 5 years attempting to sort out what to do with the validity evidence.

The result is a book that serves as a case study of test design drawing upon theory in the complex domain of English language proficiency while attempting to meet standards of educational measurement. We felt that an examination of this process would be informative to the field because it reveals how tensions between theoretical perspectives in applied linguistics and educational measurement were resolved operationally. Another book could be written about the operational issues of language test delivery over the Internet, but in this book we have set aside these complex issues to focus on the question of how validity evidence was gathered and formulated into a validity argument for the new TOEFL. Because this project aimed to develop a new TOEFL, the volume describes the TOEFL validity argument from a developmental perspective rather than as a summative evaluation. The final chapter outlines the validity argument that supports TOEFL interpretation and use at the time that the test was beginning to be used. The final chapter of the book, of course, will not prove to be the final chapter of the TOEFL validity argument, which will be ongoing as the TOEFL is used and more evidence pertaining to validity appears.

Carol Chapelle, Mary Enright, and Joan Jamieson
December 1, 2006

REFERENCES

American Educational Research Association, American Psychological Association, & National Council on Measurement in Education. (1999). *Standards for educational and psychological testing.* Washington, DC: American Educational Research Association.
Educational Testing Service. (2002). *The ETS standards for quality and fairness.* Princeton, NJ: Author.

Acknowledgments

TOEFL® iBT is the result of dedicated effort on the part of many language-testing and educational measurement experts, whose work is reflected in the references cited throughout this book. But here the editors and chapter authors wish to acknowledge the unrecognized contributions of so many others to the development of TOEFL iBT and the preparation of this book.

First we wish to thank Daniel Eignor, who, as ETS technical editor, synthesized the comments of many other reviewers and provided his own thorough reviews of many of chapters. We received helpful comments from all the following on one or more of our chapters: Lyle Bachman, Isaac Bejar, Alister Cumming, Carol Dwyer, Walter Emmerich, Phil Everson, Mary Fowles, Michael Kane, Anna Kubiak, Yong-Won Lee, Bob Mislevy, Kathy O'Neill, Liane Patsula, Willisa Roland, and Michael Zieky. We are also grateful to Kim Fryer for her help in copyediting and manuscript preparation.

In addition to contributing materials to many of the chapters and reviewing the chapters, assessment specialist leaders oversaw the development of the test and task specifications as well as the assessment tasks and test forms for prototyping and field studies and coordinated the scoring of test takers' responses. These leaders included Natalie Chen, Rob French, Robbie Kantor, Pam Mollaun, Susan Nissan, Mary Schedl, Barb Suomi, and Tina Wright.

The computer-based prototypes of new TOEFL tasks and tests were developed ably by Tom Florek and Debbie Pisacreta and usability testing was conducted by Holly Knott, Mary Lou Lennon, and Peggy Redman.

Pat Carey, Marna Golub-Smith, Ida Lawrence, and Cathy Wendler provided guidance and direction on the design of the field studies.

Over time, many different people contributed to management of data collection for the studies reported in this book. Among the staff contributing to data collection were Sandy Cool, Kathy Johnson, Tony Ostrander, Kathy Riedel, Donna Sylvester, and Ann Wydra.

ETS statistical and psychometric staff members not only conducted many of the analyses reported in the book but were also very responsive to repeated requests from authors to "do just one more analysis." Among those who carefully analyzed the data were Jill Carey, Fred Cline, Lisa Gawlick, Xiaoying Ma, Dianna Marr, Cindy Nguyen, Cathy Trapani, and Yanling Zang.

We also wish to acknowledge the contributions of TOEFL management staff at ETS who have actively supported the TOEFL revision project over the years. These efforts were brought to fruition in 2005 under the leadership of Mari Pearlman.

Finally, we wish to thank the TOEFL Board for providing financial support for the preparation of this book.

Contributors

Paul Angelis
Southern Illinois University, USA

Brent Bridgeman
Educational Testing Service, Princeton, USA

Carol A. Chapelle
Iowa State University, USA

Daniel Eignor
Educational Testing Service, Princeton, USA

Mary K. Enright
Educational Testing Service, Princeton, USA

William Grabe
Northern Arizona University, USA

Kristen Huff
The College Board, New York, USA

Joan M. Jamieson
Northern Arizona University, USA

Robert N. Kantor
Educational Testing Service, Princeton, USA

Antony John Kunnan
California State University, USA

Yong-Won Lee
Educational Testing Service, Princeton, USA

Pamela Mollaun
Educational Testing Service, Princeton, USA

Susan Nissan
Educational Testing Service, Princeton, USA

Mari Pearlman
Educational Testing Service, Princeton, USA

Donald E. Powers
Educational Testing Service, Princeton, USA

Mary Schedl
Educational Testing Service, Princeton, USA

Carol A.Taylor
Biola University, La Mirada, USA

Lin Wang
Educational Testing Service, Princeton, USA

Test Score Interpretation and Use

Carol A. Chapelle
Mary K. Enright
Joan M. Jamieson

Test users and researchers alike see test publishers as responsible for providing defensible and clear interpretations of test scores and encouraging their appropriate use. Accordingly, the TOEFL® revision was intended to result in test scores whose interpretation was transparent to test users and supported by "an overall evaluative judgment of the degree to which evidence and theoretical rationales support the adequacy and appropriateness" of their interpretation and use (Messick, 1989, p. 13). Attempting to develop theoretical rationales, designers of the new TOEFL began by exploring how theories of language proficiency would serve as a basis for test design. This chapter summarizes issues that arose during this process, explains how the test designers shifted focus to the validity argument that justifies score interpretation and use to resolve these issues, and outlines the interpretive argument that underlies the TOEFL validity argument.

LANGUAGE PROFICIENCY

Members of the TOEFL revision project believed that language proficiency theory should form the basis for score interpretation. This belief was consistent with a view prevalent in educational measurement in the early 1990s that a theoretical construct should serve as the basis for score interpretation for a large-scale test with high-stakes outcomes (e.g., Messick, 1994). However, articulating an appropriate theory of language proficiency is a divisive issue in language assessment: Agreement does not exist on a single best way to define language proficiency to serve as a defensible basis for score interpretation. Discussion of how to do so for the TOEFL drew on and contributed to an ongoing conversation in the field of language assessment (e.g., Bachman, 1990; Bachman & Palmer, 1996; Chalhoub-Deville, 1997, 2001; Chapelle, 1998; McNamara, 1996; Oller, 1979). Most language assessment specialists would agree that there is no single best way of defining language proficiency that the TOEFL project could adopt.

Two Common Beliefs

Language assessment specialists would also tend to agree on at least two other issues. One is that limiting a view of language proficiency to a trait such as knowledge of grammatical structures, knowledge of vocabulary, or reading is seldom an appropriate basis for the types of interpretations that tests users want to make. Instead, proficiency typically needs to be conceptualized more broadly as the ability to use a complex of knowledge and processes to achieve particular goals rather than narrowly as knowledge of linguistic form or a skill. Such abilities would include a combination of linguistic knowledge (e.g., grammar and vocabulary) and strategies required to accomplish communication goals. In other words, the knowledge of language is not irrelevant, but it is not enough to serve as a basis for interpreting test scores because test performance involves more than a direct reflection of knowledge. From the earliest modern conceptualization of language proficiency (e.g., Canale & Swain, 1980), some sort of strategies or processes of language use have been argued to be essential (Bachman, 1990; McNamara, 1996).

Most applied linguists would also agree that language proficiency must be defined in a way that takes into account its contexts of use because contexts of language use significantly affect the nature of language ability. In other words, the specific linguistic knowledge (e.g., grammar and vocabulary) and the strategies required to accomplish goals depend on the context in which language performance takes place. As Cummins (1983) pointed out, second language learners can be proficient in some contexts (e.g., where they discuss music and movies with their peers orally in English), but they lack proficiency in other contexts (e.g., where they need to give an oral presentation about Canadian history to their classmates in English). A conceptualization of language proficiency that recognizes one trait (or even a complex of abilities) as responsible for performance across contexts fails to account for the variation in performance observed across these different contexts of language use. As a consequence, virtually any current conceptualization of language proficiency in language assessment attempts to incorporate the context of language use in some form (Bachman & Palmer, 1996; Chalhoub-Deville, 1997; Chapelle, 1998; McNamara, 1996; Norris, Brown, Hudson, & Bonk, 2002; Skehan, 1998).

These two points of consensus about language proficiency constituted the beliefs held by TOEFL project members throughout discussion of the theoretical construct that should underlie score interpretation. Both of these beliefs had a common implication—that the new TOEFL should include more complex, performance-type assessment tasks than previous versions of the TOEFL had. While providing some common ground among participants, these beliefs were difficult to reconcile.

Two Approaches to Test Design and Score Interpretation

In educational measurement in the 1980s and 1990s, two different conceptual frameworks emerged for test design and score interpretation. Messick (1994) characterized these opposing frameworks as competency-centered and task-centered. In competency-centered assessment, a theoretical construct of language proficiency underlies score interpretation. As illustrated in Figure 1.1, the construct is conceptually distinct from the observed performance and is linked to the performance by *inference*.[1] A construct is a proficiency, ability, or characteristic of an individual that has been inferred from observed behavioral consistencies and that can be meaningfully interpreted. The construct derives its meaning, in part, from an associated theoretical network of hypotheses that can be empirically evaluated. The competency-centered perspective was therefore consistent with the belief held by the members of the TOEFL project that the type of inference to serve as the basis for score interpretation should be one that links observed performance with a theoretical construct of ability consisting of knowledge and processes.

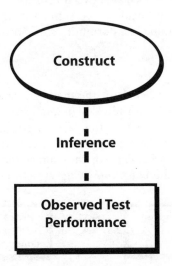

FIG. 1.1   Inference in competency-centered assessment.

From a task-centered perspective, the basis for score interpretation is the context of interest to the test user, and therefore this perspective is consistent with the second point of consensus among language assessment specialists—that the context of language use must be taken into account in conceptualizing score interpretation. From the perspective of performance testing, Wiggins (1993) claimed that judgments about whether students have the capacity to put their knowledge to use can be made only from observation of their performance on tasks that require students to perform in highly contextualized situations that are as faithful as possible to criterion situations. Answers are not so much correct or incorrect in real life as apt or inappropriate, justified or unjustified—in context. A task-centered approach to assessment focuses on identifying the types of tasks deemed important in the real world context and developing test tasks to simulate real world tasks as much as possible within the constraints of the test situation (Messick, 1994). Because the context in which performance occurs serves as a basis for score interpretation, the inference is the link between performance on test tasks and performance on tasks in the context of interest. See Figure 1.2.

Because of the different inferences assumed by competency-centered and task-centered testing, the two perspectives generate two separate and seemingly incompatible frameworks for score interpretation. Assuming different inferences underlying score interpretation, each approach draws on different types of evidence for justifying the inferences that support score interpretation. Whereas researchers working within competency-centered testing look for evidence supporting the inferential link between test scores and a theoretical construct (e.g., textual competence), those working in task-centered testing establish the correspondence between test tasks and those of interest in the relevant contexts (e.g., reading and summarizing introductory academic prose from textbooks alone in a dormitory study room).

Difficult Issues

The presuppositions and beliefs of the members of the TOEFL project fell across the two perspectives for test design and interpretation as summarized in Table 1.1. The presupposition that a theoretical construct of language proficiency should form the basis of score interpretation is consistent with competency-centered assessment, which assumes that theoretical constructs should be defined as underlying knowledge structures and processes that are

FIG. 1.2   Inference in task-centered assessment.

responsible for performance across a wide range of contexts. The belief that the construct should consist of a complex set of abilities is also encompassed within the conceptual framework of competency-centered testing even though complex, goal-oriented abilities or strategies are necessarily connected to contexts of language use. They are therefore not as universally applicable as the traits that underlie score interpretation in competency-based testing, but such abilities are theoretical constructs and therefore do not fit within task-centered assessment. The belief that context influences language performance and that it must therefore be included in score interpretation fits within a task-centered approach.

Test designers' discussion of language proficiency resulted in something of a stalemate that required them to look to a more inclusive and detailed approach for the justification of test score interpretation and use. A unified view of validity, in which multiple types of validity evidence were seen as necessary to support the interpretation and use of test scores, was well established in the field by 1990 (e.g., Cronbach, 1988; Messick, 1989). But only recently have researchers in educational measurement considered in detail how this evidence can be synthesized into an integrated evaluative judgment (Messick) or validity argument (Cronbach) for the proposed interpretation and use of test scores. Such an approach is being developed by researchers such as Mislevy, Steinberg, and Almond (2002, 2003) and Kane (Kane, 2001; Kane, Crooks, & Cohen, 1999). Their conceptual approach entails developing two types of arguments: First, an interpretive argument is laid out for justifying test score interpretation. An alternative to defining a construct such as language proficiency alone, an interpretive argument outlines the inferences and assumptions that underlie score interpretation and use. Second, a validity argument is ultimately built through critical analysis of the plausibility of the theoretical rationales and empirical data that constitute support for the inferences of the interpretive argument.

TABLE 1.1
Intersection between Beliefs about the Basis for Score Interpretation and Approaches to Test Design

The Basis for Score Interpretation	Measurement Perspective	
	Competency-centered	Task-centered
1. Should be a theoretical construct of language proficiency that accounts for language performance across a wide range of contexts	X	
2. Should include complex processes and strategies to adapt performance to different contexts	X	
3. Should take into account relevant contexts		X

INTERPRETIVE ARGUMENTS

The retrospective account of the TOEFL project given in this volume is based upon the current view that a validity argument supporting test score interpretation and use should be based on an overall interpretive argument. Development of such an interpretative argument requires at least three conceptual building blocks. The first is a structure for making an interpretive argument. More specifically tied to the TOEFL interpretive argument, the second requirement is a means of including both the competency and the task-based perspectives as grounds for score interpretation and use. The third is a conceptualization of the types of inferences that can serve in an interpretive argument for test score interpretation and use.

Argument Structure

Current approaches toward developing interpretive and validity arguments (Kane, 1992; 2001; Mislevy et al., 2002, 2003) are based on Toulmin's (1958, 2003) description of informal or practical arguments, which characterize reasoning in nonmathematical fields such as law, sociology, or literary analysis. Informal arguments are used to build a case for a particular conclusion by constructing a chain of reasoning in which the relevance and accuracy of observations and assertions must be established and the links between them need to be justified. The reasoning process in such informal arguments is different from that of formal arguments in which premises are taken as given and therefore do not need to be verified.

Mislevy et al. (2002, 2003) used Toulmin's argument structure to frame an interpretive argument for assessment, as illustrated in Figure 1.3. In such an assessment argument, conclusions are drawn about a student's ability. Such conclusions follow from a chain of reasoning that starts from data such as an observation of student performance on a test. In Mislevy's terms, conclusions drawn about test takers are referred to as *claims* because they state the claims that the test designer wants to make about a student. The claim in Figure 1.3 is that the student's English-speaking abilities are inadequate for study in an English-medium university. Claims are made on the basis of data or observations that Toulmin referred to as *grounds*. In Figure 1.3, the observation that serves as the grounds is a student presentation that is the final examination in an intensive English class. The performance that the teacher observes when the student speaks in front of the class on the assigned topic is characterized by hesitations and mispronunciations. In the interpretive argument underlying the claim about the student's readiness for university study, the relationship or inferential link between these grounds and the conclusion is not accepted as given, but rather is an assertion in need of justification.

Figure 1.3 shows the interpretive argument as consisting of one inference, which is authorized by a warrant—a law, generally held principle, rule of

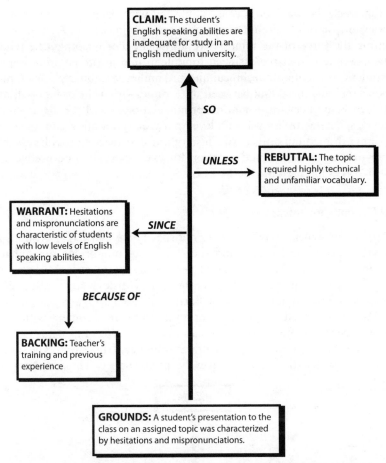

FIG. 1.3 Example structure of an interpretive argument about speaking ability. From "On the Structure of Educational Assessments," by R. J. Mislevy, L. S. Steinberg, and R. G. Almond, 2003, *Measurement: Interdisciplinary Research and Perspectives, 1,* p. 12. Copyright 2003 by Lawrence Erlbaum Associates. Adapted with permission.

thumb, or established procedure. In the example, the warrant is the generally held principle that hesitations and mispronunciations are characteristic of students with low levels of English-speaking ability who would have difficulty at an English-medium university. The warrant, in turn, needs backing, which can take a variety of forms, such as scientific theories, a body of knowledge or evidence, or precedents. In the example, backing might be drawn from the teacher's training and previous experience with nonnative speakers at an English-medium university. Stronger backing could be obtained by getting another teacher to rate the student's speaking performance and showing agreement between the two raters. For such an important final examination, the procedure would be necessary for providing backing.

Even when the warrant is well-established with backing, exceptions may be relevant, or other circumstances may undermine the inference, thereby rebutting the force of the interpretive argument. For example, the rebuttal in the example is that the assigned topic for the oral presentation required the student to use highly technical and unfamiliar vocabulary. This rebuttal weakens the inferential link between the grounds—that the oral presentation contained many hesitations and mispronunciations—and the claim that the student's speaking ability was at a level that would not allow him to succeed at an English-medium university. This argument structure provides the basic framework, components, and notation for expressing the interpretive argument that is being used for the TOEFL.

Dual Grounds for Inferences

The argument structure by itself does not specify any particular grounds and claims concerning test scores and therefore does not bridge the stalemate between competency and task-based perspectives. However, Mislevy's particular conception of the interpretive argument (Mislevy et al., 2002, 2003) offers a solution similar to that of Bachman (2002). Figure 1.4 illustrates how Mislevy specified the grounds for an interpretive argument with a two-pronged basis for score interpretation and use. One type of grounds is a statement about the observation of student performance. The second type specifies the task characteristics used to elicit the performance. These two types of

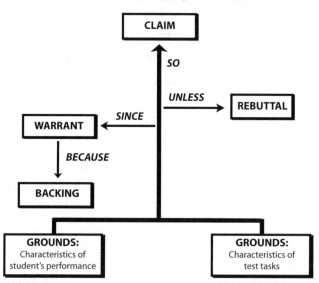

FIG. 1.4   Representation of an assessment argument based on Mislevy, Steinberg, and Almond (2003). From "On the Structure of Educational Assessments," by R. J. Mislevy, L. S. Steinberg, and R. G. Almond, 2003, *Measurement: Interdisciplinary Research and Perspectives, 1,* p. 20. Copyright 2003 by Lawrence Erlbaum Associates. Adapted with permission.

grounds are incorporated into the example in Figure 1.3: mispronunciations and hesitations (a) while speaking and (b) in a class presentation. Mislevy's approach specified that both the observation and the task characteristics that define how the observation is obtained are included as grounds because both pertain to the conclusion that can be drawn.

This representation of an interpretive argument synthesizes the points of view illustrated in Figures 1.1 and 1.2, in that the two types of grounds simultaneously provide the basis for an inference about a student's ability in a particular context. It provides a means of reconciling task-centered and competency-centered approaches to test design. However, like task-centered and competency-centered approaches to score interpretation, Figure 1.4 displays a single inference that links performance on the test to the claim. Some testing researchers find it useful to be able to specify not only the nature of the grounds for score interpretation and use but also the types of inferences that can form the basis for the interpretive argument. For the TOEFL interpretive argument, distinguishing among the types of inferences was critical for organizing the key processes and results into a coherent validity argument.

Multiple Types of Inferences

Kane (1992) argued that multiple types of inferences connect observations and conclusions. The idea of multiple inferences in a chain of inferences and implications is consistent with Toulmin, Rieke, and Janik's (1984) observation:

> ...in practice, of course, any argument is liable to become the starting point for a further argument; this second argument tends to become the starting point for a third argument, and so on. In this way, arguments become connected together in chains. (p. 73)

The complexity of the TOEFL interpretive argument suggested the utility of constructing a chain of inferences described by Kane et al. (1999).

The three-bridge argument Kane et al. (1999) illustrated an interpretive argument that might underlie a performance assessment. It consists of three types of inferential bridges. These bridges are crossed when an observation of performance on a test is interpreted as a sample of performance in a context beyond the test, as shown in Figure 1.5.

Figure 1.5 is intended to depict score interpretation as based, not on a single inference, but on three distinct inferences, each of which refers to a link, or bridge, in an argument that allows score users to move from an observation to other intermediate assertions and finally to the target score in Figure 1.5. In Toulmin's terms, the observation in Figure 1.5 would be the grounds, and the target score would be the conclusion. Figure 1.6 illustrates a sketch of an interpretative argument showing how such a chain of inferences might

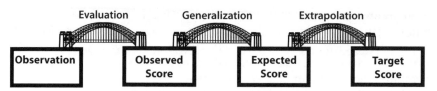

FIG. 1.5 Bridges that represent inferences linking components in performance assessment. From "Validating Measures of Performance," by M. Kane, T. Crooks, and A. Cohen, 1999, *Educational Measurement: Issues and Practice, 18*(2), p. 9. Copyright 1999 by Blackwell Publishing. Adapted with permission.

be articulated for the interpretation of the classroom assessment of speaking. Unlike the bridges in Figure 1.5, the arrows in the sketch of the TOEFL interpretive argument are intended to indicate that the direction of each inference goes one way: from the grounds or intermediate conclusion ultimately to the conclusion.

Kane's approach to the interpretive argument (Kane et al., 1999) is that each of its inferences rests on assumptions that require support. The first inference is invoked when the teacher quantifies the observation of classroom test performance by giving it a score. Such an inference, called *evaluation*, can be relatively straightforward, as when a set of dichotomously scored items is marked according to a key and the correct responses are added up or complex, as when constructed responses are evaluated according to key features of the response. The example in Figure 1.6 illustrates the latter type, which poses a critical problem for assessment of second language speaking and writing (e.g., Weigle, 2002). Unlike the example from the speaking class in the intensive program, a speaking test with high-stakes outcomes would typically require more than one expert rater and more than one sample of performance.

Kane et al. (1999) described the assumptions underlying evaluation as follows: "The criteria used to score the performance are appropriate and have been applied as intended and second, that the performance occurred under conditions compatible with the intended score interpretation" (p. 9). In language assessment, assumptions underlying the evaluation inference are investigated through research on raters, scoring rubrics, and scales (e.g., McNamara, 1996; Skehan, 1998), but in addition to these aspects of the scoring process, test administration conditions affect evaluation.

Generalization refers to the use of the observed score as an estimate of the score that would be expected of a test taker across parallel tasks and test forms. In the example, the expected score on similar test tasks would be 2. The score of 2 across all tasks was not observed, but instead was inferred on the basis of the single observed 2. In assessments with high-stake outcomes, "the evidence needed to support generalizations to the [expected] score is collected in...generalizability studies...which indicate the consistency of scores across samples of observations (e.g., across samples of raters, tasks, occasions)" (Kane et al. 1999, p. 10). In language assessment, Bachman (1990)

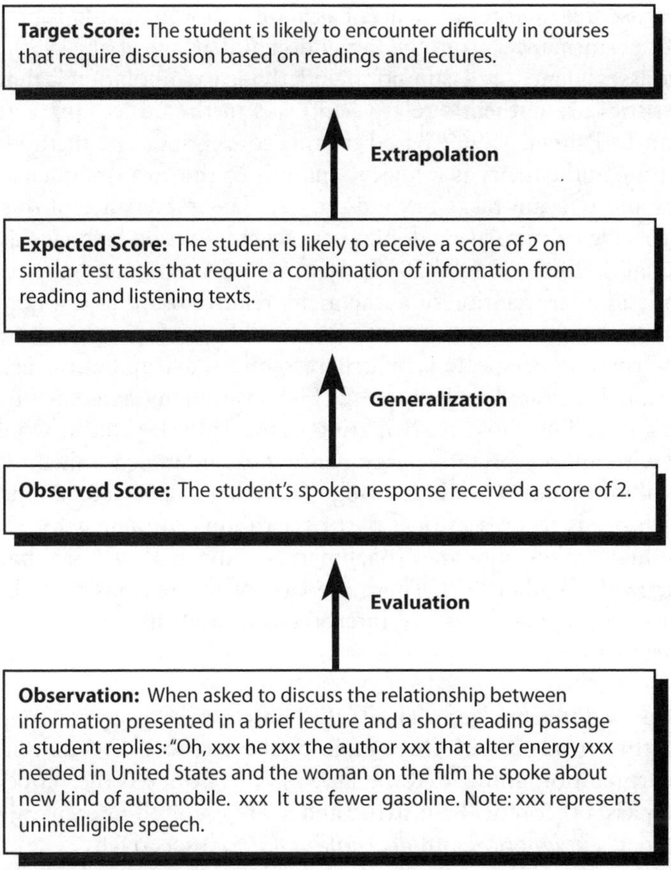

Target Score: The student is likely to encounter difficulty in courses that require discussion based on readings and lectures.

Extrapolation

Expected Score: The student is likely to receive a score of 2 on similar test tasks that require a combination of information from reading and listening texts.

Generalization

Observed Score: The student's spoken response received a score of 2.

Evaluation

Observation: When asked to discuss the relationship between information presented in a brief lecture and a short reading passage a student replies: "Oh, xxx he xxx the author xxx that alter energy xxx needed in United States and the woman on the film he spoke about new kind of automobile. xxx It use fewer gasoline. Note: xxx represents unintelligible speech.

FIG. 1.6   An illustration of an interpretative argument for interpretation and use of a speaking assessment.

described the use of g-theory to estimate the error associated with generalization of task scores across a set of language test tasks and raters. A method that has been used in numerous validation studies for language assessments, generalization is a way of conceptualizing reliability, and therefore, in some cases, assumptions underlying the generalization inference can be supported through reliability estimates. Other support for generalization comes from standardization of task characteristics and test administration conditions (Kane et al., 1999) and from score equating (Kane, 2004).

Extrapolation refers to the inference that is made when the test takers' expected score is interpreted as indicative of performance and scores that they would receive in the target setting. In the example in Figure 1.6, the expected score is interpreted to mean that the student is likely to encounter difficulty in courses requiring discussion based on readings and lectures. Assumptions underlying extrapolation can be "supported empirically by comparing assessment scores to criterion scores based on a thorough (and representative) sample of performances from the target domain" (Kane et al., 1999, p. 10). In language assessment, one assumption underlying extrapolation is that test task characteristics are authentic relative to tasks in the target language domain (Bachman & Palmer, 1996). Based on this conception, one methodology for investigating authenticity is a logical analysis of the correspondence between test tasks and relevant tasks beyond the test. The importance of this assumption underlying extrapolation dominates recent books on language assessment (e.g., Douglas, 2000; Weigle, 2002), but many issues remain about the measurement and interpretation of authenticity relative to other test qualities.

The three-bridge interpretive argument adds an important dimension to the task-centered perspective, which recognizes extrapolation as the only inference, as illustrated in Figure 1.2. However, many assessment designers and users, including those participating in the TOEFL project, would not be satisfied with an interpretative argument whose inferences failed to link to a theoretical construct. The three-bridge framework also fails to include test use, which needs to be a critical part of a validity argument for a language test with high-stakes outcomes (Bachman & Palmer, 1996; Cronbach, 1988; Messick, 1989; Wall, 1997). These are two of the reasons that the TOEFL interpretive argument for score interpretation and use includes more than three inferences.

Beyond the three bridges   The TOEFL interpretive argument expands beyond the three bridges with three additional inferences that underlie TOEFL score interpretation and use. Kane (1992; 2001) offered the scope required to encompass a theoretical construct and score use with inferences, which he referred to as *explanation* and *decision-making*, respectively.

An explanation inference refers to the link, such as the one depicted in Figure 1.1, between observed test performance and a construct. The construct responsible for explanation in the TOEFL project is the theoretical construct of academic language proficiency composed of factors assumed to influence performance. As noted earlier, experts hold diverse perspectives on the nature of language proficiency, and a formal or strong theory of language proficiency theory does not exist. Nevertheless, a theoretical language proficiency construct is relevant to score interpretation and use and therefore is included in the interpretive argument so that assumptions associated with the construct can be identified and investigated.

Decision-making links the target score to the decisions about test takers for which the score is used. This inference is different from the others because it moves the interpretive argument from interpretation of score meaning to actual score use. Kane distinguished the "descriptive interpretations" (Kane, 2002, p. 32) of the other parts of the interpretive argument from the policy-based interpretations inherent in decision-making. The latter interpretations "involve assumptions supporting the decision procedure's suitability as a policy [e.g., requiring a TOEFL score as one part of the application of international students at American universities], and policies are typically justified by claims about their consequences" (Kane, 2002, p. 32). Bachman (2005) referred to decision-making as *utilization*, which is the term we subsequently adopted for the TOEFL interpretive argument.

A third additional inference, domain definition, is included for TOEFL score interpretation and use. Kane (2004) did not include domain description as an inference, but noted the importance of a detailed definition of the target domain to guide the development of assessment tasks:

> ...if the test is intended to be interpreted as a measure of competence in some domain, then efforts to describe the domain carefully and to develop items that reflect the domain (in terms of content, cognitive level, and freedom from potential sources of systematic errors) tend to support the intended interpretation. (p. 141)

These three inferences, in addition to the three bridges—evaluation, generalization, and extrapolation—were used to develop the TOEFL interpretive argument.

Meeting the Needs of the TOEFL Project

The argument structure, dual grounds for inferences, and clarified set of multiple inferences provide conceptual tools to accommodate the perspectives of both competency-centered and task-centered assessment. Table 1.2 summarizes the relationship between the presuppositions from Table 1.1 and an

TABLE 1.2
Beliefs about Language Proficiency as They Relate to an Interpretive Argument

Belief about the Basis for Score Interpretation	Consideration in an Interpretive Argument
Should be a theoretical construct that accounts for language performance	• A claim in the interpretive argument can refer to a theoretical construct. • The explanation inference links performance to a theoretical construct.
Should include complex abilities responsible for goal-oriented performance	• A claim in the interpretive argument can refer to a construct of any level of complexity. • The explanation inference can be linked to any type of construct.
Should take into account the relevant contexts of language use	• One of the dual grounds for the interpretive argument should refer to the task characteristics, which in turn can be shown to correspond to the tasks in the contexts of interest. • The extrapolation inference can be linked to the relevant contexts of language use.

interpretive argument to support TOEFL score interpretation and use.

The beliefs of the test designers were focused on explanation in terms of a construct theory of language proficiency and extrapolation in terms of context of language use, but as Kane's discussion of interpretive arguments pointed out, the other types of inferences are relevant to the TOEFL interpretive argument and need to be explicitly stated as well. The dual grounds and the claim in an interpretive argument provide places for context and a complex construct in the interpretive argument. With these conceptual building blocks, we outline the framework used to define the interpretive argument for TOEFL score interpretation and use.

AN INTERPRETIVE ARGUMENT FOR THE TOEFL

The TOEFL interpretative argument provides a basis for validation as a scientific inquiry into score meaning and use (Messick, 1994). Drawing on the argument structure and types of potential inferences, we outline the inferences that are entailed when scores are derived from observations of test performance and used for decisions about the readiness of test takers for study in an English-medium university. We explain the inferences in the TOEFL interpretive argument through an extension of the example in Figure 1.6 of the student who received a 2 on the speaking task on the final exam in an intensive program. Rather than the classroom speaking test, however, this example refers to the speaking measure on the new TOEFL.

Types of Inferences

Figure 1.7 illustrates the types of inferences that underlie TOEFL score interpretation and use in concrete terms by describing each at a level of detail similar to that of Figure 1.6. The inferences in the TOEFL interpretive argument are the following: domain description, evaluation, generalization, explanation, extrapolation, and utilization. In Figure 1.7, they are represented by arrows that connect the grounds (the target domain and observations at the bottom), intermediate claims or implications (the observed score, expected score, and construct in the middle), and claim or conclusion (target score and test use at the top).

In the TOEFL interpretive argument, domain description links performances in the target domain to the observations of performance in the test domain, which has been identified based on the test purpose. The warrant is that the observations of test performance reveal relevant knowledge, skills, and abilities in situations representative of those in the target domain. In the example in Figure 1.7, an important performance in the target domain is described both in terms of a task that entails responding in class to questions based on assigned reading and lectures and in terms of the abilities required

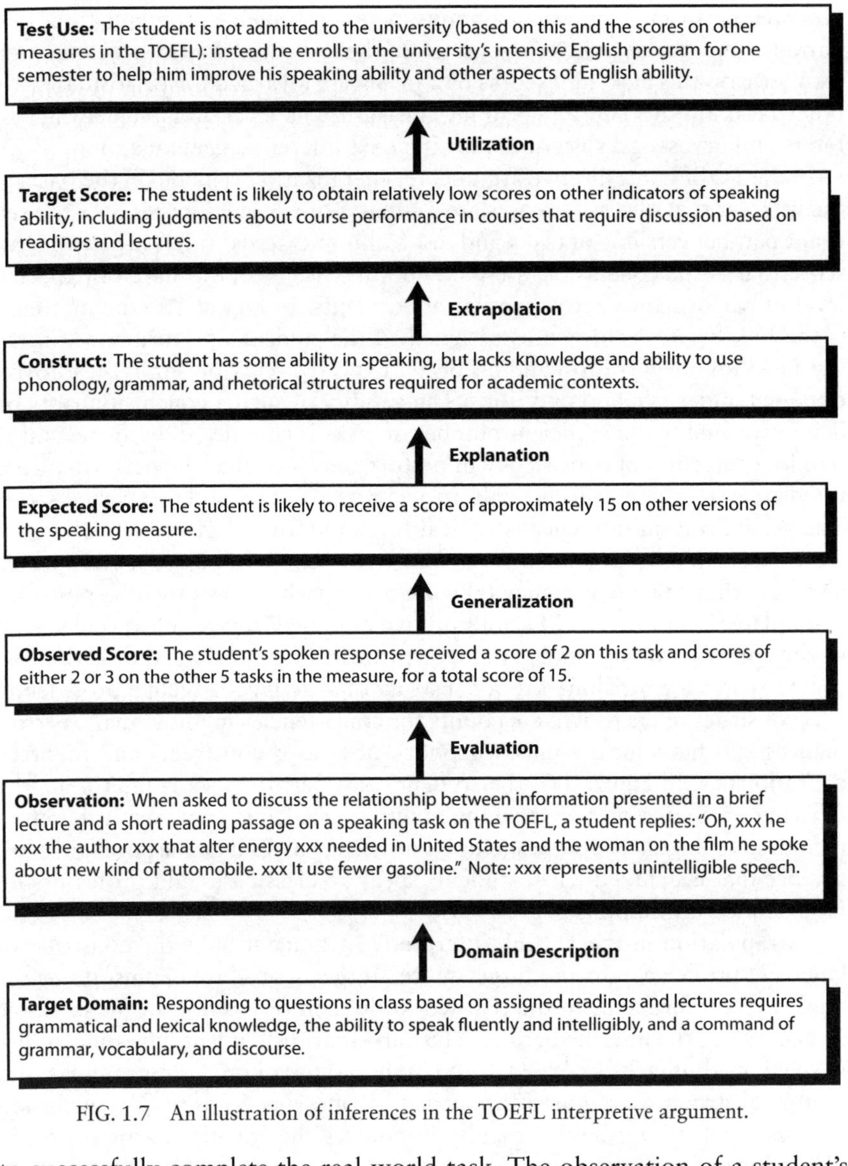

Test Use: The student is not admitted to the university (based on this and the scores on other measures in the TOEFL): instead he enrolls in the university's intensive English program for one semester to help him improve his speaking ability and other aspects of English ability.

↑ **Utilization**

Target Score: The student is likely to obtain relatively low scores on other indicators of speaking ability, including judgments about course performance in courses that require discussion based on readings and lectures.

↑ **Extrapolation**

Construct: The student has some ability in speaking, but lacks knowledge and ability to use phonology, grammar, and rhetorical structures required for academic contexts.

↑ **Explanation**

Expected Score: The student is likely to receive a score of approximately 15 on other versions of the speaking measure.

↑ **Generalization**

Observed Score: The student's spoken response received a score of 2 on this task and scores of either 2 or 3 on the other 5 tasks in the measure, for a total score of 15.

↑ **Evaluation**

Observation: When asked to discuss the relationship between information presented in a brief lecture and a short reading passage on a speaking task on the TOEFL, a student replies: "Oh, xxx he xxx the author xxx that alter energy xxx needed in United States and the woman on the film he spoke about new kind of automobile. xxx It use fewer gasoline." Note: xxx represents unintelligible speech.

↑ **Domain Description**

Target Domain: Responding to questions in class based on assigned readings and lectures requires grammatical and lexical knowledge, the ability to speak fluently and intelligibly, and a command of grammar, vocabulary, and discourse.

FIG. 1.7   An illustration of inferences in the TOEFL interpretive argument.

to successfully complete the real world task. The observation of a student's speaking performance on a test task that asks him to discuss the relationship between the information from the lecture and the reading simulates to some degree an academic task that reveals speaking abilities identified during the description of the academic domain.

Evaluation is based on the warrant that observations of performance on test tasks are evaluated to provide observed scores reflective of targeted language abilities. In the example in Figure 1.7, evaluation occurs as the student's observed performance (which contains incomprehensible pronunciation, hesitations, and errors) receives a score of 2. The score of 2 was awarded for performance on this task, and scores of 2 or 3 were awarded for performance on other tasks on the TOEFL speaking measure. The level of agreement across raters and across tasks is critical for the next inference, generalization.

In the TOEFL interpretive argument, generalization is made on the basis of the warrant that observed scores are estimates of expected scores over the relevant parallel versions of tasks and test forms and across raters. The expected score that is the conclusion for such an inference is an estimate of expected level of performance across similar assessments. In Figure 1.7, the inference is the link between the scores assigned to the student's performance on the test tasks on one test form and his or her expected score on similar test forms obtained under similar conditions. The validity of such a conclusion rests on demonstrating that a sufficient number of tasks is completed by the test taker to allow detection of consistency in performance and that the performance is rated consistently so as to provide an accurate estimate of the expected score. The generalization inference is critical for standardized assessments because we wish to claim that students' test scores are comparable no matter which test form they take, where they take the test, or who scores their responses.

Explanation in the TOEFL interpretive argument links the expected score to the construct of academic language proficiency, so the warrant is that expected scores are attributed to a construct of academic language proficiency. The construct refers to what accounts for consistencies in individuals' performances and fits logically into a network of related constructs and theoretical rationales. In Figure 1.7, the student's test performance is interpreted by drawing on a construct of speaking ability in academic contexts. It therefore includes the linguistic and pragmatic knowledge as well as the strategic competence that is entailed when students speak to classmates and professors on English-medium campuses.

Extrapolation in the TOEFL interpretive argument links the construct of language proficiency to the target score. Target scores are claims about the quality of performance in the real-world domain of interest. In the example in Figure 1.7, the intermediate conclusion—that the student has some ability in speaking, but lacks knowledge and ability to use phonology, grammar, and rhetorical structures required for academic contexts—leads to the conclusion that the student will have difficulty in courses that require participation in discussions of academic content.

The utilization inference links the target score to test use, which includes decisions about admissions and course recommendations. In the example in Figure 1.7, the conclusion that the student is likely to have difficulty in courses requiring speaking about academic materials contributes to a decision that he should not be admitted to the university, but instead he should start in an intensive English program. Such a decision would be made on the basis of the speaking score in combination with the scores on the other three parts of the

TOEFL. The actual decision would be made on the basis of a cut score set by an institution, and therefore the claim that serves as the conclusion of the TOEFL interpretive argument is that the scores will reveal distinctions in test takers that will allow institutions to set cut scores and make decisions on the basis of the cut scores that they set.

The example outlined in Figure 1.7 focuses on a speaking task, but in describing the chain of inferences that concludes with a claim about utilization, other criteria in addition to task performance had to be included: performance on all of the speaking tasks, the scores given by two raters, and ultimately scores on all of the measures of the TOEFL. The TOEFL interpretive argument encompasses all of the performances on all the measures, their scoring procedures, their scores, and the utilization of those test scores. The general framework for the TOEFL interpretive argument is shown in Figure 1.8, in which the target domain refers to language use in English-medium institutions of higher education. Observations refer to performance on the particular test tasks on the part of the TOEFL—listening, reading, speaking, writing, or the whole test—for which the interpretation is being made. Observed scores are the scores on specific tasks, measures, or the whole test. The expected score is the expected level of performance over parallel tasks, raters, and test forms. The construct is academic language proficiency, or some aspect of academic language proficiency, which is a theoretical account of consistencies in an individual's performance on academic tasks that require English language proficiency. The target score refers to claims about level of ability in the target domain. Test use means the educational decisions made on the basis of TOEFL scores.

Warrants, Assumptions, and Backing

To complete the outline of the TOEFL interpretative argument shown in Figure 1.8, the specific warrants and assumptions associated with each of the inferences need to be identified. In the speaking task example provided in Figure 1.7, the argument was presented as a series of inferences that linked the grounds to intermediate conclusions and ultimately to the conclusion about test use. The actual warrants and assumptions entailed in the TOEFL interpretive argument are shown in Table 1.3, which also provides an illustration of the type of analysis that is used to provide backing for each assumption in subsequent chapters.

In the interpretive argument, the domain description inference is based on the warrant that observations of performance on the TOEFL are representative of performances in the target domain of language use in English-medium institutions of higher education. This warrant, in turn, is based on the assumptions that assessment tasks representative of the academic domain, as well as language skills critical to success in the academic domain, can in fact be identified and that assessment tasks representative of the academic domain

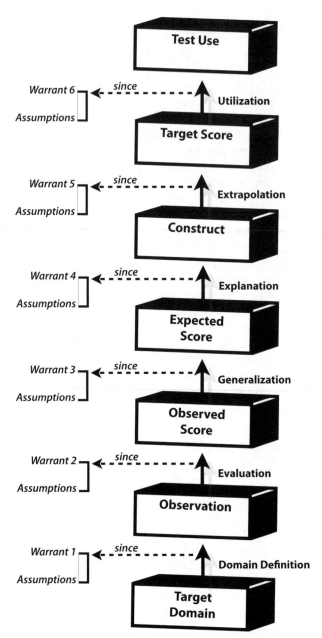

FIG. 1.8   Sketch of the TOEFL interpretive argument.

TABLE 1.3
Summary of the Warrant, Assumptions, and Backing Associated With Each Inference in the
TOEFL Interpretive Argument

Inference in the TOEFL Interpretive Argument	Warrant Supporting the Inference	Assumptions Underlying Warrant	Example of Backing Sought to Support Assumption
Domain description	Observations of performance on the TOEFL reveal relevant knowledge, skills, and abilities in situations representative of those in the target domain of language use in the English-medium institutions of higher education.	Assessment tasks that are representative of the academic domain can be identified.	Domain analysis
		Critical English language skills, knowledge, and processes needed for study in English-medium colleges and universities can be identified.	Domain analysis
		Assessment tasks that require important skills and are representative of the academic domain can be simulated.	Task modeling
Evaluation	Observations of performance on TOEFL tasks are evaluated to provide observed scores reflective of targeted language abilities.	Rubrics for scoring responses are appropriate for providing evidence of targeted language abilities.	Rubric development
		Task administration conditions are appropriate for providing evidence of targeted language abilities.	Prototyping studies
		The statistical characteristics of items, measures, and test forms are appropriate for norm-referenced decisions.	Item and test analysis
Generalization	Observed scores are estimates of expected scores over the relevant parallel versions of tasks and test forms and across raters.	A sufficient number of tasks are included on the test to provide stable estimates of test takers' performances.	Generalizability and reliability studies

(*continued*)

TABLE 1.3
Continued

Inference in the TOEFL Interpretive Argument	Warrant Supporting the Inference	Assumptions Underlying Warrant	Example of Backing Sought to Support Assumption
		Configuration of tasks on measures is appropriate for intended interpretation.	Generalizability and reliability studies
		Appropriate scaling and equating procedures for test scores are used.	Scaling and equating studies
		Task, test, and rating specifications are well defined so that parallel tasks and test forms are created.	Generalizability and reliability studies
Explanation	Expected scores are attributed to a construct of academic language proficiency.	The linguistic knowledge, processes, and strategies required to successfully complete tasks vary in keeping with theoretical expectations.	Discourse analyses and cognitive processing studies
		Task difficulty is systematically influenced by task characteristics.	Task characteristic-item difficulty studies
		Performance on new test measures relate to performance on other test-based measures of language proficiency as expected theoretically.	Concurrent correlational studies
		The internal structure of the test scores is consistent with a theoretical view of language proficiency as a number of highly interrelated components.	Studies of reliability and factor analysis
		Test performance varies according to amount and quality of experience in learning English.	Comparison studies of group differences

(*continued*)

TABLE 1.3
Continued

Inference in the TOEFL Interpretive Argument	Warrant Supporting the Inference	Assumptions Underlying Warrant	Example of Backing Sought to Support Assumption
Extrapolation	The construct of academic language proficiency as assessed by the TOEFL accounts for the quality of linguistic performance in English-medium institutions of higher education.	Performance on the test is related to other criteria of language proficiency in the academic context.	Criterion-related validity studies
Utilization	Estimates of the quality of performance in the English-medium institutions of higher education obtained from the TOEFL are useful for making decisions about admissions and appropriate curriculum for test takers.	The meaning of test scores is clearly interpretable by admissions officers, test takers, and teachers. The test will have a positive influence on how English is taught.	Standard setting studies Score interpretation materials Availability of instructional materials Washback studies

that target important skills can be simulated as test tasks. The backing for such assumptions is drawn from the analytic process of domain analysis and task construction as well as from evaluations of the success of the outcomes of these processes. These activities are described throughout this book, but Chapters 3 and 7 focus primarily on these issues.

The intermediate conclusion from domain description, the observations of performance on relevant tasks, serves as grounds for evaluation. The evaluation inference is based on the warrant that observations of performance on TOEFL tasks are evaluated to provide observed scores reflective of targeted language abilities. This warrant is based on three assumptions about scoring and conditions of task administration: (a) Rubrics for scoring responses are appropriate for providing evidence of targeted language abilities; (b) task administration conditions are appropriate for providing evidence of targeted language abilities; and (c) the statistical characteristics of items, measures, and test forms are appropriate for norm-referenced interpretations. The backing for these assumptions comes from rubric development, prototyping, and analysis of items, responses, and reliability. These studies appear primarily in Chapters 4 and 5.

Generalization is based on the warrant that observed scores are estimates of expected scores for parallel tasks, tests, and administration and rating conditions. The assumptions underlying this warrant are that (a) a sufficient number of tasks are included on the test to provide stable estimates of test takers' performances; (b) the configuration of tasks on measures is appropriate for intended interpretation; (c) appropriate scaling and equating procedures for test scores are used; and (d) task, test, and rating specifications are well-defined, so that parallel tasks and test forms are created. Backing for the assumptions associated with generalization comes from generalizability, reliability, scaling, and equating studies, as well as task design processes; these are reported in Chapters 5, 6, 7, and 8.

Explanation entails the warrant that expected scores on the TOEFL are attributed to a construct of academic language proficiency. Five assumptions underlying this warrant have been identified: (a) The linguistic knowledge, processes, and strategies required to successfully complete tasks vary in keeping with theoretical expectations; (b) task difficulty is systematically influenced by task characteristics; (c) performance on new test measures relates to performance on other test-based measures of language proficiency as expected theoretically; (d) the internal structure of the test scores is consistent with a theoretical view of language proficiency as a number of highly interrelated components; and (e) test performance varies according to amount and quality of experience in learning English. Backing for these assumptions appears throughout all of the chapters as prototyping studies, concurrent correlational studies, investigation of reliability and factor structure, and comparison of group differences.

Extrapolation is based on the warrant that the construct of academic language proficiency as assessed by the TOEFL accounts for the quality of linguistic performance in English-medium institutions of higher education. Underlying this inference is the assumption that performance on the test is related to other criteria of language proficiency in the academic contexts. Backing for this assumption is obtained from criterion-related evidence. Criterion-related studies are reported in Chapters 5, 6, and 8.

Utilization is based on the warrant that estimates of the quality of performance in English-medium institutions of higher education from the TOEFL are useful for making decisions about admissions and appropriate curriculum for test takers. This warrant is based on the assumptions that the meaning of test scores is clearly interpretable by admissions officers, test takers, and teachers and that the test will have a positive influence on how English is taught. The first assumption needs to be backed by evidence that test users have access to materials to aid score interpretation. The second assumption requires both evidence that appropriate instruction materials are available and further backing from studies of washback. Backing for these assumptions is detailed in Chapter 8.

CONCLUSION

Within an argument-based approach to validation, the justification of the validity of score interpretation and use has two aspects. The aspect for a new TOEFL, described in this and the following chapters, is the construction of an interpretative argument that lays out the grounds, inferences, warrants, and claims, all of which provide the foundation for proposed score interpretation and use. By articulating assumptions underlying the warrants, the interpretive argument serves as a guide for the collection of the backing needed for support, and a preliminary validity argument can be drafted. Sufficient backing for a warrant provides a valid bridge to the next inference. By bridging all of the inferences, links in a chain can be forged into a preliminary validity argument. The second aspect of validation is a critical evaluation of this preliminary validity argument, in which the coherence of the argument, the quality and sufficiency of the supporting evidence, and the evidence refuting alternative interpretations are weighed.

Kane (2004) saw the development of the interpretive argument as a part of the test design process and the development of the validity argument as an activity that occurs later, primarily after the test is operational. Others (Briggs, 2004; Ryan, 2002; Schilling, 2004) have argued that test design decisions and the evidence supporting these decisions contribute to the validity argument, which suggests that a draft interpretive argument would ideally be on the table during test design and field testing. Schilling, for example, pointed out that "... assessing validity during the test construction can be diagnostic with respect to test content and structure" (p. 181) and can lead to changes in the test design.

Shilling's observation is consistent with the experience in the TOEFL project: Assumptions underlying the inferences in the interpretive argument were evaluated as the test was designed even though the structure of the interpretive argument presented in this chapter had not been formally laid out. The linear structure of the TOEFL interpretative argument that we have formulated in retrospect fails to capture the dynamic process that went into its construction. The test design process itself was nonlinear and iterative. Given the various types of evidence that can be offered in support of test interpretation and use, this interpretive framework now provides us with a way to organize the evidence and its implications. As Mislevy (2004, p. 185) noted in discussing the use of argumentation in law, an interpretive argument is a way "that a mass of heterogeneous evidence becomes comprehensible only through the flow of narrative, a story as it were." The rest of the chapters in this volume are intended to convey this story to the reader.

REFERENCES

Bachman, L. F. (1990). *Fundamental considerations in language testing.* Oxford, UK: Oxford University Press.

Bachman, L. F. (2002). Alternative interpretations of alternative assessments: Some validity issues in educational performance assessments. *Educational Measurement: Issues and Practice, 21*(3), 5–18.

Bachman, L. F. (2005). Building and supporting a case for test use. *Language Assessment Quarterly: An International Journal, 2*(1), 1–34.

Bachman, L. F., & Palmer, A. S. (1996). *Language testing in practice.* Oxford, UK: Oxford University Press.

Briggs, D. C. (2004). Comment: Making an argument for design validity before interpretive validity. *Measurement, 2,* 171–91.

Canale, M., & Swain, M. (1980). Theoretical bases of communicative approaches to second language teaching and testing. *Applied Linguistics, 1,* 1–47.

Chalhoub-Deville, M. (1997). Theoretical models, assessment frameworks, and test construction. *Language Testing, 14,* 3–22.

Chalhoub-Deville, M. (2001). Task-based assessments: Characteristics and validity evidence. In M. Bygate, P.Skehan, & M. Swain (Eds.), *Researching pedagogical tasks: Second language learning, teaching and testing* (pp. 210–228). Harlow, England: Longman.

Chapelle, C. A. (1998). Construct definition and validity inquiry in SLA research. In L. F. Bachman & A. D. Cohen (Eds.), *Interfaces between second language acquisition and language testing research* (pp. 32–70). Cambridge, UK: Cambridge University Press.

Cronbach, L. (1988). Five perspectives on validity argument. In H. Wainer & H. Braun (Eds.), *Test validity* (pp. 3–17). Hillsdale, NJ: Lawrence Erlbaum.

Cummins, J. P. (1983). Language proficiency and academic achievement. In J. Oller (Ed.), *Issues in language testing research* (pp. 108–126). Rowley, MA: Newbury House.

Douglas, D. (2000). *Assessing languages for specific purposes.* Cambridge, UK: Cambridge University Press.

Kane, M. (2004). Certification testing as an illustration of argument-based validation. *Measurement, 2,* 135–170.

Kane, M., Crooks, T., & Cohen, A. (1999). Validating measures of performance. *Educational Measurement: Issues and Practice, 18*(2), 5–17.

Kane, M. T. (1992). An argument-based approach to validity. *Psychological Bulletin, 112,* 527–535.

Kane, M. T. (2001). Current concerns in validity theory. *Journal of Educational Measurement, 38,* 319–342.

Kane, M. T. (2002). Validating high-stakes testing programs. *Educational Measurement: Issues and Practice, 21*(1), 31–35.

McNamara, T. F. (1996). *Measuring second language performance.* London: Longman.

Messick, S. (1989). Validity. In R. L. Linn (Ed.), *Educational Measurement* (3rd ed.; pp. 13–103). New York: Macmillan.

Messick, S. (1994). The interplay of evidence and consequences in the validation of performance assessments. *Educational Researcher, 23*(2), 13–23.

Mislevy, R. J. (2004). Toulmin and beyond: Commentary on Michael Kane's "Certification testing as an illustration of argument-based validation." *Measurement, 2*(3), 185–191.

Mislevy, R. J., Steinberg, L. S., & Almond, R. G. (2002). Design and analysis in task-based language assessment. *Language Testing, 19,* 477–496.

Mislevy, R. J., Steinberg, L. S., & Almond, R. G. (2003). On the structure of educational assessments. *Measurement: Interdisciplinary Research and Perspectives, 1,* 3–62.

Norris, J. M., Brown, J. D., Hudson, T. D., & Bonk, W. (2002). Examinee abilities and task difficulty in task-based second language performance assessment. *Language Testing, 19*, 395–418.

Oller, J. (1979). *Language tests at school.* London: Longman.

Ryan, K. (2002). Assessment validation in the context of high-stakes assessment. *Educational Measurement: Issues and Practice, 21*, 7–15.

Schilling, S. G. (2004). Conceptualizing the validity argument: An alternative approach. *Measurement, 2*, 178–182.

Skehan, P. (1998). *A cognitive approach to language learning.* Oxford, UK: Oxford University Press.

Toulmin, S. E. (1958). *The uses of argument.* Cambridge, UK: Cambridge University Press.

Toulmin, S. E. (2003). *The uses of argument* (updated edition). Cambridge, UK: Cambridge University Press.

Toulmin, S., Rieke, R., & Janik, A. (1984). *An introduction to reasoning* (2nd ed.). New York: Macmillan.

Wall, D. (1997). Impact and washback in language testing. In C. Clapham & D. Corson, (Eds.), *Encyclopedia of language and education. Volume 7: Language testing and assessment* (pp. 291–302). Dordrecht, The Netherlands: Kluwer Academic Publishers.

Weigle, S. C. (2002). *Assessing writing.* Cambridge, UK: Cambridge University Press.

Wiggins, G. P. (1993). Assessing student performance: Exploring the purpose and limits of testing. San Francisco: Jossey-Bass.

2

The Evolution of the TOEFL

Carol A. Taylor
Paul Angelis

This chapter places the new TOEFL® in its historical context by examining the process leading up to the new TOEFL project. Did similar issues exist in 1961 when the first version of the TOEFL was conceived? How was the construct of language proficiency defined for the first TOEFL? What type of test tasks did the test consist of? How was validation approached? The TOEFL has constantly been the object of research and critical appraisal by representative test users, and therefore these basic questions have been discussed regularly throughout the history of TOEFL. Over this period, which spans more than 40 years, adjustments and additions have been made to the test format, and changing conceptions of language proficiency have been revisited regularly. Despite the fact that TOEFL revision is an ongoing process, in the interest of clarity, this chapter presents TOEFL history in three stages: the first TOEFL, the revisions beginning in the late 1970s, and first stages of the new TOEFL.

THE FIRST TOEFL

The first TOEFL was conceived by constituents with an interest in using a test of English language ability for admissions decisions about a growing number of nonnative speakers of English who were applying to North American universities in the late 1950s and early 1960s. These constituents agreed that priority should be given to the development of a test to meet the needs of colleges and universities on both undergraduate and graduate levels, but the ultimate goal should be an instrument applicable for precollege students as well. The original plans for the TOEFL were crystallized in May 1961 at a conference in Washington, DC, sponsored by the Center for Applied Linguistics of the Modern Language Association of America in cooperation with the Institute of International Education (IIE) and the National Association of Foreign Student Advisors (NAFSA). The conference report indicated that specialists described some existing testing programs and theoretical issues in English language testing and that government and university representatives indicated their needs for the test.

In the year following the conference, the National Council on the Testing of English as a Foreign Language was formed, composed of representatives of more than 30 private organizations and government agencies concerned with the English proficiency of foreign applicants to educational institutions in North America. In 1963 the Ford and Danforth Foundations provided funding to launch the TOEFL, with the Modern Language Association managing the program. The first TOEFL was administered in 1964 at 57 test centers worldwide to 920 test candidates, and test papers were returned to the United States for scoring. In the beginning, three administrations per year were given, and a new form was used for each administration during the first 2 years. Thereafter, the test material could be reused in the preparation of new forms.

In the following year, Educational Testing Service® (ETS®) and the College Board were given responsibility for continuing the operational program, which they changed gradually to meet growing demand for the TOEFL. In 1973, ETS was given sole responsibility for TOEFL test development, operations, and finances. To maintain control over testing policy issues, however, a TOEFL Policy Council was created at the same time to represent the interests of the original constituents. The council was composed of members representing the College Board, the Graduate Record Examinations® Board, and a number of agencies and associations concerned with the admission of international students to colleges and universities in the United States and Canada.

In retrospect, it is interesting to note that participants at the first TOEFL meeting in 1961 addressed the same types of issues that members of the new TOEFL revision project were faced with again in the 1990s: what the test should measure, what content the test should include, and how validity should be justified. Moreover, at that single meeting in 1961, many of the initial decisions were made about the test construct and content and the validation research, as summarized in Table 2.1. It is worth looking in greater detail at these issues from 1961 that had become so complex 30 years later.

What the Test Should Measure

Members of the first TOEFL planning committee recognized the diverse set of linguistic skills that would be required of the students for whom the test was being developed: "It is recognized that different academic tasks and training

TABLE 2.1
Decisions about Testing Issues for the First TOEFL

Testing Issue	Decisions
Construct: What should the test measure?	The test should consist of an "omnibus battery testing a wide range of English proficiency and yielding meaningful (reliable) subscores in addition to total scores" (*Testing the English Language Proficiency of Foreign Students*, 1961, p. 3). The construct can be defined as a list of components of language knowledge and skills that would be expected to affect performance across a wide range of relevant situations.
Content: What should the test consist of?	The test battery will contain sections for the measurement of: (a) control of English structure, (b) auditory comprehension, (c) vocabulary and reading comprehension, and (d) writing ability. All sections will consist of multiple-choice items.
Validation: How can test use be justified?	The test should be pretested on a wide range of nonnative speakers of English as well as native speakers of English. Correlations between the new test and existing tests should be obtained and reported.

programs call for different levels of English proficiency and make greater demands on some linguistic skills than on others" (*Testing the English Language Proficiency of Foreign Students*, 1961, p. 3). The approach therefore was to attempt to identify a common core of language abilities that would be relevant to the range of situations in which students would find themselves at the university. Carroll (1961, p. 35) identified "separate aspects of language competence [that] might be considered in drawing up specifications for a proficiency test":

1. Knowledge of structure
2. Knowledge of general-usage lexicon
3. Auditory discrimination (of phonemes, allophones, and suprasegmentals)
4. Oral production (of phonemes, allophones, and suprasegmentals)
5. Reading (in the sense of converting printed symbols to sound)
6. Writing (in the sense of converting sound to printed symbols, i.e., spelling)
7. Rate and accuracy of listening comprehension
8. Rate and quality of speaking, as in an interview situation
9. Rate and accuracy of reading comprehension
10. Rate and accuracy of written composition

This list fits well within the ability approach to language testing that dominated thinking in educational measurement as well as with theory in linguistics that viewed language as composed of separately definable components such as a sound system, grammar, and vocabulary. Coming at the same time as similar proposals from Lado in his newly published book, *Language Testing* (1961), Carroll's list found strong support as targets for the test being considered.

At the same time, Carroll suggested that the discrete knowledge and skills to be tested be accompanied by an integrative approach that would require examinees to draw on their knowledge of discrete linguistic items as well as their knowledge of context to construct and produce meaning from language. In other words, he was hinting at what years later became the presuppositions for test developers, described in the first chapter. Prevalent views in linguistics and measurement in the early 1960s, however, found more support for a discrete language testing model.

Test Content

The presentations at the 1961 conference served as input to test design by identifying areas that could be tested. The difficult areas proved to be speaking and writing, Numbers 8 and 10, respectively, on Carroll's list. The decision of how to test speaking was deferred to later versions of the test, and the recommendation was made "that research on techniques for measuring oral production skill be undertaken at once for the possible inclusion of such devices in later test forms" (*Testing the English Language Proficiency of Foreign Students,* 1961, p. 4). Writing ability was to be tested by objective techniques, not by the scoring of writing samples. However, it was decided that an unscored composition would be furnished to test users to use as they pleased. The other aspects of the construct were measured by four separate sections, each providing a separate subscore: Listening Comprehension, English Structure, Vocabulary, and Reading Comprehension.

The constructs believed to define the relevant language abilities were one important source of content ideas, but another came from examples of existing English language tests. One such test, the American University Language Center test, was a combination of the *Aural/Oral Rating Sheet,* used to score auditory comprehension and oral production in an interview setting, and the *English Usage Test,* which consisted of 150 three-choice objective items testing control of English inflections, grammatical structure, word-order patterns, and idioms. Two additional components of that testing system were just then being introduced and played a role in shaping plans for the TOEFL. One was the *Vocabulary and Reading Test,* containing 60 four-choice items divided into three parts: general vocabulary, two-word verbs, and reading comprehension. The second was the *Listening Test,* in which examinees listened to 40 short statements and questions, and, after hearing each utterance, chose the most appropriate of four printed answers or interpretations. Other tests considered were those used in Britain and other Commonwealth countries: the *University of London Certificate of Proficiency in English for Foreign Students* and the *University of Cambridge Certificate of Proficiency*. Summaries were also given of testing operations in Australia, New Zealand, Canada, India, and a number of African countries. Despite some differences among these tests, the number of similarities was far greater, and the content of the TOEFL followed these models.

Validation Issues

In 1961, professional practice in educational measurement suggested that the technical quality of the items should be assured through pretesting and item revision and that the reliability and validity of the test scores should be demonstrated. The members at the conference suggested that pretesting might be carried out on such groups as students attending summer IIE institutes, ICA College Preparatory Workshop participants, students attending the ASAF Language School at Lackland Air Force Base, and students attending U.S. English language institutes. It was also recommended that *native* speakers of English be tested to obtain initial information on difficulty and to provide a check against faulty items, misleading directions, and the like (*Testing the English Language Proficiency of Foreign Students*, 1961, pp. 3–6). These pretesting data were to contribute to the TOEFL validation strategies, which, in turn, provided impetus for considering the larger issue of a research agenda for the TOEFL program.

TOEFL validation strategies Consistent with practice at that time, TOEFL validation was approached from three perspectives. Content validity was addressed through formation in 1967 of the TOEFL Committee of Examiners (COE), a group of language teaching and testing specialists outside of ETS who were given oversight responsibilities for test design and content. The discussion and approval of test content by this outside committee of experts on English language teaching was intended to support the content validity of the TOEFL.

Empirical studies investigating correlations of the TOEFL with criterion measures constituted the primary approach to validation. Many of these studies were included in the comprehensive collection of TOEFL related studies conducted from 1963 to 1982, compiled by Hale, Stansfield, and Duran (1984). Predictive validity studies such as those by Chase and Stallings (1966) and Gue and Holdaway (1973) pointed out that although correlations between TOEFL performance and academic success generally were low, these were considered not to detract from the validity of the TOEFL because language ability and academic performance were not considered the same. Studies investigating concurrent validity looked at performance on the TOEFL in relation to performance on other recognized tests of similar abilities. Among studies cited from the early TOEFL period were those by Maxwell (1965),

Upshur (1966), and Pack (1972). For the most part, correlations between the TOEFL and other similar tests were quite high, providing evidence for the concurrent validity of the TOEFL.

The two most prominent approaches for seeking construct validity evidence in support of the inferences made from TOEFL scores came from (a) comparisons of native speaker performance with TOEFL candidates' performance on the TOEFL and (b) correlations of the TOEFL with other second language tests (i.e., concurrent validity studies). In studies by Angoff and Sharon (1970) and by Clark (1977), the evidence indicating clear differences in performance between native and nonnative speakers was cited as support for the appropriateness and validity of the TOEFL for decisions about the language ability of nonnative speakers. Likewise, when nonnative speakers showed significantly different performance on the test, compared with their performance on tests of other abilities as well as aptitude measures, this was cited as evidence for TOEFL performance being something different and valid in its own right. Among such studies were those by Schrader and Pitcher (1970), Scoon and Blanchard (1970), and Angelis, Swinton, and Cowell (1979).

TOEFL research agenda   During the early TOEFL years, no formal research program existed for the TOEFL, nor was an impetus for research provided by an external research committee. As the first decade of the TOEFL drew to a close, however, pressure increased for research to become a regular part of the TOEFL program, for the initiation of a formal process by which TOEFL research could be planned with input from those in the growing field of language testing research, and for increased and regular communication between TOEFL developers and the language testing community. The late 1970s saw a rapid confluence of interest and focus on language testing research, which was mirrored by the response made within ETS for the TOEFL. The TOEFL program instituted the TOEFL Research Committee, which was composed of external specialists in language testing who could advise and direct research on TOEFL. Procedures were established to facilitate communication between the TOEFL Research Committee and the TOEFL COE; the chairs of these two committees were given standing places as members of the TOEFL Policy Council, which is composed of score users outside ETS from whom the TOEFL program takes direction. Moreover, a regular portion of the TOEFL program budget was designated to support the work of the TOEFL Research Committee, to fund research projects, and to disseminate research results as published reports and conference presentations.

One of the first of the studies launched within this structure (Pike, 1979) was a concurrent validity study based on data from 418 speakers of Spanish and Japanese who completed the existing TOEFL, a rewriting task (Hunt, 1970), a cloze measure, and four alternative multiple-choice subtests meant to explore effects of item presentation and response. Participants were also given an oral interview and asked to write four short essays, each on a different topic. Based on correlational data, the study concluded that there was a sufficiently strong relationship between performance on the listening comprehension section and oral interviews (evidence of concurrent validity) to warrant maintaining a listening component to test oral/aural skills. The relationship between the multiple-choice writing ability section and essay performance was also strong. In a similar fashion, the vocabulary and writing ability sections seemed to be highly correlated and to match performance on external measures such as words in context, sentence combining, and paragraph completion. The results of this study played a large role in the decision to change the TOEFL to a three-section test. Listening comprehension remained a separate section. English structure and writing ability were combined to form a new section called structure and written expression. Reading comprehension and vocabulary were combined to form a new section called reading comprehension. Research like Pike's was useful for better understanding language testing and the TOEFL in particular; therefore, such studies continued to be conducted, and over the following years the TOEFL underwent a number of revisions.

Summary

In 1961 these issues of construct, content, and validation were seen not only as technical and addressing scientific concerns, but also as issues to be communicated to test users. The testing program was intended to include a range of services to help users to understand the test and its scores: interpretive manuals and specimen tests for test users, materials explaining norms, and validation, including correlations with existing tests. These forms of communication, as well as the practice of rotating members on TOEFL test committees, provided a mechanism for shaping TOEFL's research agenda, maintaining fruitful discussion of issues, and informing subsequent TOEFL revisions.

TOEFL REVISIONS

In the latter part of the 1970s, the unresolved issues raised in 1961—the inclusion of a measure of integrative language proficiency as well as an assessment of speaking and writing—received greater attention. Some score users questioned the extent to which the TOEFL was fulfilling its intended purpose, in part because of new demands that arose with the rapidly growing pool of international students coming to the United States. One concern was the need for adequate oral skills on the part of graduate-level applicants who were to be considered for assignments as teaching assistants. The need to assess the speaking ability of international graduate students forced the issue that assessment of linguistic production was essential, and therefore the TOEFL program developed a new test for this purpose, the Test of Spoken English™

TABLE 2.2
Decisions About Testing Issues for the Revised TOEFL Suite of Tests

Testing Issue	Decision
Construct: What should the test measure?	The original constructs of the test (listening, reading, and structure and written expression) were retained, but two additional ones were added: writing and speaking. The construct definition remained the list of components expected to affect English language performance across the wide range of relevant situations, but added two separate constructs of writing ability and speaking ability, tested by the TSE and TWE.
Content: What should the test consist of?	The main part of the test retained multiple-choice sections: English structure, listening comprehension, vocabulary, and reading comprehension. The TWE required examinees to write an essay in response to a prompt, and the TSE required examinees to give spoken responses to a set of recorded prompts, many of which targeted specific areas of speaking.
Validation: How can test use be justified?	A program for exploring communicative competence, investigating issues leading to development of the TSE and TWE, and developing a research agenda was implemented.

(TSE®). A second concern was the dissatisfaction expressed by the testing community and teachers of English as a second language about the use of the TOEFL Structure and Written Expression section as a measure of writing. In response, the TOEFL program developed a measure requiring written production, the Test of Written English™ (TWE®). The introduction of the TSE and TWE tests motivated continued exploration of basic issues in assessment, as outlined in Table 2.2.

What the Test Should Measure

By the 1980s, Carroll's 1961 idea of integrative language ability had been expanded and explored by researchers in applied linguistics using terms such as *communicative competence*. The TOEFL program attempted to gather information and conduct analyses that would help to determine how communicative competence could be measured by the TOEFL. An invitational conference was held in 1986 with the purpose of analyzing the implications of communicative competence theory for the TOEFL. The summary statements made by Tucker at the conference (Tucker, 1986) identified some of the key issues at that time as ones surrounding the notions of context and discourse and their implications for test design and content. In line with some research already begun, Tucker highlighted as well the need to "describe better the language tasks or the demands that are made on students in an American academic context" (p. 194), but referred at the same time to the emphasis placed by many of the conference presenters on examining for possible testing of the compensatory strategies that nonnative speakers employed. However, little action was taken on the basis of this exploration of communicative competence during this period.

Test Content

The 1980s saw a special focus given to explorations of issues with direct links to test content and format. For this reason, the TOEFL Research Committee and TOEFL COE decided to hold joint meetings for 3 consecutive years (1981, 1982, and 1983) with a particular focus on implications of communicative competence for the test. Despite plenty of discussion, immediate content implications proved to be difficult to determine. The dramatic changes in content during this period were probably motivated more directly by perceived needs of the test users for scores on tests of writing and speaking ability.

The introduction of the TWE was met with much support from the language teaching community because the test required actual writing. Not only was this seen as a sign of a move toward testing of real language abilities but also as support for the teaching of writing. Particularly in ESL settings such as intensive English programs in the United States, teachers had long bemoaned the fact that their efforts at teaching writing had been met with little enthusiasm from students because the students knew that the test they would take as part of their pursuit of university admission was a completely multiple-choice test. For much of its initial period, however, the TWE was offered as a separate test from the TOEFL. Those who took the TOEFL did not necessarily take the TWE. A number of factors soon led to the decision to include the TWE as part of selected TOEFL test administrations, but a similar decision was not made for the TSE, perhaps because of logistics and cost. Rather than considering the addition of a new component of TOEFL that could address speaking proficiency for all test takers and hence be administered with the TOEFL, the TSE was developed primarily to address the need to assess prospective graduate teaching assistants, and because of this, the TSE needed to be administered as a separate test.

Validation

During this period, a number of validation concerns were raised and addressed, but particular attention was given to providing a research basis for the new TWE and TSE and attempting to provide some data to complement the theoretical perspectives offered on communicative competence.

The TWE and TSE In preparation for the TWE, some critical studies were carried out to investigate the character and importance of writing demands for foreign students in American universities. The first of these gathered data to identify the writing tasks required of undergraduate and graduate international students (Bridgeman & Carlson, 1983). The second examined the relationship of admission test scores to writing performance of both native and nonnative speakers of English (Carlson, Bridgeman, Camp, & Waanders, 1985). This research and the development of the TWE addressed some concerns about the assessment of writing, but criticisms were made about the research as well as about operational practices such as the manner for determining topics for writing and scoring responses (Raimes, 1990). For the TSE, research investigated content issues, such as performance on a range of test item types relative to performance on an oral interview (Clark & Swinton, 1979), and provided data upon which decisions were made affecting the final version of the TSE. Once in use, further studies examined the role of that test in actual instructional settings (Clark & Swinton, 1980) and then for special populations other than international teaching assistants. One of the first such populations was health professionals (Powers & Stansfield, 1983).

Communicative competence   A number of studies were undertaken seeking evidence for the extent to which the existing TOEFL could be considered a measure of communicative competence. One study examined the content of the items on the TOEFL from the perspective of communicative competence (Duran, Canale, Penfield, Stansfield, & Liskin-Gasparro, 1985). Others investigated factors underlying performance on the existing TOEFL sections (Boldt, 1988), the relationship between examinees' major field and performance on reading comprehension passages (Hale, 1988), and the relationship between familiarity with American culture and performance on TOEFL items that employ an American context or setting (Angoff, 1989). Another study investigated faculty perceptions of the importance of various listening skills and activities for academic success. In a study by Powers (1985), faculty views about the appropriateness of alternative methods of assessing these skills were also obtained. Of particular interest was the question of framing the minitalks that served as input for some of the listening items. This referred to providing an announcement at the start of the minitalk to indicate the setting (place, interlocutors, etc.) for what examinees would then hear.

The most comprehensive study done during this period explored how communicative competence could be interpreted within the TOEFL context and sought to demonstrate empirically the degree to which TOEFL and other similar tests could assess communicative competence. Henning and Cascallar (1992) identified the problems associated with defining communicative competence and detailed many of the limitations associated with the skills/components model of language and of testing prominent in much of the work of Carroll (1961) and Lado (1961), which had formed the basis for the TOEFL. Henning and Cascallar summarized the linguistic, discourse, sociolinguistic, and strategic competence features of the communicative competence models put forward at that time but pointed out that "little empirical evidence had yet been found for any hierarchical ordering of the constituent components of these models" (p. 3). Even more important and significant for the time was these authors' summary comment that "there is no one ultimate model of communicative competence. Nor is it expected that any one model will serve all purposes equally well" (p. 5).

TOEFL research agenda   Under the joint leadership of key individuals in the ETS research and program divisions and with the aid of the TOEFL Research Committee, the first TOEFL research agenda (Alderman, 1979) was developed as a means of looking ahead to plan research studies and looking back to assess their impact for the test. This agenda reflected the conception of validity dominant in language testing with inclusion of content, predictive, concurrent, and construct components. In an effort to follow the lines of research being explored within the larger network of second language testing, additional studies were undertaken at a much faster pace from this time forward.

Summary

Activities during the 1980s forecasted many issues that became the concerns of the new TOEFL project. The TOEFL COE and the TOEFL Research Committee were beginning to wrestle with the need for integrative measures requiring constructed responses and the complexities introduced by communicative competence theory. At the 1986 conference, Tucker even broached the idea that alternative delivery mechanisms were becoming available, pointing out examples of places where some breakthroughs had been made with computer-assisted or other modes of interactive systems. During this period, however, the focus remained on the new operational challenges of meeting test users' immediate concerns by providing scores for examinees' constructed written and oral responses on the TWE and the TSE, respectively.

Many test users were satisfied that these additional tests indicated one step forward, but at the same time, communication of score meaning was awkward, with the maintenance of separate scores for the TOEFL (which was composed of the three subscores) and for the add-on tests in writing and speaking. The TWE was given at some of the administrations of the TOEFL, but even under this arrangement, a clear distinction between the two tests remained in that TWE had its own scoring system using a 6-point holistic scale. Score reports showed both the traditional two-digit part scores and three-digit total score for the TOEFL plus the separate 0–6 score for the TWE. With increasing numbers of persons taking both the TOEFL and the TWE, it became easier to collect data on the comparative performance on these two measures, but questions concerning the interpretation of these dual sets of scores sparked much debate concerning broader issues of validity and the appropriateness of the tests. The inherent problems in trying to combine two very different score scales were investigated but not resolved at this time. Instead, the TOEFL Policy Council felt that it would be worthwhile to attempt to reconceptualize the TOEFL in a manner that would draw upon communicative competence theory to design a new test.

Initial Work on the New TOEFL

The events of the 1980s left the TOEFL program with a number of unresolved tensions. Although content changes had been made to address needs expressed by users, the basis for score interpretation had been questioned by the content experts who hoped to see the implications of communicative competence take a more central role. Interpretation of the awkward dual TOEFL and TWE scores on the score report was not evident; pressures for exploring technology were on the horizon, and how validation should be conceived and conducted was debated. The new TOEFL project was born out of these tensions that surfaced regularly at meetings of the TOEFL COE, the TOEFL Research Committee, and the TOEFL Policy Council. The tensions prompted the TOEFL program to return to the initial questions that had been posed at the 1961 meeting: the purpose of the test, the operational issues affecting test delivery, and reasonable goals for the revision project.

Reestablishing TOEFL's Purpose

To investigate TOEFL's purpose in the 1990s, program staff and external consultants conducted TOEFL score user focus groups, telephone interviews, and a mail survey. The focus groups and telephone interviews (Educational Testing Service [ETS], 1993b) invited comment from official test score users, including undergraduate and graduate admissions officers, graduate deans, department chairs, and directors of intensive English programs in North America. This initial score user group represented large and small institutions, public and private schools, and 2-year, 4-year, and comprehensive degree programs. The focus groups and telephone interviews were used to develop a mail survey, sent to institutions and sponsoring agencies that regularly received official test score reports. Collectively these users provided information in four principal areas: (a) decision-making purpose(s) for which TOEFL scores were used, (b) international student enrollment trends, (c) current uses of TOEFL, and (d) perceived needs for the new TOEFL. These test users reaffirmed that the primary use of the new TOEFL would be to inform admissions decisions with respect to the English language proficiency of nonnative speakers of English.

They also confirmed what the TOEFL committees had called for in a new test that would (a) be more communicative, (b) include more constructed-response tasks and direct measures of speaking and writing, (c) include tasks that integrated language modalities, and (d) provide more information than existing TOEFL scores about the ability of international students to use English in an academic environment. There was fairly strong consensus among score users that descriptors similar to those provided with TSE and TWE scores would make test scores more meaningful. While many score users wanted richer score interpretation that provided language performance information by modality (i.e., reading, writing, listening, speaking), they also continued to want a single, total test score for initial selection of the most qualified among large numbers of students. Results further indicated that score users:

- supported the idea of a new computerized TOEFL test but advised continuing to offer the paper-based test
- were concerned about examinees' familiarity with and access to computers
- were tolerant of increased fees if the new test provided additional information about examinees' English proficiency
- desired direct measures of writing and speaking in the new test
- desired expedited score reporting processes
- requested assistance with interpreting TOEFL scores (Grant & Ginther, 1995)

As project staff and consultants considered feedback from official score users, they also identified three major trends in the test-taking population. First, in a study published in 2001, Powell reported a shift from undergraduate to graduate international students studying in the United States during the 1990s. Taylor (1994) reported a similar trend, based on TOEFL examinees' self-reported reasons for taking the TOEFL. Second, using Institute of International Education and UNESCO data, Powell (2001) reported a shift in the international student population such that the majority of international students studying in the United States were Asian. Again, TOEFL data (ETS, 1998a, 1999) were consistent with these reports and also revealed that international graduate students arrived with less need for intensive English study than their undergraduate counterparts. The 1997–1998 TOEFL data showed that the mean total scaled score for graduate students was 543, compared to 521 for undergraduate students. Finally, considering the 39.9% growth in the Overseas Institutional Testing Program volumes between 1993 and 1998, Powell concluded that the number of intensive and semi-intensive English language and TOEFL test preparation programs outside the United States had likely increased considerably. These trends suggested that the new test should extend the upper end of its scale to have better performance discrimination among its more English-proficient examinees bound for graduate programs.

Operational Issues

By the 1990s, developments affecting learning and assessment in higher education had evolved sufficiently to suggest the need to revisit operational possibilities for the new test. This was done through development of a list of constraints and working assumptions (Schedl, 1995), which included the factors shown in Appendix A. More dramatic than any of these constraints that had developed through discussion with consultants and test users was the interest expressed by ETS to move the TOEFL to computer. If the test were to be computer-based, a number of daunting new operational issues faced the project. No other existing computerized testing program at ETS used test tasks that included audio components. How would TOEFL transmit audio files, capture spoken responses, and transmit them for scoring? Would the test be linear or adaptive or some combination? Moreover, it was unclear how developing substantially larger item pools could be done efficiently if the test were to be computer adaptive.

Three monographs were therefore commissioned to review technology-related issues for the new TOEFL. Hansen and Willut (1998) considered current computer and communications technologies in colleges and universities in North America and projected how changes in these technologies by the year 2000 might change the way in which students did their work. The authors offered findings with respect to tools, instruction, testing, and administrative information (pp. 3–4):

1. Students had access to and were expected to use an increasing array of computer-related tools. These included personal computers and word processors, spreadsheets, presentation and database software, fax machines, modems, and online information systems.
2. While computer and communications technologies in instructional settings were diverse, they tended to be ancillary to the main instruction, in which lecture continues to dominate.
3. Computer and related technologies were widely used in testing, but the actual use of computer-based tests was still new and untried in many domains.
4. With respect to administrative information, students increasingly accessed information and registered for courses online. This area of computer use was expected to increase dramatically.

Hansen and Willut's (1998) main conclusion was that change toward a virtual classroom or campus would be fairly slow and evolutionary rather than revolutionary. They predicted the major change would be in the areas of increased use of tools such as word processing, e-mail, and Web-based services with easier and more rapid access to information. A major implication for test design was that "the increasing diversity of information media may increase the importance of the ability to coordinate and switch between different communication modalities and between different representational systems" (p. 27).

The second technology review (Frase et al., 1997) considered current and emerging technologies relevant to language testing from the perspective of a large-scale testing organization. Recognizing that the use of new technologies had ramifications for all aspects of test development, Frase et al. focused their review and recommendations in four broad areas—management strategies, new technologies, test development, and research processes. They recommended a flexible and cautious approach that would allow ETS to back out of a computer application when it did not appear to work well. They also identified existing technologies and projected when emerging technologies might actually be available to support computer-based testing of more communicative and integrated language performance.

Given the need to include a speaking component in a new test, a third review examined current and emerging capabilities of computer-based speech technology. Burstein et al. (1999) concluded that, while technologies existed that could capture and transmit speech, state-of-the-art commercial technology for speech recognition was not yet ready for high stakes applications like large-scale, computer-based testing of communicative language ability. These monographs underscored the challenge ahead for ETS and TOEFL to produce a computer-based test that would include all four modalities with performance-based language tasks. While technology was not intended to drive test design, it became clear that it would provide both new opportunities and constraints to the project, including concerns about the cost of the test that had been administered to nearly one million test takers in 1996–1997.

Goals for the New TOEFL

Teams of specialists composed of ETS staff and external consultants were called together to begin the task of investigating the implications, extent, and scope of work that lay ahead in the ambitious venture of creating a new TOEFL. A project team established in the fall of 1993 reviewed the work of the TOEFL COE and discussions that had occurred with the TOEFL Policy Council and other TOEFL committees. From this work, the team identified a set of project goals that would determine a work plan for the next phase of the project. According to the initial planning document (ETS, 1993a, 1994), these goals included creating a new TOEFL that would:

- reflect current theories of communicative language use in an academic context
- result in valid and reliable decision making and fairness to examinees
- provide more information to score users

- be offered internationally
- be fiscally responsible
- incorporate appropriate technological capabilities
- provide opportunity for expanded services
- offer the possibility of continuous improvement.

While not explicitly stated at this point, an additional goal was to create a test that would be more aligned with current language teaching practice and thus create a test with more positive washback than the existing TOEFL. These goals, supplemented by the advice and ongoing review of the TOEFL Policy Council and committees, informed the project work plan that was composed of several parallel, interrelated efforts to help to define what the test should be measuring, what the content should consist of, and what validation work would be needed. The directions identified for each area are summarized in Table 2.3.

What the Test Should Measure

The process of exploring communicative competence as a basis for score interpretation made explicit the presuppositions and beliefs that were introduced in the previous chapter: that a theoretical construct should form the basis for score interpretation, that the construct should comprise the complex abilities responsible for performance, and that score interpretation should take into account the relevant contexts of language use. These perspectives were evident in the first paper that was written to record the discussions of the TOEFL COE in the early 1990s about communicative competence for the new TOEFL (Chapelle, Grabe, & Berns, 1997) as well as in several other papers that were commissioned to elaborate on particular aspects of communicative competence.

TABLE 2.3
Directions Identified for the New TOEFL

Testing Issue	Direction
Construct: What construct should the test measure?	The test should more accurately reflect communicative competence, which refers to the ability to put language knowledge into use in relevant contexts. Scores based on measurement of the construct should discriminate at the high end of the TOEFL scale.
Test content: What should the test consist of?	Test tasks should require examinees to perform on tasks that resemble those that they will encounter in the academic setting.
Validation: How can test use be justified?	The test should be subject to ongoing investigations that help to provide evidence about score meaning and the consequences of score use.

Communicative competence   Chapelle et al. (1997) documented consensus among members on the TOEFL COE in the early 1990s by drawing on the conceptions of communicative competence put forward by Canale and Swain (1980) and Bachman (1990), which included knowledge of language (e.g., grammatical, sociolinguistic, and textual knowledge) as well as strategic competence and the context of language use. The TOEFL COE's working model of communicative language use in an academic context included these same basic aspects to attempt to conceptualize the relevant aspects of language use in an academic context, as shown in Figure 2.1. The model included language knowledge, procedural competence, and the context of language use, which

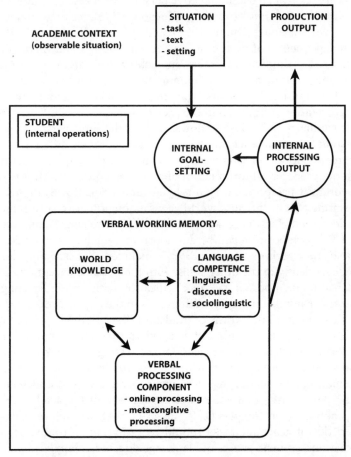

FIG. 2.1   A working model of communicative language use in an academic context. From *Communicative Language Proficiency: Definition and Implications for TOEFL 2000* (TOEFL Monograph No. 10), by C. Chapelle, W. Grabe, and M. Berns, 1997, Princeton, NJ: Educational Testing Service. Copyright 1997 by Educational Testing Service. Adapted with permission.

for academic language use is defined through a combination of texts, tasks, and settings.

The TOEFL program sought more insight and input into the process of understanding the constructs that might form a basis for score interpretation by commissioning papers to explore each of the areas for which scores might ultimately be reported—reading, writing, listening, and speaking. With the goal of linking prior research in these areas to the TOEFL COE's working model of communicative language use in an academic context, the authors of the papers were sent a draft of the paper by Chapelle et al. (1997) as a starting point for their contribution. Each author or set of authors was then asked to provide a critical review of literature and research related to the assessment of each skill area from a communicative perspective. These four monographs, dealing with the domains of reading (Hudson, 1996), writing (Hamp-Lyons & Kroll, 1996), listening (Rubin, 1993), and speaking (Douglas, 1997), were written independently of each other in the early 1990s and represented the perspectives of the individual experts in each of these areas. Summarized in Table 2.4, the resulting analyses of communicative competence and each language skill instantiated elements from the three beliefs about the basis of score interpretation introduced in the previous chapter.

As the summary in Table 2.4 shows, each of the three perspectives is evident to some extent in each of the papers even though differences appear as a matter of degree of emphasis. For example, the paper on writing relied least on a theoretical formulation of a writing construct. After reviewing some theoretical perspectives, Hamp-Lyons and Kroll (1996) quoted Johns (1990), stating that "...because world views among theorists, researchers and teachers in both the first language and ESL differ...no single, comprehensive theory of ESL composition can be developed on which all can agree" (p. 9). Unlike the other authors, Rubin (1993) concluded that listening should be tested independently of the other skills, with the possible exception of allowing students to take notes or ask for clarification with certain listening tasks. However, more notable than these differences in the papers is their agreement on two areas. First, in the words of Hudson (1996) in the paper on reading, "There is no assertion that this will be easy" (p. 13). The complexity of each of the areas covered and the implications for testing were acknowledged by all authors. Second, all agreed that in view of the important role of context in performance, an essential step in moving forward was to understand better the academic tasks that examinees would face in the academic setting. In the speaking paper, Douglas (1997) asserted that research revealing these characteristics of academic tasks should be drawn upon to give examinees "...instructions, content, genre, and language directed at [applicants to North American colleges and universities]" (p. 18).

Academic tasks   In an attempt to better understand academic tasks, another set of reviews was commissioned to consider research related to the

TABLE 2.4
Summary of Reviews of Five Domains Relevant to New TOEFL Score Interpretation From the Early 1990s

Domain	*Perspective Reflected in the Reviews*[a]		
	A theoretical construct is needed	*The construct should be a complex of knowledge and abilities*	*Context of language use should be included*
Communicative competence (Chapelle, Grabe, & Berns, 1997)	Draws on communicative competence, functional linguistics, and sociolinguistic theory	Defines specific aspects of linguistic knowledge, psycholinguistic processes, and procedures, postulated to account for performance	Defines context through texts, tasks, and settings
Reading (Hudson, 1996)	Draws on psycholinguistic theory	Discusses processes (e.g., automaticity), content and formal schemata, strategies and metacognitive skills, and reader purpose	Identifies context of reading and types of texts as important
Listening (Rubin, 1993)	Draws on theory of auditory perception and processing	Identifies sociolinguistic knowledge and memory as significant	Identifies multiple contextual factors, discourse markers, pause and hesitation, text difficulty, text type, and academic tasks
Writing (Hamp-Lyons & Kroll, 1996)	Draws on second language acquisition and composition theory, but acknowledges that no single theory exists	Defines knowledge and abilities as discourse competence	Suggests that tasks, texts, and raters all affect writing
Speaking (Douglas, 1997)	Draws on a psycholinguistic model of speech production	Defines language knowledge, psycholinguistic processes, and metacognitive strategies	Identifies a range of contextual features viewed from the perspective of test method characteristics

[a] The three beliefs about the basis of score interpretation described in Chapter 1.

language needs of students in North American academic settings. Ginther and Grant (1996) reviewed the research on native English-speaking students, and Waters (1996) reviewed research on nonnative English speaking students. Based on both of these reviews, Ginther and Grant concluded the following:

> Because the focus has been on instruction rather than on testing, and because instruction takes place over a period of time of at least a quarter in university

settings, insights that might be derived to inform test design are limited. Indeed, this review may offer more insight into what TOEFL 2000 cannot be rather than what it should be or will be. (p. 1)

Thus, it is critical that a plan guide the data collection. Going out into the universe of possible tasks, sampling those tasks, categorizing those tasks, and then deriving information that will inform test design from those tasks may be impossible in one lifetime; it seems more logical to determine the domain of interest using a defensible rationale prior to the study, collect information according to a specific plan, and finally utilize that information collected as a means of validating the construct. (p. 30)

In short, all attempts to better understand the role of communicative competence as a construct that could improve score interpretation in the early 1990s revealed issues of increased complexity rather than a clear path for moving forward.

Test Content Issues

In 1995, certain aspects of the test were changed as a first step toward a more communicative approach to language testing. Single-statement listening comprehension items were eliminated, the academic lectures and longer dialogues used in the listening section were increased in number, and vocabulary tasks were embedded in reading comprehension passages to test vocabulary in context (ETS, 1998b). While research on these changes revealed some evidence of increased construct validity over the previous test configuration (Freedle & Kostin, 1996; Nissan, DeVincenzi, & Tang, 1996; Schedl, Thomas, & Way, 1995), these changes reflected relatively minor progress toward the more comprehensive test redesign that was a primary goal of the new TOEFL. Nevertheless, the changes constituted some clear test content redesign that provided a better link to communicative competence theory.

More dramatic test content changes were also explored by the project team, who met with a subgroup of the TOEFL COE and brainstormed what tasks a new test might consist of. One approach discussed was to create a set of modules of test tasks based on a day in the life of a student. This was quickly abandoned because of test length that such an approach would require. Following this meeting, prototyping teams at ETS operationalized critical aspects of communicative competence into several modules of test tasks, referred to as *clay models*. Retention of these modules served the purposes of (a) presenting for consideration sets of test tasks that were thought to take into account both the TOEFL COE's model and what TOEFL constituents had called for in a new TOEFL and (b) identifying research and development issues emanating from discussion of these clay models for consideration in the next phase of the project. The modules included extended reading and listening passages that were contextualized and linked thematically. They also contained integrated, performance-based writing and speaking tasks. With this integration, writing and speaking tasks were derived from thematically linked reading texts and listening stimuli. The modules included printed text, visuals, and videotaped lectures and discussions. As such, these test tasks represented a dramatic departure from the TOEFL paper-based test (PBT) in terms of content, task types, and scoring.

These modules revealed critical issues for project staff when they were considered in the context of large-scale testing, with the potential need for large task banks. These efforts were further complicated by ETS's shift of a number of its major testing programs to computer and an expressed interest in also moving TOEFL to computer. After reviewing the set of prototype modules, the project team did not see a way of presenting such modules on a computer in either a continuous or episodic testing situation without their content quickly becoming compromised. The test tasks based on extended communicative contexts appeared to be considerably more memorable than stimuli and tasks with less context, such as discrete grammar items. But of more critical concern was that a test with a limited number of extended tasks and linked topics would of necessity include fewer test tasks and topics than the current discrete-point test. This raised issues of construct underrepresentation and test fairness. With far fewer tasks linked to one or two topics, some examinees would likely be advantaged because of greater background knowledge related to the topic of the module while others would be disadvantaged. Rather than reducing construct underrepresentation through creation of more complex tasks, it appeared that the modules increased construct underrepresentation and would likely add sources of construct-irrelevant variance by drawing less on language knowledge and more on content knowledge. In addition, a test with a relatively small number of tasks would likely result in less reliable scores than those obtained from the existing discrete-point test.

Validation

Although the majority of the effort in the early 1990s was directed toward examining the nature of communicative competence theory and its implications for test design and delivery, the concomitant need for a relevant program of research remained a concern. The changes in validation perspectives emphasizing multiple strands of evidence to support score interpretation, as well as the role of consequences in validation, were evident in a number of the papers on test validity from this period. Intending to reflect these current perspectives on validation explicitly, Brown, Perkins, and Upshur (1995) created a research agenda to help inform the test development process for the new test and subsequently to provide technical information and guidance in interpreting score data from new forms of the test (see Appendix B). Their work focused specifically on research questions related to imminent test revisions and validity issues. They proposed 20 research questions grouped by:

(a) construct/domain, (b) task validity, (c) task reliability, (d) task fairness, and (e) delivery. These issues reflect a number of the familiar validation issues, but they also hint at one validation issue that dominated discussion of the new TOEFL during this period, the issue of the consequences of the TOEFL.

As the TOEFL grew to be taken by close to a million examinees each year, the effects, or washback, of TOEFL on instruction were a constant source of concern. The increased use of the test in intensive English programs outside the United States suggested more careful consideration of issues of test washback. Powell's (2001) analysis of the relationship of intensive English programs (IEPs) to TOEFL concluded the following:

> It is no striking disclosure to assert that the TOEFL is a primary impetus for IEP enrollment by students intending to pursue a degree in the United States, nor is it breaking news that IEPs are pressured to respond curricularly to the perceived needs of their learners. Of the 530 intensive programs described in English Language and Orientation Programs in the United States, 362 reported use of the Institutional TOEFL; 280 programs expressly included mention of a TOEFL preparation course in their curricular offerings. (p. 31)

From discussions with TOEFL committee members and other language teachers and testers, the TOEFL program knew that many individuals were dissatisfied because of the perceived negative effects of the multiple-choice TOEFL on language instruction. While the addition of the TWE and the TSE were viewed by some as important enhancements to the overall testing program from a washback perspective, they were also viewed by some to be of limited value because they were not directly incorporated into the TOEFL and total test score. In addition, in 1993 the TWE was administered at only 5 of the 12 official TOEFL test administrations, and score users reported that limited access to the test was the primary reason that they did not require TWE scores for admissions purposes. Language teachers also wanted high-stakes tests to reflect more authentic tasks and situations that would reinforce a communicative language curriculum. While not formally documented in prior TOEFL research, these concerns had appeared in documents addressing the broader field of English as a second language testing (Alderson & Wall, 1993; Hughes, 1993).

For a more thorough consideration of washback issues, the project team commissioned a review of literature and research on TOEFL washback. This work was intended to review issues of consequential validity and provide a research direction for the development project and later for the new test. Bailey (1999) began her review of literature by noting the longstanding assertion that "tests exert a powerful influence on language learners who are preparing to take these exams, and on the teachers who try to help them prepare" (p. 1). Bailey concluded the first section of her review with four observations: (a) language testing washback had often been discussed, (b) it was widely held to exist, (c) there was no unified point of view about what the construct of washback encompassed, and (d) positive washback should be given consideration in the development and evaluation of language tests. She then created a model for washback in language testing based on Hughes' (1993) distinction among participants, processes, and products. Bailey concluded her monograph with a recommendation for a triangulated approach to studying washback for the TOEFL, arguing for the collection and use of both quantitative and qualitative data over time in order to provide evidence of the extent to which the introduction of a new TOEFL would impact language instruction and learning. While there was some discussion of the consequences of testing at this phase of the project and how the impact of the current test on instruction provided impetus for a new test, it was not until the next phase of the project, discussed in Chapter 3, that development teams asked how to know that the test is better, and improved washback became an explicit goal of the project.

Summary

Because this overview cannot capture the complexity of the many overlapping processes that occurred during this period of gathering information and generating ideas, Appendix C outlines key project efforts and decisions. It should be evident from the review of the beginning of the new TOEFL exploration that this phase created more questions than answers. Each of the aspects of the test and testing program that had been defined in the 1961 meeting, and revised during the 1980s, was reviewed, questioned, and once again put on the table for discussion. Table 2.5 summarizes the changing status of each of the key areas of the testing program as decisions gave way to questions during the 1990s.

The questions raised about the test construct, content, and validation, in turn, brought up additional challenges, not the least of which was a psychometric model appropriate for meeting the needs of the new test. It was unclear whether existing psychometric models could be applied to language testing data that included test tasks that integrated two or more modalities, which appeared to be a reasonable demand in communicative competence theory. Another challenge was how to undertake targeted research in a timely fashion and provide results for development. An alternative model to the semi-annual TOEFL Research Committee meetings was needed that would allow for a much more timely development of an integrated research agenda, have significantly increased funding available for research and development efforts, and accommodate monthly cycles of review with project liaisons who would monitor project completion. These issues were contemplated during a transition period for TOEFL.

TABLE 2.5
Testing Issues and Their Responses by the First TOEFL, the Revised TOEFL, and the New
TOEFL

	Decisions and Questions Raised at Each Stage of the TOEFL		
Testing issue	First TOEFL	Revised TOEFL	New TOEFL
Construct: score interpretation	English proficiency: subscores and a total score. The construct is a list of components affecting performance across situations.	Same as the original construct, but writing ability and speaking ability were added as separate constructs.	How can an appropriate theoretical perspective based on communicative competence be articulated to underlie score interpretation?
Test content	Multiple-choice sections for English structure, listening, vocabulary, and reading comprehension.	Multiple-choice sections for English structure, listening, vocabulary, and reading comprehension. Separate tests for writing ability and speaking ability.	How can test tasks be conceptualized to tap into theoretically-defined abilities and to reflect the tasks learners will confront in the academic setting?
Validation: justifying test use	Pretesting and correlations with other tests and performance	Investigations leading to development of the writing and speaking tests	How can the appropriate inferences and assumptions be articulated in a way that will form a basis for the interpretive argument that includes utilization of test scores?

A Transition Period for TOEFL

A review and advisory meeting was held in the fall of 1994 with three language testing experts, Lyle Bachman, Merrill Swain, and J. Charles Alderson. Shortly thereafter in 1995, project staff (Taylor, Eignor, Schedl, & DeVincenzi, 1995) reviewed the results of the cumulative efforts and discussed them with the TOEFL committees and consultants. Both of these reviews made it apparent that, collectively, the papers synthesizing prior theory and research did not provide a framework that test developers could use to build a new test with multiple forms. The papers identified challenges and posed large research questions, but they did not provide a clear course for developing a language test. Moreover, by this time others had also found it difficult to connect existing research on communicative competence to a test framework. McNamara (1996) provided an extensive critique of attempts to build tests using communicative competence models and also underscored the difficulty of linking theory and testing practice.

It was apparent that a new project infrastructure and longer development and implementation time frame would be required to create, research, and implement a new TOEFL that responded to constituencies' concerns and needs. The resulting consensus was that the development effort should be bifurcated. ETS would move the TOEFL PBT to computer with some important design enhancements drawn from the foundational work of the new TOEFL project. The original vision of the TOEFL project would then continue to be pursued within the Research division of ETS.

This incremental approach to test revision would allow the TOEFL to build on existing work while exploring future test innovations. Some members of the project team were charged with conducting the research to inform the TOEFL computer-based testing (CBT) design and others were reassigned to develop the computer-based TOEFL. New test design features were identified, computer-based prototypes were created and piloted, a study of TOEFL examinees' computer familiarity and performance on computer-based test tasks was undertaken, and TOEFL CBT implementation plans were developed. Several TOEFL research reports detail this research and describe in detail the new task types created for TOEFL CBT (Eignor, Taylor, Kirsch, & Jamieson, 1998; Jamieson, Taylor, Kirsch, & Eignor, 1999; Kirsch, Jamieson, Taylor, & Eignor, 1998; Taylor, Jamieson, Eignor, & Kirsch, 1998). With the implementation of the TOEFL CBT underway, in the fall of 1996 new TOEFL project staff resumed work on conceptualizing test frameworks, developing a new research oversight and funding model, and pursuing research to inform test design, as described in the next chapter.

REFERENCES

Alderman, D. (1979). *TOEFL research agenda* (internal TOEFL report). Princeton, NJ: Educational Testing Service.

Alderson, J. C., & Wall, D. (1993). Does washback exist? *Applied Linguistics, 14*, 115–129.

Angelis, P. (1982). Academic needs and priorities for testing. *American Language Journal, 1*, 41–56.

Angelis, P., Swinton, S., & Cowell, W. (1979). *The performance of non-native speakers of English on TOEFL and verbal aptitude tests* (TOEFL Research Rep. No. 3). Princeton, NJ: Educational Testing Service.

Angoff, W. H. (1989). *Context bias in the Test of English as a Foreign Language* (TOEFL Research Rep. No. 29). Princeton, NJ: Educational Testing Service.

Angoff, W. H., & Sharon, A. T. (1970). *A comparison of scores earned on the Test of English as a Foreign Language by Native American college students and foreign applicants to U.S. colleges* (ETS Research Bulletin No. RB-70-08). Princeton, NJ: Educational Testing Services.

Bachman, L. F. (1990). *Fundamental considerations in language testing*. Oxford: Oxford University Press.

Bailey, K. M. (1999). *Washback in language testing* (TOEFL Monograph No. 15). Princeton, NJ: Educational Testing Service.

Boldt, R. F. (1988). *Latent structure analysis of the Test of English as a Foreign Language* (TOEFL Research Rep. No. 28). Princeton, NJ: Educational Testing Service.

Bridgeman, B., & Carlson, S. (1983). *Survey of academic writing tasks required of graduate and undergraduate foreign students* (TOEFL Research Rep. No. 15). Princeton, NJ: Educational Testing Service.

Brown, J. D., Perkins, K., & Upshur, J. (1995). *Research recommendations for the TOEFL 2000 project* (internal TOEFL 2000 report). Princeton, NJ: Educational Testing Service.

Burstein, J. C., Kaplan, R. M., Rohen-Wolff, S., Zuckerman, D. I., & Lu, C. (1999). *A review of computer-based speech technology for TOEFL 2000* (TOEFL Monograph No. 13). Princeton, NJ: Educational Testing Service.

Canale, M., & Swain, M. (1980). Theoretical bases of communicative approaches to second language teaching and testing. *Applied Linguistics, 1,* 1–47.

Carlson, S., Bridgeman, B., Camp, R., & Waanders, E. (1985). *Relationship of admission test scores to writing performance of native and nonnative speakers of English* (TOEFL Research Rep. No. 19). Princeton, NJ: Educational Testing Service.

Carroll, J. B. (1961). Fundamental considerations in testing for English proficiency of foreign students. In *Testing the English proficiency of foreign students* (pp. 31–40). Washington, DC: Center for Applied Linguistics.

Chapelle, C., Grabe, W., & Berns, M. (1997). *Communicative language proficiency: Definition and implications for TOEFL 2000* (TOEFL Monograph No. 10). Princeton, NJ: Educational Testing Service.

Chase, C. I., & Stallings, W. M. (1966). *Tests of English language as predictors of success for foreign students* (Indiana Studies in Prediction No. 8). Bloomington: Bureau of Educational Studies and Testing, Indiana University.

Clark, J. L. D. (1977). *The performance of native speakers of English on the Test of English as a Foreign Language* (TOEFL Research Rep. No. 1). Princeton, NJ: Educational Testing Service.

Clark, J. L. D., & Swinton, S. S. (1979). *An exploration of speaking proficiency measures in the TOEFL context* (TOEFL Research Rep. No. 4). Princeton, NJ: Educational Testing Service.

Clark, J. L. D., & Swinton, S. S. (1980). *The Test of Spoken English as a measure of communicative ability in English-medium instructional settings* (TOEFL Research Rep. No. 7). Princeton, NJ: Educational Testing Service.

Douglas, D. (1997). *Testing speaking ability in academic contexts: Theoretical considerations* (TOEFL Monograph No. 8). Princeton, NJ: Educational Testing Service.

Duran, R., Canale, M., Penfield, J., Stansfield, C., & Liskin-Gasparro, J. (1985). *TOEFL from a communicative viewpoint on language proficiency: A working paper* (TOEFL Research Rep. No. 17). Princeton, NJ: Educational Testing Service.

Educational Testing Service. (1993a). *Project plan for TOEFL 2000* (internal TOEFL 2000 report). Princeton, NJ: Author.

Educational Testing Service. (1993b). *Initial information gathering from TOEFL score users and overview of preliminary findings* (internal report to the TOEFL Policy Council). Princeton, NJ: Author.

Educational Testing Service. (1994). *TOEFL 2000 Stage I task assignments and timeline* (internal TOEFL 2000 report). Princeton, NJ: Author.

Educational Testing Service. (1998a). *1997–1998 TOEFL volumes and trends.* Princeton, NJ: Author.

Educational Testing Service. (1998b). *Computer-based TOEFL score user guide* (1998–1999 ed.) Princeton, NJ: Author.

Educational Testing Service. (1999). *TOEFL test and score data summary* (1998–1999 ed.) Princeton, NJ: Author.

Eignor, D., Taylor, C., Kirsch, I., & Jamieson, J. (1998). *Development of a scale for assessing the level of computer familiarity of TOEFL examinees* (TOEFL Research Rep. No. 60). Princeton, NJ: Educational Testing Service.

Frase, L. T., Gong, B., Hansen, E., Kaplan, R., Katz, I., & Singley, K. (1997). *Technologies for language testing* (TOEFL Monograph No. 11). Princeton, NJ: Educational Testing Service.

Freedle, R. O., & Kostin, I. W. (1996). *The prediction of TOEFL listening comprehension item difficulty for minitalk passages: Implications for construct validity* (TOEFL Research Rep. No. 56). Princeton, NJ: Educational Testing Service.

Ginther, A., & Grant, L. (1996). *A review of the academic needs of native English-speaking college students in the United States* (TOEFL Monograph No. 1). Princeton, NJ: Educational Testing Service.

Gough. D. (1993). *Trends in international student enrollments in colleges and universities in North America* (internal TOEFL 2000 report). Princeton, NJ: Educational Testing Service.

Grant, L., & Ginther, A. (1995). *TOEFL 2000 score user survey report* (internal TOEFL 2000 report). Princeton, NJ: Educational Testing Service.

Gue, L. R., & Holdaway, E. A. (1973). English proficiency tests as predictors of success in graduate studies in education. *Language Learning, 23,* 89–103.

Hale, G. A. (1988). *The interaction of student major-field group and test content in TOEFL reading comprehension.* (TOEFL Research Rep. No. 25). Princeton, NJ: Educational Testing Service.

Hale, G. A., & Hinofotis, F. (1981). *New directions in English language testing* (internal TOEFL Research Committee report). Princeton, NJ: Educational Testing Service.

Hale, G. A., Stansfield, C. W., & Duran, R. P. (1984). *Summaries of studies involving the Test of English as a Foreign Language, 1963–1982* (TOEFL Research Rep. No. 16). Princeton, NJ: Educational Testing Service.

Hamp-Lyons, L., & Kroll, B. (1996). *TOEFL 2000—Writing: Composition, community, and assessment* (TOEFL Monograph No. 5). Princeton, NJ: Educational Testing Service.

Hansen, E. G., & Willut, C. K. (1998). *Computer and communications technologies in colleges and universities in the year 2000* (TOEFL Monograph No. 12). Princeton, NJ: Educational Testing Service.

Henning, G., & Cascallar, E. (1992). *A preliminary study of the nature of communicative competence* (TOEFL Research Rep. No. 36). Princeton, NJ: Educational Testing Service.

Hudson, T. (1996). *Assessing second language academic reading from a communicative competence perspective: Relevance for TOEFL 2000* (TOEFL Monograph No. 4). Princeton, NJ: Educational Testing Service.

Hughes, A. (1993). *Backwash and TOEFL 2000.* Unpublished manuscript, University of Reading, UK.

Hunt, K. (1970). Syntactic maturity in school children and adults. *Society for Research in Child Development, 35,* 1–67.

Jamieson, J., Jones, S., Kirsch, I., Mosenthal, P., & Taylor, C. (2000). *TOFFL 2000 framework: A working paper* (TOEFL Monograph No. 16). Princeton, NJ: Educational Testing Service.

Jamieson, J., Taylor, C., Kirsch, I., & Eignor, D. (1999). *Designing and evaluating a computer-based TOEFL tutorial* (TOEFL Research Rep. No. 62). Princeton, NJ: Educational Testing Service.

Johns, A. M. (1990). L1 composition theories: Implications for developing theories of L2 composition. In B. Kroll (Ed.), *Second language writing: Research insights for the classroom* (pp. 24–36). New York: Cambridge University Press.

Kirsch, I., Jamieson, J., Taylor, C., & Eignor, D. (1998). *Computer familiarity among TOEFL examinees* (TOEFL Research Rep. No. 59). Princeton, NJ: Educational Testing Service.

Lado, R. (1961). *Language testing.* New York: McGraw-Hill.

Maxwell, A. A. (1965). *A comparison of two English as a foreign language tests.* Unpublished manuscript, University of California, Davis.

McNamara, T. F. (1996). *Measuring second language performance.* London: Longman.

Nissan, S., DeVincenzi, F., & Tang, K. L. (1996). *An analysis of factors affecting the difficulty of dialog items in TOEFL listening comprehension* (TOEFL Research Rep. No. 51). Princeton, NJ: Educational Testing Service.

Pack, A. C. (1972). A comparison between TOEFL and Michigan Test scores and student success in (1) freshman English and (2) completing college programs. *TESL Reporter, 5,* 1–7, 9.

Pike, L. (1979). *An evaluation of alternative item formats for testing English as a foreign language* (TOEFL Research Rep. No. 2). Princeton, NJ: Educational Testing Service.

Powell, W. (2001). *Looking back, looking forward: Trends in intensive English program enrollments* (TOEFL Monograph No. 14). Princeton, NJ: Educational Testing Service.

Powers, D. E. (1985). *A survey of academic demands related to listening skills* (TOEFL Research Rep. No. 20). Princeton, NJ: Educational Testing Service.

Powers, D. E., & Stansfield, C. W. (1983). *The Test of Spoken English as a measure of communicative proficiency in the health professions* (TOEFL Research Rep. No. 13). Princeton, NJ: Educational Testing Service.

Raimes, A. (1990). The TOEFL Test of Written English: Causes for concern. *TESOL Quarterly, 24,* 427–442.

Rubin, J. (1993). *TOEFL 2000: Listening in an academic setting* (internal TOEFL 2000 report). Princeton, NJ: Educational Testing Service.

Schedl, M. (1995). *TOEFL 2000 design framework: A working draft* (internal TOEFL 2000 report). Princeton, NJ: Educational Testing Service.

Schedl, M. A., Thomas, N., & Way, W. D. (1995). *An investigation of proposed revisions to section 3 of the TOEFL test* (TOEFL Research Rep. No. 47). Princeton, NJ: Educational Testing Service.

Schrader, W. B., & Pitcher, B. (1970). *Interpreting performance of foreign law students on the Law School Admission Test and the Test of English as a Foreign Language* (Statistical Rep. No. 7025). Princeton, NJ: Educational Testing Service.

Scoon, A. R., & Blanchard, J. D. (1970). *The relation of a test of English as a second language to measure intelligence, achievement, and adjustment in a sample of American Indian students.* Paper presented at TESOL, San Francisco. (ERIC Document Reproduction Service No. ED039530).

Taylor, C. (1994). *Profile of TOEFL score users and TOEFL examinees* (internal TOEFL 2000 report). Princeton, NJ: Educational Testing Service.

Taylor, C., Eignor, D., Schedl, M., & DeVincenzi, F. (1995, March). *TOEFL 2000: A project overview and status report.* Paper presented at the annual meeting of Teachers of English to Speakers of Other Languages (TESOL), Long Beach, CA.

Taylor, C., Jamieson, J., Eignor, D., & Kirsch, I. (1998). *The relationship between computer familiarity and performance on computer-based TOEFL test tasks* (TOEFL Research Rep. No. 61). Princeton, NJ: Educational Testing Service.

Testing the English language proficiency of foreign students. Report of a conference sponsored by the Center for Applied Linguistics in cooperation with the Institute of International Education and the National Association of Foreign Student Advisers. (1961). Washington, DC: Center for Applied Linguistics.

Tucker, G. R. (1986). Closing remarks. In C. Stansfield (Ed.), *Toward communicative competence testing: Proceedings of the second TOEFL invitational conference* (TOEFL Research Rep. No. 21). Princeton, NJ: Educational Testing Service.

Upshur, J. A. (1966). *Comparison of performance on "Test of English as a Foreign Language" and "Michigan Test of English Language Proficiency."* Unpublished manuscript, University of Michigan.

Waters, A. (1996). *A review of research into needs in English for academic purposes of relevance to the North American higher education context* (TOEFL Monograph No. 6). Princeton, NJ: Educational Testing Service.

3

Frameworks for a New TOEFL

Joan M. Jamieson
Daniel Eignor
William Grabe
Antony John Kunnan

Exploration of fundamental testing issues over the first half of the 1990s resulted in questions that had to be resolved if a new TOEFL® was going to be developed. The papers written during that period had identified issues and perspectives on language proficiency, but in order to move forward with test design and validation, the challenge was to articulate a framework incorporating communicative competence to underlie score interpretation. This meant that, in addition to a theoretical perspective on language proficiency, a psychometric approach was needed to link scores to substantive meanings. This chapter describes how project members addressed this challenge in 1996 and 1997 by articulating a construct of communicative competence within the psychometric approach of proficiency scaling. At this stage, the interpretive argument outlined in the first chapter was just beginning to be sketched through the implicit assumptions of those who tackled this challenge. Even at this stage, however, the inferences in the emerging interpretive argument were based on assumptions that had implications for a test design framework and initial research, both of which are described in this chapter.

PROFICIENCY SCALING AND COMMUNICATIVE COMPETENCE

Proficiency scaling and communicative competence were joined in the *TOEFL 2000 Framework* (Jamieson, Jones, Kirsch, Mosenthal, & Taylor, 2000), which outlined the need for proficiency scaling as a basis for understanding score meaning that could be communicated to users. The first part of this chapter summarizes the justification made in the *TOEFL 2000 Framework* for proficiency scaling and offers a retrospective analysis of the assumptions and implications of the proficiency scaling and communicative competence perspectives for the *TOEFL 2000 Framework*.

Why Proficiency Scaling

The *TOEFL 2000 Framework* (Jamieson et al., 2000) described the value of the proficiency scaling approach with reference to its success in developing interpretable scales in literacy projects at Educational Testing Service® (ETS®) beginning in 1985. It linked the need for proficiency scales to the test purpose of the TOEFL (i.e., making high-stakes admissions decisions about applicants to North American universities). In their literacy projects, Kirsch, Jungeblut, and Mosenthal (1998) developed tasks from a variety of printed materials (e.g., ads, bills, newspaper articles, bus schedules); the tasks involved a variety of uses of these materials with the intention of assessing prose, document, and quantitative literacy. The first survey, the Young Adult Literacy Survey, tested the hypothesis that the interaction between the type of material and its particular use would define task difficulty and its placement on one of the three literacy scales—prose, document, and quantitative (Kirsch & Jungeblut, 1986). Once the tasks had been administered, analyzed, and placed on a scale, they were subsequently analyzed to explore other characteristics besides type of material and type of use. This ex post facto analysis revealed that a relatively small set of variables seemed to affect the difficulty of many of the tasks.

Kirsch and Mosenthal (1990) further investigated factors associated with task difficulty on the document scale, and after analyzing patterns in their data, they came up with three main categories of variables: those related to the structure/complexity of the stimulus material, those related to the type of task required, and those related to the processes/strategies required to connect the information given in the question or directions to the information contained in the text. Regression analyses yielded a set of five variables that significantly accounted for task difficulty across a number of subgroups in the sample (the variance accounted for ranged from 89% for the total group to 56% for those who reported 0–8 years of school).

In a second literacy survey, the U.S. Department of Labor Survey, Kirsch and his colleagues (Kirsch et al., 1998) refined the set of variables they had found to be significant. In this survey, they again had three literacy scales (prose, document, and quantitative), and again they used a variety of authentic materials and uses. This time, however, they used three variables for the prose and document scales—plausibility of distracters, type of match, and type of information—to create new assessment tasks and to predict task difficulty. Kirsch et al. labeled these variables *process variables* because the variables called for processes or strategies for relating the information requested in the question or directive to the information contained in the text or document.

Having coded all tasks for the values of these variables, Kirsch and his colleagues were successful in accounting for 75% to 87% of the variance in task difficulty (Kirsch et al., 1998). For this survey, they also used the information from the scaled scores and the values of the variables to create a reporting summary that contained five levels of performance, descriptions of the tasks at each level, and the probability that someone who scored at a given level could perform the tasks at each of the other levels. The score reports made use of these proficiency scales. In a third survey, the National Adult Literacy Survey, Kirsch and his colleagues (Kirsch et al., 1998) used some of the old tasks and created some new tasks using the same variables included in the Department of Labor Survey. Again, they found that they could explain considerable amounts of the variance in task difficulty on each of the three literacy scales.

The clarity of results yielded from the proficiency scaling approach in the literacy projects was in sharp contrast with the murkier issues characterizing communicative competence theory, as outlined in Chapter 1, that what underlies score interpretation should:

1. be a *theoretical construct* that accounts for language performance across a wide range of contexts,
2. include *complex abilities* responsible for accomplishing a particular range of goals, and
3. take into account relevant *contexts*.

The proficiency scaling-communicative competence union was accomplished in two ways. First, the proficiency scaling approach called for identification of task characteristics that would ultimately figure into the descriptions of the proficiency scales. This idea was combined with the third assumption above, derived from communicative competence theory, to describe contexts in terms of task features. The authors of the *TOEFL 2000 Framework* (Jamieson et al., 2000) indicated that "[w]e begin with Bachman and Palmer's (1996) notion that a finite number of task characteristics influence students' communicative competence in a given language, as measured by a test" (p. 13). The combined proficiency-scaling communicative competence concept of task characteristics included those that might be related to language performance in any way, rather than only those that were hypothesized to be responsible for task difficulty. The task characteristics included in the *TOEFL 2000 Framework*, therefore, intertwine the types of situational or contextual features identified in theories of communicative competence with test task characteristics identified by Bachman and Palmer and those theorized to predict difficulty in keeping with the proficiency scaling approach. The second accommodation made to connect the two was to include provision for a theoretical construct composed of complex abilities (i.e., characteristics of the first two points of communicative competence, as stated above) as a means of explaining performance in addition to task characteristics.

Assumptions and Implications

The *TOEFL 2000 Framework* argued for the need for a test framework "to give meaning and interpretability to [scores]" (Jamieson et al., 2000, p. 7) obtained by examinees. In the terms used in the first chapter, the focus was on the utilization inference, that estimates of the quality of performance in the English-medium institutions of higher education obtained from the TOEFL would be useful for making decisions about admissions and appropriate curriculum for test takers. The assumptions underlying this warrant are that the meaning of test scores would be clearly interpretable by admissions officers, test takers, and teachers and that the test would have a positive influence on how English is taught, as shown in the last row of Table 3.1. The final column of that row shows the two implications of those assumptions from the perspective of the *Framework* writers. First, linking test scores to descriptions of what examinees know and can do based on an analysis of test-task characteristics provides test score users with more useful information than does a test score. Another way of expressing this is to say that an examinee's abilities can be expressed meaningfully in terms of the probability of correct performance on a particular set of tasks. Second, communicative language ability needs to be reported on four scales corresponding to the four skills: listening, reading, speaking, and writing. These scales were thought to be easily understood by test score users, a belief supported by surveys of test score users indicating their desire for scores in each of these skills, as well as the fact that in applied linguistics teachers are trained, texts are written, and language classes are offered in these four skills.

The writers of the *TOEFL 2000 Framework* (Jamieson et al., 2000) also held assumptions associated with the other inferences in what would become the interpretive argument for TOEFL. An assumption underlying the domain description inference was that assessment tasks that require important skills and are representative of the academic domain could be simulated. The implication that the *TOEFL 2000 Framework* writers saw was that a test-task framework should guide test developers to identify important tasks in an academic setting because modeling test tasks on important real world tasks would insure that appropriate knowledge, skills, and abilities would be assessed and that the context of language use would be taken into

TABLE 3.1
The Inferences, Assumptions, and Implications Implicit in the Framework

Assumptions Underlying Warrant in the mid-1990s	*Implication for Test Design and Validation within a Proficiency Scaling-Communicative Competence Perspective*
	Domain Description
Assessment tasks that require important skills and are representative of the academic domain can be simulated.	A test-task framework should guide test developers to identify important tasks in an academic setting. Modeling test tasks on important real world tasks will insure that appropriate knowledge, skills, and abilities are assessed and that the context of language use is taken into account.
	Evaluation
The statistical characteristics of items, measures, and test forms are appropriate for norm-referenced decisions.	Tasks that vary in difficulty need to be defined and constructed. A scale appropriate for norm-referenced decisions can be constructed through the use of IRT to place examinees' scores and tasks on the same metric. Examinees' responses should be scored in a way that allows for the use of IRT for item analysis. The use of IRT with a variety of task types should be explored to better understand the psychometric implications for different ways of scoring tasks.
	Generalization
Task and test specifications are well-defined so that parallel tasks and test forms are created.	Precise task specifications need to be developed to guide task creation. Parallel tasks can be constructed through a framework specifying which task variables do and do not affect task difficulty.
	Explanation
A theoretical construct consisting of a complex of abilities and processes underlies performance across contexts. The abilities and processes used to explain test scores are defined by task characteristics shown to be significant predictors of task difficulty.	Validation research should seek evidence supporting hypothesized levels of difficulty for test tasks, particularly through multiple regression analysis.
	Extrapolation
Performance on the test is related to other criteria of language proficiency in the academic context.	Criterion-related validity studies should be conducted.

(*continued*)

TABLE 3.1
Continued

Assumptions Underlying Warrant in the mid-1990s	Implication for Test Design and Validation within a Proficiency Scaling-Communicative Competence Perspective
	Utilization
The meaning of test scores is clearly interpretable by admissions officers, test takers, and teachers.	Linking test scores to descriptions of what examinees know and can do, based on an analysis of test task characteristics, provides test score users with more useful information than does a test score.
The test will have a positive influence on how English is taught.	Communicative language ability will be reported on four scales that correspond to the four skills.

account. TOEFL project members relied on logical and empirical analysis of the domain to inform the design of test-task framework. The logical analysis consisted of the identification of task characteristics that would help to establish correspondence between test tasks and academic language tasks. The empirical analysis involved the collection and analysis of a corpus of academic language as well as job analysis.

An assumption associated with the evaluation inference was that the statistical characteristics of items, measures, and test forms would be appropriate for norm-referenced decisions. The *TOEFL 2000 Framework* writers (Jamieson et al., 2000) interpreted this to mean that tasks that vary in difficulty needed to be defined and constructed. Because of the decision that proficiency scaling should be used, the use of item response theory (IRT) was also assumed to be the psychometric approach for handling examinee responses. Thus, the implications in the *TOEFL 2000 Framework* were that a scale appropriate for norm-referenced decisions should be constructed through the use of IRT to place examinees' scores and tasks on the same metric. This further implied that examinees' responses should be scored in a way that would allow for the use of IRT for item analysis and that the use of IRT with a variety of task types should be explored to better understand the psychometric implications for different ways of scoring tasks. The implication for the TOEFL project was the need to examine issues such as the extent to which polytomously scored items could be analyzed using existing IRT software and whether dichotomously scored and polytomously scored items from different modalities could be included on a single scale. An assumption underlying the generalization inference was that task and test specifications are well-defined, so that parallel tasks and test forms can be created based on the specifications. The implications for the *TOEFL 2000 Framework* writers were that precise task specifications needed to be developed to guide task creation and that parallel tasks could be constructed through a framework specifying which task variables do and do not affect task difficulty.

Assumptions about the explanation inference were based on a theoretical construct consisting of a complex of abilities and processes underlying performance across contexts and the belief that the abilities and processes used to explain test scores are defined by task characteristics shown to be significant predictors of task difficulty. The proficiency scaling approach to explanation consists of statements about the probability of an examinee at a particular level completing a task at a particular level of difficulty. This technical procedure for testing the explanatory power of the task variables is a multiple regression analysis with task characteristic variables as independent variables and item difficulty as the dependent variable. Success in explanation is gauged by the percentage of variance in item difficulty accounted for by variables of the task characteristics that are identified as those that should affect difficulty. The implication was that the TOEFL framework had to identify the task characteristics that should explain variance in task performance. Communicative competence theory suggests that complex abilities and processes are responsible for performance, but it does not suggest specific implications for validation. The extrapolation inference was based on the assumption that performance on the test would be related to other criteria of language proficiency in the academic context, and the implication would be that criterion-related validity studies would be needed.

The proficiency scaling approach was attractive to the authors of the *TOEFL 2000 Framework* (Jamieson et al., 2000) because it offered some prescribed steps forward, particularly in the area of domain definition. Once the relevant domain of tasks has been identified, researchers are able to describe task characteristics that can be operationalized by variables that will prove useful for subsequent analysis. The implications of this assumption are evident in the *TOEFL 2000 Framework,* which consisted largely of descriptions of task characteristics and variables that pertain to the analysis of academic tasks. Communicative competence theory also stresses the importance of task characteristics, but this is because of the interaction between context and linguistic variation. The coupling of proficiency scaling and communicative competence set into motion development of test frameworks, research, and investigation of psychometric issues.

THE TOEFL FRAMEWORK FOR DOMAIN DEFINITION

The *TOEFL 2000 Framework* (Jamieson et al., 2000) consisted of a statement of the test's purpose, a set of task characteristics, and variables associated with each task characteristic that would be tested to determine which variables affected test performance to the greatest extent. The test purpose was similar to that which had been set for the previous iterations of the TOEFL revision: The TOEFL would measure English language proficiency to be used in admissions decisions to North American universities. However, the *TOEFL 2000 Framework* added that test tasks would reflect what students would find in academic settings, that abilities would be reported along one or more scales, and that scores might also be used for "guiding English language instruction, placement decisions, and awarding certification" (Jamieson et al., 2000, p. 10).

The General Framework

The general framework outlined in Jamieson et al. (2000) identified relevant task characteristics and variables of academic language tasks that would be used in research and development. A large portion of the *TOEFL 2000 Framework* consisted of an example of TOEFL items that were analyzed based on some of these variables and an explanation of how one would develop a scale from such an analysis.

Task characteristics and variables   A *task* was defined as the material with which a test taker was presented as well as what the test taker was expected to do based on that material. The basic features in a task were described by situation, text material, and test rubric, as illustrated in Figure 3.1. The authors of the *TOEFL 2000 Framework* (Jamieson et al., 2000) provided the reasons for selection of each of these task features and some variables that might be considered for each of the three.

Situation   Jamieson et al. (2000) formulated the situation component of the task definition in the *TOEFL 2000 Framework* on the basis of communicative competence theory. Rather than constituting independent variables in the prediction of task difficulty, the variables of situation were intended to address the third implication of communicative competence theory, that

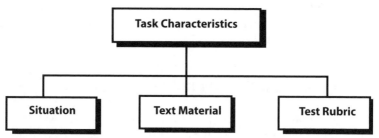

FIG 3.1   Three aspects of task characteristics. Note. From *TOEFL 2000 Framework* (TOEFL Monograph No. 16, p. 13) by J. Jamieson, S. Jones, I. Kirsch, P. Mosenthal, and C. Taylor, 2000, Princeton, NJ: Educational Testing Service. Copyright 2000 by Educational Testing Service. Reprinted with permission.

test score interpretation should take into account relevant contexts. In other words, the variables of situation provided an analytic means of supporting a domain description. These variables were identified based on research in applied linguistics investigating language use, particularly from Bachman and Palmer's (1996) framework in language assessment that identifies test-task characteristics relevant to the domain description:

> ...in order to justify the use of language tests, we need to be able to demonstrate that performance on language tests corresponds to language use in specific domains other than the language test itself. One aspect of this pertains to the correspondence between the characteristics of the TLU [target language use] tasks and those of the test task. (p. 23)

The authors of the *TOEFL 2000 Framework* (Jamieson et al., 2000) defined *situation* through the variables that represent aspects of a context believed to affect language use: the participants (e.g., gender, ethnicity, age, role), content (e.g., academic, class-related, extracurricular), setting (e.g., instructional milieu, academic milieu, nonacademic milieu), purpose (e.g., heuristic, instrumental, personal), and register (e.g., formal, consultative, informal).

Text material   Also drawing from communicative competence theory and intending it to be useful for the domain description, Jamieson et al. (2000) defined *text material* to include the language features an examinee read or listened to as well as the language features produced in texts written or spoken by examinees. Text material consisted of grammatical features (e.g., vocabulary, syntax), pragmatic features (e.g., expository, argumentative, persuasive, socializing), and discourse features (e.g., rhetorical properties, text structure properties).

The test rubric   Guided by prior work using proficiency scales, Jamieson et al. (2000) intended the test rubric variables to affect task difficulty, and therefore the variables ultimately would be useful for the explanation of test scores. The test rubric consisted of the questions/directions (e.g., type of information requested, type of match, plausibility of distracters; these were defined as they had been in the National Adult Literacy Survey [Kirsch et al., 1998]), the response formats (e.g., multiple choice, constructed response), and the rules for scoring both selected and constructed responses (e.g., dichotomous right/wrong, partial credit, holistic, primary trait). The *TOEFL 2000 Framework* provided examples from adult literacy to show how these features might affect task difficulty. Table 3.2 gives a summary of the task characteristics, variables, and their definitions.

Although we have highlighted the influence of the proficiency scaling and communicative competence perspectives, the creation of the *TOEFL 2000*

TABLE 3.2
Summary of Task Characteristics and Variables Outlined in the TOEFL 2000 Framework

Task Characteristics	Task Variables	Definition of Variable
Situation	Participants	The people involved in the language act and their relationships (e.g., student, faculty).
	Content	The subject matters included in the language tasks. General types are academic, class-related, and extracurricular.
	Setting	The place where the language act occurs. Three general types are instructional, academic, and nonacademic milieu.
	Purpose	Reasons for engaging in tasks. These are defined by functional terms such as instrumental and regulatory.
	Register	Degree of formality on the language. Three levels are defined as formal, consultative, and informal.
Text material	Grammatical features	Grammatical features (e.g., relative clauses, vocabulary, and frequency).
	Pragmatic features	Pragmatic function (e.g., expository).
	Discourse features	Rhetorical properties of a text that realize the author's goal.
Test rubric	Questions/ directives	The types of information that readers and listeners need to find to respond to the question.
	Response formats	The way that the examinee is directed to respond to a task prompt.
	Rules for scoring	The procedures for assigning a value to examinees' responses.

Framework (Jamieson et al., 2000) entailed considerable synthesis of perspectives and research traditions. The resulting framework was a novel creation, which then was further stretched and reshaped as teams used it for developing separate skills frameworks.

From General to Four Skills Frameworks

Because the proficiency scaling assumptions suggested that the scales and their task descriptors needed to be clear and recognizable to test score users, Jamieson et al. (2000) argued that the framework should be developed further by dividing the test into the familiar four skills. Although resembling the skills/ability combinations used for the paper-based TOEFL and by language testers in the 1960s, the skill frameworks were intended to reflect current theories of communicative competence by including a combination of language features, purposes, and contexts. Moreover, Jamieson et al. argued that the skill frameworks could treat skills both individually and in an integrated, or more complex, manner; college students take writing classes but often combine speaking, reading, and writing; language students take conversation classes but often listen and read in these classes.

Skills teams were convened beginning in June 1997 to write framework documents using the *TOEFL 2000 Framework* (Jamieson et al., 2000) as a guide. Each of the four teams was composed of one ETS assessment specialist, one ETS researcher, two applied linguists from outside ETS, and one member from the original *TOEFL 2000 Framework* team. Each team was to conceptualize its assigned skill by identifying a set of variables for the task characteristics outlined in the *TOEFL 2000 Framework* and to create a research agenda. However, like the skills papers of the previous phase of the project (described in Chapter 2), each team emphasized some perspectives over others. Whereas teams had been charged with defining the variables of situation, text type, and test rubric, they each chose three or four of the following: purposes, abilities, tasks, text types, expected performance, and qualities of expected responses. Table 3.3 summarizes the categories developed by the four skills teams, with the last row delineating the relationship between these task characteristics and the ones in the general framework paper.

All of the skills teams were able to define something they called *task type*, but in the *TOEFL 2000 Framework* (Jamieson et al., 2000), task had been the superordinate term that was to be further delineated by the situation, text type, and test rubric. Listening and reading included abilities, and reading included purpose, as well. Purpose was a variable under situation in the *TOEFL 2000 Framework*, but abilities were not included in the *TOEFL 2000 Framework*. Text type, which appears in the original *TOEFL 2000*

TABLE 3.3
Summary of the Categories in the Four Skills Frameworks Relative to those in the General Framework

Framework	Characteristics in TOEFL Testing Frameworks					
	Purposes	Abilities	Task type	Text type	Expected performance	Qualities of response
Listening		X	X	X		
Reading	X	X	X	X		
Speaking			X		X	X
Writing			X		X	X
General	A variable under situation	Does not exist	Used as a superordinate term	Called text material	A variable under test rubric	A variable under test rubric

Framework as one of the task components, is used in the *Listening Framework* (Bejar, Douglas, Jamieson, Nissan, & Turner, 2000) and the *Reading Framework* (Enright, Grabe, Koda, Mosenthal, Mulcahy-Ernt, et al., 2000), and it is included as a first level category rather than as a component of the task. The *Writing Framework* (Cumming, Kantor, Powers, Santos, & Taylor, 2000) and the *Speaking Framework* (Butler, Eignor, Jones, McNamara, & Suomi, 2000) included expected performance and qualities of response, which were variations on two of the variables that had been included in the testing rubric of the *TOEFL 2000 Framework*. Why were the resulting skill frameworks different from the general framework from which they were modeled? Are there inherent differences across skills that defy their classification within a common perspective? It may not be possible to answer these questions completely, but to address them, we examine the development of the frameworks for each of the skills.

The Listening Framework

The listening team attempted to follow closely the task model presented in the *TOEFL 2000 Framework* (Jamieson et al., 2000; i.e., situation, text, and test rubric) but in doing so created a long list of variables rather than any actual tasks for the test (Bejar et al., 2000). For example, situation variables included who the participants are, where they are, the type of text they expect (e.g., if a professor is in front of a large classroom, the test takers can expect to hear a lecture), the number of speakers and their relationship (i.e., whether or not it is symmetrical), academic content (life sciences, social sciences, humanities and arts, and physical sciences), class-related content (e.g., assignments, due dates, text books), and campus-related content (e.g., registration, faculty advisor, library help). While these are precisely the types of variables that sociolinguists would agree affect language use, additional analysis was needed to construct a framework that would be a useful representation for testing.

Test rubric was only briefly discussed in the *Listening Framework* (Bejar et al., 2000). Instructions, questions, and rules for scoring were described, as were item-text interaction variables of type of match, type of information, and plausibility of distracters. Response formats were described as selected responses or oral and written constructed responses, but these were not developed.

Having abandoned the situation and test rubric terminology of the *TOEFL 2000 Framework* (Jamieson et al., 2000), the listening team defined their framework by focusing on specification of the task in terms of two task characteristics, task type and text type. In a subsequent paper, the listening team added an additional component to the framework, abilities. These three categories—abilities, task type, and text type—were specified and defined as a

TABLE 3.4
Characteristics in the Listening Framework

Listening abilities	Tasks	
	Task types	Text types
1. Understand important details	Identify—who, what, when, or where questions Explain—how or why questions	
2. Understand main ideas, topics, goals	Identify or explain main ideas	
3. Understand key vocabulary	Identify or explain key vocabulary	
4. Understand communicative function of utterances	Identify the function or purpose of an utterance Identify what aspect of an utterance signals function	Lectures, consultations, and conversations
5. Make inferences about relationships among ideas	Identify and explain relationships among ideas in text	
6. Integrate information with own knowledge	Relate text information to own knowledge	
7. Integrate information from more than one listening text	Analysis and synthesis of information across texts	
8. Integrate information from listening and reading texts	Analysis and synthesis of information across texts	

three-dimensional cube, which was intended to express the interaction among three dimensions, but in the final listening framework there was a one-to-one or a one-to-two correspondence between specific abilities and task types, while all text types were relevant to all task types. Table 3.4 summarizes the components of the listening framework that resulted from the cube representation.

Listening abilities   The listening abilities reflected a cognitive or psycholinguistic perspective, referring to unobservable processes (e.g., understand the function or purpose of an utterance). These abilities reflect the first of the two stages of the listening process that is conceptualized in the framework and cube documents as consisting of a listening stage and a response stage. In the listening stage, an acoustic signal is received, and as the signal is being acted upon by specialized receptive processes and general cognitive processes, at least three types of knowledge are accessed in real time (situational knowledge, linguistic knowledge, and background knowledge). This incoming stimulus is mentally represented as a set of propositions. To infer that the listener has understood the meaning of a text, one must rely on some external response (an outcome of the listening comprehension process) that is manifest via another modality—such as reading multiple-choice options, writing, or speaking—because there is no direct access to the internal workings of a listener's mind (Brown, 1995; Buck, 1997). How well the response demonstrates comprehension is mediated by the representation of the stimulus, which in turn is mediated by knowledge and cognitive factors.

Task type   The task type ended up being defined by what the learner had to do to complete the task (e.g., identify). These descriptors are similar to, but more general than, the descriptors under *question/directive*, which was part of the test rubric in the *TOEFL 2000 Framework* (Jamieson et al., 2000).

Text types   Texts were described as consisting of three types, but this was the result of many iterations of considering the nature of text types. The *Listening Framework* (Bejar et al., 2000) defined spoken text as the detailed collection of features including discourse and pragmatic features. The description of these features was strongly influenced by the work of Bachman and Palmer's (1996) language and task characteristics. Grammatical features of listening texts that were studied included phonology, vocabulary, and syntax. Aspects of phonology that were going to be operationalized and investigated further were pauses, speech rate, sandhi variation, stress and intonation, and accent. Four vocabulary variables were identified that could affect the difficulty of listening comprehension items: the number of infrequent words; frequently repeated word sequences; technical terms; and hedges, emphatics, and vague words. It is generally assumed that a text's syntactic complexity is related to difficulty in listening comprehension, and a number of studies had investigated one or two measures of syntactic complexity. The team decided it would be better served by thinking of clusters of features that co-occur and referred to Biber's multidimensional analyses of over 50 surface linguistic markers to account for discourse complexities within the spoken register (Biber, 1988, 1992, 1995). Discourse features of listening texts that were identified as salient to difficulty were described in three groups: propositional structure, propositional density, and propositional complexity. A number of coding schemes were reviewed (Brown & Yule, 1983; Hansen, 1994; Kintsch, 1974; Schiffrin, 1987; Young, 1994), but none seemed to provide a feasible methodology to use in large-scale test development.

Pragmatic features of listening texts included the purpose of the speaker, the degree of planning, and text type. The purpose of the speaker was described as the speaker's reason for the speech event, such as giving directions, giving an opinion, predicting, or inviting. Degree of planning (planned, somewhat planned, and unplanned) was included to characterize the scriptedness of oral texts; it was hypothesized that grammatical features such as type of vocabulary or sandhi variation would co-occur with this variable. Three text types were of interest: lectures, consultations, and student interactions. In reaction to criticisms against the inauthentic speech in the current TOEFL (often referred to as *TOEFL talk*) and to the inclusion of authenticity as a quality indicator in language-testing literature, the listening team considered various methods of text creation and decided that a corpus of actual academic language should be commissioned. This corpus could then provide an assessment specialist with either stimulus material or models from which stimuli could be created.

The *Listening Framework* (Bejar et al., 2000) covered additional ground that described the rationale for delimiting the way that listening was conceived. For example, technical and administrative decisions required the test to measure only transactional listening (i.e., listening for a specific purpose), although in the real world, listening is also interactional (i.e., listening to maintain social relations). Also, relatively easy tasks involving simple linguistic subskills were not included in the construct because of the desire to increase the difficulty of the test in order to better assess the more proficient students who were coming to North American universities. The *Listening Framework* mentioned the inclusion of video but indicated that video was probably beyond the technological capabilities at the current time and might be something to include in future modifications of the test. In view of these and other issues, the listening team moved forward into development of prototype items using the framework in Table 3.4.

The Reading Framework

The *Reading Framework* (Enright et al., 2000) might have been expected to follow directly from the *TOEFL 2000 Framework* (Jamieson et al., 2000) in view of the prior successes with a proficiency-scaling framework in prose literacy. Instead, the *Reading Framework* pointed out that three perspectives could be used to explain reading comprehension—a processing perspective, a task perspective, and a reader-purpose perspective. However, team members felt that a reading construct defined from a task perspective would not adequately reflect the domain of academic reading if the skills underlying reading were not also posited. At the same time, they felt that even though processes such as word recognition fluency, processing efficiency, inferencing, and text-model building were important to understanding reading comprehension, in and of themselves these processes did not constitute an interpretable hierarchy of proficiency; rather, they were viewed as skills that were called upon in differing degrees of emphasis for different reading purposes. *Purpose*, therefore, became the controlling task characteristic for the reading framework, which is shown in Table 3.5.

TABLE 3.5
Characteristics in the Reading Framework

Reading Purposes	Abilities	Task Types	Text Types
Reading to find information	Recognize and identify words efficiently	Scanning	
Reading for basic comprehension	Comprehend the essential meaning of major propositions	Sentence simplification	
	Efficiently comprehend major propositions	Reading efficiency	
Reading to learn	Integrate and/or remember major ideas and supporting information in a text, organize important information from the text Remember important details from a text Express major ideas and supporting information in a text	Prose and schematic summaries of information in the text (complex selected response) Sentence recognition Productive summaries— answer questions about important ideas and supporting information in the text by writing or speaking	Historical narration, exposition, argumentation, evaluation
Reading to integrate information across texts	Generate organizational framework and relate ideas and information from two or more sources	Prose and schematic summaries of information from two texts (complex selected response) Productive summaries— organize and relate ideas and supporting information from multiple sources by writing or speaking	

Purpose   Like the listening team, the reading team devised its own set of terms, redefined task types, redefined text types, and added abilities to their reading framework. Whereas in the *TOEFL 2000 Framework* (Jamieson et al., 2000), test rubric was defined explicitly as consisting of questions/directives, response formats, and rules for scoring, the reading team considered it

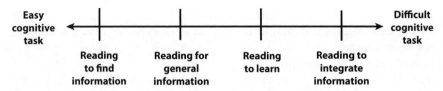

FIG. 3.2   Hypothesized implicational scale for reading purposes.

to be the implicit relationship among types of texts, reader tasks, and reader purpose.

Purpose is the only situational feature from the *TOEFL 2000 Framework* (Jamieson et al., 2000) that appears in the *Reading Framework* (Enright et al., 2000). The reading team felt that the scale of increasingly complex purposes for reading could be used effectively to build an interpretive score scale. They also felt that the reading purposes could incorporate components of reading processes and task features as variables that contribute to differences between better and weaker readers (Goldman, 1997; Perfetti, 1994, 1997; Perfetti, van Dyke, & Hart, 2001). The four purposes were reading to find information, reading for general information, reading to learn, and reading to integrate. With other factors being equal, the purposes for reading were hypothesized to constitute a hierarchical scale (Carver, 1992, 1997; Enright & Schedl, 2000), as illustrated in Figure 3.2.

Enright and Schedl (2000) specified in detail the cognitive and linguistic abilities called upon by each reading purpose and the kinds of tasks that would engage those abilities. Reading to find information was described from two different perspectives. One approach explains performance in terms of the development of reading efficiencies and rapid, automated word recognition skills. A hierarchical relationship between these skills and more complex reading abilities such as comprehension was proposed (Carver, 1992; 1997; Perfetti, 1994). Some tasks used to assess this aspect of reading included skimming and scanning, in which specific words in a text were to be located rapidly (Carver, 1997). A different conceptualization of finding information in texts was found in the work of Guthrie and his associates (Guthrie, 1988; Guthrie & Kirsch, 1987; Guthrie & Mosenthal, 1987). This model drew on theories of search and problem-solving processes to explain performance on tasks that required locating information in a wide variety of documents, including articles, manuals, tables, and schematics. Furthermore, Guthrie and his associates proposed that reading comprehension and finding information were independent rather than hierarchical processes. Enright and Schedl concluded that the approach to reading to find information that emphasized rapid and efficient word recognition skills was more consistent with the *Reading Framework* (Enright et al., 2000). Although finding information in this sense was assessed indirectly in the TOEFL, they concluded that more direct assessment of finding information could be explored through scanning and skimming tasks.

Reading for basic comprehension, as described in the *Reading Framework* (Enright et al., 2000), "requires a reader to understand the main ideas or the main points of the text or to form some understanding of the main theme of the text, but does not necessarily require an integrated understanding of how the supporting ideas and factual details of the text form a coherent whole" (p. 6). For this reading purpose, readers must comprehend most of the individual propositions and sentences in the text and be able to understand some of the relationships between sentences. However, this reading purpose does not require the construction of a more enduring, well-organized, and detailed representation of the text. Enright and Schedl (2000) concluded that the reading skills underlying basic comprehension were assessed by the item types on the existing TOEFL and made only one recommendation for a new type of question, sentence simplification. The proposed task would assess the reader's ability to simplify or clarify utterances in the text. Examinees would be asked to compare several sentences to a complex sentence taken from the passage text and to choose the one that most closely retained the meaning of the original. The correct answer would be a simplification that retained the basic ideas of the original while simplifying its lexical and/or syntactic content.

Reading to learn was described by Enright and Schedl (2000) from two related but distinct perspectives. One perspective described learning from text as the integration of the text with prior knowledge. The second perspective emphasized the development of an organized mental representation of a text that supports the recollection and reconstruction of the ideas in the text. The latter perspective was seen as more consistent with the concept of reading to learn as proposed in the *Reading Framework* (Enright et al., 2000): "Reading to learn requires readers to integrate and connect detailed information from the text in a manner that is consistent with the rhetorical pattern of the text" (p. 32). From this perspective, they suggested aspects of reading to learn that were not assessed on the existing TOEFL reading measure. These aspects included distinguishing between essential and unessential information in a text, remembering information from a text, organizing information from a text, and reconstructing information from a text. Examples of tasks were developed to illustrate how reading to learn, which was defined as "developing an organized mental representation of a text that supports the recollection and reconstruction of the ideas in the text" (p. 18), might be assessed. Most of these tasks shared features with summary tasks in that they required the examinees to select and organize information from a significant portion of the text. Both selected-response and constructed-response tasks were proposed. Two types of selected-response tasks were proposed. One required completing a prose summary of the text by identifying sentences that would be appropriate to include in a summary. Another required completing schematic summaries, such as tables or diagrams, by indicating how information from the text should be organized. Constructed-response reading-to-learn tasks would require a written or oral summary of important information in the text. Furthermore, both selected-response and constructed-response tasks might directly assess memory for the text, depending on whether the text was available when the task was completed.

Reading to integrate was discussed in the *Reading Framework* (Enright et al., 2000) in terms of integrating information found in different texts. The reason for this emphasis was the idea that "such tasks require a reader to. work across two or more texts and generate an organizing frame that is not explicitly stated" (p. 6). Other key features of this reading purpose were that the relationship between sources needs to be recognized and that the specific relationships between the detailed information conveyed by the two sources also needs to be identified by the reader. The research on reading multiple texts illustrated the need, in some academic situations, for a reader to recognize differences and similarities in content, in points of view, and in the rhetorical devices of different authors. This research did not exclude the possibility that these types of differences may also be found within a single text. The distinction between reading to learn and reading to integrate may lie in what the focal aspects of a text are for a reader, what kinds of relationships among ideas a reader must notice, and what a reader must do in response to a text. Thus this reading purpose required a text or texts that include(s) multiple rhetorical functions/positions/points of view and tasks that require the reader to address the complexities of the text. In terms of task format, reading to integrate could be demonstrated in many of the same ways as reading to learn—by answering multiple-choice questions, by completing prose or schematic summaries, or by constructing written or oral response to questions.

Text types The *Reading Framework* (Enright et al., 2000) defined text type in terms of pragmatic, rhetorical, and linguistic and discourse features. The pragmatic and rhetorical features are shown in Table 3.6. Linguistic features

TABLE 3.6
Specification of Types of Texts by Pragmatic Features and Corresponding
Rhetorical Features

Pragmatic Features	Rhetorical Features
Historical narration	Narrate
Exposition	Define, describe, elaborate, illustrate Compare-contrast, classify Problem-solution
Argumentation, evaluation	Explain Justify

included emphasis on vocabulary knowledge, anaphoric reference, and discourse signaling. Grammar was identified as important but not identified as a predictor to be isolated in planning for task difficulty. Discourse features were included such as main idea position, transitional marking, the overall organization, given and new information, and noun-predicate density.

Enright and Schedl (2000) also considered practical constraints such as time and cost as they proposed tasks. On the basis of these considerations, the reading team launched their program of task development.

The Speaking Framework

Speaking was conceptualized as the use of oral language to interact directly and immediately with others. For the TOEFL, these interactions would be limited to academic settings in which participants were engaged in acquiring, transmitting, and demonstrating knowledge (Butler et al., 2000). The speaking team hoped to create a measure of oral communication in an academic context that would provide scores that could be extrapolated to speaking performance across disciplines and that would include tasks across a variety of genres, functions, and situations. The tasks would simulate realistic communicative situations with integrated tasks, including listening and speaking or reading and speaking. However, the speaking team faced obstacles in working within the proficiency scaling approach of the *TOEFL 2000 Framework* (Jamieson et al., 2000), which had been used for developing scales for a receptive skill. Use of the proficiency scaling approach for a productive skill did not prove to be straightforward. Moreover, compared to reading, the language skill of speaking has no first-language research base relevant to assessment goals. The second-language research on speaking was conflated with other issues such as communication strategies, pragmatics, conversational analysis, and interview-assessment practices. The distance between the various goals of this research and those of the *Speaking Framework* (Butler et al., 2000) posed a challenge.

Drawing on Skehan's (1998) research on factors affecting task difficulty, the *Speaking Framework* (Butler et al., 2000) suggested that tasks might be designed according to variables that affect difficulty such as number of participants, concrete/abstract information, immediate/remote communication, retrieval/transformation of information, familiar/unfamiliar audience, and visual support. The idea was that such variables could serve as proficiency descriptors based on the participants' roles (number, age, gender, ethnicity, occupation, educational level) and relationships (symmetric and asymmetric) and the number of participants in addition to the speaker (the test taker)—one-to-one, a small group, a small audience, and a large audience. Four general topics that would be appropriate to academic settings were enumerated: academic subjects, organization of learning activities, rules of academic life, and daily living events that occur on a campus. Features affecting the formality of the language were identified as the degree to which (a) the language is expected to satisfy formal rules of grammar, (b) focus is given to the quality of the language, (c) spoken contributions are phrasal or sentential, (d) time is available to plan an utterance, and (e) the interaction is co-constructed or scripted.

The *Speaking Framework* (Butler et al., 2000) also suggested that tasks could be designed to affect particular aspects of speaking ability and that different, appropriate rating criteria could be established. For example, tasks containing familiar material could be scored for fluency, tasks with differentiated outcomes could be scored for syntactic complexity, and well-structured tasks could be scored for accuracy. The *Speaking Framework* reinterpreted the text features in the *TOEFL 2000 Framework* (Jamieson et al., 2000) to refer to the examinee's expected response. The characteristics include expected performance and quality of performance, rather than test rubric. The speaking framework that was ultimately used in task development is outlined in Table 3.7.

Task type   The situational features were ultimately set aside, leaving task type as the only specification of the way the task would be configured. Tasks

TABLE 3.7
Characteristics in the Speaking Framework

Task Type	Expected Performance	Qualities of Response
Independent speaking	Produce monologic spoken discourse on a range of topics, drawing on own knowledge and/or experience and using a range of rhetorical/pragmatic functions	Intelligibility, fluency
Integrated reading/ speaking	Use information from a variety of academic reading texts as the basis for producing monologic discourse drawing on one or more rhetorical/pragmatic functions	Intelligibility, fluency, content, coherence, organization
Integrated listening/ speaking	Use information from a variety of consultations and student interactions (dialogic stimuli) as the basis for producing monologic discourse drawing on one or more rhetorical/pragmatic functions Use information from a variety of lectures (monologic stimuli) as the basis for producing monologic discourse drawing on one or more rhetorical/pragmatic functions	Intelligibility, fluency, content, coherence, organization

were defined as either *independent* or *integrated*. An independent task would require the examinee to speak about a topic that is known to each individual examinee (e.g., personal point of view) that would not require the examinee to comprehend material from another source. An integrated task, in contrast, would require the examinee to speak about a topic for which information had been supplied from another source. The latter type of task stretched the original framework most dramatically because it actually entailed assessment of two skills simultaneously. For example, if an examinee had to comprehend a written argument about fishing rights and responsibilities in the Pacific Northwest before speaking on his opinion about the topic, the task performance would have to be considered a combination of reading and speaking rather than a measure of speaking as an independent skill.

Expected performance   Three types of response formats were considered in the *Speaking Framework*: reading aloud, elicited sentence repetition, and constructed response. The first two response types were limited to certain structural features of speaking, such as control of phonological features, but these had the advantage of being scorable by a computer. Constructed responses would provide a much richer assessment of speaking and could be scored for all of the structural features of interest. In their discussion of length of response, the authors of *Speaking Framework* (Butler et al., 2000) surveyed existing ESL speaking tests and reported that they ranged in length from 8 to 35 minutes. They stated that the speaking assessment should give a test taker the opportunity to produce 10–15 minutes worth of speech so that the candidate's linguistic, sociolinguistic, functional, and discourse abilities could be measured.

Discourse features were composed of generic/pragmatic features and structural features. Generic/pragmatic features exist at both the micro and macro levels. The micro level was defined by short turns and could be characterized either by functions from speech act theory or by conversational analysis. The macro level was defined by extended discourse and could be characterized by either rhetorical functions or genres. Structural features included elements such as the following: accomplishment of task, sufficiency of response in terms of length and complexity, comprehensibility, including control of phonological and prosodic features, adequacy of grammatical resources, fluency, cohesion, and range and precision of vocabulary. The *Speaking Framework* (Butler et al., 2000) suggested that the relative importance of various structural features could be varied according to task and that rating could be conducted using different scoring schemes.

Quality of performance   The section of the *Speaking Framework* (Butler et al., 2000) titled "Quality of Performance" was subdivided into six parts: Levels of Scoring, Method of Scoring, Criteria for Scoring, Mode of Capturing Responses and Scoring, Types of Integrated Tasks, and Factors Influencing Task Difficulty. For levels of scoring, the speaking tasks could be scored either dichotomously (present/absent) or polytomously (evaluated for different levels of correctness); the team envisioned most tasks being scored polytomously, using perhaps a generalized partial-credit IRT model for scoring these tasks and a Rasch or two-parameter IRT model for scoring the dichotomous items. In terms of method of scoring, rating scales would be used. Two families of rating scales were described: holistic/analytic, which are rather generic and can be used across several different tasks, and primary/multitrait, which are specific to particular tasks (Turner & Upshur, 1996).

The speaking team noted that the holistic scales used with the Test of Spoken English™ (TSE®) seemed to mask differences in difficulty among tasks. They argued that since proficiency scales are one of the goals of the new TOEFL project and since the position of tasks on a scale may be related to task difficulty, use of a holistic scale should be questioned. The primary/multitrait family of rating scales uses one or more scales to indicate how well a test taker has accomplished a specific task; however, the viability of these methods was questioned from a financial perspective. The *Speaking Framework* (Butler et al., 2000) presented the possibility of scoring speaking on some of the following criteria: pronunciation, vocabulary, cohesion, organization, grammatical accuracy, comprehensibility, fluency, and length of response. Regarding the mode of capturing responses and scoring, the team assumed that the tasks would be delivered to the test taker on a computer rather than by an interlocutor and that the responses would be saved in a computer file to be judged at a later time by a human rater. They speculated that with developments in speech recognition, computers could be used in the future to judge some features while the human rater scored others.

The *Speaking Framework* (Butler et al., 2000) included other considerations such as speculation about the role of computer-assisted scoring of examinees responses, the use of cloze and elicitation tasks as indirect measures of linguistic ability in grammar or pronunciation, and inclusion of a combination of short-answer tasks that would focus on linguistic ability, which could be computer-scored. They acknowledged the constraints on interaction that are imposed by direct assessments such as oral interviews and even more so with semi-direct tests such as the speaking team was envisioning. The nature of the tasks that the interaction requires, the roles of the interlocutors, and the conditions under which interlocutors perform are different from interactions outside of the test. Despite these limitations, the *Speaking Framework* outlined a way of moving forward into prototyping of tasks.

The Writing Framework

The writing team faced a challenge similar to that of the speaking team: The proficiency scaling approach of the *TOEFL 2000 Framework* (Jamieson et al., 2000) had been conceived and implemented for the assessment of a receptive skill. Recognizing the limited applicability of the *TOEFL 2000 Framework*, the team approached the *Writing Framework* (Cumming et al., 2000) by focusing on the examinees' expected performance and how it could be evaluated.

Although the writing team could have drawn on many years of experience in assessing writing on the Test of Written English™ (TWE®), they started the process of test development anew by outlining eight requirements that they wanted the test to meet:

1. Require examinees to produce sustained, coherent, appropriate, and purposeful texts in response to the task presented
2. Involve a total writing time of 60–75 minutes
3. Require examinees to produce writing integral to academic environments and contexts
4. Include tasks that can maximally generalize across disciplines
5. Contain writing tasks involving reading and listening skills—writing that occurs in response to content
6. Assess both the written product and a variety of writing processes
7. Include tasks that discriminate across the mid to upper proficiency levels
8. Require raters to consider both the written text and the scorer's processes of reading the texts in assigning scores to writing tasks. (Writers need to know who the reader is and how the text will be evaluated for a given task.)

Over the course of working with these parameters, the writing team defined the three characteristics that ended up as critical to the *Writing Framework* (Cumming et al., 2000), as summarized in Table 3.8.

Task types The task definitions were intended to operationalize the way that writing in an academic setting was defined in the *Writing Framework* (Cumming et al., 2000). In most academic settings, writing represents a response to learning a set of material, synthesizing information, or building an argument from previously reviewed resources. Writing has to reflect specific academic genres and subdomains of academic writing so that students can display the knowledge they are acquiring. The focus of writing tasks therefore needed to be on transmitting and adapting information rather than on creating new knowledge (Hale et al., 1996; Waters, 1996). Three types of writing

TABLE 3.8
Characteristics in the Writing Framework

Task Types	Expected Performance	Qualities of Response
Independent	State, explain, and support an opinion	Organization of discourse and ideas Language use
Integrated text-based task	Organize the major ideas/important information in a reading text or a lecture, select important information to include, and accurately communicate via another modality these ideas and this information as requested in a directive	Organization of discourse and ideas Language use Content responsibility
Integrated situation-based response	Based on an exchange between or among students or between a student and staff or faculty member, describe a problem and propose a solution or synthesize and summarize information in writing	Organization of discourse and ideas Language use Content responsibility

tasks were proposed to test this construct of academic writing. An independent writing task would encourage the test taker to express his/her ideas on a topic with supporting ideas based on experience. A writing sample based on input from a written or spoken text could be either a brief response (in which the test taker displayed knowledge of the input text) or an extended response (in which the test taker would identify, select, and manipulate information from the input text). A situational writing task would have the test taker read or listen to a brief text and respond by writing a few sentences that would be appropriate in terms of the content, setting, and purpose. This combination would provide a variety of tasks and contexts for writing and was thought to be feasible in the allowable time.

Expected performance To develop the three types of writing tasks, the team also delimited the rhetorical functions that would best reflect informational writing: Based on the evidence they reviewed, they argued that writing tasks should focus on (a) categorization and analysis, (b) problem and solution, and (c) suasive argumentation. They decided that narrative writing and creative expression did not represent appropriate tasks for the overall test purpose. Because topic characteristics are a source of variation in writing (Brossell, 1986; Hidi & McLaren, 1990; Tobias, 1994), the three writing tasks proposed would have different topics. Examples of characteristics that may affect difficulty included the extent of required background knowledge, emotional appeal, number of options available, topic abstractness, and cognitive demands. How topic variation and related variables affected the construct would be a focus of future research.

Qualities of response   The writing framework indicated that evaluative criteria for scoring texts should be based on an examinee's ability to organize and present ideas. Ideas need to reflect a reasonable hierarchical structure; introductory and transitional framing for the information should be appropriate; and thematic coherence should be maintained. Examinees should demonstrate vocabulary range and appropriate word choice. Similarly, conventions of grammar, usage, and formatting should be demonstrated. Finally, writers should use appropriate logic and rhetorical devices to sustain reader attention. These evaluation criteria were spelled out in more detail as part of a text characteristics model.

Writers need to know what readers will be looking for when they evaluate texts. In the independent writing task, the writer should assume that the reader knows the prompt, the task, and the time limit. The reader would not have any biases on the topic but would notice anomalous information. The writer could assume that the reader was proficient and would make an appropriate effort to comprehend the text. At the same time, the reader would notice problems in syntax, word choice, formatting, and spelling. In the writing tasks requiring a response to external stimuli, the reader would expect that the content information would not be distorted and would present sufficient and specific information. The reader would know the source material and would have expectations about appropriate paraphrasing, quoting, and citing.

In evaluating the writing, the reader would use the earlier evaluative criteria based on discourse organization of ideas and substantive content and the accurate use of English structure and vocabulary. More specifically, the reader would focus on four discourse variables: organization (the reader could follow ideas), coherence (there would not be any anomalies or contradictions), progression (there would not be any glaring gaps or redundancies), and development (there would be sufficient details, examples, and reasons). The reader would focus on four language use variables: range and appropriateness of vocabulary, appropriate language and discourse connections, accuracy of syntax and morphology, and accurate spelling and punctuation.

Other considerations were raised in the *Writing Framework* (Cumming et al., 2000), such as the view that writing could not be limited to the product itself; the process was seen as equally important. However, the writing team decided not to address process. Students could use various approaches (outlining, note taking, revising, mapping), but no attempt would be made to judge the processes that they used. The framework shown in Table 3.8 provided a structure which was further explored in the studies of task design.

Summary

Why were the four skill frameworks different from the general framework from which they were modeled? The reasons probably depended on a number of factors, including the individuals on each team, but some skill-related differences can be identified. For example, both the *Listening Framework* (Bejar et al., 2000) and the *Reading Framework* (Enright et al., 2000) added a cognitive ability perspective that was not included in the *TOEFL 2000 Framework*. It would be difficult to argue that this addition was due to an inherent difference in the listening and reading skills the TOEFL assessed from the reading skills in the adult literacy project; it would be better explained, however, by the teams' preference for explanation to draw on cognitive ability perspectives rather than solely on task characteristics.

The *Speaking Framework* (Butler et al., 2000) and the *Writing Framework* (Cumming et al., 2000) described skills in terms of the relationship between the speaker/listener and the writer/reader, respectively, and therefore the characteristics of the response and its evaluation were central to these frameworks. Whereas the procedures for assigning a value to examinees' responses were included in the general framework, these procedures and the nature of the expected performance played a much larger role in the *Speaking Framework* and *Writing Framework*. Despite discussions about including integrated tasks within each of the skill areas, in the end the speaking and writing teams were the ones that carefully considered integrated tasks by using reading and/or listening material as the basis for the content of test takers' responses.

The *Listening Framework* (Bejar et al., 2000) and *Speaking Framework* (Butler et al., 2000) relied heavily on L2 studies that had not been synthesized into a coherent perspective for assessment. The listening and speaking teams began by enumerating the variables that were defined and outlined in the general framework, but in both cases the result was a long list of variables that proved difficult to use as a guide for constructing test tasks. It was a fragmented description of the aspects of the construct to be represented. The reading and writing teams chose among well-articulated and well-researched perspectives. Nevertheless, by the end of this period of development process, parallels between the frameworks emerged. The final frameworks look similar for listening and reading and for speaking and writing even though the paths to their development were different.

Each of the four frameworks also included an agenda outlining a research and development process that would take place over the next 3 years to move the project through four stages: construct refinement, usability and prototype testing, pilot testing, and field testing. These stages, which did not materialize precisely as outlined by the four teams, are described in the following three chapters. In the rest of this chapter, we describe the implications of the frameworks for research pertaining to domain definition.

RESEARCH RELEVANT TO DOMAIN DEFINITION

The assumption and implications summarized in Table 3.1 provided impetus for two large-scale studies to provide a basis for domain definition. The supporting assumption associated with domain definition requires that test tasks be modeled on the tasks examinees will perform in the domain of interest, and therefore research was conducted to gather evidence about the language of academic tasks and the relative importance of the variety of tasks of potential interest.

The Language of Academic Tasks

The *Listening Framework* (Bejar et al., 2000) and *Reading Framework* (Enright et al., 2000) suggested research using a corpus of academic language to analyze the rhetorical and linguistic features of authentic university language. Results would serve as a basis for defining task features associated with language (referred to as text material in the *TOEFL 2000 Framework*). Biber and colleagues (Biber, Conrad, Reppen, Byrd, & Helt, 2002 and Biber, Conrad, Reppen, Byrd, Helt, Clark, et al., 2004) undertook a study to construct and analyze a corpus of academic language, called the TOEFL 2000 Spoken and Written Academic Language (T2K-SWAL) Corpus. The purposes of this project were (a) to describe the linguistic features of spoken and written registers that are encountered by North American students in English-medium university classes, (b) to construct tools for test developers to explore the grammatical characteristics of the corpus during task design, and (c) to serve as a potential source for aural texts for listening tasks.

Methods   The first phase of the research was the corpus design, construction, and grammatical tagging. The corpus was designed to allow for systematic investigation of differences in linguistic patterning across registers, academic disciplines, and academic levels. The corpus consisted of 1.67 million words from 251 texts of spoken language and 1.07 million words from 172 texts of written language. Spoken registers included classroom teaching, classroom management, labs and in-class groups, office hours, study groups, and service encounters. Written registers included textbooks, course packs, course management, and other campus writing (e.g., catalogues, Web sites). In addition to these spoken and written registers, the corpus was designed to represent major academic disciplines (business, education, engineering, humanities, natural science, and social science) and three academic levels (lower division undergraduate—freshman and sophomore; upper division undergraduate—junior and senior; and graduate). The spoken texts were collected from Northern Arizona University; Georgia State University; Iowa State University; and California State University, Sacramento campuses by students and faculty who agreed to use tape-recorders for a 2-week period. Spoken texts were transcribed using a consistent convention, and written texts were scanned into computer text files. Each text file was labeled according to features such as register, discipline, academic level, and status of speaker. Each text was then grammatically annotated; each word was tagged for its part of speech and particular grammatical function or larger syntactic structure.

In the second phase of the study, the researchers undertook linguistic analysis of the corpus, seeking general descriptive results to characterize the similarities and differences among various categories of texts. In the third phase, tools were developed allowing task designers and test developers to make queries to the corpus to evaluate potential texts for the TOEFL relative to the academic corpus.

Results Results indicated that mode and register predicted linguistic variation much more than did academic discipline or level, to the point that discipline and level did not determine the language choices investigated. This means that students tend to encounter the same structural linguistic features, regardless of their academic field or level of study. Large linguistic differences appear across registers, and larger differences appear between spoken and written modes. In addition, the results provided linguistic descriptions for many of the types of texts that were being considered for inclusion in the TOEFL such as textbooks, lectures, service encounters, office hours, and study groups.

The following software tools and resources were completed over the course of the project: CorpusManager, which located texts; databases for vocabulary and lexical bundle distributions; and tools to compare newly created texts by assessment specialists at Educational Testing Service with the texts in the T2K-SWAL Corpus to assess the extent to which the language used in assessment tasks is representative of real-life language use.

The exploration of the corpus as source for aural texts for listening tasks resulted in the decision that overall corpus excerpts were unusable for developing test tasks. First, many excerpts could not pass ETS sensitivity review. For example, corpus lectures on spousal abuse (from a sociology class) and on cancer death rates (from a statistics class) would be potentially upsetting to some students and therefore not appropriate in a test with high-stakes outcomes. Second, excerpts that were too closely tied to knowledge of American culture were not appropriate for a test that would be taken by many students who had never been to the United States. Third, some lectures could not be adequately comprehended without background knowledge from a previous lecture. Fourth, some excerpts contained so many digressions that the main idea could not be easily grasped. Fifth, some lectures relied on visual materials that were not captured in the excerpts that were audiotaped (videotaping was considered but rejected as too cumbersome and intrusive). Sixth, comprehension frequently required skills other than the English language skills that the TOEFL is intended to assess, such as the math skills needed to understand a business lecture on interest rates. Finally, some excerpts contained factual errors that could confuse students who knew the correct answer; for example, in one case a student tutor confirmed, incorrectly, that Alexander Hamilton was the fourth president of the United States.

Implications   The corpus research provided empirical evidence for many issues that were being discussed in the design of the new TOEFL. It helped to resolve questions as to whether different versions of the test should be developed for different groups of students. The findings of no linguistic differences between the graduate and undergraduate levels and only slight differences among the academic disciplines supported the decision to have only one version of the TOEFL. The finding that mode of production was the most important predictor supported the decision for separate scores on the listening and reading measures. The study also pointed out important registers that had not been considered for inclusion in the TOEFL but that represented different language students encounter, such as classroom/course management and institutional written material. Overall, the research provided basic results that support domain definition, in addition to a corpus and analysis tools that provide a valuable resource for future research studies and test development.

Language Use in Academic Tasks

A second study surveyed university instructors and students to discover their perception of the importance of the types of tasks proposed for the TOEFL. Rosenfeld, Leung, and Oltman (2001) described their research as the type of job analysis that is suggested for investigation of the content representativeness of tests (American Educational Research Association, American Psychological Association, & National Council on Measurement in Education, 1999), which is one approach to domain definition. The two major questions were whether (a) instructors and international students perceived the tasks identified as important academic tasks and (b) instructors and students thought that more successful students performed these tasks better than less academically able students.

Methods   The study was conceived of as a job analysis of the academic tasks requiring English language proficiency that students need to succeed in their course work. Rosenfeld et al. (2001) oversaw the process of generating sets of task descriptions consistent with the skill frameworks that were hypothesized to be important for competent academic performance. Initially, each of the four skills teams generated a list of task statements that they felt were consistent with their frameworks and with competent academic performance. This draft was reviewed by a TOEFL committee and by faculty and students, who were encouraged to identify any tasks that they thought were important to academic performance but were missing from the list. The survey instrument was piloted and finalized to include 42 ratable task statements and a few demographic questions.

A survey was used to collect responses to the set of task statements from undergraduate and graduate faculty and undergraduate and graduate students. The range of schools and academic disciplines included was based on *Open Doors 1994/1995: Report on International Education Exchange* (Davis, 1995). Six subject areas were included because of their high enrollment of international students (chemistry, computer and information science, electrical engineering, business/management, history, and psychology). The top 100 schools in terms of international student enrollment were selected as the basis from which to sample. Schools were then selected based on geographic diversity, size, whether they were public versus private, and whether they had undergraduate and graduate majors in each of the six subject areas. The response rate was good (59% for undergraduate faculty; 81% for graduate faculty; 78% for undergraduate students; 92% for graduate students) and roughly represented the demographics of the group sampled.

Results Large majorities of both undergraduate and graduate faculty and students judged all 42 listening, reading, speaking, and writing tasks to be relevant aspects of the job of undergraduate and graduate students. Even though faculty and students rated all tasks as important or very important, some tasks were rated as more important than others. For example, all four groups rated the following task statements very highly:

1. Read text material with sufficient care and comprehension to remember major ideas.
2. Organize writing in order to convey major and supporting ideas.
3. Understand the main ideas and supporting information when listening.

Other statements that received lower importance rating by all four groups of participants included:

1. Recognize the use of examples, anecdotes, jokes, and digressions (when listening).
2. Demonstrate facility with standard spoken language...while...describing objects.

Across the faculty and within all six subject areas, mean ratings on the scale assessing relationship to success indicated that undergraduate and graduate faculty perceived that the more academically successful nonnative speakers of English either generally or almost always performed all 42 tasks better than the less academically successful nonnative speakers (Rosenfeld et al., 2001, pp. 46–47).

Implications   The design of this study permitted examination of potential differences between academic levels and academic disciplines in regard to which tasks were important for course completion. No strong evidence was found to support a claim for any differences in the kinds of tasks undergraduates or graduates have to do or for the kinds of tasks graduate students in different disciplines have to do. Lack of such evidence supported the decision to create only one version of the TOEFL for all students. Furthermore, the data on faculty and student judgments of the relative importance of tasks were available for consideration in the design of test tasks and criterion measures.

Summary

These two studies by Biber and his colleagues (Biber et al., 2002; Biber et al., 2004) and Rosenfeld et al. (2001) took priority over other research suggestions in the frameworks (Bejar et al., 2000; Butler et al., 2000; Cumming et al., 2000; Enright et al., 2000), which identified a range of issues in task design and development, including the ease with which tasks could be duplicated, the amount of time a task took, the ease with which test takers understood what was required of them in performing a task, automated speech recognition, automated ratings of essays, and online scoring by human raters, to name just a few. Many of these issues were explored later and are described in Chapters 4 and 5.

PSYCHOMETRIC ISSUES FOR EVALUATION AND EXPLANATION

Proficiency scaling made some rigorous assumptions affecting how evaluation and explanation inferences were to be justified psychometrically, whereas communicative competence theory did not. Among the basic assumptions underlying proficiency scaling is that IRT is the psychometric model used to estimate the statistics for task quality to justify evaluation inferences (see Table 3.1). The proficiency-scaling approach to explanation—showing task characteristics to be significant predictors of task difficulty—assumes that task difficulty will be estimated through the use of IRT because of the sample-independent estimates of difficulty that IRT produces. The implication for the TOEFL project was that the use of IRT with a variety of scales and test tasks needed be explored. This exploration ran up against some of the inconsistencies between proficiency scaling and communicative competence.

Evaluation

The proficiency-scaling approach to evaluation inferences assumed that a meaningful scale would be constructed through the use of IRT to place examinees' scores and tasks on the same metric, and accordingly examinees' performance needed to be scored in a way that allowed for the use of IRT for item analysis. These assumptions created practical challenges for two of the testing practices that would be considered consistent with the communicative competence approach: polytomously scored items and integrated tasks. At the same time, the use of IRT raised issues about the administration conditions of testing.

Polytomously scored items   Whereas the use of IRT as a model underlying analysis of dichotomously scored items had become relatively commonplace in operational testing programs at ETS such as the TOEFL by the middle of the 1990s, much less common were the more complicated IRT models for polytomously scored items (i.e., items scored by making use of multiple score points or levels and not just right or wrong). However, if test tasks were to reflect communicative language use, constructed responses would have to be required and evaluation would have to produce scores allowing for levels of correctness. Fundamental questions existed about implementing such a polytomous scoring model using IRT in an operational program. Moreover, it was very likely that polytomously scored items in certain of the TOEFL sections might be augmented with dichotomously scored items (i.e., the usual sort of TOEFL multiple-choice items). Such a mix of dichotomous/polytomous items added an additional layer of unexplored issues.

Tang (1996) began to investigate these issues with a review of the most promising polytomous IRT models, with a particular focus on the most commonly used computer program for implementing such models, PARSCALE (Muraki & Bock, 1999). She found that either of the more general polytomous models typically employed, the generalized partial-credit model (Muraki, 1992) or the graded response model (Samejima, 1969), could be implemented with the constructed response tasks under consideration for the new TOEFL. She also found that the PARSCALE program had been successfully applied in the calibration of combinations of dichotomously and polytomously scored items. Hence, it appeared that IRT could be employed with the sections of the TOEFL under consideration. These were positive results in view of the proficiency scaling assumption that IRT would provide certain measurement advantages over traditional test theory procedures (see Gulliksen, 1950) with the new test.

Tang and Eignor (1997) followed up by implementing the IRT models Tang had reviewed with existing TOEFL data. Underlying the Tang and Eignor investigation was the assumption that it might be reasonable to combine dichotomously scored TOEFL reading comprehension items with polytomously scored TWE tasks in forming a reading/writing score and to combine dichotomously scored TOEFL listening comprehension items with polytomously scored TSE tasks to form a listening/speaking score. Tang and Eignor employed the three-parameter logistic model with the dichotomously scored items and used first the generalized partial-credit model and then the graded response model with the polytomously scored tasks. They succeeded in calibrating all the various section and model combinations, but their results indicated some preference for using the generalized partial-credit model with the three-parameter logistic model when calibrating items using PARSCALE. Overall, the results of this analysis painted a positive picture for the use of PARSCALE with the types of data that were being discussed for the TOEFL, but because the items that Tang and Eignor experimented with were not al-together similar to those that would appear in the new TOEFL, additional work was needed.

Integrated tasks   Communicative competence theory implied that inte-grated tasks requiring performance on tasks linked to one another should be included on the test, but such tasks would violate the IRT assumption that test tasks on a single scale be conditionally independent. That is, for a given level of ability, the response to one item should be independent of the response to another item. Integrated tasks, where a common listening stimulus might be used for listening to multiple-choice items and speaking constructed-response tasks, do not lend themselves to a traditional IRT-based modeling approach. Set-based items, such as reading comprehension items that share a common reading stimulus, also cannot be considered to be independent. However, un-like the listening/speaking integrated task mentioned above, such items can be modeled using standard IRT procedures by considering the set of items to be one polytomously scored *macro-item* with as many score levels as there are actual items. The polytomously scored macro-item can then be modeled using any of the available IRT models for polytomously scored items, such as the generalized partial-credit model.

The work reviewed by Carey (1996) and Tang (1996) and implemented by Tang and Eignor (1997) was based on the use of items in studies with-out built-in dependencies (except for set-based items, which were treated as macro-items). However, Mislevy (1995) began to work on task dependence issues in new TOEFL, taking a different approach to modeling—Bayesian inference networks (or Bayes nets). Bayes nets are graphical models that help statisticians carry out probability-based inference when dealing with complex networks of interdependent variables. The level of complexity of the Bayes net is a function of the level of complexity of the relationships assumed in the behavior and between tasks and variables. However, during the course of the TOEFL project, the study of Bayes nets represented research in progress rather than an operational psychometric model that was ready for use.

Administration conditions   Prospective use of IRT raised operational issues such as whether or not the TOEFL would be delivered as an adaptive test. Adaptive testing depends on being able to immediately derive a score on the item or task just presented, so that that information can be used in the process of choosing the next item or task to be administered. From the inception of the new TOEFL, many project members expected that items in the listening and reading sections would be like those in the existing paper-based and computerized tests (i.e., multiple-choice or extended multiple-choice). Hence, adaptive delivery was certainly a possibility with these sections. In contrast, it was anticipated that open-ended polytomously scored tasks would be employed in the speaking and writing sections. Adaptive testing was not a viable option for the speaking and writing sections because they could not be scored automatically in real time for use in selecting subsequent tasks. Although there had been recent advances involving automated scoring of linguistic responses (Burstein, Kaplan, Rohen-Wolff, Zuckerman, & Lu, 1999), it was felt that such scoring could not be accomplished within the small window of time available for scoring responses in a computerized adaptive test (CAT). Given all this, any response to a speaking (or writing) task would need to be directed to a human rater for scoring or scored via computer outside the actual testing process.

Adaptive testing programs usually involve the administration of tests on a continuous or close-to-continuous basis, but nothing precludes administration of these tests within a number of noncontinuous blocks of time. If it were decided that a computerized test would not be adaptive, two possible delivery scenarios existed. The test, which would need to be assembled in an intact linear fashion, much like a paper-based test, could be constructed via computer immediately, using computerized test assembly procedures (referred to as linear-on-the-fly testing or LOFT; see Eignor, 1999), like the reading section of the TOEFL computer-based test (CBT). Alternatively, the test form could be constructed offline, likely employing computerized test assembly procedures, and then later delivered via computer. The difference between the two approaches is that with LOFT, a sufficient item pool needs to exist to support immediate construction of a linear form for the particular individual being tested, whereas with the other approach, one or a small number of linear forms simply need to be constructed beforehand. Given the problems involved in maintaining the security of item pools (Wainer & Eignor, 2000), LOFT was not considered for any of the sections of the new TOEFL. Hence, linear forms were planned for the new test, and each form would only be administered within a short window of time.

If adaptive and LOFT testing, both of which require that items be calibrated via IRT procedures, were ruled out, the use of IRT would no longer be an absolute necessity for purposes other than proficiency scaling, or possibly for test equating. Further, while IRT had been used with the paper-based version of the current TOEFL for test assembly and test-equating purposes, procedures that make use of traditional non-IRT-based item or score statistics were seen as viable alternatives. Hence, depending on decisions that would be made later in the project, constructed forms might be equated via classical test-equating procedures (see Kolen & Brennan, 1995), and, if computer assembly of these forms was seen as advantageous, via assembly procedures that made use of classical item statistics (see Stocking, Swanson, & Pearlman, 1993).

Explanation

The proficiency scaling approach to the explanation inference assumes the use of IRT for obtaining item difficulty statistics, which are used as the dependent variable in a multiple regression analysis. Explanation is empirically supported to the extent that the hypothesized combinations of task characteristics predict task difficulty. The communicative competence approach to explanation suggests that a theoretical construct consisting of a complex of abilities and processes underlies performance across contexts, but the approach does not make any specific suggestions about how evidence supporting this assumption can be obtained. The fact that proficiency scaling had a concrete method for approaching explanatory inferences and communicative competence theory had none accounts for the way that the *TOEFL 2000 Framework* (Jamieson et al., 2000) was originally conceived.

Rather than attempting to develop a basis for the explanation inference from the integrated tasks implied by communicative competence theory, the framework development was divided into four skills, within which task characteristics could presumably be identified. The *TOEFL 2000 Framework* (Jamieson et al., 2000) justified this path with the claim that "score users such as admissions officers and graduate deans...requested that scores be reported for speaking, writing, listening, and reading because these skills relate to the kinds of decisions that need to be made" (p. 12). Moreover, the argument was made that if the scales upon which scores were to be reported were to be informative to test score users, the scales needed to be based on a frame of reference recognizable to test score users. The idea was that discussions beginning from the four skills would ultimately provide a useful way to describe authentic language tasks in academic settings. These tasks could then provide the frame around which the test would be created, and integrated skills tasks would emerge. Indeed, the *TOEFL 2000 Framework* claimed "that speaking, writing, listening, and reading can be tested both integratively and independently" (Jamieson et al., 2000, p. 12), but during development of the skills frameworks, any movement in this direction raised concerns about the effects of integrated tasks on the consistency and interpretability of each scale. As a consequence, most of the time and effort spent on framework development was devoted to defining the four skills rather than defining a single integrated construct (Angelis & Chapelle, 1999), and the need to theorize and incorporate integrated tasks was largely unmet through the end of 1999, when integrated tasks on the speaking and writing scales were added.

In this sense, the *Speaking Framework* (Butler et al., 2000) and *Writing Framework* (Cumming et al., 2000) best realized the vision of the *TOEFL 2000 Framework*'s (Jamieson et al., 2000) suggestion that each of the four skills could be assessed though the use of a combination of independent and integrated tasks: "...integrated tasks will provide information about examinees' ability in more than one skill area" (p. 12) and that "...integrated tasks will be combined with information from the independent tasks to construct a profile of language abilities for each examinee" (p. 13). The psychometric problem was, however, that IRT was not a suitable psychometric model to implement this.

A second psychometric problem pertained to the need for an interpretable overall score on the TOEFL. Despite the claim in the *TOEFL 2000 Framework* (Jamieson et al., 2000) that test score users are interested in obtaining scores on the skills, admissions officers and faculty use overall scores for admissions decisions, and these decisions are the current primary use of the TOEFL. Many methods of deriving a total score from the four skills scores were considered, but without a means of communicating its score interpretation to users, a satisfying result was not found. The paradox was that the proficiency scaling approach had set expectations for the way in which explanatory inferences were to be justified and laid out parameters for frameworks that would work toward these expectations. However, the score that would ultimately be used for the central decision-making purpose of the TOEFL would not be interpretable according to the proficiency scaling expectations because no proficiency scaling framework could be constructed for communicative competence.

In short, the assumption that IRT should be used as the appropriate model for analysis of test items was interconnected with task design, administration conditions, and explanations. As a consequence, throughout the development of the frameworks, the assumptions associated with IRT were raised repeatedly, and the need for a different approach was recognized.

CONCLUSION

Proficiency scaling and communicative competence theory served as points of departure for developing a general framework, but the authors of the specific skills frameworks for listening, reading, speaking, and writing modified the components of the general framework. The skills frameworks (Bejar et al., 2000; Butler et al., 2000; Cumming et al., 2000; Enright et al., 2000) each recommended extensive research, but this chapter included only two of the initial studies as well as psychometric issues that were salient during this stage. This chapter described the research focused on domain definition and the investigation of psychometric issues, both of which were prompted by the frameworks. Despite the initial motivations guiding the *Framework*, by 1999 no specific plans were developed to have proficiency scales in place when the new TOEFL was introduced. The reasons are more complex than this chapter has revealed, and they extend into the next chapter, which discusses research results that indicated no support for the task characteristics as predictors of difficulty.

This chapter contained a relatively neat retrospective account of what was a dynamic process with multiple orthogonal perspectives converging on the problem of how to best move the project forward. At its height, the project received input regularly from at least 30 people, who discussed the contents of the frameworks, the research priorities, and test-task development. Moreover, as this and the previous chapter have demonstrated, the issues involved in creating such a test were not well understood, leaving the process open to negotiation and guidance from outside the project staff. Nevertheless, by 1998 test tasks were being created in a manner that had been influenced by the frameworks. These tasks were piloted in the initial small-scale research conducted to gather data on learners' performance and insight into the process of task creation. The specific area of research targeted in this stage of the project and the results are described in the following chapter.

REFERENCES

American Educational Research Association, American Psychological Association, & National Council on Measurement in Education. (1999). *Standards for educational and psychological testing*. Washington, DC: American Educational Research Association.

Angelis, P., & Chapelle, C. (1999). *TOEFL 2000: An integrated measure of academic language ability*. Unpublished manuscript.

Bachman, L. F., & Palmer, A. (1996). *Language testing in practice*. Oxford: Oxford University Press.

Bejar, I., Douglas, D., Jamieson, J., Nissan, S., & Turner, J. (2000). *TOEFL 2000 listening framework: A working paper* (TOEFL Monograph No. 19). Princeton, NJ: Educational Testing Service.

Biber, D. (1988). *Variation across speech and writing*. New York: Cambridge University Press.

Biber, D. (1992). On the complexity of discourse complexity: A multidimensional analysis. *Discourse Processes, 15*, 133–163.

Biber, D. (1995). *Dimensions of register variation: A cross-linguistic comparison.* Cambridge: Cambridge University Press.

Biber, D., Conrad, S., Reppen, R., Byrd, P., & Helt, M. (2002). Speaking and writing in the university: A multidimensional comparison. *TESOL Quarterly, 36*, 9–48.

Biber, D., Conrad, S. M., Reppen, R., Byrd, P., Helt, M., Clark, V., et al. (2004). *Representing language use in the university: Analysis of the TOEFL 2000 spoken and written academic language corpus* (TOEFL Monograph No. 25). Princeton, NJ: Educational Testing Service.

Brossell, G. (1986). Current research and unanswered questions in writing assessment. In K. Greenberg, H. Wierner, & R. Donovan (Eds.), *Writing assessment: Issues and strategies* (pp. 168–182). New York: Longman.

Brown, G. (1995). Dimensions of difficulty in listening comprehension. In D. Mendelsohn & J. Rubin (Eds.), *A guide for the teaching of second language listening* (pp. 59–73). San Diego, CA: Dominie Press, Inc.

Brown, G., & Yule, G. (1983). *Discourse analysis.* New York: Cambridge University Press.

Buck, G. (1997). Testing listening skills. In C. Clapham & D. Corson (Eds.), *The encyclopedia of language and education: Vol 7. Language testing and assessment* (pp. 65–74). Dordrecht, the Netherlands: Kluwer.

Burstein, J. C., Kaplan, R. M., Rohen-Wolff, S., Zuckerman, D. I., & Lu, C. (1999). *A review of computer-based speech technology for TOEFL 2000* (TOEFL Monograph No. 10). Princeton, NJ: Educational Testing Service.

Butler, F. A., Eignor, D., Jones, S., McNamara, T., & Suomi, B. K. (2000). *TOEFL 2000 speaking framework: A working paper* (TOEFL Monograph No. 20). Princeton, NJ: Educational Testing Service.

Carey, P. A. (1996). *A review of psychometric and consequential issues related to performance assessment* (TOEFL Monograph No. 3). Princeton, NJ: Educational Testing Service.

Carver, R. P. (1992). Reading rate: Theory, research, and practical implications. *Journal of Reading, 36*, 84–95.

Carver, R. P. (1997). Reading for one second, one minute, or one year form the perspective of Rauding theory. *Scientific Studies of Reading, 1*, 3–43.

Cumming, A., Kantor, R., Powers, D., Santos, T., & Taylor, C. (2000). *TOEFL 2000 writing framework: A working paper.* (TOEFL Monograph No. 18). Princeton, NJ: Educational Testing Service.

Davis, T. M. (Ed.). (1995). *Open doors 1994/95: Report on international educational exchange.* New York: Institute of International Education.

Eignor, D. (1999). Selected technical issues in the creation of computer-adaptive tests of second language reading proficiency. In M. Chaloub-Deville (Ed.), *Issues in computer-adaptive testing of reading proficiency.* Cambridge: Cambridge University Press.

Enright, M. K., Grabe, W., Koda, K., Mosenthal, P., Mulcahy-Ernt, P., & Schedl, M. (2000). *TOEFL 2000 reading framework: A working paper* (TOEFL Monograph No. 17). Princeton, NJ: Educational Testing Service.

Enright, M. K., & Schedl, M. (2000). *Reading for a reason: Using reader purpose to guide test design.* Unpublished manuscript. Princeton, NJ: Educational Testing Service.

Goldman, S. (1997). Learning from text: Reflections on the past and suggestions for the future. *Discourse Processes, 23*, 357–398.

Gulliksen, H. (1950). *Theory of mental tests.* New York: Wiley Press.

Guthrie, G. T. (1988). Locating information in documents: Examination of a cognitive model. *Reading Research Quarterly, 23*, 178–199.

Guthrie, J. T., & Kirsch, I. S. (1987). Distinctions between reading comprehension and locating information in text. *Journal of Educational Psychology, 79*(3), 220–227.

Guthrie, J. T., & Mosenthal, P. (1987). Literacy as multidimensional: Locating information and reading comprehension. *Educational Psychologist, 22,* 279-297.

Hale, G. A., Taylor, C., Bridgeman, B., Carson, J., Kroll, B., & Kantor, R. (1996). *A study of writing tasks assigned in academic degree programs* (TOEFL Research Rep. No. 54). Princeton, NJ: Educational Testing Service.

Hansen, C. (1994). Topic identification in lecture discourse. In J. Flowerdew (Ed.), *Academic listening* (pp. 131-145). New York: Cambridge University Press.

Hidi, S., & McLaren, J. (1990). The effect of topic and theme interestingness on the production of school expositions. In H. Mandl, E. DeCorte, N. Bennet, & H. F. Friedrich (Eds.), *Learning and instruction in an international context* (vol. 2.2, pp. 295-308). Oxford: Pergamon.

Jamieson, J., Jones, S., Kirsch, I., Mosenthal, P., & Taylor, C. (2000). *TOEFL 2000 Framework: A working paper* (TOEFL Monograph No. 16). Princeton, NJ: Educational Testing Service.

Kintsch, W. (1974). *The representation of meaning in memory.* Hillsdale, NJ: Erlbaum.

Kirsch, I., & Jungeblut, A. (1986). *Literacy: Profiles of America's young adults* (NAEP Rep. No. 16-PL-01). Princeton, NJ: Educational Testing Service.

Kirsch, I. S., Jungeblut, A., & Mosenthal, P. B. (1998). The measurement of adult literacy. In T. S. Murray, I. S. Kirsch, & L. B. Jenkins (Eds.), *Adult literacy in OECD countries: Technical report on the First International Adult Literacy Survey* (NCES 98-053; pp. 105-134). Washington, DC: U.S. Government Printing Office.

Kirsch, I., & Mosenthal, P. (1990). Exploring document literacy: Variables underlying the performance of young adults. *Reading Research Quarterly, 25,* 5-30.

Kolen, M. J., & Brennan, R. L. (1995). *Test equating: Methods and practices.* New York: Springer-Verlag.

Mislevy, R. J. (1995). Test theory and language-learning assessment. *Language Testing, 12,* 341–369.

Muraki, E. (1992). A generalized partial credit model: Application of an EM algorithm. *Applied Psychological Measurement, 16,* 159–176.

Muraki, E., & Bock, D. (1999). PARSCALE 4—IRT scaling, item analysis, and scoring or rating scale data [Computer software]. Chicago, IL: Scientific Software, Inc.

Perfetti, C. (1994). Psycholinguistics and reading ability. In M. A. Gernsbacher (Ed.), *Handbook of psycholinguistics* (pp. 849–894). San Diego, CA: Academic Press.

Perfetti, C. (1997). Sentences, individual differences, and multiple texts: Three issues in text comprehension. *Discourse Processes, 23,* 337–355.

Perfetti, C., van Dyke, J., & Hart, L. (2001). The psycholinguistics of basic literacy. *Annual Review of Applied Linguistics, 21,* 127–149.

Rosenfeld, M., Leung, P., & Oltman, P. K. (2001). *The reading, writing, speaking, and listening tasks important for academic success at the undergraduate and graduate levels* (TOEFL Monograph No. 21). Princeton, NJ: Educational Testing Service.

Samejima, F. (1969). Estimation of latent ability using a response pattern of graded scores. *Psychometrika Monograph,* No. 17.

Schiffrin, D. (1987). *Discourse markers.* New York: Cambridge University Press.

Skehan, P. (1998). *A cognitive approach to language learning.* Oxford: Oxford University Press.

Stocking, M. L., Swanson, L., & Pearlman, M. (1993). Application of an automated item selection method to real data. *Applied Psychological Measurement, 17,* 151–168.

Tang, K. L. (1996). *Polytomous item response theory models and their applications in large-scale testing programs: Review of literature* (TOEFL Monograph No. 2). Princeton, NJ: Educational Testing Service.

Tang, K. L., & Eignor, D. R. (1997). *Concurrent calibration of dichotomously and polytomously scored TOEFL items using IRT models* (TOEFL Technical Rep. No. 13). Princeton, NJ: Educational Testing Service.

Tobias, S. (1994). Interest, prior knowledge, and learning. *Review of Educational Research, 64,* 37–54.

Turner, C., & Upshur, J. (1996). Developing rating scales for the assessment of second language performance. In G. Wigglesworth & C. Elder (Eds.), The language testing cycle: From inception to washback [Special issue]. *Australian Review of Applied Linguistics, Series S, 13,* 55–79.

Wainer, H., & Eignor, D. (2000). Caveats, pitfalls, and unexpected consequences of implementing large-scale computerized testing. In H. Wainer (Ed.), *Computerized adaptive testing: A primer* (2nd ed., pp. 271–299). Mahwah, NJ: Erlbaum.

Waters, A. (1996). *A review of research into needs in English for academic purposes of relevance to the North American higher education context* (TOEFL Monograph No. 6). Princeton, NJ: Educational Testing Service.

Young, L. (1994). University lectures—Macro-structures and micro-features. In J. Flowerdew (Ed.), *Academic listening* (pp. 159–176). New York: Cambridge University Press.

4

Prototyping New Assessment Tasks

Mary K. Enright
Brent Bridgeman
Daniel Eignor
Robert N. Kantor
Pamela Mollaun
Susan Nissan
Donald E. Powers
Mary Schedl

In many testing applications, the framework for the test is specified initially, and this specification subsequently guides the development of items and scoring procedures. Empirical relationships may then be used to inform decisions about retaining, rejecting, or modifying items. Interpretations of scores from tests developed by this process have the advantage of a logical/theoretical and an empirical foundation for the underlying dimensions represented by the test. (American Educational Research Association, American Psychological Association, & National Council on Measurement in Education [AERA, APA, & NCME], 1999, p. 41)

This statement of guidance from the *Standards for Educational and Psychological Testing* draws a clear line between the type of conceptual frameworks outlined in the previous chapter and the empirical research described in this and many of the following chapters. However, the *Standards* also states, "The procedures used to develop items and scoring rubrics and to examine item characteristics may often contribute to clarifying the framework" (AERA, APA, & NCME, 1999, p. 41). This was the case for the new TOEFL® project—the conceptual and theoretical issues of framework development discussed in the previous chapter took place in constant conversation with the empirical research discussed in this and the following chapters. This empirical research occurred in successive phases that focused on the prototyping and trialing, first of tasks, then of measures,[1] and third of test forms. These preliminary phases of test design are detailed in this and the following two chapters. In this chapter, we discuss the task prototyping process during the period of 1999–2000 that allowed the project to evolve from the conceptualization set forth in frameworks to a preliminary design for an assessment with high-stakes outcomes.

GUIDING QUESTIONS FOR THE FIRST PROTOTYPING PHASE

The initial prototyping phase of the new TOEFL project provided experience using task frameworks to create new assessment tasks. We examined test takers' performance on these tasks under a variety of administration conditions and developed preliminary scoring rubrics. We also gathered data to determine if task characteristics affected task difficulty and if performance was consistent with our theoretical expectations about the processes and skills involved in completing the tasks. As these tasks were created and pilot-tested, the four skill teams posed a number of specific questions that they sought to answer. Although an explicit interpretative argument was not specified at this time, relationships between the questions posed and the assumptions underlying inferences and warrants in the interpretative argument can be traced in retrospect. Table 4.1 summarizes the relevance of the questions posed to the assumptions associated with three of the inferences in the emerging interpretative argument: domain definition, evaluation, and explanation.

Use of the task frameworks for development of prototype test tasks pertains to the warrant underlying the domain definition inference that the performances on the test are representative of performances in the academic domain. The approach to domain description embodied in the framework had to be operationalized in exemplars of new assessment tasks. All four skills teams addressed questions concerning the creation of exemplar assessment tasks that would ultimately support domain definition inferences by modeling a wider variety of tasks in the academic domain than those tasks used on prior versions of the TOEFL, TSE®, and TWE®. For all four skills, assessment specialists needed to develop new types of test questions. For listening and reading skills, assessment specialists also needed to find or develop texts in which the language more broadly represented the academic domain.

Investigations of test takers' performance on the exemplar tasks focused on three assumptions underlying the warrant entailed by evaluation inferences that performance on test tasks could be scored to reveal evidence of language proficiency. The speaking and writing teams used methodical processes to develop rubrics appropriate for providing evidence of language abilities. All skills teams sought to establish what task and administration conditions would be optimal for observing evidence of the abilities to be assessed. For

TABLE 4.1

Questions Investigated in the First Prototyping Phase Relevant to Assumptions Underlying
Warrants and Inferences in the TOEFL Interpretative Argument

Assumptions Underlying Warrant	Related Questions
Domain description	
Assessment tasks that require important skills and are representative of the academic domain can be simulated.	Can a wider variety of assessment tasks be created to provide better coverage of tasks in the academic domain? Can academic language be simulated better on test tasks?
Evaluation	
Rubrics for scoring responses are appropriate for providing evidence of targeted language abilities.	What type of rubrics would be appropriate for evaluating spoken and written responses?
Task administration conditions are appropriate for providing evidence of targeted language abilities.	How do task characteristics and administration conditions affect the opportunity to observe evidence of target abilities?
Explanation	
Task difficulty is systematically influenced by task characteristics.	Could task difficulty be manipulated by varying task characteristics?
The linguistic knowledge, processes, and strategies required to successfully complete tasks are in keeping with theoretical expectations.	Were the strategies engaged by tasks construct relevant and in accord with theoretical expectations?

example, computer delivery of the test required that an easily navigable interface be developed so that the technology would not interfere with the assessment of test takers' language abilities. Interface issues were of particular importance for the reading and speaking tasks.

Even at this early stage of development, we sought empirical evidence to support the warrant underlying the explanation inference that test scores could be attributed to a construct of academic language proficiency. All four teams sought evidence that a theoretical model of language proficiency could be substantiated by demonstrating how task characteristics influenced task difficulty, as had been proposed within the proficiency scaling approach. Listening and reading teams also sought evidence as to whether the processes engaged by tasks were in accord with their expectations.

Despite the common areas of inquiry among the skills that are evident, the detailed report of the research reveals variation among areas in the ways questions were investigated. Because the skills teams were working more or less independently of each other, each group defined its own path through the process of evidence-seeking at the task design stage, each one building upon the framework that it had designed.

LISTENING

As discussed in Chapter 3, the *Listening Framework* (Bejar, Douglas, Jamieson, Nissan, & Turner, 2000) was further elaborated to specify the interaction among abilities, task types and text types. As a result, eight listening abilities, ten tasks types, and three text types were identified (see Table 3.3 in Chapter 3). This broad framework implied a number of assumptions that needed to be investigated before more specific decisions could be made about the form of the listening tasks on the TOEFL. In particular, the listening team identified three critical areas, stating questions whose answers would eventually provide evidence relevant to the inferences of domain definition, evaluation, and explanation.

DOMAIN DEFINITION AND TASK DESIGN

The domain definition inference for the TOEFL assumes a correspondence between the test tasks and academic tasks, particularly between the language used on the test and that typical of academic settings. Therefore, the listening team worked on defining and developing task types based on a framework intended to represent a range of relevant academic tasks as summarized in Table 4.2. In addition, the listening team explored two questions relevant to improving the authenticity of the language used in listening tasks. Could the corpus (see Chapter 3) be used to improve the naturalness of speech in the lectures and conversations heard in the listening tasks? What would be the impact of including nonnative accented speech on these listening tasks?

Task Types

As the listening team engaged in a process of prototype task development and small feasibility studies, they clarified the relationship between task types and three general abilities—basic understanding, pragmatic understanding, and integrating information, as described in Table 4.2.[2] Tasks intending to assess pragmatic understanding and integrating information (i.e., Task Types 5–9 in Table 4.2) were explored with particular emphasis because these abilities were not a distinct focus of assessment on the current listening measure of the TOEFL. The results of this initial exploration indicated that the task framework was useful for generating new, relevant task types, and therefore it should continue to be used. The one exception was Task Type 9, requiring integration across two different texts that assessment specialists found very difficult to produce.

TABLE 4.2

Description of Tasks Proposed for a New TOEFL Listening Measure

General Abilities	Task Types	Text Types
Basic understanding—ability to understand the main ideas, important details, and key vocabulary of an aural text	1. Identify—who, what, when, or where questions 2. Explain—how or why questions 3. Identify or explain main ideas 4. Identify or explain key vocabulary	
Pragmatic understanding—ability to understand the pragmatic information (stance of the speaker and the function of what the speaker is saying) of an aural text	5 Identify the function or purpose of an utterance 6. Identify what aspect of an utterance signals function	Lectures, consultations, and conversations
Integrating information—ability to identify the organization of the text(s) and to identify the relationships between the ideas in the text(s) (e.g., inferring, predicting, comparing, contrasting, drawing logical conclusions).	7. Identify and explain relationships among ideas in text 8. Relate text information to own knowledge 9. Analyze and synthesize information across texts	

Listening Texts

The linguistic features of the texts chosen for the TOEFL were considered carefully through an examination of the corpus of oral academic language and a study of the effects of nonnative language on listening comprehension.

Use of language from the corpus   The listening team wanted to include aural language on the test that replicated more natural speech patterns than were evident on the existing TOEFL. Oral texts for the existing TOEFL listening tasks were created, rather than taken from authentic sources as were reading texts. The speech patterns of these created materials have been criticized as a poor representation of natural speech, with the implication that performance in the test situation would not be reflective of performance in actual academic situations. The previous chapter described the research that compiled a corpus of authentic academic language of over a million spoken words, containing interactions in lectures, in-class discussions, service encounters, and study groups at five tertiary-level institutions in North America. Throughout the prototyping phase, the corpus was used as a basis for materials development to insure the authenticity of the aural input. Based on initial piloting, we learned that short verbatim segments from the corpus, taken out of context, were frequently not a good basis for developing discrete test questions, as explained in the previous chapter.

Despite the problems with using the corpus verbatim, it proved useful for prompting ideas for authentic topics. Given the corpus-inspired beginning, the excerpts were rewritten and, where necessary and appropriate, information was added from other sources to make the stimulus comprehensible in the testing situation. Further, the corpus is currently used for training assessment specialists so that the stimuli they write contain features such as false starts, sentence fragments, and digressions that are frequently found in speech. It is also used as a model for professional speakers producing test stimuli in the recording studio, so that the general pace and rhythm of real speech is retained.

Effects of nonnative accent   One characteristic of oral academic language in North American classrooms is that it includes a variety of nonnative accents. It might be argued that such accents should therefore be represented in the language that the test takers are exposed to on the test. At the same time, however, such authentic language risks disadvantaging test takers. Major, Fitzmaurice, Bunta, and Balasubramanian (2002) explored the effect of accents on listening comprehension, which they viewed in terms of a tension between fairness and authenticity:

> If a test of listening comprehension is to reflect the authentic language of important listening contexts at the university, it should include accented English. However, accented language may affect the listening comprehension of ESL listeners differently depending on their native languages. Such effects would constitute bias, which would be considered evidence against the test's construct validity. Do test developers need to sacrifice the construct validity of listening tests in order to ensure their authenticity? (p. 174)

To explore the issue of potential bias due to the inclusion of accented speech in the listening measure of the new TOEFL, Major et al. (2002) examined the effects of nonnative accents on listening comprehension. They sought to determine if listeners perform significantly better when the speaker is a native speaker of their own language. Lectures and listening comprehension questions that had been previously administered on TOEFL tests were used. Two native speakers (one male, one female) from four different language backgrounds (Chinese, Japanese, Spanish, and standard American English) recorded all eight lectures. Groups of listeners whose native languages were Chinese, Japanese, Spanish, and standard American English participated in the study. These languages were selected for inclusion because Chinese and Japanese represented the most common languages of TOEFL test takers in 1997–1998, and Spanish represented an Indo-European language. Eight subgroups of listeners (two per native listener group) heard one of eight different audiotapes that included eight lectures, each one delivered by a different native language speaker.

Major et al. (2002) reported some unexpected findings. Spanish listeners performed best when the speaker was Spanish, but Chinese listeners performed worst when the speaker was Chinese, and Japanese listeners performed worst when the speaker was Japanese. Unfortunately, as Major et al. acknowledged, the study's design did not control the difficulty of the lectures across different speaker-language–listener-language pairings, so the results cannot be clearly interpreted. However, the authors tackled important issues: how authenticity should be determined and whether authenticity contributes to test bias. The authors pointed out a lack of data about the frequency of various nonnative accents among instructors and professors. In the absence of such data, there would be no rationale for which accents should be sampled in assessment materials. Their results also illustrate the dangers of introducing uncontrolled sources of variability into the assessment situation and the potential for bias that this introduces.

INVESTIGATIONS RELEVANT TO EVALUATION

One task administration procedure that was contemplated for the listening measure on a new TOEFL was to allow notetaking, which had not been permitted on previous versions of the TOEFL. The change was motivated by a belief that allowing notetaking would better simulate the college classroom experience. Furthermore, because an increase in the length of the mini-lectures was being contemplated, notetaking might be an important aid for test takers. With these issues in mind, Carrell, Dunkel, and Mollaun (2002, 2004) investigated the effects of lecture length (2.5 vs. 5 minutes), topic (science vs. humanities) and notetaking (allowed vs.disallowed) on listening comprehension. Secondary analyses were performed to investigate the contribution of short-term memory and listening comprehension ability to the outcomes. Interpretations of the effects of the central variables were qualified by interactions among the factors.

Notetaking was found to enhance performance for shorter but not longer lectures and for humanities but not physical science topics. Longer lectures resulted in a decrement in performance for participants with higher listening comprehension abilities but not for participants with lower listening comprehension abilities. Analyses of participants' responses to a debriefing questionnaire clearly indicated participants felt more comfortable when they were allowed to take notes and believed that notetaking facilitated their performance. Given the results of this study, notetaking was recommended for listening tasks on the new TOEFL. The reasoning was that notetaking had a facilitative effect under some conditions, contributed to test taker comfort level, and did not appear to have a deleterious effect under any conditions.

INVESTIGATIONS RELEVANT TO EXPLANATION

For listening, two areas of investigation were germane to explanation. Special emphasis was placed on exploring the tasks intended to assess listening abilities that were thought not to be assessed on the existing TOEFL. These included pragmatic understanding and integrating information from multiple sources. Evidence was sought that would justify interpretations of performance on Task Types 4 and 7 in Table 4.2 in terms of these abilities. The listening team was also concerned with the extent to which hypothesized task characteristics would affect task difficulty as described in the previous chapter.

Study of Abilities and Processes: Pragmatic Understanding

The fourth task type listed in Table 4.2 is intended to assess understanding of the communicative function of utterances, an ability referred to as pragmatic understanding. Pragmatics items largely draw on the test taker's understanding of language in which the speaker's purpose or stance may or may not coincide with the surface expression of his or her utterance. Spoken utterances are often intended to be understood on different levels that lie beyond, or beneath, the surface content. A prototyping project investigated the feasibility of creating tasks to assess this ability.

Method   Twelve listening tasks were created; each task consisted of a listening text and a set of four to six questions, some of which assessed basic understanding while others assessed pragmatic understanding. The questions were presented aurally and followed by written multiple-choice answer options. The pragmatics questions assessed three aspects of pragmatic language: rhetorical function, speaker attitude (such as certainty or doubt), and whether the speaker was expressing facts or opinions. The experimental tasks were administered by computer to 20 students (15 nonnative speakers of English and 5 native speakers). The students were divided into four ability groups. The nonnative speakers were divided into three ability groups based on their TOEFL scores, and the native speakers constituted the highest ability group.

Results   Both the basic understanding and pragmatics items had the expected differences across these ability groups, and the total proportion correct for both question types was about the same. In separating the ability groups, however, the pragmatics items appeared to be slightly better than the basic understanding items.

Questionnaire responses suggested that pragmatics questions did indeed require different thought processes than the basic understanding questions. Strategies used more frequently on the basic understanding questions were lexical recall, specific content recall, general content recall, repetition, picture/

graphic, process of elimination, and guessing. Strategies used more frequently on the pragmatics questions were inference and intonation.

Conclusion   Overall, the pragmatics questions appeared to be at an appropriate difficulty level and to tap aspects of comprehension not well addressed by the basic understanding questions. The recommendation was to continue the development of pragmatics questions.

Study of Abilities and Processes: Integrating Information

A prototyping study was conducted to evaluate the characteristics of questions designed to assess skill in listening to integrate information. This ability to connect information within an aural text or from two texts had been identified as a key listening ability. The ability requires:

1. linking two or more pieces of explicit information and applying it to a problem or identifying the relationship, and
2. making inferences about relationships within or between texts; such as, predicting outcomes from events described, drawing conclusions, evaluating information, inferring causal or comparative links, and drawing accurate generalizations or logical inferences.

Method   Four text sets were developed for the prototype. Three were paired sets, and the fourth was a single longer lecture. The paired sets covered a single topic in two different settings. For example, a lecture on biology was paired with a discussion of this lecture in a study group. In another paired set, a study group discussion was followed by a visit to a professor's office to discuss the same topic. In addition to the questions on integrating information, questions assessing basic understanding were also presented. The questions required a variety of response modes—selected response, written response, and spoken response. The selected response items were not all standard multiple-choice questions; some required the selection of more than one correct answer. Others required putting options in a sequence that could be either temporally based (which happened first) or logically based (e.g., "place the animals below from least complex to most complex," with choices ranging from sponge to earthworm).

Each text set also had an integrating information item that required an extended written or spoken response. These responses received two scores—one for listening and one for either writing or speaking. For the listening score, a 4-point scale was developed with scores ranging from 0 = provides no or very little evidence of understanding to 3 = addresses all aspects of prompt accurately (although response may contain minor inaccuracies in supporting ideas or examples). The written and spoken constructed responses were scored with standard TWE and TSE rubrics, respectively. Thus, each task yielded both a listening score and a writing or speaking score.

Thirteen students from New Jersey and 20 from Arizona participated in the prototyping effort. Because the integration tasks were expected to be difficult, participants were selected primarily at the high end of the TOEFL range to see whether these tasks were useful for making discriminations at this level. Thirteen students had TOEFL scores over 600, and an additional six were native speakers of English. Eleven students were native speakers of Asian languages; the remainder were speakers of European languages. Tasks were administered by computer. Spoken responses were recorded by the computer, but essays were handwritten.

Results   The integrating information items showed a broad range of item difficulties, with proportions correct ranging from .25 to .83. The most difficult problem required the test taker to put four events in order from a list of five events; there was only one correct arrangement out of the 120 possible arrangements. Another item required the test taker to recall information that had been acquired from two different sources. This item was originally coded as assessing integration of information, but after much discussion we decided that merely requiring memory of information from two sources is not the same as the integration of two ideas. This item was recoded as a basic understanding item, and we concluded that in the future items of this type should not be used to assess a separate skill related to integrating information.

In general, as intended, the integrating information items were more difficult on average than the basic understanding items, but there was also considerable overlap. It was possible to write relatively easy integrating information items as well as relatively difficult basic understanding items. Both selected response and productive (writing and speaking) formats were able to elicit evidence related to integrating information.

Conclusion   Integrating information from two different texts was not necessarily more difficult than integrating information within a single text. Indeed, in the small set of texts studied, the most difficult questions required integration of information from a single text. This was most likely due to the particular single text used rather than suggesting that integrating information within a single text is inherently more difficult than cross-text integration. However, this result did call into question whether a distinction between integrating information within a text or from more than one text could be supported.

Study of Task Difficulty

Speech rate and sentence structure (fragments vs. complete grammatical sentences) were identified as potential sources of difficulty in listening prompts, and a study was designed to determine the effects of these prompt features on question difficulty. Although these two features are independent of each other, they were investigated in a single study for ease of materials development and test administration.

Method A sample of 275 test takers was recruited from populations of English as a second language (ESL) students at four domestic sites and two overseas sites. The experimental test consisted of a disclosed TOEFL paper-based test (PBT) listening measure and eight prototype listening sets (four conversations and four lectures). There were four versions of the aural stimulus for each prototype set. Three versions were recordings of identical scripts in which only the rate at which the scripts were spoken was varied. Slow, normal, and fast versions were created. The speed differences were defined from a review of 45 texts from the Biber corpus (Biber et al., 2004) and 60 TOEFL computer-based test (CBT) listening stimuli (30 short conversations and 30 mini-talks). Since the rate of speech for conversations tended to be significantly faster than for lectures, two normal rates of speech were determined, one for conversations and one for lectures. Normal rate of speech for conversations was set at 195 words per minute (wpm); for lectures, normal rate of speech was set at 155 wpm. Fast and slow rates were set at 25% faster and slower than normal.

The fourth version of the aural stimulus was identical to that of the other three except that it contained no sentence fragments, only complete sentences. (The other three represented the level of fragmentation typically found in samples from the corpus.) A *fragment* here refers to a fragment of a syntactic clause. A true *grammatical* fragment may or may not count as a fragment for the purposes of the study; such as,

(MA)   Why isn't the registration form complete?
(WB)   Because the department office gave me the wrong information about how to fill it out. [Technically this is a sentence fragment because it's a subordinate clause standing on its own, but the intended meaning is completely expressed, so this as a not fragment for the study's purposes.]
versus

(MA)   Why isn't the registration form complete?
(WB)   Because when I went to the department office to find out how to fill it out—OK, so they had these instructions there, and those instructions said to just fill in parts A and C. [The first clause in WB's response is syntactically incomplete and would count as a fragment.]

The fragmented version was recorded at a normal rate of speech. The four versions were spiraled into four forms so that they could be randomly

administered to the students in the sample. The test takers were classified
into four English language ability levels, based on their performance on the
TOEFL PBT listening measure. Because speech rate was not crossed with
fragmentation level in the design, these issues were addressed separately. Also,
conversations and lectures were analyzed separately.

Results For each conversation, mean scores were highest for the slow
presentation speed, and means for the mid-rate speed were generally very
close to the means for the slow speed. In the 3 (speeds) x 4 (ability levels)
analysis of variance (ANOVA), the speed effect was statistically significant
($p < .01$) in one conversation and was very close to conventional significance
levels in two other conversations ($p < .065$ and $p < .053$, respectively). Effect
sizes comparing the fastest and slowest speeds ranged from 0.2 to 0.3 (in
standard deviation units) across the four conversations. There were no significant interactions with ability, suggesting that the speed effect is relatively
constant across ability levels.

As with the conversations, there was a tendency for higher scores when the
lecture was presented more slowly. The ANOVA indicated that the difference
was statistically significant for one lecture ($p < .02$) and marginally significant
for another lecture ($p = .065$). Effect sizes over the four lectures ranged from
0.0 to 0.4. No interactions with ability were noted.

For the analysis of fragmented conversations, means tended to be slightly
higher for stimuli with fragmented sentences than for stimuli with complete
sentences. However, the difference was statistically significant for only one of
the four conversations ($p < .01$; effect size 0.2), and again there were no interactions with ability. It may be somewhat counterintuitive that fragmented
speech would be easier to comprehend, but this finding may be related to
speech rate. As noted above, slow speech appears to be easier to comprehend,
and because the fragmented speech also tended to be slower, the apparent
fragmentation difference is likely just another manifestation of the speed difference. The number of meaning units to be processed in a given amount of
time is higher with complete sentences than with fragmented speech. Differences between means for fragmented and nonfragmented speech in lectures
were very small, and none even approached statistical significance. There
were no significant interactions with English language ability.

Conclusion The listening team recommended that speech rate not be
used as a way to manipulate difficulty in TOEFL listening comprehension
stimuli because to achieve significant effects, the rate of speech would have
to be increased or decreased beyond the range of natural-sounding speech.
Furthermore, a uniform rate of speech throughout a conversation or a talk is
artificial in most cases. Speech rate tends to vary in the course of a lecture or a
conversation, and these variations are often context- or situation-dependent,
usually involving speakers' slowing down their pace for emphasis or to en-

sure comprehension or speeding up their pace in order to move on to another thought, to finish up a lecture, and so on. Because sentence structure (fragments vs. complete sentences) does not appear to affect difficulty in TOEFL listening comprehension stimuli, the team further recommended that listening stimuli incorporate sentence fragments of the same types and in roughly the same proportions as found in authentic conversations and lectures.

OUTCOMES OF LISTENING TASK PROTOTYPING

The listening task prototyping studies, combined with experience with the current TOEFL, suggested that six of the seven task types in Table 4.2 would be feasible for assessing the desired abilities. A task type to assess an eighth ability (integrating information from listening and reading texts) was not addressed in this round of studies as priority was placed on first obtaining information on integrating information from two listening texts. Questions based on integrating information across or within listening texts could cover a wide difficulty range, and within-text questions were not necessarily easier than across-text questions. Difficulty could be influenced by speech rate, but only by increasing or decreasing the rate to unrealistic levels. Fragmented speech was more realistic and no more difficult than speech in complete sentences.

READING

The *Reading Framework* (Enright et al., 2000) defined what the reading measure of the TOEFL was intended to assess and hypothesized a number of task characteristics that might affect task difficulty, including the organizing aspects of the construct, reading purpose. In the prototyping phase of the project, the primary questions centered on issues of domain definition and evaluation (identifying and constructing tasks that test takers could perform in an operational testing setting) and explanation (collecting evidence as to whether performance on tasks was in accord with theoretical expectations). The investigation of these three types of issues flowed through a research process with a design phase—consisting of task definition, task construction, and usability testing—and an experimental phase—consisting of an empirical study.

DOMAIN DEFINITION AND TASK DESIGN

The reading team approached the design of assessment tasks via an analysis of the research in cognitive and educational psychology on reading (Enright & Schedl, 2000). The tasks proposed for development were selected because they were expected to engage a complex of abilities, processes, and strategies that were appropriate for different reading purposes. It was thought that this would broaden the representation of academic reading activities beyond those assessed on most reading tests. Furthermore, new longer, more complex texts would be required to assess these reading purposes.

Task Types

Based on a review of cognitive and educational research of reading, Enright and Schedl (2000) identified a number of task types that they argued might be used to assess the four reading purposes outlined in the *Reading Framework* (Enright et al., 2000). The proposed tasks are described in Table 4.3, along with the reading purpose(s) each is proposed to assess. More than one type of task was proposed for the assessment of three of the four reading purposes, although in some cases they were existing TOEFL tasks.

The existing TOEFL is believed to assess the ability to find information indirectly through items that require test takers to locate a word or phrase mentioned in a question as a starting point to search for the answer to the question. However, a scanning task was developed to assess more directly the ability to rapidly recognize words. This task required test takers to rapidly locate specific words within a reading passage. The score on the task was to be the number of words located within a limited amount of time.

The existing TOEFL also purports to assess basic comprehension abilities, but two new tasks, sentence simplification and reading efficiency, were proposed as well. The proposed sentence simplification task, based on work by Sarig (1987), was designed to assess the ability of readers to simplify or clarify information in the text. Test takers were asked to compare a complex sentence taken from the passage text with a set of four new sentences and to choose the one that most closely retained the essential meaning of the original while simplifying its lexical and/or syntactic content.

Basic comprehension requires a reasonably efficient reading rate (Enright et al. 2000), but reading efficiency is not directly assessed on the existing TOEFL. Therefore, a reading-efficiency task to assess this aspect of basic comprehension abilities was also developed. Test takers were allowed a limited amount of time to read a text, and then the text was removed, and three multiple-choice items about the main ideas in the passage were presented.

None of the items on the existing TOEFL was thought to assess reading to learn, and therefore four task types were developed to investigate how different aspects of reading to learn might be assessed. Three of these represented selected response versions of summary tasks that required the test takers to select and organize information from a significant portion of the passage. The three task formats included (a) prose summaries, (b) outlines, and (c) tables. After test takers read the passage and answered a number of regular multiple-choice questions about the text, they were to complete these tasks.

TABLE 4.3
Description of Tasks Proposed for a New TOEFL Reading Measure

Reading Purpose Tasks are Intended to Measure	Task Type	Task Requirement
Reading to find information—locate discrete pieces of information in a text	Scanning task	Test takers locate specific words in the text quickly (cf. Carver, 1990, 1997).
Reading for basic comprehension— understand the main ideas or the main points of the text or form some understanding of the main theme of the text	Sentence simplification task	Test takers identify essential information in a complex sentence from the text (cf. Sarig, 1987).
	Reading efficiency task	Test takers read the text within a short period of time and answer questions about the main ideas when the text is no longer available.
Reading to learn—develop an organized understanding of how the main ideas, supporting information, and factual details of the text form a coherent whole	Summary completion task (prose summaries)	Test takers select sentences to construct a summary of the text.
	Schematic summary task (complete an outline or table)	Test takers organize information from the text into a framework such as a table or outline.
	Sentence recognition task	Test takers verify whether a sentence is an accurate representation of information in the text when the text is no longer available (cf. Royer, 1990).
Reading to integrate (when two texts are used in the prompt)—generate an organized understanding of the relationships among the kinds of information found in different sources	Summary completion task (prose summaries)	Test takers select sentences from the two texts to construct a summary of the texts.
	Schematic summary task (complete an outline or table)	Test takers organize information from the two texts into a framework such as a table or outline.

In addition, the reading-to-learn tasks may or may not assess memory for the text, depending on whether or not the passage was still available as the task was completed. Finally, a fourth task simply required test takers to recognize, when the text was no longer available, whether individual sentences were accurate restatements of information that had appeared in the text. Three task formats, similar to those developed for reading to learn, were developed for reading to integrate information across texts. These included (a) prose summaries, (b) outlines, and (c) tables. These tasks differed from the reading-to-learn tasks in that these tasks required test takers to select and organize information from two separate passages providing different information or perspectives on the same topic.

Reading Texts

The *Reading Framework* (Enright et al., 2000) called for longer and more complex texts than those on the existing TOEFL to assess higher level reading purposes. Texts on the existing TOEFL were typically 300 to 350 words long and followed a simple expository organization. These short, simple texts would not provide sufficient material to assess test takers' ability to organize information. Texts recommended for use on a new TOEFL would be longer (550–700 words) and would be chosen in accord with the definition in the *Reading Framework* of the pragmatic text types and their rhetorical features (see Table 3.6 in Chapter 3).

In view of the many new task types and the need for specific types of longer texts than assessment specialists were using at the time, the task development process addressed the most basic questions about feasibility of finding materials needed to construct tasks according to specifications.[3] Assessment specialists sought to discover (a) whether or not new text types of an appropriate length with the rhetorical and pragmatic properties proposed in the framework could be found in sufficient quantities to sustain an operational test and (b) to what extent such texts could be classified reliably with respect to the features of interest to maintain comparability across forms.

The challenge of finding texts with more complex organizations in the range of 550 to 700 words was met. In addressing the question of classification, however, we recognized the need to reconsider how texts should be classified. In particular, the rhetorical features described in Table 3.4 in Chapter 3 were often found within the same text. The most important feature of texts that appeared to support more complex tasks was not a specific rhetorical organization per se but simply having more than one organizational dimension.

INVESTIGATIONS RELEVANT TO EVALUATION

At this point in development, the primary concern for reading relevant to evaluation focused on the computer-presentation of reading tasks. Anyone who has tried to navigate through a poorly designed computer program can attest to the fact that a bad interface interferes with the completion of a task. To ensure that the interface for the new TOEFL was transparent to users, a series of usability studies was carried out in conjunction with the development of an interface and tutorials during this period.

The TOEFL CBT contained item types that did not involve a particularly complicated user interface. The kinds of interactions test takers had to perform were limited to scrolling or pointing and clicking on defined screen areas (e.g., bubbles for multiple-choice items or individual words and phrases in sentences or paragraphs). Plans for the new TOEFL included expanding the range of stimulus materials and response modes. Audio segments, multiple text passages, and integrated tasks (where test takers read a passage or listened to audio and then discussed either orally or in writing information from the text) were among the new item types under consideration. These new item types presented test takers with a broader range of interactions and, as a result, posed new and more complex design considerations. Instead of merely pointing and clicking, test takers might be required to control the display of multimedia or move between multiple stimulus materials. As a result, a number of new interface requirements needed to be designed and tested.

Interface design and usability testing proceeded through a series of stages, focusing on different aspects of the interface. In each stage, small groups of 10 to20 ESL participants were observed navigating through computer screens and were interviewed about what difficulties they encountered and their preferences for different designs. Participants varied in degree of computer familiarity, level of English proficiency, and first language background. Initially, tools to control multimedia presentation and to move among integrated tasks were designed and tested. Then the general screen layout (e.g., the size and location of the stimulus/item presentation windows and the location of navigation icons) as well as presentation templates for a variety of item types were developed. A third stage focused on how users would navigate through the test. This included designing how test takers would move from item to item, how help screens would function, and how test takers would review items in sections where that was permitted. The final stage was to develop tutorials that would familiarize the test takers with how to use the tools, complete test tasks, and navigate through the test.

The interests of the four skills teams converged in the area of interface design because of the need for consistency in the presentation format for all four skills and for integrated tasks. However, this work was of particular importance for the reading team for two reasons. First, some of the tasks or task variables of interest could only be presented or controlled via computer presentation. This included tasks that required time limits on text presentation or the collection of response time (scanning and reading efficiency tasks) or that required restricting access to the text while questions were answered. Second, presenting some of the tasks on the computer might be so complicated that the task might not be considered feasible for CBT.

For reading, a small set of computer-based versions of the tasks was developed and subjected to usability testing. This initial work was carried out with a set of 14 academic texts that had some of the pragmatic and rhetorical features described in Table 3.6 in Chapter 3. The set of texts included two paired texts on the same topic that could be used for reading to integrate. Examples of the types of interface issues investigated for reading included how to display longer texts and to navigate between texts and complex selected response items. One option to display longer texts was to allow test takers to scroll though the text. Another option was to provide icons to switch between pages. Most candidates did not easily understand the paging icons, whereas the scrolling version caused no obvious problems. Because some new item types could not be displayed on the same screen with the reading passage due to their width, icons that enabled candidates to toggle back and forth between the test and the questions were created and tried out. While candidates found these icons easy to use once they understood them, it was clear that information about these icons needed to be part of the tutorial. Based on the results of these trials, interface issues were resolved; tasks were selected for additional evaluation; and a tutorial was developed.

Overall, usability testing resulted in an interface that test takers found easy to navigate and the identification of information needed in tutorials. The two tasks that presented the most difficulties were the scanning task and reading-to-integrate task. Participants found the scanning tasks confusing—they did not readily understand what was expected. The reading-to-integrate task was most awkward for computer presentation as test takers had to navigate among three screens—two presenting each a different text and one presenting a complex response format (a schematic).

INVESTIGATIONS RELEVANT TO EXPLANATION

Explanatory inferences were addressed by investigating hypotheses about task difficulty. In the *Reading Framework* (Enright et al., 2000), the four reading purposes were conceptualized as representing a continuum from lower level abilities—rapid and efficient word recognition—to higher level abilities—organizing and integrating information from one or more texts. Reading purpose was viewed as one variable that might affect task difficulty, with tasks that assess the lower level abilities being easier than those that assess higher level abilities. As models of new tasks to assess these reading purposes were developed, the reading team specified other variables that might affect the difficulty of specific task types. For example, the amount of time available to read a passage was expected to affect the difficulty of the scanning and reading efficiency tasks. These hypotheses were explored in an experimental study in which the administration conditions for the different task types were manipulated to test these theoretical predictions about task difficulty. The results of this study, along with the information gathered in the usability studies and provided by assessment specialists, informed decisions about the whether the new assessment tasks provided evidence consistent with the intended interpretations of performance in terms of reading for different purposes.

Method

Three texts were selected for the study. For each text, a scanning task, a reading efficiency task, reading-to-learn tasks, and a set of four-option, multiple-choice, basic comprehension items were developed. The basic comprehension items included a sentence simplification item. For the scanning task and the reading efficiency task, the impact of different time limits on performance was investigated. For both of these tasks, we expected that more time to complete the task would result in better performance. For reading-to-learn tasks, we investigated how the availability or unavailability of the text affected performance. We expected that the tasks would be more difficult if the test takers could not review the text as they were completing the reading-to-learn tasks.

Six base forms of an experimental instrument were created for computer administration. Each form included all three texts, but the type of tasks and task administration conditions were varied between forms. On each form, either a scanning task or reading efficiency task was presented first with one of the three texts. (Within a given form, the timing of the scanning or reading efficiency tasks was varied for each text.) The scanning or reading efficiency task was followed by a set of basic comprehension items about text. The text was accessible while these items were completed. Next, a reading-to-learn summary task was presented. Within a form, only one type of summary task was presented (i.e., a form would have a table associated with each text). On half the forms, the text was not available when the summary task was completed. Finally, a sentence recognition task was presented, with the text no longer available.

For each of the six base forms, three subforms were created in which the order of the texts was counterbalanced so that each text and its associated questions appeared in each position equally often. (The order of items associated with a text was constant across forms). The resulting 18 forms were randomly administered to participants at three domestic sites and three overseas sites. The participants also completed the reading measure of a PBT in the 2 weeks preceding the administration of the computer-based instrument. Overall, the reading mean scaled score for the participants on the PBT was 54.7 (SD = 7.20, n = 294). A scaled score of 54 represents the 49th percentile and a score of 56 represents the 61st percentile of the scores of more than 750,000 test takers who took the test in a 1-year period. Thus, the study participants were fairly representative of the target population in reading comprehension ability.

Results: Assessment of Intended Abilities and Processes

The study results, combined with the experience of assessment specialists and observations from the usability studies, provided a basis for appraising whether the performance on the tasks intended to assess the four reading purposes reflected construct-relevant or -irrelevant factors. The outcomes for tasks designed to assess basic comprehension and reading to learn were mixed. Performance on some tasks was judged to provide appropriate evidence of the intended construct, while on other tasks, performance was affected by construct-irrelevant factors. The tasks designed to assess reading to find information and reading to integrate were judged to be unsuitable because construct-irrelevant factors affected performance.

Reading to find information   The data from the pilot test of the scanning task was lost due to a programming error. However, throughout the developmental process, assessment specialists and study participants frequently expressed concerns about the face validity of the reading to find information tasks as well as the validity of the strategies that might be used on the tasks. Based on these experiences, we decided not to pursue further development of this type of task, at least for inclusion in an assessment with high-stakes outcomes.

Reading for basic comprehension   An example of the sentence simplification item was developed for each of the three passages in this study. The proportion correct for these items were 38%, 54%, and 74%, and their correlations with the reading score for the PBT were .38, .05, and .37, respectively. Thus, the items represented a wide range of item difficulties, and two of the three items discriminated appropriately among test takers with respect to their basic comprehension ability. This task appeared to be a promising way to assess an important aspect of basic comprehension—comprehension of individual sentences—more directly. This type of task was recommended for further development.

For the reading efficiency task, the three reading passages, which ranged from 434 to 547 words, had been presented to test takers for 2, 2.5, or 3 minutes. Then the test takers answered three multiple-choice questions about ideas in the passage when the passage was no longer available. Our expectation was that more correctly answered questions would be associated with longer times to read the passages. However, we did not observe the expected relationship between reading time and accuracy for two of the three passages.

While it is certainly possible that the expected relationship might be observed if the reading times had been shorter or the questions more difficult, we thought that further exploration of these issues would require more resources (particularly time) than were available. Thus, this task was eliminated from further consideration.

Reading to learn   The reading-to-learn tasks were developed to assess the ability to construct an organized mental representation of a text. This representation includes main ideas, supporting information, and the relationships among them. Reading to learn was hypothesized to rely more on knowledge of discourse features than basic comprehension. Furthermore, we expected that these tasks would be more difficult if the text was no longer available when the task was completed. Three selected response tasks developed to assess reading to learn were a prose summary, a table, and an outline. In our usability studies, we found that test takers readily understood how to complete these tasks.

For the purposes of this study, a simple partial credit model—a count of the number of options correctly selected and placed in the appropriate category—was used to score these tasks. No significant differences in performance related to the availability of the text were found when ANOVAs were conducted for the table tasks, the summary completion tasks, or the outline tasks. The availability of the text did not have a consistent effect on performance. Sometimes performance was better when a text was available, and sometimes it was better when a text was unavailable. The effect sizes for differences in performance related to text availability ranged from –.17 to .42 for summary completions tasks, from –.08 to .27 for table tasks, and from .28 to .70 for the outline tasks.

Based on the results of the usability studies, assessment specialists' experience in developing new tasks, and the results of the study, we decided to continue development of the summary completion task and the table completion task. The outline task was judged to focus too much on details and to overlap with the type of information that could better be assessed with simple multiple-choice items. Furthermore, given the inconsistent results for text availability, we decided to make the text available for the reading-to-learn tasks.

Finally, the fourth reading-to-learn task, recognizing whether individual sentences were accurate restatements of information that had appeared in the text when the text was no longer available, was eliminated from further consideration. The focus of the task was remembering important details rather than main ideas. During usability testing, we found that few of the test takers could accurately remember details from the text when tested using a true/false format. In addition, assessment specialists often disagreed on the accuracy of the restatements. In effect, this task appeared to be too ambiguous to present on a test with high-stakes outcomes.

Reading to integrate   In the *Reading Framework,* reading to integrate was discussed in terms of integrating information found in different texts. The reason for this emphasis was the idea that "such tasks require a reader to work across two or more texts and generate an organizing frame that is not explicitly stated" (Enright et al., 2000, p. 6). Although we did create some computer-based prototypes of tasks that required integrating the information from two different texts, research on this type of task was not pursued for two reasons. First, if we used longer texts (600–700 words) as recommended in the Reading Framework, we would be able to present only three texts, given time constraints. If we further limited content coverage by presenting two texts on the same topic, generalizability would likely be reduced because so few topics would be sampled. Secondly, an interface that required navigation between two long texts and questions about the text was found to be awkward and time-consuming.

Informed by the assessment specialists' experience and test takers' reactions and performance, we further constrained directions for development. A number of tasks were eliminated from further consideration. The reasons for discontinuing development of other tasks included a lack of face validity and concerns whether the appropriate processes were engaged by the task (scanning task), failure of performance to be in accord with theoretical expectations (reading efficiency task), difficulty in creating unambiguous options (sentence recognition task), and complexity of computer-based presentation and potential reduction in generalizability (reading to integrate two texts).

Results: Prediction of Task Difficulty

In the *Reading Framework* (Enright et al. 2000), an implicational hierarchy among reading purposes had been proposed as one of the variables that might contribute to task difficulty. That is, proficiency on certain types of tasks was hypothesized to be required for success on other tasks, provided that other factors were held equal. Evidence about the difficulty of tasks was expected to be relevant to verifying this hypothesis. However, even in the *Reading Framework*, it was recognized that "easy tasks could be designed for reading to learn or reading to integrate and difficult tasks asking test takers to find discrete information or read for general comprehension" (p. 6). The experience in this study also highlighted another issue that would make it difficult to support empirically the hypothesis of a hierarchy among reading purposes. Given that the reading-to-learn items were polytomous and that there were dependencies among the possible response selections, a rationale for scoring these items would need to be developed. Establishing a difficulty hierarchy between polytomously scored tasks and dichotomously scored tasks when there was discretion in creating the scoring rubric for the polytomous tasks would be questionable.

Finally, the idea that a certain variable might affect the difficulty of specific tasks was not supported in the pilot study. For the reading efficiency task, more time to read the passage did not result in better performance on basic comprehension questions. For reading-to-learn summary tasks, the availability of the text had inconsistent effects on performance.

OUTCOMES OF READING TASK PROTOTYPING

Experience with task definition, usability testing, and pilot testing had important implications for further development of tasks to assess independent reading abilities. From the new task types proposed to assess independent reading, we decided three—sentence simplification, a prose summary task, and a schematic summary task—were the best candidates for further development, given our present state of knowledge. The sentence simplification task was consistent with our conceptualization of reading for basic comprehension and was presented in a well-established format, simple multiple-choice. However, summary tasks to assess reading to learn did present challenges for further development. These included item design issues such as determining an optimal score range for items (e.g., the number of answer spaces in an outline or table) or the number of distracters included with the keys. There was a related psychometric issue about how to score the tasks. Finally, there were construct issues, such as whether these task types actually are any different from traditional multiple-choice items in terms of the cognitive processes or linguistic knowledge required for their completion. Some of these issues would be explored in the next stages of development.

SPEAKING

The *Speaking Framework* (Butler, Eignor, Jones, McNamara, & Suomi, 2000) articulated many of the issues that would need to be considered in designing tasks and distinguished *independent* from *integrated* tasks, which were intended to correspond to different types of tasks in the academic domain. Since the latter were new for TOEFL, they were the object of careful examination throughout every phase of the research. Practical considerations constrained the types of tasks that could be administered and the nature of the scoring rubric, which in turn affected domain definition, evaluation, and explanation inferences.

DOMAIN DEFINITION AND TASK DESIGN

The degree to which test tasks could be modeled on speaking tasks in the academic context was limited by practical considerations. Given the volume of test takers tested each year (approximately 750,000) and the plans for the computer delivery of speaking tasks, the assessment would, of necessity, have to be of an indirect nature. The use of the computer also restricted the range of discourse employed to monologic. Further discussions of what type of speech could be assessed under high-volume, computer-administered

TABLE 4.4
Description of Tasks Proposed for a New TOEFL Speaking Measure

Task Type	Expected Performance	Qualities of Response
Independent speaking	Produce monologic spoken discourse on a range of topics, drawing on own knowledge and/or experience and using a range of rhetorical/pragmatic functions	Intelligibility, fluency
Integrated reading/ speaking	Use information from a variety of academic reading texts as the basis for producing monologic discourse drawing on one or more rhetorical/ pragmatic functions	Intelligibility, fluency, content, coherence, organization
Integrated listening/ speaking	Use information from a variety of consultations and student interactions (dialogic stimuli) as the basis for producing monologic discourse drawing on one or more rhetorical/ pragmatic functions	Intelligibility, fluency, content, coherence, organization
	Use information from a variety of lectures (monologic stimuli) as the basis for producing monologic discourse drawing on one or more rhetorical/pragmatic functions	Intelligibility, fluency, content, coherence, organization

conditions resulted in the formulation of more specific descriptions about the types of tasks that might be developed, the kinds of performances to be expected, and the qualities of the discourse that should be produced in response to these tasks. These descriptions are presented in Table 4.4. Despite the practical considerations that constrained the characteristics of speaking tasks, the speaking team expected the inclusion of integrated tasks to broaden the representation of academic speaking on the assessment. The assumption here, reflected in the description of qualities of response, was that the characteristics of spoken text produced by test takers would differ for different task types. However, investigations relevant to this assumption could not be pursued until much later in development, when a sufficient corpus of test-taker speech samples was available.

INVESTIGATIONS RELEVANT TO EVALUATION AND EXPLANATION

Issues relevant to evaluation inferences included the need to develop a computerized interface for the presentation of speaking prompts and collection of speaking responses and to develop scoring rubrics. An issue relevant to explanation was whether different task administration conditions impacted task difficulty. A series of small-scale studies was conducted to test the usability of computer-based task presentation, to provide speech samples for rubric development activities, and to investigate the impact of certain task characteristics that were hypothesized to impact task difficulty. These investigations afforded opportunities to gather backing for both evaluation and explanation inferences.

Computer-Based Administration of Speaking Tasks

In the first stages of usability testing, we determined what tools for audio functions (play, record, volume control, length indicators, timers) and associated icons were most easily understood by test takers. Based on these results, a number of speech tasks were packaged for computer administration to a few participants. The goal of this initial tryout was to obtain preliminary information about performance on a variety of speaking tasks, to identify other usability issues that would need additional consideration, and to collect speech samples for preliminary rubric development activities.

Method Twenty-two locally recruited test takers took part in the pilot; ten were undergraduate students, and twelve were graduate students. An attempt was made to locate students representing a range of native languages and academic disciplines. Four native speakers (two undergraduate, two graduate) also participated.

The study was carried out in two rounds, both of which were administered via computer. Participants were tested individually and interviewed after they completed all the tasks. For the first round, 16 independent speaking tasks were developed. These speaking tasks represented a variety of rhetorical functions (narrate, hypothesize, inform, persuade, compare/contrast, state/support opinion, describe, recommend, and give directions). Some of the tasks were modeled after TSE tasks, and some were created new for the pilot. Two forms of eight tasks each were created. In the second round, a small number of integrated reading/speaking and listening/speaking tasks were added. In Round 2, each independent speaking task was given a standard 30 seconds of preparation time; test takers could start recording whenever they were ready and could progress to the next task when ready.

Results Test takers reported they had no difficulty with the computer delivery of the tasks, even the integrated tasks. Both undergraduate and graduate students were able to respond successfully to the independent speaking tasks and to the integrated tasks given in the second round. There seemed to be no particular difficulty for test takers in dealing with the various rhetorical functions employed.

Conclusion   The results of this pilot supported computer delivery of both independent and integrated tasks, supported the use of the list of rhetorical functions under consideration, and demonstrated that the tasks constructed were viable for both undergraduate and graduate test takers.

Developing Rubrics

In view of the extended constructed responses that were required of test takers on the speaking test, rubrics specifying how test takers' performance should be evaluated to yield a score needed to be developed. Preliminary rubric development was informed by the expertise of many individuals experienced in evaluating the speaking abilities of second language learners.

A series of five workshops was held to develop the rubrics. The first four workshops separately utilized the expertise of a different group that worked with the TOEFL population in institutions of higher education: (a) ESL instructors, (b) oral proficiency raters, (c) academic administrators (university, departmental, or program administrators), and (d) applied linguists. The fifth workshop consisted of a representative from each of the first four groups. Each group was expected to help identify salient characteristics of successful speaking performance in an academic setting.

In each workshop, speech samples, which had been collected from in the preliminary computer-based pilot study and represented a range of proficiency levels, were employed. The prompts used to elicit those samples were reviewed. Each group of experts listened to a set of samples for each task and rank-ordered the samples from high to low (5–1) based on overall performance. The participants were asked to identify the salient features of performance that differentiated speakers at high, middle, and low levels of proficiency. Participants then shared their rankings and the characteristics they had identified as representative of each of the five levels. The results of the discussions in each group were then summarized in a preliminary rubric, listing the salient speech characteristics at each level of proficiency.

Assessment specialists at ETS® collated the results from the four workshops into draft speaking rubrics. At the fifth workshop, participants further refined the rubrics. The outcomes of the workshops were a 4-point holistic scoring scale for the integrated tasks and a slightly modified 5-point holistic scoring scale (modified from the TSE scale) for the independent speaking tasks. Subsequent to the five workshops, the speaking team met and reviewed the rubric for the integrated tasks that would soon be used for scoring purposes.

Effects of Task Characteristics

The integrated tasks were considerably different from anything that had been attempted on the TSE, and a variety of potential task characteristics and scoring rubrics could be envisioned. A series of pilot studies of reading/speaking and listening/speaking tasks was carried out to explore two issues: the appropriateness of alternative scoring rubrics and the impact of a variety of task characteristics on task difficulty. The former issue was relevant to the evaluation inference, and the latter was relevant to the explanation inference.

Investigations of reading/speaking tasks   The first two pilot studies were designed to inform decisions about variables that might affect task difficulty: (a) text type (narrative vs. expository text) and (b) task administration conditions. The task administration variables were characterized as either providing or not providing support for speaking responses.

Four reading texts and associated prompts for the spoken responses were developed. In each case, the related speaking prompt required the test takers to answer orally a substantive question about the content of the reading text. Two of the four reading texts were narrative, and the other two were expository. The four reading texts and associated speaking prompts were used to compare subsequent speaking performance under three support conditions. Two support conditions that were expected to facilitate performance included (a) allowing notetaking and (b) providing a bulleted list of points to be covered in the response as part of the prompt. Neither of these supports was provided in a third, no-support condition. These pilot studies were administered using tape recorders and paper-and-pencil materials to save the additional time it would take to put them on the computer. Test takers had 15 minutes to read a passage and then to answer a set of four to seven reading comprehension questions. Test takers were then allowed 90 seconds to review the text to prepare to speak about the passage. The speaking prompt was presented, and the test takers had 90 seconds to record a response. Two raters, using a 4-point holistic rubric, rated responses independently.

In one pilot study, two groups of 12 test takers each were administered the four reading texts and associated speaking prompts in a partially counterbalanced order to study the impact on speaking of the presence of the bulleted list versus the notetaking condition. Group means and standard deviations were calculated for each of the four text topics for each of the two conditions (notes vs. bullets). The eight resulting means were the average across the two ratings for test takers falling in each of the eight cells in the design. Marginal means and standard deviations, derived by collapsing either across conditions or text topics, were also calculated.

The data suggested that the two groups of test takers were not equal in speaking ability, with one group scoring higher than the other group on all four tasks. Given the small sample sizes and the nonequivalent groups, it was decided not to employ tests of statistical significance across prompts or conditions. Nevertheless, certain effects were evident in the data. For example, support conditions (notes vs. bullets) did not appear to affect overall performance, with means for both conditions being 2.0 (on the 4-point scale). Also, performance on the two tasks based on narrative texts (mean of 2.1) did not differ greatly from the performance on the two tasks based on expository texts (mean of 1.9), although the narrative-based tasks did appear to be a little easier.

In a second pilot study, another two groups of 12 test takers each were administered the four reading texts and associated speaking prompts in a partially counterbalanced order to study the impact on speaking of the presence of the bulleted list as part of the prompt versus the condition where no support was provided.

Group means and standard deviations were again calculated for each of the four text topics for each of the two conditions (bullets vs. no support). The eight resulting means were the averages across the two ratings for test takers falling in each of the eight cells in the design. Marginal means and statistical deviations were calculated by collapsing across conditions or text topics. Again, the two groups did not appear to be equal in ability. However, the results did replicate the first set of results. The support conditions (bullets vs. no support) did not appear to greatly affect overall performance, with the two means being 2.5 and 2.6. Performance on the two narrative-based tasks (mean of 2.6) did not differ greatly from the performance on the two expository-based tasks (mean of 2.5), although the narrative-based tasks again appeared to be a little easier. The two groups employed in this part of the study appeared to be a good deal more able than the two used in the previous analysis (means of 2.5 vs. 2.0). Since the experimental conditions employed were set up to ensure these four groups would be of comparable ability, the results seen seem to have been caused by the very small sample sizes and again point to the inadvisability of employing tests of statistical significance.

These results must be interpreted with caution due to the small sample sizes and resultant lack of equivalent groups, but (a) no empirical reason was found to prefer one support condition over the other two, and (b) while narrative-based tasks appear to be a little easier than expository-based tasks, the differences in means are close enough that, given the sample sizes, none of the text types can be claimed to be superior to the others.

Rating issues   For these pilot studies, two raters used the original 4-point holistic rubric to rate the speech samples. Correlations between ratings from the two raters varied from .70 to .79 across the four topics, indicating acceptable rater consistency when employing the 4-point holistic rubric.

However, it was decided that consistency in the size of the scales used for rating the independent and integrated speaking tasks might help raters in the rating process. Therefore, a 5-point rubric for the integrated tasks was also developed and tried out.

Using the documents from the earlier workshops and the 4-point rubric previously developed, assessment specialists at ETS analyzed sets of responses against the criteria identified in these materials. From these working sessions, versions of draft 5-point rubrics evolved. The 5-point reading/speaking rubric was then applied to the speech samples and further refined and applied to these samples.

The two raters, after rating all responses on a 4-point holistic scale, then went back and independently rated each response on a 5-point holistic scale. Within-rater correlations using the 4-point and 5-point ratings for each topic were calculated. These correlations ranged from .73 to .88, with all but two of the eight correlations above .80. Clearly, the raters were using the two scales to rank order in much the same way.

In conclusion, the data suggested that switching from a 4-point holistic scale for reading/speaking to a 5-point holistic scale, to be consistent with the number of scale points used for independent speaking, would be a reasonable thing to do. The raters made other recommendations to be considered in preparing materials for raters. First, guidelines for dealing with the incorporation of source-text language into the test takers' responses were needed because reading verbatim from the source makes it difficult to assess the real speaking proficiency of the test taker. Second, the provision of key points to guide the assessment of content, along with guidelines about how much weight to put on content and linguistic ability in the rating when a single overall holistic score is employed, would also be helpful.

Investigations of listening/speaking tasks   This pilot study was designed to investigate what type of listening text to employ in eliciting speech samples, the support and timing conditions that might be used in obtaining the speech samples, and the nature of the scale or scales to be employed in scoring.

Six listening texts and associated prompts for the spoken responses were administered to a pilot study group of 110 test takers under a variety of conditions. In each case, the related speaking prompt required the test taker to answer orally a substantive question about the content of the listening text, employing one of a number of standard rhetorical functions. Two of the six listening texts were campus conversations, and they were used to compare subsequent speaking performance under two conditions: when the speaking task did or did not follow multiple-choice listening comprehension questions. Another two of the listening texts were academic conversations, and they were used to compare subsequent speaking performance under two conditions: when the test taker had 60 seconds speaking time and when the test taker had 120 seconds. (The second academic conversation was subsequently dropped from the study because the raters for this study felt that this text and associated prompt did not elicit scorable speech.) The final two listening texts, which were lectures, were used to compare subsequent speaking performance under two conditions: when the test taker has 90 seconds speaking time and when the test taker has 150 seconds.

The total group of 110 test takers was randomly assigned to one or the other of two groups (Group 1 and Group 2), and the test takers in the two groups each spoke based on the six prompts associated with the six listening texts that were administered in a counterbalanced order within text type. The listening texts and the prompts used to elicit the speech samples were administered together via tape recorder, and each spoken response was recorded on tape.

This overall design, with related ordering of prompts/texts within the two groups, can be subdivided into three components. Each subcomponent then constitutes a separate study of the condition combinations listed above. The listening texts and associated prompts for each condition combination were administered in counterbalanced order, so as to minimize the possibility of text order effects.

For each response, two raters provided ratings on three different 5-point scales: The overall holistic scale (similar to the one used for reading/speaking tasks), a content-based scale (which provided an assessment of the completeness and accuracy of the information from the listening text), and a linguistic ability scale (which provided an assessment of the linguistic features of the response). While only two raters rated any test taker's speaking response to a particular listening text and associated prompt, a total of eight raters was involved in the study. For the analyses that are described next, scores on an overall 5-point holistic rubric were employed.

Group means and standard deviations were calculated for each of the two campus conversations in the two speaking conditions: speaking following multiple-choice and speaking alone. Marginal means were then calculated by collapsing across the two experimental conditions or collapsing across the two campus conversation text topics. The marginal means for the two conditions were 3.3 both for speaking following multiple-choice and for speaking alone. The marginal means for the two campus conversations differed slightly (3.3 vs. 3.2). An ANOVA with two between-group factors (text topic and condition) was run, and no significant effects related to text topic or the inclusion of multiple-choice items were found.

Group means and standard deviations of the speaking scores were calculated for the one scorable academic conversation text topic for the two relevant conditions: when the test takers had 60 seconds and 120 seconds to speak. The mean for the 120-second condition (3.2) turned out to be a bit higher than the mean for the 60-second condition (2.9). While the mean for the 120-second condition was higher, an ANOVA run on the data indicated that the observed difference in the means was not statistically significant.

Group means and standard deviations of the speaking scores were also calculated for each of the two listening lecture text topics for the two conditions being studied: when the test takers had 90 seconds and 120 seconds to speak. Marginal means were also calculated by collapsing across conditions and across listening lecture text topics. The mean for the 90-second condition (3.2) turned out to be a little higher than the mean for the 150-second condition (3.1). The mean for the second of the two lectures (3.3) turned out to be quite a bit greater then the mean for the first lecture (3.0). However, the

ANOVA run on the data indicated that both sets of differences could not be considered statistically significant, nor could the lecture topic by condition interaction.

To determine whether significant differences appeared in test takers' speaking performance across the three listening text types employed, mean scores were compared for groups listening to campus conversations, academic conversations, and lectures. Although the mean for the campus conversations (3.3) was somewhat higher than those for the single academic conversation (3.0) and the lectures (3.1), these differences did not prove to be statistically significant based on the ANOVA run on the data.

Although the analyses carried out were not very sensitive in view of the small sample sizes, the results suggested a number of conclusions to be drawn about the conditions (presence or absence of multiple-choice listening comprehension items, amount of speaking time) and the sort of listening text employed (campus conversation, academic conversation, lecture). There were no significant differences across all conditions compared, nor were there any significant differences in performance across the three types of listening texts employed. These findings allowed for considerable latitude in designing the large-scale pilot study that is described in the next chapter.

Rating issues   Overall, the means and standard deviations observed for all the conditions investigated seemed reasonable for a 5-point holistic scale.

Further analyses were conducted to appraise the value of analytic versus holistic scales. Combining across the five listening topics employed and then looking at individual within-rater correlations between scores on three scales, the overall holistic-content correlations ranged from .81 to .97 across the eight raters, the overall holistic-linguistic ability correlations from .81 to .98, and the content-linguistic ability correlations from .61 to .88. Combining across the eight raters, and looking at the within-listening prompt correlations between scores on the three scales, the overall holistic-content correlations ranged from .87 to .93 across the five prompts, the overall holistic-linguistic ability correlations ranged from .87 to .94, and the content-linguistic ability correlations ranged from .76 to .82. Collapsing across both listening prompts and raters, the overall holistic-content correlation was .90, the overall holistic-linguistic ability correlation was .91, and the content-linguistic ability correlation was .78. There were 72% of the ratings provided that were the same, and 98% were the same or one score point apart. Looking at the overall holistic and linguistic ability ratings, 78% of the ratings provided were the same, and 99% were the same or one score point apart. Finally for the content-linguistic ability ratings, 53% of the ratings were the same, and 96% were the same or one score point apart.

While it seems that the content and linguistic ability 5-point scales may be measuring slightly different things, the relationship of both of these scales to the single overall 5-point holistic scale supports the conclusion that little would be gained by using the two in lieu of the single overall holistic scale. This has clear implications with respect to cost and time spent on scoring for the integrated listening/speaking tasks to be considered for an operational assessment.

OUTCOMES OF SPEAKING TASK PROTOTYPING

An interface for the computer delivery of speaking tasks was successfully developed. Rubric development drew on the expertise of many individuals who worked with ESL students in academic contexts. Both 4-point and 5-point rubrics were explored, as were analytic and holistic scales. A recommendation to use 5-point holistic rubrics for both independent and integrated tasks was made based on these investigations.

No evidence for a relationship between task characteristics and task difficulty, as proposed in the previous chapter, was found in these pilot studies. For the reading-speaking task, we found that aids, such as providing a list of bulleted points to address in the response or allowing notetaking, did not seem to enhance performance when compared with conditions where no aid was provided. While narrative texts appeared to be slightly easier than expository texts, these differences were not large. Speaking performance was found to be unaffected by type of listening text: campus conversation, academic conversation, or lecture. Two administration conditions that were varied, presence or absence of multiple-choice items and the different time limits for responding, did not affect speaking performance.

These results had two implications. On the one hand, they indicated that speaking performance was robust and that minor task variations would not have large effects on performance. The absence of performance differences associated with task characteristics and administration conditions allowed latitude in the design of speaking tasks. Other factors—such as domain coverage, expert opinion, availability of text materials, and cost of development—would be more important in task design. On the other hand, these results suggested that, given the types of tasks envisioned, it would not be easy to identify task characteristics that could be used to explain performance. Therefore, other approaches would need to be sought for supporting explanatory inferences.

WRITING

The *Writing Framework* (Cumming, Kantor, Powers, Santos, & Taylor, 2000) called for sampling *sustained* writing in an academic context, writing that would be in response to a particular assigned task, *coherent, appropriate*, and *purposeful*. It also called on the assessment to facilitate a variety of writing processes and to vary tasks with respect to their dependence on listening and reading materials. The emphasis of the test takers' performance directed research at the design phase to the exploration of the task framework—linked to domain definition inferences—on the scoring rubrics and administration conditions required for support of evaluation inferences and to the impact of task characteristics on task difficulty as entailed by the explanation inference.

DOMAIN DEFINITION AND TASK DESIGN

The task descriptions intended to support domain definition inferences were centered on the three writing tasks described in Table 4.5. More than 10 years of experience with the TWE indicated that the independent task did not demand extensive research beyond reconsideration of scoring rubrics. This independent task would provide a prompt from which test takers would formulate and express ideas on their own. The integrated tasks would require comprehension of academic information and sustained written responses based on comprehension of that information. The responses to the two types of integrated tasks were expected to vary in register or the formality of the language used. Implicit in this description of possible tasks was that multiple-choice grammar items or short constructed-response tasks (single sentences) would not produce evidence relevant to the construct of sustained writing described in the *Writing Framework* (Cumming et al., 2000).

TABLE 4.5
Description of Tasks Proposed for a New TOEFL Writing Measure

Task Type	Definition
Independent	An invention essay in which the writing prompt would provide just enough information "to stimulate the examinee to generate his/her own ideas on the topic with supporting reasons and examples drawn from observation, experience, or reading" (Cumming et al., 2000, p. 11)
Integrated[a] text-based	Responses that would require test takers to "display knowledge...derived" from a reading passage or a lecture; this would require test takers to "identify, select, and manipulate the relevant information in the text" (Cumming et al., 2000, p. 20)
Integrated situation-based	Responses that would elicit written responses summarizing or responding/reacting to campus-based situations (as presented in conversations or perhaps e-mails)

[a] In the *Writing Framework* (Cumming et al., 2000), the term interdependent was used to refer to tasks that required integration of two or more modalities. As work progressed, the term integrated replaced interdependent.

INVESTIGATIONS RELEVANT TO EVALUATION AND EXPLANATION

Many alternatives for integrated writing tasks existed, and the advantages and disadvantages of the alternatives needed to be weighed. In examining these alternatives, we had to address several issues germane to the evaluation inference. One issue was how different types of prompts, which were meant to sample a variety of academic contexts and communicative situations in which purposeful, sustained writing could be observed, would provide opportunities to observe evidence of different aspects of writing ability. Scoring rubrics needed to be developed and tried out. At the same time, an issue relevant to the explanation inference, whether certain task characteristics would influence task difficulty, was also explored. These issues were addressed in an iterative fashion. As tasks were trailed and modified, rubrics based on the test takers' responses were developed and refined, and the impact of task characteristics on the qualities of writing and on task difficulty were assessed.

Preliminary Trial of Writing Tasks

Due to the lack of experience with the integrated writing tasks, uncertainty existed concerning the effects of the many possible variations in task types. As a consequence, a small-scale trial of a variety of writing prompts was designed. The purpose of this trial was to investigate the appropriateness of different task types for providing evidence of academic writing skills and the qualities of responses valued by raters.

Five prototype task types were developed. Examples of integrated text-based tasks included writing summaries of a lecture, a reading passage, and a transcription of a lecture. Examples of integrated situation-based tasks included writing a note after reading a transcription of a conversation and writing a note after listening to a conversation. Eight ESL students were interviewed as they completed the tasks.

Experience in developing the tasks and the observations of the students' performances had numerous implications for further task design. Listening-related tasks based on both formal text-based lectures and the situation-based conversations were seen as successful. Reading-related tasks were especially problematic if they asked test takers to go *beyond* what was in the academic subject matter text and relate it to their own experience. Such tasks might differentially depend on knowledge of academic subject and introduce a potential for bias related to disciplinary background. For situation-based prompts, listening-related ones were seen as a better direction for further development than reading-based ones.

A decision was made to leave the text available when the test takers are writing a response based on a reading. This decision was based partly on examination of student responses, but mainly on the desire to ensure that the tasks primarily measured writing ability instead of placing undue burden on memory. An inspection of test-taker responses revealed very little of what might be considered to be plagiarism. It was acknowledged, however, that the situation might be different when the stakes are higher than they are in a research study. The writing team felt, however, that extensive plagiarism, if it occurred, could be considered during the scoring process.

When test takers were asked to respond to a reading, some test takers tended to express an opinion instead of responding to the prompt. Therefore, directions for the reading/writing task were modified to discourage expressing an opinion and encourage better understanding of the task requirement to base the response to the prompt on information in the text.

Timing limits needed to be determined to make the tasks accessible to the majority of the test takers. The trial for the reading/writing task established that it could be accomplished in under 30 minutes, and the listening/writing trial found that 15 minutes would be satisfactory for formulating a response to the question.

Studies of Rater Cognition

The question of how responses to the writing tasks might be evaluated was addressed in the *Writing Framework* (Cumming et al., 2000). After considering a variety of possibilities, the writing team set forth the evaluative criteria shown in Table 4.6, which were to be considered in the development of formal scoring rubrics.

TABLE 4.6
Evaluative Criteria to Be Used as Basis for Developing Scoring Rubrics

Aspect of Writing	*Criteria*
Organization of discourse and ideas	Organization (a reader should be able, without undue rereading, to follow and understand what the writer is saying and why it is being discussed in relation to the prompt)
	Coherence (a reader should be able to derive meaning from sentences and not find logical contradictions)
	Progression (there should be no glaring gaps, redundancies, or digressions)
	Development (specificity, quality, and quantity of information and ideas)
Language use	Appropriateness and range of vocabulary
	Appropriateness and effectiveness of language used to manage discourse connections
	Accuracy, appropriateness, and range of syntax and morphology
	Spelling, punctuation, and other orthographic conventions
	For integrated tasks—appropriate use of paraphrase, reported speech, and summation

Because the exact nature of the constructs assessed by holistic rating schemes is often ill defined, Cumming, Kantor, and Powers (2001, 2002) investigated raters' decision-making processes to develop a descriptive model of rater behaviors. Such a model was expected to clarify the meaning of holistic scores in terms of the test-taker abilities and to provide a preliminary framework for scoring independent essays and new types of integrated writing tasks. The framework was developed and refined in three related studies. First, the authors empirically derived a preliminary framework to describe the decision-making behaviors of ten raters with experience in evaluating independent essays written by ESL students. In their second study, the researchers collected verbal reports of decision-making from seven raters who had experience evaluating the essays of English mother-tongue (EMT) students as they evaluated some of the same essays. In the third study, the framework was extended to describe the decision-making behaviors of the ESL-experienced raters as they evaluated ESL student responses to the novel integrated writing tasks.

In the first study, the text qualities that raters mentioned as characteristic of effective writing included rhetorical organization, expression of ideas, accuracy and fluency in language used, and the amount of text produced. In the second study, ESL raters placed relatively more emphasis on the linguistic characteristics of essays than on the rhetorical and ideational qualities, while EMT raters attended to both equally. Furthermore, both groups of raters attended more to rhetorical and ideational qualities for essays rated high than for essays rated low. In the third study of the integrated writing tasks, raters focused more on the influence of the prompt materials than they had in rating independent essays. They attended to the writers' understanding of the listening and reading materials and how they used source materials in the essay. Compared with independent essays, raters increased attention to task completion, relevance, and style while decreasing attention to length.

This series of studies has a number of implications for understanding the writing qualities underlying holistic rating scales and for improving the rating process. First, linguistic qualities are weighed more heavily than rhetoric and ideas for essays receiving low scores. Second, raters did attend to different qualities in independent and integrated essays. Third, both rater characteristics and task characteristics influenced rater decision processes. Cumming et al. (2001, 2002) noted that these factors are important to acknowledge in training materials and, more specifically, that raters would need guidance on how comprehension and use of source materials should be evaluated for integrated tasks.

The insights gained from the qualitative investigations of task administration conditions and the rater cognition studies informed two subsequent pilot studies of integrated writing tasks.

Effects of Task Characteristics

Investigations of the integrated writing tasks paralleled those of the integrated speaking tasks in many ways. In pilot studies of reading/writing tasks and listening/writing tasks, the issues of the appropriateness of scoring rubrics, relevant to the evaluation inferences, and the issue of the impact of task characteristics on task difficulty, relevant to the explanation inference, were explored. However, the writing team also considered another issue relevant to the evaluation inference—how task characteristics affected opportunities to observe evidence of writing abilities.

Investigation of reading/writing tasks   Issues addressed in the pilot study of integrated reading/writing tasks included the impact of passage length/complexity on writing performance, the development of an appropriate scoring rubric, and the effects of multiple-choice reading comprehension questions on task difficulty.

Approximately 100 ESL students (of low, medium, and high English language ability at three U.S. colleges) wrote substantive responses to questions based on four reading passages. Two passages were typical of TOEFL PBT reading passages (300–350 words), and two were novel, more complex passages (600–700 words) used for the new reading comprehension tasks. Prior to completing the writing task, participants answered reading comprehension questions for two of the four passages so researchers could assess the impact of this factor on writing. Which passages had associated reading comprehension questions and which did not were counterbalanced over groups of study participants, as was order of task administration.

The reading passages, but not the comprehension questions, were available to study participants when they responded to the prompt. To evaluate the resulting writing samples, experienced readers applied a scoring rubric that was developed jointly by ETS assessment specialists and university professors.

Four university professors with experience in writing assessment and ETS assessment specialists met over a 4-day period to analyze the writing samples and to develop a preliminary rubric for the integrated reading/writing tasks. Prior to the meeting, all participants reviewed the task materials and a sample of responses. During the meeting, an inductive process was used to develop a rubric. Each participant holistically rated each sample essay as to the degree to which the writer demonstrated the expected performance. The participants also entered into a database the characteristics of the essay that influenced their judgments. These ratings and descriptors were then compiled for each essay and provided the starting point for developing a consensus about qualities of essays at different score levels. Subsequently, the rubric was further refined by the ETS assessment specialists, and the writing samples associated with the two longer passages were scored by experienced raters using this rubric.

Five-point holistic rubrics were developed that directed raters' attention to language use, discourse organization, and appropriate use of content from the reading passage. Appropriate use of language to report the ideas of others was incorporated into the reading/writing rubric so that, for reading/writing tasks, the related issues of (a) copying from the text and (b) accurately representing the content of the text could be dealt with in scoring.

One outcome of the analysis and scoring was a decision that the shorter reading passages, typical of the current TOEFL, did not provide enough substance for writing: Many of the responses were essentially one- or two-sentence top-level summaries. Alternatively, some writers regarded all the information in these tightly written shorter texts to be salient and important and found little reason to be selective in reorganizing information for efficient expression. As a consequence, little evidence of writing abilities could be discerned, and the responses to the shorter passages were not evaluated further.

For the other tasks, raters exhibited similar levels of scoring agreement, regardless of the reading passage that was used as the stimulus for writing, agreeing exactly more than half the time and exactly or within 1 point more than 90% of the time. The calculation of Cohen's coefficient kappa revealed a level of agreement that has been characterized as moderate.

The distribution of ratings for participants' writing samples based on the longer passages was skewed, indicating that the writing tasks were somewhat difficult, with mean scores in the range of 2.1 to 2.4 on a 5-point scale. Nonetheless, the full range of possible scores was invoked when study participants' performances were evaluated. A comparison of the means and standard deviations of the writing scores for the two passages in the two experimental conditions (following reading comprehension questions vs. no reading comprehension questions) revealed that the main effect of passage, the presence of reading comprehension questions, and their interaction did not influence writing scores significantly.

When asked about the amount of time they had to write their responses, a near majority of the participants indicated that they needed more time. Participants who answered reading comprehension questions prior to writing were somewhat less likely to report insufficient time than did those who did not. It is important to note that answering the reading comprehension questions did *not* impact writing performance; it impacted only the time pressure experienced by study participants.

Test takers varied widely with regard to their perceptions of task difficulty, with test takers perceiving the tasks to be very easy about as often as they regarded them to be very difficult. Actual performance on the tasks, however, suggested that the tasks were relatively difficult for study participants. With respect to overall impression, most participants felt that the reading/writing task was at least a somewhat good measure of their ability to read and explain their understanding of the passage. Finally, a substantial majority of study participants felt that the writing tasks were at least somewhat similar to the kinds of tasks required in their academic work.

A consensus was reached by the writing team about the issues and amount of training that would be needed to evaluate responses to the reading/writing tasks. One aspect of training that distinguishes the reading/writing task type from the independent task is that readers will have to become very familiar with the reading passages on which responses are based. Finally, it was determined during the course of developing items that, once the proper stimulus is identified, integrated reading/writing prompts require about the same level of effort to develop as independent writing tasks.

Conclusion The major experimental manipulation (i.e., whether test takers answered reading comprehension questions before they wrote their responses) appeared to have little if any effect on the quality of writing responses or task difficulty. Test takers did, however, report somewhat less time pressure in writing when they were able to answer reading comprehension questions first, possibly because answering these questions afforded them slightly more time to think about the reading stimulus in preparation for writing. These findings therefore suggest little if any reason for *not* administering reading comprehension questions before test takers are asked to write, and, in fact, they suggest that there may be a slight advantage to presenting such questions first.

STUDY OF LISTENING/WRITING TASKS

A second study addressed the suitability for the listening/writing tasks of (a) asking multiple-choice questions prior to writing and (b) using *directed* listening stimuli/prompts. The objective was to determine whether these two factors would affect task difficulty. The first factor was whether multiple-choice questions should be inserted between the end of the lecture and writing the essay. The second factor was whether students should be provided with a list of specific points to be addressed in the written response. (Prompts with specific points enumerated were called *directed* prompts.)

The hypothesis was that multiple-choice questions could affect test performance positively by providing additional context and focus for the essays. (On the other hand, the questions could interfere with test performance by increasing the time interval between the end of the stimulus and the beginning of the writing.) Similarly, the list of specific points could have either positive or negative consequences. For example, they might enhance memory, thus assuring that relevant points were covered and that poor responses were not simply a function of poor memory. If, however, they provided too much structure, the usefulness of the essay as a measure of the test taker's organizational abilities could be compromised.

Method   To study this issue, study participants wrote essays in response to two conversations and four lectures. Each participant wrote one response under each of six experimental conditions. For conversations, the experimental conditions were whether the writing task was preceded by multiple-choice reading comprehension questions. For lectures, there were four experimental conditions, representing combinations of the variables (a) with or without a directed prompt and (b) with or without multiple-choice reading comprehension questions. The pairing of the lectures and conversations with the different experimental conditions was counterbalanced for groups of study participants. The study participants, recruited from five colleges in the United States, were 138 ESL students of varying English language ability and from a variety of native language backgrounds.

A procedure similar to the one used to develop rubrics for the integrated reading/writing tasks was followed for the listening/writing tasks. Through an iterative process of analyzing and discussing the qualities of test taker responses, a team of expert essay readers—both ETS staff and external consultants—decided that the most salient features of test-taker responses could best be captured by a 5-point holistic rubric that described four aspects of responses—organization, content, language/syntax, and vocabulary—to be considered in scoring. ETS assessment specialists subsequently refined the rubric by considering additional test-taker responses. The final rubric was similar to the rubric for the reading/writing tasks in that it directed raters' attention to language use (including both language/syntax and vocabulary), discourse organization, and appropriate use of content. The resulting revised rubric was applied to the participant responses that were collected for the study.

Results   The preliminary reading of a sample of the essays based on conversations indicated that they did not provide the kind of evidence needed to support the writing claims. Therefore, these types of tasks were dropped from further consideration. In addition, scoring of the essays written in response to one of the lectures (history) was problematic, and these essays also were dropped. The remaining three essays, based on three of the lectures, appeared to yield a good range of scorable responses on the 1–5 holistic scale although, like the reading/writing tasks, the listening/writing tasks were somewhat difficult, with mean scores ranging from 2.0 to 2.3. Unfortunately, the elimination of one of the prompts resulted in an unbalanced design, thus confounding groups and experimental conditions. Consequently, the empirical results were less conclusive than hoped.

Nonetheless, there was little indication that the quality of the writing was affected significantly by first asking multiple-choice questions or by using prompts that cued test takers to focus on specific points. (According to readers, however, directed prompts may have hindered reliable judgments of writing ability when writers leaned too heavily on language from prompts.)

Differences between mean test scores in the various conditions were small by conventional standards and therefore of little practical concern.

Participants rated lectures as being considerably more difficult than conversations. There was, however, little variation in the perceived difficulty of the four lectures. Most participants reported having had little if any prior knowledge of the content of lectures. Most students reported taking notes at least sometimes during the exam, and most students felt that their notes were useful in answering the question. Students generally reported having enough time to answer the multiple-choice questions, and most students thought they had the right amount of time to write each of the compositions. A majority of test takers thought that writing a composition about lectures and conversations was a good way to demonstrate their writing ability. Despite only a negligible impact on test performance, most students perceived both the list of points and the multiple-choice questions as being at least a little helpful for writing their responses.

Conclusion   First, tasks that involve understanding and writing about lectures are much more likely to yield information to support claims about students' writing skills than are tasks that involve conversations. Second, the question remained largely unanswered of whether the multiple-choice questions that preceded the writing prompt provided test takers with content and focus that aided them in writing their essays. This is because there was no consistency across sets in what kind or degree of overlap existed between multiple-choice questions and writing prompts. That is, although the study found that performance on the writing tasks was not significantly affected by the presence of preceding multiple-choice questions, the study was not designed to manipulate the kind and degree of overlap between multiple-choice questions and the writing prompt.

OUTCOMES OF WRITING-TASK PROTOTYPING

The results of these preliminary studies of integrated writing tasks led to revisions in the types of tasks proposed to represent the target domain, decisions about the administration conditions and text characteristics that best provided opportunities to observe evidence of writing abilities, and the development of scoring rubrics. Of the task types proposed in Table 4.5, the integrated text-based tasks (based on reading passages and lectures) were found to reveal academic writing abilities, but the integrated situation-based tasks (based on conversations) did not. For reading/writing tasks only, the longer texts provided enough substance for writing tasks. As in the case of speaking, administration conditions, such as the presence or absence of multiple-choice questions, had little observable effect on performance, although they appeared to affect test-taker perceptions of factors such as time pressure.

Both reading/writing and listening/writing tasks were found to be somewhat difficult. The rubrics developed for both reading/writing and listening/writing tasks focused attention on similar qualities of responses and could be applied reliably by raters. However, it was recognized that copying from the text might create difficulty for raters scoring reading/writing tasks.

IMPLICATIONS FOR TEST DESIGN

The process of developing task frameworks, designing prototype materials, and conducting pilot studies resulted in a number of implications for the design of

TABLE 4.7
Summary of Outcomes and Implications for Further Development as They Relate to the Inferences in the Interpretative Argument

Outcomes	*Implications*
Domain definition	
Listening—Development of all seven task types proposed to represent academic tasks was feasible. Verbatim materials from the corpus materials required background knowledge for comprehension. The use of nonnative accented speech in listening materials might result in bias for some language groups.	Continue development of all task types. Text will not be drawn directly from the corpus; the corpus would be used to establish characteristics of authentic speech to guide materials development. Nonnative accented speech will not be used.
Reading—Tasks proposed to assess two of the four reading purposes were successfully developed. Longer, more complex reading texts to assess reading to learn were found.	Continue development of sentence simplification task and reading-to-learn tasks. Texts should be chosen on the basis of complexity of rhetorical organization rather than the type of organization.
Speaking—Three tasks types modeled on academic speaking tasks were successfully developed.	Computer delivery of the speaking tasks constrained the types of task to be monologic. Continue development of all three tasks types
Writing—Independent and integrated text-based tasks were successfully developed, but integrated situation-based tasks were not.	Continue development of independent and integrated text-based tasks
Evaluation	
Listening—Notetaking had a facilitative effect under some conditions, had no deleterious effects under any conditions, and contributed to test taker comfort.	Notetaking should be allowed.
Reading—An interface to present longer reading texts and more complex question formats was designed. Reading to integrate information across two texts was too complex for computer presentation.	Continue development of tasks requiring integration of information within but not across two texts. Rationale for scoring rubric for complex tasks needs to be developed.

(continued)

TABLE 4.7
Continued

Outcomes	Implications
Speaking—An interface to support the presentation of speaking tasks was developed. Both 4-point and 5-point holistic scales functioned well for integrated tasks. There was a strong relationship between two analytic scales and a holistic scale. All tasks appeared to be at an appropriate level of difficulty.	Computer presentation of speaking tasks was feasible. Use of a 5-point holistic rating scale for both integrated and independent speaking tasks was recommended.
Writing—Integrated text-based writing tasks based on lectures or longer reading passages provided evidence of academic writing abilities, but those based on conversations or shorter reading passages did not. Although integrated writing tasks were somewhat difficult, a full range of score points was observed. A 5-point holistic rubric including attention to language use, organization, and content was developed for integrated tasks.	Continue development of integrated writing tasks based on longer academic reading texts and lectures. Raters would need guidance about what content was relevant in responses to integrated tasks and how to score responses that included verbatim materials from the texts.

Explanation

Listening—Strategies used for pragmatics items differed from those used for basic understanding. Integrating information items were more difficult on the average than basic comprehension items. Integrating information from two texts was not more difficult that integrating information across a single text. A fast speech rate had some effect on task difficulty. Fragmented speech did not affect task difficulty.	Continue development of pragmatic understanding tasks and of tasks requiring integration of information within but not across two texts. Since only abnormal speech rates affected difficulty, speech rate would not be used to manipulate task difficulty. Fragmented speech would be used to simulate authentic speech.
Reading—Three of the proposed new task types were judged to provide evidence of reading abilities. No evidence to support predictions of task difficulty was found.	Continue development of sentence simplification, prose summary, and schematic summary tasks. Pursue approaches other than difficulty prediction for explanation.
Speaking—Variations in task characteristics did not impact task difficulty.	Other approaches to explanation should be sought because variables affecting task difficulty were not identified. Task characteristics were chosen based on other considerations.
Writing—Variations in task characteristics did not impact task difficulty.	Other approaches to explanation should be sought because variables affecting task difficulty were not identified. Task characteristics were chosen based on other considerations.

the test that was developed for the next phase of prototyping. Table 4.7 summarizes these implications, along with their basis, for each part of the test as they related to the inferences in the interpretative argument. The implications of the outcomes of this phase pertained primarily to details of task design and administration, required for support of domain definition and evaluation inferences, respectively. The tasks for listening, reading, speaking, and writing also underwent analysis to determine whether hypothesized sources of difficulty appeared to affect the observed difficulties of the tasks. No evidence suggested that task difficulty could be predicted by the task features, and therefore, after these pilot studies, this approach was abandoned as a potential method to support the explanation inference. Support for explanation inferences would need to be based on alternative kinds of assumptions.

Like the results of prior phases of the project, the results obtained in the task-prototyping phase contained some similarities across skill areas, but they also reflected the idiosyncratic concerns of development teams in each area. Domain definition inferences were taken to the next phase by testing the extent to which the thinking captured in the TOEFL 2000 frameworks (Bejar et al., 2000; Butler et al., 2000; Cumming et al., 2000; Enright et al, 2000) could be implemented in practice, but the extent to which each framework specified a task framework differed across groups, and therefore the outcomes differed. The task administration conditions raised different concerns for each area. For example, whereas the listening team was focused on notetaking, the reading team was concerned with the computer interface. The speaking and listening teams were concerned with development of scoring rubrics. All teams sought support concerning prediction of difficulty. Although the particular predictors were different across the teams, all were equally unsuccessful at manipulating difficulty. Despite the differences in research paths, the investigations all sought appropriate support for the primary inferences of concern at this stage and offered some insight into how the first test blueprint should be drafted.

A DRAFT BLUEPRINT FOR A NEW TOEFL

The results of the pilot studies were combined with the conceptual issues laid out in the previous chapter and prior experience with the TOEFL to draft the blueprint for a new TOEFL, which is summarized in Table 4.8. The test tasks were selected and specified on the basis of outcomes summarized in Table 4.7. For example, test takers would be allowed to take notes while listening because of the results of the notetaking study, which suggested the positive affective effect of notetaking and the lack of effect on scores. Similarly, the task types specified in the blueprint were informed by research results. For example, the types of reading tasks selected for further development would include the complex selected-response tasks (reading to learn) but not scanning or reading efficiency tasks. It was decided that approximately 3 1/2 hours

TABLE 4.8
Potential Configuration for a New TOEFL Test

Test Tasks	Response Format	Time
Listening measure		
Conversation 1		
Conversation 2	Simple and complex selected	40 minutes
Lecture 1	response items	
Lecture 2		
Reading measure		
Passage 1		
Passage 2	Simple and complex selected	75 minutes
Passage 3	response items	
Speaking measure		
Speaking based on Conversation 1		
Speaking based on Lecture 1		
Speaking based on Passage 1	Constructed responses	20 minutes
Independent speaking tasks		
Writing measure		
Writing based on Lecture 2		15 minutes
Writing based on Passage 2	Constructed responses	25 minutes
Independent essay		30 minutes

would be appropriate, and the timing for each measure was based on observations of task completion time during pilot testing. As originally intended, four scores would be produced from the testing. In addition, during piloting, the decision was made to include the scores on the integrated tasks in the writing and speaking measures.

This blueprint configuration allowed us to focus on central issues that would have to be resolved before a new TOEFL, including the complex tasks we were considering, could be administered worldwide as a secure test with high-stakes outcomes via computer to hundreds of thousands of test takers each year at a reasonable cost. These issues were particularly prominent given this blueprint. One was the reliability and generalizability of speaking or writing measures that included only a small number of tasks. A second was the development of evidence that linked performance on the test to performance in the academic domain (extrapolation). These issues stimulated the next phase of pilot testing described in the following chapter.

CONCLUSION

The development and pilot testing of tasks described in this chapter, which represented the first empirical stage of the development of a new TOEFL, revealed that we were able to construct a variety of complex tasks that test takers were capable of performing and that computer presentation of these tasks did not appear to be a barrier for these students. The experience gained in task development also further delimited the scope of the domain definition inference implicit in the TOEFL frameworks. The evaluation inference would be strengthened through the iterative process, gathering expert judgment to construct scales and expert raters to use the scales on responses from pilot testing, used to develop rubrics for the speaking and writing measures of the new TOEFL. The evaluation inference would have a stronger basis also as the result of the examination of the effects of the administration of task characteristics. Finally, since no support existed for hypotheses about what task variables would affect task difficulty, a more sustained research and development effort would be needed to establish other sources of explanation and other methods to provide descriptive score information. This was one of the objectives of the larger scale study reported in the following chapter.

NOTES

1. Traditionally, separate TOEFL test sections corresponded to measures of separate language skills, so terms such as *listening section* and *listening measure* were interchangeable. This was not always the case for the prototyping studies for new TOEFL, e.g., some test sections included tasks that contributed to measures of different skills. Therefore, in this and the following chapters, we use the term *measure* to refer to the score on a series of tasks assessing the same skill, and the term *section* to refer to a block of tasks.
2. Versions of a tenth task type (integration of information from listening and reading texts, Table 3.3 in Chapter 3) were eventually investigated for the speaking and writing measures.
3. Reading texts were not selected from the corpus for two reasons: Authentic academic reading materials were readily available, and TOEFL reading texts always had been taken from entry level college textbooks that presume no subject-specific knowledge on the part of the reader. Despite their authenticity, the corpus texts are either too advanced or require background knowledge the reader has gained from earlier parts of the textbooks.

REFERENCES

American Educational Research Association, American Psychological Association, & National Council on Measurement in Education. (1999). *Standards for educational and psychological testing.* Washington, DC: American Educational Research Association.

Bejar, I., Douglas, D., Jamieson, J., Nissan, S., & Turner, J. (2000). *TOEFL 2000 listening framework: A working paper* (TOEFL Monograph No. 19). Princeton, NJ: Educational Testing Service.

Biber, D., Conrad, S. M., Reppen, R., Byrd, P., Helt, M., Clark, V., et al. (2004). *Representing language use in the university: Analysis of the TOEFL 2000 spoken and written academic language corpus* (TOEFL Monograph No. 25). Princeton, NJ: Educational Testing Service.

Butler, F. A., Eignor, D., Jones, S., McNamara, T., & Suomi, B. K. (2000). *TOEFL 2000 speaking framework: A working paper* (TOEFL Monograph No. 20). Princeton, NJ: Educational Testing Service.

Carrell, P. L., Dunkel, P. A., & Mallaun, P. (2002). *The effects of notetaking, lecture length, and topic on the listening component of the TOEFL 2000 test* (TOEFL Monograph No. 23). Princeton, NJ: Educational Testing Service.

Carrell, P. L., Dunkel, P. A., & Mollaun, P. (2004). The effects of notetaking, lecture length, and topic on a computer-based test of ESL listening comprehension. *Applied Language Learning, 14,* 83–105.

Carver, R. P. (1990). *Reading rate: A review of research and theory.* San Diego, CA: Academic Press.

Carver, R. P. (1997). Reading for one second, one minute, or one year form the perspective of Rauding theory. *Scientific Studies of Reading, 1,* 3–43.

Cumming, A., Kantor, R., & Powers, D. E. (2001). *Scoring TOEFL essays and TOEFL 2000 prototype writing tasks: An investigation into raters' decision making and development of a preliminary analytic framework* (TOEFL Monograph No. 22). Princeton, NJ: Educational Testing Service.

Cumming, A., Kantor, R., & Powers, D. E. (2002). Decision making while rating ESL/EFL writing tasks: A descriptive framework. *The Modern Language Journal, 86,* 67–96.

Cumming, A., Kantor, R., Powers, D., Santos, T., & Taylor, C. (2000). *TOEFL 2000 writing framework: A working paper* (TOEFL Monograph No. 18). Princeton, NJ: Educational Testing Service.

Enright, M., Grabe, W., Koda, K., Mosenthal, P., Mulcahy-Ernt, P., & Schedl, M. (2000). *TOEFL 2000 reading framework: A working paper* (TOEFL Monograph No. 17). Princeton, NJ: Educational Testing Service.

Enright, M. K., & Schedl, M. (2000). *Reading for a reason: Using reader purpose to guide test design* (internal report). Princeton, NJ: Educational Testing Service.

Major, R. C., Fitzmaurice, S. F., Bunta, F., & Balasubramanian, C. (2002). The effects of nonnative accents on listening comprehension: Implications for ESL assessment. *TESOL Quarterly, 36*(2), 173–190.

Royer, J. M. (1990). The sentence verification technique: A new direction in the assessment of reading comprehension. In S. Legg & J. Algina (Eds.), *Cognitive assessment of language and math outcomes* (pp. 144–191). Norwood, NJ: Ablex.

Sarig, G. (1987). High-level reading in the first and in the foreign language: Some comparative process data. In J. Devine, P. L. Carrell, & D. E. Eskey (Eds.), *Research in reading in English as a second language.* Washington, DC: Teachers of English to Speakers of Other Languages.

5

Prototyping Measures of Listening, Reading, Speaking, and Writing

Mary K. Enright
Brent Bridgeman
Daniel Eignor
Yong-Won Lee
Donald E. Powers

During a second prototyping phase of the new TOEFL® project from 2000 to 2001, we sought evidence for the quality of the measures in the proposed blueprint that had been the end result of the first phase (the blueprint is summarized in Table 4.8). Our focus in this second phase broadened from issues related to the design of tasks to those related to the design of measures composed of these tasks. The research in this phase was motivated primarily by the need to support the generalization inference. The scores that the test takers obtained on each of the four measures would be interpreted as reflective of scores that would be obtained on parallel versions of the measures. In particular, the design of the speaking and writing measures needed to take into account the many factors that would affect score generalizability, as well as practical constraints. These measures were composed of different task types that varied in their dependence on input from other modalities and that required complex constructed responses. Only a few of these tasks, which were time-consuming to administer and were costly to score, could be included on a test form. Therefore, a study was designed to assess of the impact of different task configurations and rating designs on the reliability of the test measures.

In this chapter, we discuss the questions that motivated research during this phase in terms of their relevance to the assumptions underlying inferences and warrants in the evolving interpretative argument. We describe the design and methodology of the central study. The data and responses collected in this study provided grist for many different analyses and for other studies. The findings of these analyses are reported here as they pertain to the inferences in the interpretative argument. We conclude with a summary of how the results of these studies contributed to an emerging consensus about the design of a new TOEFL.

GUIDING QUESTIONS FOR THE SECOND PROTOTYPING PHASE

The test blueprint shown in Table 4.8 and the conclusions about task design discussed in the previous chapter provided the impetus for the research and analyses conducted during this second prototyping phase. The critical questions at this point were relevant to the assumptions associated with the generalization inference because of the need to justify the composition of the speaking and writing measures, but questions relevant to the assumptions associated with the evaluation, explanation, and extrapolation inferences were also posed. The questions that guided research and analyses in this phase are presented in Table 5.1 as they relate to the assumptions underlying the warrants and inferences in the TOEFL interpretative argument.

Three questions were relevant to the assumptions associated with the evaluation warrant that observations of performance on the test are evaluated to provide scores that reflect targeted language abilities. A rationale to justify the scoring of complex selected-response formats for listening and reading, which could be scored in a variety of ways, was needed. For constructed-response tasks, preliminary scoring rubrics had been developed in the previous phase. During this phase, the collection of more spoken responses provided an opportunity to conduct a further empirical evaluation of the proposed speaking rubric. Another question concerned the statistical characteristics of tasks and measures and whether they would support norm-referenced decisions.

The questions motivated by the need to support the generalization warrant—that observed scores are estimates of expected scores over parallel versions of tasks and test forms and over raters—were central to the design of speaking and writing measures. One question we considered was whether differences among tasks, task types, and ratings (the facets of measurement) introduced variability into test scores that would undermine the inferences we wish to make about consistency in the measurement of individual differences in the abilities that were the target of the assessment. Another area of investigation was optimal scenarios for maximizing consistency in measurement, given many sources of variability and time and cost constraints. For the speaking and writing measures, we investigated how different numbers of tasks and ratings would affect generalizability. For the listening, speaking, and writing measures, we investigated how different combinations of task

TABLE 5.1

Questions Investigated in the Second Prototyping Phase Relevant to the Assumptions
Underlying the Warrants and Inferences in the TOEFL Interpretative Argument

Assumptions Underlying Warrant	Related Questions
Evaluation	
Rubrics for scoring responses are appropriate for providing evidence of targeted language abilities.	How should complex selected-response tasks be scored? Are the proposed rating scales for speaking appropriate?
The statistical characteristics of items, measures, and test forms are appropriate for norm-referenced decisions	What are the statistical characteristics of the tasks and measures?
Generalization	
The number of tasks and ratings are sufficient to provide stable estimates of test takers' performances.	What is the relative contribution of different facets of measurement to score variability? How do various assessment scenarios for the total test (i.e., the number of tasks and ratings, rating designs) affect score reliability?
Configuration of tasks on measures is appropriate for intended interpretation.	How does the composition of a composite measure (i.e., different configurations of task types and number of tasks within task type) affect score reliability? Is reporting a composite score composed of scores on different task types justified psychometrically?
Explanation	
Performance on new test measures relates to performance on other test-based measures of language proficiency as expected theoretically.	Do the prototype measures assess language skills in a manner that is similar to or different from other standardized language tests?
The linguistic knowledge, processes, and strategies required to complete tasks successfully are in keeping with theoretical expectations.	Do the qualities of speech vary with proficiency level and task type as hypothesized?
The internal structure of the test scores is consistent with a theoretical view of language proficiency as a number of highly interrelated components.	What was the internal structure of the prototype test?
Extrapolation	
Performance on the test is related to other criteria of language proficiency in the academic context.	How did performance on the prototype measures relate to students' and instructors' assessments of students' English language skills?

types and number of tasks within task type affected generalizability.[1] Finally, from the beginning of the design phase, there was a particular concern as to whether there would be sufficient consistency in an individual's scores for different task types (e.g., independent vs. integrated tasks) to warrant their inclusion on a composite measure.

Research questions relevant to the explanation warrant—that test scores are attributed to a construct of academic language proficiency—were also posed. Traditionally, measurement specialists have sought both structural and substantive evidence to support theoretical explanations for test performance (Messick, 1989). An examination of the relationships among measures that purport to assess similar or different skills may provide evidence about the structural aspects of the assessment that are consistent with theoretical assumptions. Correlations between the prototype measures and existing standardized tests of language proficiency were explored to determine if the prototype measures were assessing language proficiency in a distinctive way. The internal relationships among the prototype measures were also examined.

Substantive evidence that the cognitive processes and knowledge engaged by test tasks are consistent with theoretical expectations also strengthens the explanation inference. During the task-prototyping phase described in the previous chapter, results suggested that an assumption about the relationship of task characteristics to task difficulty, a potential source of substantive evidence, could not be supported at this time. In this phase, the features of spoken responses were closely examined to support another substantive assumption—that the linguistic knowledge, processes, and strategies engaged by test tasks were consistent with theoretical expectations.

We also sought evidence for the extrapolation of the scores obtained on each measure to performance in the academic context. For all four of the measures, the question was how performance on the new measures related to criteria of English language proficiency in an academic setting, where criteria included nontest indicators of English language ability, such as students' and instructors' judgments of students' language skills.

Methodology

Addressing the many questions described in Table 5.1 required administering a number of instruments, which assessed language proficiency in various ways, to a sample of participants that was large enough ($n\sim500$) to provide reasonably accurate and stable estimates of relevant statistics. Given that the questions we were addressing were formative and exploratory in nature, we planned to examine patterns in the data rather than engaging in extensive hypothesis testing. Prototype measures of listening, reading, speaking, and writing tasks were developed to investigate issues of generalizability for an assessment instrument based on the blueprint in Table 4.8. Support for extrapolation inferences required alternative, nontest measures of language proficiency. Existing standardized tests of language ability were administered to evaluate the representativeness of the study sample and to evaluate the relationship of the new measures to existing measures of language proficiency.

Participants

Participants were volunteers who were studying and teaching English as a second language (ESL) in nine locations across sites in Australia, Canada, Hong Kong, Taiwan, and the United States. At each of the data collection sites, ESL students were chosen to represent a range of proficiency levels, graduate and undergraduate status, and Asian and Non-Asian language backgrounds. Each student was paid up to $175 for completing three sessions of testing. In addition, they were sent reports of their scores on two of the tests they took, the TOEFL paper-based test (PBT) and PhonePass. A small number of native English-speaking students were tested at three locations. At the sites where students were recruited, ESL instructors willing to rate the English language skills of their participating students were identified. Instructors were paid $150 to complete the rating instruments.

Materials

The materials consisted of prototype TOEFL measures, a background questionnaire for students, and criterion measures. The criterion measures included alternative measures of language proficiency as well as existing standardized tests of language ability.

PROTOTYPE TOEFL MEASURES

Performance on multiple exemplars of the tasks shown in the blueprint (see Table 4.8) was needed to support analyses of score reliability and generalizability. We therefore developed a prototype computer-based instrument (CBI) composed of listening, reading, speaking, and writing tasks. As suggested by the blueprint, the sections of the CBI were not constructed to provide evidence relevant to the assessment of only a single skill. Therefore, some sections of the CBI included both receptive and productive tasks based on the same stimulus material. The six test sections included listening and writing, reading and writing, independent writing, listening and speaking, reading and speaking, and independent speaking. Based on the tasks in these six sections, we proposed to provide scores for four measures. For example, the score for the writing measure would be based on the writing tasks in the listening and writing section, the reading and writing section, and the independent writing section.

Because of the large number of tasks included in the instrument, we developed two test modules, to be administered in separate sessions. One module included listening, reading, and writing tasks (Sections 1, 2, 3). The other module included listening, reading, and speaking tasks (Sections 4, 5, 6), as illustrated in Table 5.2. Participants were allowed to choose whether to hand-

TABLE 5.2
Composition of Sections of the Computer-Based Prototype of Listening, Reading, Speaking, and Writing Measures

Module and section	Tasks	
	Text	Questions
Module 1. Listening, reading, and writing		
Section 1. Listening/writing: 85 minutes total, including 15 minutes for each written response	3 conversations	6 basic understanding items 3 pragmatic understanding items 5 integrating information items
	3 lectures	7 basic understanding items 3 pragmatic understanding items 4 integrating information items 3 writing prompts
Section 2. Reading/writing: 80 minutes total, including 25 minutes for each written response	2 passages	10 basic comprehension items 2 reading-to-learn items (table completion) 2 writing prompts
Section 3. Independent writing: 30 minutes		1 writing prompt
Module 2. Listening, reading, speaking		
Section 4. Listening/speaking: 65 minutes total (speaking tasks: preparation time 60—90 seconds, speaking time 60–120 seconds per item)	3 conversations	4 basic understanding items 3 pragmatic understanding items 3 integrating information items 3 speaking prompts
	3 lectures	6 basic understanding items 4 pragmatic understanding items 4 integrating information items 3 speaking prompts
Section 5. Reading/speaking: 50 minutes total (speaking tasks: preparation time 90 seconds, speaking time 90 seconds per item)	3 passages	17 basic comprehension items 3 reading-to-learn items (1 summary completion, 2 table completion) 2 speaking prompts
Section 6. Independent speaking: 12 minutes total (speaking tasks: preparation time 30 seconds, speaking time 60 seconds per item)		5 speaking prompts

write or to type their responses to the writing tasks, and they were permitted to take notes throughout the CBI sessions.

Module 1 included listening, reading, and writing tasks. The listening tasks in Module 1 included three conversations and three lectures with accompanying multiple-choice items to assess listening. There were three 15-minute integrated listening/writing tasks. Each of these integrated listening/writing tasks, based on the content in the lecture, was presented immediately following the listening multiple-choice items for each lecture. The reading tasks included two passages with multiple-choice items and a new, selected-response complete-a-table item type. After completion of both reading comprehension sets, integrated reading/writing tasks, based on the content of the reading passages, were presented in a separate section. The reading passages were available for review in the reading/writing section, and 25 minutes were allowed for each reading/writing task. Finally, a 30-minute independent writing task from the Test of Written English™ was included. Total testing time for Module 1 was 3 hours and 15 minutes.

Module 2 included listening, reading, and speaking tasks. Again, the listening tasks included three conversations and three lectures with accompanying listening multiple-choice items. In addition, a speaking task accompanied each listening stimulus, for a total of six listening/speaking tasks. The reading tasks included three reading comprehension passages with multiple-choice items. One passage was followed by a selected-response, complete-a-summary item, and the other two passages were followed by selected-response, complete-a-table items. Speaking tasks were also associated with two of the three passages. For each listening comprehension or reading comprehension set, the speaking tasks immediately followed the listening comprehension or reading comprehension questions. For the reading/speaking tasks, the passage was available when the participant completed the speaking task. Finally, the participants completed five independent speaking tasks. Total testing time for Module 2 was 2 hours and 7 minutes.

Background Questionnaire

The background questionnaire was designed to gather relevant information about the sample in order to estimate the degree of match between the sample and the typical TOEFL population. It asked questions about the test takers' age, gender, objective for taking the TOEFL, and first language.

Test-Based Criterion Measures

A number of test-based criterion measures were administered. The TOEFL paper-based test (PBT) included the following measures: listening comprehension, structure and written expression, and reading comprehension. The total test time was approximately 115 minutes. The 35-minute listening measure, composed of 50 multiple-choice items, required group administration as test takers listen to spoken texts (i.e., dialogues, conversations, mini-lectures) from an audio cassette. The 25-minute structure and written expression measure contained 40 multiple-choice items on English grammatical structure. The 55-minute reading measure contained five texts of about 350 words in length and 50 multiple-choice items. Raw scores for each measure were converted to scaled scores; the scales for listening and structure and written expression were 20–68; for reading, the scale was 20–67.

PhonePass Spoken English Test (SET) 10,[2] an automated listening and speaking assessment that was delivered via a 10-minute phone interaction, was also administered. The tasks included reading sentences aloud, repeating sentences heard, naming opposites, and answering simple questions. Speech samples were automatically scored for listening vocabulary, repeat accuracy, pronunciation, reading fluency, and repeat fluency. These five subscores and an overall score that represented a weighted combination of the subscores were reported.

Measures of Other Criteria

Three additional criterion measures of the test takers' language proficiency were obtained through the use of test takers' judgments about their own ability, their class placements, and their instructors' judgments. Test takers were asked to rate how difficult it was for them to use English for 16 academic tasks on a scale of 1 (not difficult) to 5 (extremely difficult). The task statements were developed, in part, on the basis of the faculty and student survey of the language tasks that are important for success in North American universities (Rosenfeld, Leung, & Oltman, 2001). Site administrators at three North American sites provided information about participants' class placement (i.e., whether or not participants were required to take ESL support classes).

In addition, we developed a questionnaire for ESL instructors to rate the English language skills of students with whom they were familiar. Instructors rated (on a 5-point scale from clearly insufficient to highly developed) the students' abilities in six areas—reading comprehension, listening comprehension, writing about personal experiences and opinions, writing about academic topics, speaking about personal experiences and opinions, and speaking about academic topics.

Procedures

The test instruments were administered in the period from November 2000 through January 2001. Data were collected at nine sites, each of which satisfied the requirements for the research, including the ability to recruit ESL students, the technology required to conduct the study, and professionals willing to serve as site coordinators. Sites were located in Australia, Canada, Hong

Kong, Taiwan, and the United Sates. Pentium-based computers were used for the CBI modules. Access to touch-tone telephones was required for the PhonePass test, and a tape player was necessary for the TOEFL PBT.

Site coordinators were asked to recruit students with varying levels of English language proficiency, based on previous TOEFL scores. If TOEFL scores were not available, or the scores were not current, other criteria, such as instructors' evaluations or course placement, could be used to gauge language ability level. Coordinators were asked to recruit equal numbers of undergraduate and graduate students or equal numbers of students preparing for undergraduate and graduate study in English language institutions within each ability group. For the lower-level and medium-level students at English speaking sites, coordinators were asked to identify ESL instructors who would ask their students to participate and who were willing to rate the English language proficiency of any of their students who participated.

Three test sessions were completed within a 1-month period at all sites. The site coordinator determined the interval between sessions according to the availability of the facilities. During the first session, the participants completed the TOEFL PBT and the background questionnaire. They were given instructions on how to take PhonePass, which was to be completed between the first and second test sessions. Whether PhonePass was administered in a proctored or unproctored setting was left to the discretion of the site coordinator because of differences in the availability of a sufficient number of phones at the testing sites.

The computer-based modules were administered in two subsequent sessions. All participants at a particular site took the two modules in the same order, but the order of the modules was varied across sites. Participant responses were returned to ETS® via the Internet and stored on a server for later scoring.

Instructors' ratings were obtained after students had completed the TOEFL PBT. Site coordinators at English speaking sites distributed the rating instruments to ESL instructors who had agreed to evaluate the students participating in the study. Instructors were asked to review the scales for rating the students, observe the students for a week with the scales in mind, and then complete the scales and return them to the site coordinators.

Sample Demographics

The characteristics of the study participants were inspected to evaluate the degree of fit between the study sample and the population the participants are intended to represent. Descriptive statistics from the demographic questionnaire demonstrated a good match between the study sample and the population of TOEFL test takers. Characteristics of the participants are summarized next to corresponding data representing the larger TOEFL population in general in Table 5.3. Data are reported for participants who completed three sessions of testing (N = 475). The nonnative English speakers who completed all three sessions were tested in Australia (n = 95), Canada (n = 60), Hong Kong (n = 89), Mexico (n = 81), Taiwan (n = 24), and the United Sates (n = 126).

Despite the overall similarities between the participants in the TOEFL population and those of the sample, the participants in this study differed from those of the TOEFL population in three ways. Fewer of the study participants were preparing for or engaging in graduate studies, and more were enrolled in intensive English programs and other programs of study. More Spanish and Chinese speakers were in our sample than in the TOEFL population, reflecting the limited number of testing sites in this study. Finally, the overall English language ability of the sample was slightly higher than that of the TOEFL

TABLE 5.3
Background Characteristics of Study Participants and 2000–2001 TOEFL Population

	Study Participants (N = 475)	TOEFL Population (2000–2001)
Gender		
Female	48.9%	47.0%[a]
Objective		
Bachelors degree	20.5%	30.0%a
Graduate degree	30.2%	52.4%[a]
Intensive English only	22.1%	NA[b]
Other/No response	27.2%	15.3%[a]
First language		
Chinese	38.1%	23.3%[a]
Spanish	21.5%	5.5%[a]
Korean	8.4%	12.2%[a]
Thai	6.7%	2.3%[a]
Japanese	4.6%	13.5%[a]
Other	20.7%	43.2%[a]
TOEFL PBT scaled scores		
Listening—M (SD)	55.9 (6.1)	52.1 (6.4)[c]
Structure—M (SD)	55.9 (6.8)	55.6 (7.2)[c]
Reading—M (SD)	55.5 (7.15)	54.4 (6.7)[c]
Total—M (SD)	557.8 (60.7)	540.0 (61.0)[c]
PhonePass	5.5 (1.09)	NA[b]

[a] Data for 703,021 TOEFL CBT and PBT test takers (combined) tested between July 2000 and June 2001.
[b] Information not available for TOEFL population.
[c] Based on 230,877 test takers who took the TOEFL PBT between July 2000 and June 2001.

population. The standard deviations for the study sample indicate that the participants varied considerably in proficiency.

FINDINGS

Outcomes related to the evaluation inference include the development of a scoring scheme for complex selected-response items; the results of a rater cognition study for speaking; and the statistical characteristics of the prototype measures of listening, reading, speaking, and writing. We describe univariate and multivariate generalizability studies and other analyses of reliability that were conducted to provide support for the generalization inference. In light of theoretical assumptions relevant to explanation, we explore the structure of the prototype assessment by inspecting correlations among the prototype and existing measures of the four skills. Finally, we review evidence germane to the extrapolation inference: the relationship of test scores to self-assessments, academic placement, and instructors' ratings of students.

Outcomes Relevant to Evaluation

Three issues explored at this juncture were how to score complex selected-response items, how appropriate the rubrics were for scoring speaking samples, and whether the measures provided a range of scores sufficient to support decisions about the relative degree of proficiency among test takers. The development of the scoring rules for complex selected-response items drew on an analysis of the implications of different scoring scenarios (dichotomous vs. partial credit). For speaking, Brown, Iwashita, and McNamara (2005) conducted an ancillary study of raters' cognitions as they scored a subset of spoken responses from the central study. Descriptive statistics for the four measures were inspected to establish if the test scores would support norm-referenced decisions.

SCORING COMPLEX SELECTED-RESPONSE TASKS

Based on the experience of creating the reading-to-learn tables during the task prototyping phase, we decided to use tables with either five or seven correct options. We needed to develop a rationale for partial-credit scoring of these complex selected-response items. Test takers had to complete a table by selecting either five or seven targets from a larger set of options. Because of the dependencies among the five to seven targets, we thought a single table should not receive the same weight given to a combination of five or seven independent multiple-choice items. Although these tables were measuring more complex, higher level abilities than the multiple-choice items, each table was focused on a few interrelated elements of the text—fewer elements than one would expect to assess with five or seven discrete multiple-choice items. Thus, we needed to convert the original 5-point and 7-point raw response scales to new scales with fewer score points. We considered several scoring options that might be implemented to achieve this goal.[3]

1. Score each table dichotomously (i.e., right/wrong,[4] wrong = 0, right = 1). This was rejected on several grounds. First, the content experts were in agreement that each of these tables was measuring more than a single multiple-choice item and should receive more credit than that awarded for a single multiple-choice item. Second, there was some concern that once test takers became familiar with the scoring of the new test, there would be little incentive to spend much time on a complex item that was worth no more than a multiple-choice item, and many would choose to spend their time reviewing their answers to other items instead. If this were true, then scores on the tables would reflect not only language ability but also test-taking strategy. While strategy always plays a role, it seemed that this scoring scheme could substantially increase the effects of test-taking strategy and thereby reduce the relationship between test scores and reading ability.

2. Score each table dichotomously, using a scoring scheme in which more than 1 point was awarded for a correct response (right/wrong, wrong = 0, right = 2 or 3). This was rejected because it would likely produce a score distribution with peaks and valleys.

3. Collapse scores to produce the desired score range. For example, on a 5-point table, we could convert raw scores of 0 and 1 to 0, 2 and 3 to 1, 4 and 5 to 2. While this approach has considerable appeal, it also collapses scores throughout the entire scale, which reduces the ability of these complex items to make fine discriminations among moderate to high ability test takers.

4. Set a threshold for each table type, below which no points will be awarded, thus reducing the maximum points per table to an appropriate value. For example, on a 5-point table, we could convert raw scores of 0, 1, or 2 to 0; a score of 3 to 1; a score of 4 to 2; and a score of 5 to 3. Thus, in contrast with Option 3, finer distinctions would be maintained between moderate and higher levels of performance. This is the strategy that we finally adopted for the complex table items. Given the very high probability of getting several targets correct purely by chance (discussed below), this strategy was expected to increase item discrimination for these tables.

Having settled on option four as the most appropriate procedure, we needed to determine where to set a threshold. A simulation was conducted to determine that the probability of getting each score purely by chance. For

TABLE 5.4

Probabilities of Achieving Each Possible Score by Chance Alone on Five- and Seven-Target
Complex Tables and on Five- and Seven-Item Sets of Multiple-Choice Items

Raw Score	Rounded Probability of Scoring at or above each Score Point by Chance Alone					
	2 columns 7 targets	3 columns 7 targets	7 discrete MC items[a]	2 columns 5 targets	3 columns 5 targets	5 discrete MC items[a]
7	< 1%	< 1%	< 1%			
6	1%	< 1%	< 1%			
5	9%	3%	1%	1%	1%	< 1%
4	28%	15%	7%	5%	3%	2%
3	59%	44%	25%	27%	**16%**	10%
2	84%	80%	56%	61%	48%	37%
1	98%	97%	87%	91%	82%	76%
0	100%	100%	100%	100%	100%	100%

Note. Boldface indicates preliminary scoring thresholds, below which no points will be awarded (discussed in text).
[a]Assuming four answer options per item.

complex tables with seven targets, the probability of getting at least one of the seven targets correct purely by chance was more than .97; for tables with five targets, the probability ranged from .82 to .91, depending upon the particular table configuration. The probabilities of getting scores close to the midpoint of the scale were also very high. For example, on tables with two columns, a test taker who responded randomly (without even looking at the item) would be expected to get a score of 2 or higher on the five-target tables and 3 or higher on the seven-target tables about 60% of the time. As shown in Table 5.4, these probabilities were much higher than the chance probabilities of getting comparable numbers of items correct in a set of five or seven multiple-choice items.

The thresholds for the complex table items were set on the basis of consideration of the probability of chance responses at each level. First, for each of the four table types, we determined the cumulative probability of scoring at or above each raw score point (see Table 5.4) by chance alone. After comparing the probability distributions across table types, we decided to set a preliminary threshold at the raw score that a random responder would be expected to reach less than 40% of the time. This produced a threshold of 3 points for each of the five-target tables, and a threshold of 4 points for each of the seven-target tables. Thus, for the five-target tables, any raw score below 3 would be converted to 0, and scores of 3, 4, and 5 would be converted to 1, 2, and 3. For the seven-target tables, anything below 4 would be converted to 0 and scores of 4, 5, 6, and 7 would be converted to 1, 2, 3, and 4, respectively. Next, we considered how much each table was worth in terms of the content and skills being measured. Our initial judgment was that the selected thresholds produced approximately the right number of score points for each of the items. When this approach to scoring was applied to the table items in this study, three of the tables had a maximum score of 4 points, and one table had a maximum score of 3 points.

The scoring issues were simpler for the summary completion items. For the summary completion item in this study, an introductory sentence was provided, and test takers selected three additional sentences from five options. This task was fairly easy, so it was scored dichotomously. However, it was decided that in future versions of this item type, the items would include an additional option and would be worth 0 to 2 points, with no points awarded for selecting one correct response, given the high probability (.5) of this occurring by chance. Both of these analyses helped us to make decisions about evaluation of performance on the complex selected-response tasks called for in the blueprint.

APPRAISALS OF SPEAKING SAMPLES BY ENGLISH LANGUAGE SPECIALISTS

Brown et al. (2005) investigated the appropriateness of the proposed rating scales for speaking in a study of how experienced English language specialist raters judged test-taker responses to both independent and integrated speaking tasks. These specialists provided verbal protocols as they rated a selected sample of test taker responses that previously had been scored holistically. The sample included 200 responses, eight at each of five score levels for five tasks (two independent and three integrated). Brown et al. reported that these raters used four central conceptual categories—linguistic resources, phonology, fluency, and content—to evaluate test taker responses. The investigators noted that the raters' attention to content contrasted with other studies of rater cognition in which raters evaluated general or nonacademic tasks such as interviews. In such cases, the raters focused primarily on linguistic resources.

The profiles or distributions of comments by these raters for the four conceptual categories varied with holistic score level. The raters' attention to phonology and fluency decreased with score level, and attention to linguistic resources and content increased. The profiles or distributions of the raters' comments for the four conceptual categories for the task types were not as consistently differentiated as they were for score level. Content was as important a focus for the independent tasks as for the integrated ones. However, the criteria the raters used to evaluate the content of independent and integrated tasks did differ. For independent tasks, raters referred to the relevance and sophistication of ideas, while for integrated tasks, the judges referred to the inclusion of key information and organization of ideas. Finally, Brown et al. (2005) compared the draft descriptions for the holistic scales with the raters' conceptual categories and found much overlap.

This study demonstrated that raters attended to more than grammatical competence and phonology when assessing these speech samples—they attended to content as well. This attention to content provided support for the rationale for including these tasks on the test—the tasks would be more representative of the academic domain where *what* is said is as important as *how* it is said. The variety of features that raters mentioned was consistent with the draft ETS rating scales. However, the attention to content and variability in what different raters thought was appropriate indicated a need to provide raters in the future with an outline of what content was key when they evaluated different tasks.

Prototype TOEFL Measures

The descriptive statistics for the prototype measures were examined to determine if the tasks were of an appropriate level of difficulty overall and if there was sufficient variation in test taker performance to differentiate levels of proficiency among test takers. Table 5.5 presents the summary statistics for the prototype measures of the four skills.

For a variety of reasons, many of the speech samples were lost or were unscorable. For example, about 25% of the reading/speaking samples were not scored because the participants read directly from the passage rather than constructing their own response. Other reasons samples were not scored included participants electing not to respond, poor audio quality, missing files, and mechanical problems. Because the greatest loss of data was associated with the reading/speaking tasks, scores on these tasks were not included in the speaking score total in some analyses.

Prototype listening measure   Initially, 52 listening comprehension items were associated with six campus conversations and six lectures, but after we inspected the item statistics, two of the items were eliminated. The lectures and conversations were based on samples of actual campus conversations and lectures in the TOEFL corpus (Biber et al., 2004). The reliability of this measure was .85.[5]

TABLE 5.5
Summary Statistics for Unscaled Scores for Prototype Measures of Listening, Reading, Speaking, and Writing

Measures	N	Mean	SD	Min.	Max.	N Items	Total Points
Listening	472	35.3	7.74	11.0	49.0	50	50
Reading	476	23.1	8.54	5.0	40.0	29	40
Speaking	334	35.8	8.94	15.5	55.0	11	55
Writing	457	16.5	4.69	6.0	29.5	6	30

Although the idea that an analysis of task difficulty would provide a basis for a proficiency scale no longer appeared practicable overall, the descriptive statistics for listening revealed that the hypothesized differences on difficulty received some support. The hypothesis was that basic understanding items would be the easiest, pragmatic understanding items would be of intermediate difficulty, and connecting information items would be the most difficult. This hierarchy was supported by results showing that basic understanding items ($n = 23$, $M = .75$, $SD = .16$) were significantly easier than pragmatic understanding items ($n = 13$, $M = .70$, $SD = .18$, $t = 9.07$, $df = 471$, $p < .001$) and connecting information items ($n = 14$, $M = .65$, $SD = .18$, $t = 18.2$, $df = 472$, $p < .001$). Pragmatic understanding items were also easier than connecting information items ($t = 7.81$, $df = 474$, $p < .001$). Nevertheless, there was a lot of overlap in the distribution of item difficulties for the three item types, suggesting that it would not be easy to control item difficulty more precisely.

Prototype reading measure   Twenty-nine reading items were based on reading passages, which were longer and more complex in organization than the passages in the then existing TOEFL. At least one of the new selected-response item types, either summary-completion or table-completion, was included for each passage. After inspection of the item statistics for the 27 basic comprehension items, 3 were eliminated. The basic comprehension items, which had a four-option multiple-choice format, were scored dichotomously, as was the summary completion item. The reading-to-learn table items were scored according to the rationale discussed previously. Three of these items were scored using a 0–4 scale and one using a 0–3 scale. Thus, the maximum reading score of 40 points reported in Table 5.5 is based on 24 dichotomously scored regular multiple-choice items, 1 dichotomously scored summary completion item, and 4 partial-credit table items. The reliability of this reading measure was .86.

Prototype speaking measure   Of 13 speaking tasks included in the study, 5 were independent speaking tasks, 6 listening/speaking tasks, and 2 reading/speaking tasks. Experienced raters scored the speech samples using a 5-point holistic scale for each task. Each sample was scored by two raters independently, and if the raters disagreed by more than 1 point or if one rater was unable to score the sample, a third rater scored the sample. Raters were also asked to comment on problems they encountered in rating the samples.

Many of the speaking samples were lost or unscorable, particularly reading/speaking tasks because some test takers read sections of the passage aloud rather than develop their own responses. Therefore, the reading/speaking tasks were not included in the preliminary analyses. There were 334 participants who had scores on the other 11 speaking tasks. The mean scores and the score distributions for these 11 speaking tasks are presented in Table 5.6. The new integrated listening speaking tasks were similar to independent

TABLE 5.6
Means, Standard Deviations, and Score Distributions for Speaking Tasks (n = 334)

Speaking tasks	M	SD	Percentage of Scores at each Score Level								
			1.0	1.5	2.0	2.5	3.0	3.5	4.0	4.5	5.0
Listening/speaking											
Task 1	3.17	0.99	3.0	4.2	10.5	14.4	24.0	18.0	9.0	9.6	7.5
Task 2	3.40	0.80	0	1.2	5.1	11.7	31.1	19.8	15.0	8.7	7.5
Task 3	3.18	0.99	3.3	4.5	10.2	13.5	22.5	17.1	14.4	7.8	6.9
Task 4	3.07	1.07	5.1	6.9	11.7	13.8	22.2	13.5	10.5	8.7	7.8
Task 5	3.01	1.13	6.9	7.5	13.5	12.3	21.0	12.6	9.3	8.1	9.0
Task 6	3.33	0.97	2.1	1.8	10.8	12.9	21.6	15.9	15.6	10.5	9.0
Independent speaking											
Task 7	3.32	0.92	1.2	3.0	7.2	13.5	27.5	17.1	12.6	9.0	9.0
Task 8	3.30	0.87	0.3	1.8	9.6	14.4	26.6	16.8	15.0	8.4	7.2
Task 9	3.37	0.93	0.9	4.8	5.1	12.0	25.7	16.5	15.9	10.5	8.7
Task 10	3.27	0.94	0.9	3.0	10.2	17.1	22.2	14.1	15.9	9.0	7.8
Task 11	3.39	0.91	0	2.4	9.0	13.2	22.8	18.9	14.7	9.3	9.9

speaking tasks in difficulty (with average means 3.2 and 3.3, respectively) but the variability was somewhat larger for the integrated listening/speaking tasks than for the independent speaking tasks (with average standard deviations of .99 and .91, respectively). The reliability of the speaking measure, based on these 11 tasks, was .95.

Prototype writing measure   The participants completed six writing tasks, five of which were based on listening materials or reading passages, and one of which was an independent task from the Test of Written English (TWE®). The TWE rubric was used for the independent writing sample. The TWE rating scale has 6 points, but this scale effectively functions as a 5-point scale because a score of 1 is seldom given. Rubrics had been developed during previous pilot testing for the five integrated writing tasks, and a 5-point scale was used to score the integrated tasks. Two raters scored each writing sample and, if the raters disagreed by more than 1 point, a third rater scored the sample. The score given to each sample in the preliminary analyses represented the mean of the two ratings. In the case of third ratings, either the mean of the two closest ratings or—if the third rating fell in between the two other ratings, the middle rating—was used.

The mean scores and the score distributions for the six writing tasks are presented in Table 5.7. For this analysis, the 6-point TWE scale was converted to a 5-point scale by treating scores of 2 or lower as equal to 1 and subtracting 1 from the remainder of the scores. This made it easier to compare the relative difficulty of the independent and integrated tasks. Some of the new integrated writing tasks were more difficult than the independent writing tasks. The mean scores for the integrated reading/writing tasks and one of the listening/writing tasks were nearly one standard deviation lower than the mean scores for the independent writing task and one of the other listening/writing tasks. In contrast with the speaking tasks, there was more variation in difficulty associated with the writing tasks. The reliability of the writing measure, consisting of six tasks, was .88.

SUMMARY

The descriptive statistics reveal that the participants understood the task requirements and were able to fulfill them with varying degrees of success. For all four measures, a wide range of scores was observed, a requisite for creating scales that would differentiate among test takers at different levels of proficiency. The distributions of the listening/speaking and independent speaking tasks were approximately normal, with the distribution centered at the midpoint of the scoring scale. There was more variation in difficulty among the listening/speaking tasks than among the independent tasks. Overall, the writing tasks varied more in difficulty than the speaking tasks. The two reading/writing tasks were the most difficult, the independent writing task was of intermediate difficulty, and the listening/writing tasks were variable in difficulty.

Three observations raised concerns that would have to be addressed in further development. One was the problem, also noted in the previous task prototyping phase, of copying from the reading passages if they were available

TABLE 5.7
Means, Standard Deviations, and Score Distributions for Writing Tasks (n = 473–493)

Writing task	M	SD	Percentage of Scores at each Score Level								
			1.0	1.5	2.0	2.5	3.0	3.5	4.0	4.5	5.0
Reading/writing											
Task 1	2.42	1.01	16.1	12.2	17.5	19.7	12.6	9.6	8.5	2.6	1.2
Task 2	2.31	0.96	17.0	15.8	16.6	19.1	13.3	8.8	7.2	1.4	0.6
Listening/writing											
Task 3	3.20	0.95	2.2	4.5	10.6	13.1	21.1	20.2	12.9	9.8	5.5
Task 4	2.80	1.11	9.5	10.5	14.8	13.6	15.8	15.0	9.7	6.3	4.7
Task 5	2.49	1.00	12.3	14.1	16.4	18.4	15.4	11.3	8.0	2.5	1.6
Independent writing											
Task 6	3.14	0.90	2.3	3.6	9.7	16.7	24.5	18.8	12.9	6.8	4.7

when related speaking and writing tasks were completed. Raters would need training and guidance on how to score responses that varied in the amount of verbatim information from listening and reading materials. Another was the uncontrolled variation in task difficulty for the integrated writing and speaking tasks. Measures composed primarily of performance tasks are difficult to equate because test equating over many successive test forms requires some exposure of the tasks. Because only a few constructed-response items appear on a test form, they are usually highly memorable, and the exposure necessary for equating poses security risks. Thus, other evidence of task comparability across forms (e.g., task specifications and rubrics, consistency in task difficulty, and rater reliability) are used to support the comparability of scores from different test forms. Finally, the score distribution for the reading/writing tasks and one of the listening/writing tasks indicated that many of the participants, who were somewhat more proficient than the overall population, found these tasks to be difficult. Whether these tasks would be of an appropriate level of difficulty for the population would require further investigation.

Outcomes Relevant to Generalizability

The measures in this study were composed of many more items or tasks, which were differentiated with respect to task type, than the blueprint called for within the 3½ to 4 hour time frame proposed for the new TOEFL. For the reading measure, any subset of tasks chosen for the new TOEFL would be expected to accurately reflect the larger set because the reading passages were varied in content, but not differentiated with respect to register (e.g., materials sampled from academic textbooks and articles). For the listening measure, in contrast, the differences in the registers (conversations vs. lectures) that test takers heard on the test were potentially a source of unpredictable variation in test scores that would negatively affect generalization to a single universe of tasks. Therefore, we sought to determine how different configurations of tasks would affect the internal consistency of a listening measure.

Scores on the speaking and writing measures were each subject to variation due to tasks, task types, and raters. These measures included both independent and integrated tasks. The different task types were associated with different types of input (e.g., a stand-alone prompt, a lecture, a reading passage). Potentially each of these task types might be tapping a somewhat distinct aspect of speaking or writing, and if a composite score were based on heterogeneous tasks or task types, its reliability would be compromised. Furthermore, inconsistency among raters when rating tasks could also contribute to less reliable scores. Factors that would improve reliability, such as increasing the number of tasks and the number of ratings per task, add to the cost of scoring and the time required to complete the tests. Therefore, the speaking and writing measures needed to be designed in a way that balanced the impact of these many factors in an optimal way.

To address these issues, Lee (Lee, 2005; Lee & Kantor, 2005) used generalizability (G) theory (Brennan, 2001; Cronbach, Gleser, Nanda, & Rajaratnam, 1972). G-theory is a statistical procedure for evaluating assessment designs that have multiple sources of error (e.g., a design in which test takers take multiple tasks that are rated by multiple raters) through a two-staged investigation including *generalizability* (G) and *decision* (D) studies. In the G-study, the relative contribution of each source of variation to the total variance in scores can be estimated and evaluated, whereas the impact of various changes in the measurement design (e.g., different numbers of tasks or raters) on score reliability is investigated in the D-study. G-theory offers a superior alternative to internal consistency and interrater reliability measures in classical test theory (CTT) when task and rater reliability need to be examined within a single analysis. G-theory allows us to estimate variance components associated with effects involving persons, tasks, and raters and their interactions and to disentangle multiple sources of measurement error.

Reliability of the Listening Measure

CTT estimates of internal consistency were computed to determine how different configurations of text type (conversation or lecture) and number of items would impact the reliability of the listening measure. The listening measure in this study was made up of six conversations and six lectures, for a total of 50 items. Given that the listening measure of the new TOEFL was unlikely to have more than 30 to 36 questions, an analysis was conducted to estimate the impact of different configurations of text types/numbers of items on reliability. The data were used to simulate five different test configurations, which were composed of tasks with different text type (conversations or lectures) and a varying number of items per text, to estimate the reliability of each configuration.

Two procedures for simulating these different configurations were used. Seven listening comprehension sets, composed of three conversations and four lectures and associated multiple-choice items, were selected to serve as the base configuration. The number of items associated with each text was manipulated in two ways: (a) by adding items from another five sets not used in the base configuration and (b) by counting some of the items more than once within a set in the base configuration. Table 5.8 contains the estimated reliability results for the five configurations. In the calculations, the set of items related to the each of the listening texts was treated as a testlet and scored as a unit to capture the dependency within each set. Results for configurations of the measure are presented in Table 5.8. For example, configuration A consisted of two conversations and four lectures with five items per text for a total of 30 items. Configuration E had three conversations with five items each and four lectures with seven items per lecture, for a total of 43 items.

TABLE 5.8

The Reliabilities of Alternative Configurations of Text Types and Number of Items per Text for a Listening Comprehension Measure

Text type	Configuration					
	Base	A	B	C	D	E
Conversation 1	5	5	5	5	5	5
Conversation 2	4	5	5	5	5	5
Conversation 3	4			5	5	5
Lecture 1	5	5	6	6	6	7
Lecture 2	5	5	6	6	6	7
Lecture 3	5	5	6	6	7	7
Lecture 4	5	5	6	6	7	7
Total items	33	30	34	39	41	43
rp[a]		.78–.80	.78–.82	.79–.84	.79–.85	.79–.85
r[b]		.80	.82	.84	.85	.85

[a] A range is reported for each configuration, with the lower value derived when items within a set in the base configuration were counted more than once to reach the desired number. The upper value was derived when items from sets not used in the base configuration were added to items in the base configuration to reach the desired number.

[b] A decision was made to use the upper value as the best estimate of reliability. When an item is counted more than once in the calculations, there is no covariance between the item and itself, resulting in a reliability estimate that must be too low.

The overall result was that particular configurations had little impact on score reliability over and above the impact associated with the number of items. Thus, the configuration with two conversations and two lectures that was specified in the blueprint needed to be increased to include more conversations or more lectures. However, in terms of reliability, it didn't matter which of the two were increased, provided a sufficient number of items could be administered within the 40 minutes allotted. Decisions about the number of conversations versus lectures would need to be made on the basis of other factors, such as the time needed to administer different configurations or the relative difficulty of creating more stimuli versus the difficulty of creating more items per stimuli.

Generalizability Analysis for Speaking Scores

For the Speaking measure the questions we addressed were more complex because of the many factors that could influence generalizability of measures composed of complex, time-consuming performance tasks. Potential sources of variability in scores included test taker ability, the leniency or harshness of ratings, inconsistency in ratings, variations in task difficulty, and variation in test taker performance across tasks. The first of these factors was the intended target of the assessment, while the other factors, if uncontrolled, could reduce the reliability in the measurement of test taker ability. Therefore, the impact of these factors on score reliability was examined by modeling different possibilities for the design of the speaking measure. Four particular issues were addressed by Lee (2005):

1. What is the relative contribution of different measurement facets to score variability?
2. How do various assessment scenarios for the total test (i.e., the number of tasks and ratings, rating designs) affect score reliability?
3. How does the composition of a composite measure (i.e., different configurations of task types and the number of tasks within a task type) affect score reliability?
4. Is reporting a composite score composed of scores on different task types justified psychometrically?

Generalizability analyses were conducted on the data from participants who had scores for at least two tasks of each of the three types (listening/speaking, reading/speaking, and independent speaking) because we were interested in the effects of task types. Two listening/speaking tasks based on academic conversations were excluded from the analyses because, upon further evaluation of the responses, it was determined that they did not provide enough substance for spoken responses. Therefore, this analysis was conducted on the scores of 261 participants on 11 tasks (4 listening/speaking, 2 reading/speaking, and 5 independent tasks). The speaking responses were rated on a scale of 1 to 5 by two independent raters from a pool of 22 raters.

Two sets of analyses, univariate and multivariate, were conducted on this data. Both univariate and multivariate models have been developed within the same G-theory framework, but the models differ in that the former is suited to analyzing scores from a single test in which content categories are not differentiated as levels of a fixed facet, whereas the latter can also handle scores from multiple subsections of the test simultaneously by differentiating each of the subsections as a level of the fixed facet (see Brennan, 2001). In the univariate analysis, Lee (2005) examined the effect of different rating designs on score reliability without considerations of task type. In the multivariate analysis, Lee focused on the impact of different configurations of task types, the number of tasks within task types, and the number of ratings on score reliability. In both of these analyses, the relative contributions of different aspects of the assessment to score variability were noted.

In the D-studies in both the univariate and multivariate analyses, generalizability and dependability coefficients were estimated for scenarios in which the number of tasks was varied from 1 to 12 and the number of ratings was either 1 or 2. The discussion below reports the results for the generalizability coefficient, analogous to a reliability coefficient in CCT, which is useful for evaluating the appropriateness of using a test score for norm-referenced decisions, such as a relative comparison of individuals for selection.

Contribution of different measurement facets to score variability   The univariate and multivariate G-studies provided estimates of the proportion of total variance associated with different measurement facets for single observations. The D-studies provided estimates of the proportion of total variance associated with different measurement facets for multiple observations of tasks and ratings. A question of central interest in the D-studies was the comparison of an efficient design in which responses to 5 tasks each received a single rating versus a liberal design in which responses to 12 tasks were each rated twice.

In both the univariate and multivariate G-studies, the greatest source of variation in scores (51.3% to 56.3%) was due to differences among test takers, a necessary condition for assessing individual differences in speaking reliably. Little variance was associated with the task main effect (.3% to 1.7%), indicating that the speaking tasks did not vary greatly in difficulty. The effects of ratings and task-by-rating interactions also were minimal. However, the person-by-task interactions, which accounted for between 11.4% and 17.3% of the total variance in both analyses, indicated that the rank-ordering of test takers varied for different tasks. This is consistent with the results in many other studies. Effects associated with tasks and person-by-task interactions account for a greater portion of score variance than do effects associated with raters or ratings and their interactions with persons (Brennan & Johnson, 1995; Gao, Shavelson, & Baxter, 1994; Linn, Burton, DeStefano, & Hanson, 1996; Miller & Linn, 2000; Shavelson, Baxter, & Gao, (1993).

The person-by-task-by-rating interaction plus undifferentiated error effect also accounted for a large proportion of the total variance for a single observation in the G-studies (i.e., about 20% to 28%).

As expected, the proportion of variance associated with test takers increased as the number of observations did. In the univariate D-study, about 82% of the total variance was explained by differences among test takers for the 5-task-and-single-rating scenario, whereas about 93% was explained for the 12-task-and-double-rating situation. The relative proportion in the total variance of the person-by-task-by-rating interaction plus undifferentiated error variance component was greatly reduced—from 28% to 9%—when the number of tasks was increased to 5 for the single rating scenario. Nevertheless, when the number of tasks and ratings were further increased to 12 and 2, respectively, this proportion decreased to 2%, which could be seen as a small change for adding 7 more tasks and one more rating per essay.

Effect of the number of tasks and ratings on score reliability   Lee (2005) examined the impact of the number of tasks (1 to12) and the number of ratings (1 or 2) on the generalizability coefficient in the univariate D-study. For a single rating scenario, Lee found a very large increase (.31) in the generalizability coefficient—from .52 to .83—as the number of tasks increased from 1 to 5. However, increasing the number of tasks from 5 to 12 resulted in a much smaller gain of .07 in the generalizability coefficient. Similarly, a relatively small difference in the coefficient was observed for single versus double ratings. In the case of 5 tasks, an increase of .05 between the single-rating and double-rating scenarios was observed for the generalizability coefficient. Furthermore, when the number of ratings was held constant (e.g., 2 tasks × 2 ratings each versus 4 tasks × 1 rating each), increasing the number of tasks was found to improve generalizability more than increasing the number of raters, a result consistent with previous findings (e.g., Breland, Bridgeman, & Fowles, 1999).

Effect of the composition of a composite measure on score reliability The multivariate D-study allowed Lee (2005) to assess the impact on reliability of different configurations in the number of listening-speaking, reading-speaking, and independent speaking tasks for a measure of a fixed length. For example, a total number of five tasks could result from different combinations in the number of tasks types, such as one listening/speaking, one reading/speaking, and three independent speaking tasks versus two listening/speaking, two reading/speaking, and one independent speaking tasks. When Lee examined six different combinations of task types for a composite measure of a fixed length of five tasks, he found generalizability coefficients ranging from .82 to .86. These differences in the range of generalizability coefficients were deemed small enough to suggest that other factors, such as content coverage, should be given more weight in deciding the final composition of the measure.

Justification for reporting a composite score In the multivariate analyses, the universe (i.e., true) score correlations among the subsections were very high (listening/speaking and reading/speaking =.98; reading/speaking and independent speaking = .95; listening/speaking and independent speaking = .89), justifying the computation of a composite speaking score based on these three tasks types.

Summary The univariate and multivariate G-studies established that, for a single observation, the proportion of variance associated with test takers was relatively large and that proportions of variance associated with tasks, ratings, and the task-by-rating interaction were minimal. These results indicate that the tasks were primarily assessing differences in test takers' abilities, that the tasks did not vary greatly in difficulty, that the ratings of tasks did not vary in severity, and that the ratings did not vary for different tasks. However, the person-by-task interactions were also noticeable, indicating that the rank ordering of test takers was somewhat inconsistent across different tasks, a common finding in research on performance tasks. Nevertheless, the univariate D-study illustrated how the proportion of variance associated with persons increased and that associated with the person-by-task interaction decreased as the number of tasks was increased, leading to a more reliable assessment of test takers' abilities.

A particular focus of the univariate D-study was to determine the reliability of rating scenarios composed of different numbers of task and ratings. Large increases in reliability were reported as the number of tasks increased from 1 to 5, and relatively smaller increases were found as the number of tasks increased from 5 to 12. Furthermore, when the number of ratings was fixed, scenarios that included more tasks and single ratings were more reliable than scenarios that included fewer tasks and double ratings.

Finally, the multivariate analyses indicated that combining different task types on a single speaking measure was justified psychometrically and that differences in the number of tasks within task types for a fixed test length had small effects on reliability. In sum, these results indicated that a speaking measure composed of five tasks that were rated only once would be reasonably reliable. Another implication of the findings was that the composition of the measure in terms of different task types could be made on the basis of other factors, such as content domain coverage and task development effort.

Generalizability Analysis for Writing Scores

Like the speaking scores, the writing scores were potentially affected by many factors, so Lee and Kantor (2005) conducted univariate and multivariate generalizability analyses to address for writing the same issues as Lee (2005) had addressed for speaking.

One difference between the analyses for speaking and for writing was that the writing analysis compared the effects of using *raters*, as opposed to *ratings*, as a facet in the analysis. This was to address another rating design issue—the impact of a rating design in which each writing task was scored only once and each writing sample from a particular test taker was scored by a different rater.[6] The analyses for speaking did not distinguish between a single-rating scenario in which some or all the responses from an test taker would be scored by the same rater and one in which each response from an test taker would be scored by a different rater. To conduct analyses relevant to this rating design, it was necessary to obtain additional ratings of the essays. Six raters who had participated in the original rating of the essays were asked to re-rate the essays from a subgroup of 162 participants so that each essay was rated by six raters. This resulted in a complete data matrix for a fully crossed person-by-task-by-rater design.

Lee and Kantor (2005) carried out a univariate analysis of this data to evaluate the impact of different rating designs on score reliability. The complete data matrix allowed the researchers to evaluate the impact of number of tasks, number of raters, and a rating procedure in which different raters scored each sample from a particular test taker. The original rating procedure did not ensure that different raters scored each writing sample for a particular test taker. This procedure was attractive because it would ensure that a test taker's responses would be seen by more than one rater even though each response was rated only once.

Lee and Kantor (2005) also carried out multivariate analyses to investigate the impact of different configurations of task types and number of tasks within task type on reliability and to determine if a composite score based on different task types was justified psychometrically. The fact that there was only one independent writing task meant that this data was less than ideal for evaluating a writing measure that might be composed of listening/writing, reading/writing, and independent writing tasks because more than one example of each task type was required for the multivariate analysis. Therefore, these researchers conducted two multivariate analyses—one for a measure composed of listening/writing and reading/writing sections and a second for a measure composed of listening/writing and reading/writing plus independent writing sections.

Contribution of different measurement facets to score variability   In the univariate and multivariate G-studies of the re-rated data, the largest variance components were associated with persons, explaining about 43.4% to 55.4% of the total variance. Other large effects that were evident included task main effects (0.8% to 10.2%). The smallest of these task main effects was for the reading/writing section in the first multivariate analysis, reflecting the fact that the two reading/writing tasks were of equal difficulty. However, when the reading/writing tasks and the independent task were combined into a section in second multivariate analyses, the task main effect was larger because of the difference in difficulty between the two task types (see Table 5.7).

Person-by-task interactions (15.2% to 17.0%) were large and of the same magnitude in all the analyses as were person-by-task-by-rater interactions plus undifferentiated error effects (17.4% to 26.5%). These effects indicated that test takers were not rank-ordered in the same way, not only for different tasks, but also for different task-by-rater pairs. In the multivariate analyses, the relative proportion of variance for this interaction was larger for the sections that included the reading/writing tasks than for the sections that included the listening/writing tasks in both the first analysis (26.5% vs. 17.4%) and the second analysis (24.2% vs. 17.4 %). The researchers suggested that this difference might have reflected difficulties in rating essays in which the test takers copied phrases and sentences verbatim from the reading text. Although raters were instructed to assign the lowest scores to essays that included extensive verbatim material, it may have been difficult to apply this criterion consistently.

The effects associated with raters (raters, person-by-raters, and task-by-raters) were very small, ranging from 1% to 2.3%.

Effect of assessment scenarios on reliability Having a complete data matrix in which each rater rated all the responses from each test taker allowed Lee and Kantor (2005) to investigate the generalizability of scores for different assessment scenarios, given a particular rating design. As noted previously, the rating design of interest was one in which each response would be rated only once but, for any test taker, each response was rated by a different rater.

The researchers reported that, when the number of total ratings was held constant, the reliability estimates were higher for the single rating scenario than for the double rating scenario. For example, the generalizability coefficient for one task rated by two raters was .59 while that for two tasks, each rated once, was .70.

Effect of the composition of a composite measure on score reliability In the multivariate analyses, the estimates of the reliability of measures composed of different types of writing tasks did not vary for different configurations when the number of tasks was fixed. For example, the generalizability coefficients for four different configurations of three task types were between .77 and .80. These results parallel those for listening and speaking in that they indicate that the composition of a measure with respect to task type had little impact on reliability or generalizability other than that associated with number of tasks.

Justification for reporting a composite score Finally, in both multivariate analyses, the universe correlation between sections was greater than .90, providing justification for reporting a composite score based on different task types.

Summary Overall patterns regarding the relative effects of persons, tasks, and raters on writing scores were consistent with the results of the analyses of the speaking scores and many other studies of performance assessments. The largest source of variation in scores was associated with individual differences in writing ability as measured by these tasks. As has been found in many other studies, relatively large person-by-task interactions in the G-study indicated that persons were not rank-ordered consistently across tasks. Although *raters* (rather than *ratings*) were used in the analyses of writing, this source of variance was still small overall. This increased our confidence in the results of the speaking analyses, in which *ratings* was used as a measurement facet.

Other implications of these analyses were consistent with those found for speaking. When the number of total ratings is held constant, the reliability estimates favored single rating scenarios. Furthermore, a rating scenario in which each response from a test taker would be rated by a different rater was explored in the writing analyses. This rating scenario may have advantages from both sampling and cost perspectives. From the perspective of sampling, the more tasks that are administered, the better the coverage of the domain will be. And if each response by a test taker is scored by a different rater, better sampling of raters for individual test takers is assured. From a cost perspective, there would be savings if task development costs are less than the costs of multiple ratings per task.

The results of the multivariate analyses for both speaking and writing demonstrated that the configuration of the measure with respect to different tasks types did not affect reliability over and above the number of tasks included and that the inclusion of different task types in the measure was justified psychometrically.

Nevertheless, the reliability of the writing measure is not likely to be as high as the speaking measure because, given testing time constraints, no more than two or three such tasks are likely to be administered for writing. Nor is it likely to be as reliable as a measure composed of many multiple-choice questions such as the SWE measure (cf. Table 5.9, α =.87). However, two effects evident in the multivariate analyses might lead to further improvements in reliability with further investigation. For one, relatively larger effects were associated with tasks and in particular, with listening/writing tasks for writing. A better understanding of sources of task difficulty could reduce the systematic variation in scores associated with this factor. A second area of concern is the relatively large proportion of the variance associated with the person-by-task-by-rater interaction for reading/writing. Perhaps either raters need clearer directions or more training to score such tasks consistently, or the administration conditions for the task should be reconsidered.

Outcomes Relevant to Explanation

As noted in Chapter 1, a strong theory of language proficiency is more of an ideal than a reality at present. The test design process, however, provides an opportunity to refine and clarify construct theories and how they are realized in test performance. Therefore, we examined the structural relationships among the test measures and their relationships to other measures of language proficiency in light of an assumption that different aspects of language proficiency might be assessed by different methods. We also investigated how the internal structure of the prototype test corresponded to theoretical views about the structure of language abilities. In their study of rater cognition described previously, Brown et al. (2005) conducted an analysis of the discourse features of responses to the speaking tasks to determine if these features varied with proficiency level and task type in accordance with theoretical assumptions.

Analysis of Test Structure and Relationships to Other Standardized Measures of Language Proficiency

The two questions relevant to theoretical issues concerned the relationship of the prototype measures of four skills to other standardized tests of these skills and the internal structure of the prototype instrument. To gain insight into these issues, we explored the correlations among measures presented in a multitrait-multimethod matrix in a heuristic manner (Campbell & Fiske, 1959). Table 5.9 presents the correlations among measures of the four skills—reading, listening, writing, and speaking—on the two methods of measurement for a sample of 351 participants for whom we had data on all the prototype measures. The reliabilities for each of the language skill measures are presented in parentheses along the diagonal of the upper right and lower left matrix. The correlations in Table 5.9 have been corrected for measurement error because, for this type of analysis, we are interested in what the correlations would be among the measures in the absence of measurement error.

Relationships between the prototype measures and other language tests One of the beliefs that motivated the design of a new TOEFL was that language proficiency includes the ability for use as well as static linguistic knowledge. As a consequence, productive tasks were to be included on the test. Evidence that some of the prototype measures assessed language ability

TABLE 5.9
Disattenuated Correlations among Four Language Skills Measured by Two
Different Methods (N = 321)

		TOEFL PBT/PhonePass				Prototype Measures			
		Read	Listen	SWE[a]	PhonePass[b]	Read	Listen	Write	Speak
TOEFL PBT/ PhonePass	Reading	(.83)							
	Listening	.83	(.87)						
	SWE[a]	.91	.79	(.87)					
	PhonePass	.64	.79	.66	1.00[b]				
Prototype measures	Reading	.95	.80	.83	.64	(.86)			
	Listening	.87	.94	.82	.78	.93	(.84)		
	Writing	.80	.75	**.79**	.75	.87	.89	(.86)	
	Speaking	.69	.80	.73	**.84**	.78	.87	.89	(.96)

Note. Boldface indicates correlation between the same language skills measured by different instruments.
[a] SWE = structure and written expression.
[b] A measure of internal consistency could not be computed for PhonePass. If a reliability of 1 is assumed, the corrected correlations between PhonePass and other measures represent conservative, lower-bound estimates.

in a different way than did existing tests would support this belief. The correlations in bold along the diagonal in the lower left section of the matrix are pertinent to this issue. These are the correlations between the same language skills measured by different instruments. For reading and listening, these correlations are very high and are somewhat higher than their correlations with other language skills. This suggests there was no method effect for these two measures, a result that was not surprising given that there was much overlap in the types of items on both instruments. A different pattern is evident for the structure and written expression measure and the prototype writing measure. The correlation between the former and the latter is the lowest of the same skill/different method pairs and is no higher than the correlations between the structure and written expression measure and the prototype reading or listening measures. Thus, the prototype writing measure, composed of constructed-response tasks, did appear to assess writing ability in a way that was different from a multiple-choice test of knowledge of structure and written expression. The correlation between PhonePass and the prototype speaking measure was also quite high, although not as high as those for the measures of listening and reading. Again, this was not surprising because PhonePass and the prototype speaking measure were both productive tasks.

Internal structure of the prototype instrument   Historically, debates about the structure of language proficiencies contrasted a unitary competence model, in which one general factor was expected to explain a large amount of common variance among language tasks, with a divisible competence model, in which specific, independent factors were associated with individual skills crossed with linguistic components. As theorizing about language proficiency matured and statistical methodology became more sophisticated, these positions were synthesized into the current consensus that language proficiency is best described as a hierarchy with a common factor presiding over some specific factors (Sasaki, 1999). While this consensus implicitly underlays the communicative perspective that informed the conceptualization of the new TOEFL, the implications of this model for score reporting were a source of contention. On the one hand, some argued that this theoretical position implied a single test score would be most appropriate. On the other hand, some stakeholders desired separate scores for the four skills. This conflict between theory and practical needs motivated empirical investigation about the degree of commonality among the four skills and circumstances under which four separate skill scores would provide useful information. Given the test design we were envisioning, there were two factors that might increase the convergence among the measures of the four skills and one factor that might reduce it. The factors that might increase convergence were (a) using common stimulus materials for the receptive and productive tasks and (b) using more authentic academic materials and tasks. A factor that might moderate convergence among the measures was response format because the receptive skills were assessed by selected-response formats and the productive skills by constructed-response formats.

What would the structure of a test that included paired-skills tasks look like? For reading, listening, and writing measures, scores on the TOEFL PBT and on the new tasks represented the different methods. For speaking, the different methods were PhonePass and a score based on the new speaking tasks.

One of the most interesting results evident in Table 5.9 is that the correlations among all four skills are higher for the prototype measures than for the existing instruments, possibly because of construct-relevant factors such as the fact that the new tasks were designed to assess a common core of language abilities—for example, discourse competence—that contribute to performance in all four skill areas. The tasks have greater overlap in terms of type of required abilities. Some speaking and writing tasks depend on comprehension of academic materials, a requirement not present in the TOEFL PBT.

Other potential explanations for the high correlations are the similar aspects of test method among the prototype tasks, such as content overlap. Most of the writing tasks were based on the same materials as the reading and listening tasks, and many of the speaking tasks were based on listening materials. However, the correlations between skills tested with nonoverlapping content (listening/reading and writing/speaking) also are highly correlated. Other construct-irrelevant factors could be novelty effects, motivation, or computer familiarity. Some test takers may have responded positively to the challenge of new, more complex tasks, while others may have become anxious or less motivated, given that there were no consequences for lack of effort. Other sample-dependent effects, such as language learning and environmental experiences, may have also affected the relationships among skills.

This examination of data relevant to the issue of test structure was only preliminary, and the issue would be revisited in subsequent phases of development. The difficulty of interpreting the results of this analysis not only reflects methodological factors but also illustrates the theoretical ambiguities about the degree to which measures of specific skills should correlate.

An Analysis of Speech Samples

To complement their investigation of raters' cognition described earlier, Brown et al. (2005) analyzed the nature of the discourse characteristic of speech samples at different levels of ability and for different task types. They focused on features of the speech samples that reflected aspects of performance associated with categories used by the raters, such as linguistic resources, phonology, fluency, and content. Many of the features—grammatical accuracy and complexity, vocabulary, pronunciation, speech rate, amount of content—in each of the categories were found to vary with score level, although the effect sizes for individual measures tended to be medium or small.

While we expected the integrated tasks to be more challenging, there is no consensus in theoretical expectations about the impact of task complexity on performance features. Brown et al. (2005) noted that some theories propose that greater cognitive load should lead to heightened concentration and better performance. Other theories predict that greater task complexity should lead to fewer resources to coordinate and manage linguistic resources. In general, there were fewer and smaller differences in the features of speech samples for different task types than there were across levels of performance. When compared with performances on independent tasks, performances on integrated tasks had a more complex schematic structure, were less fluent, and included more sophisticated vocabulary. The latter effect was expected because of the availability of an input text. In sum, Brown et al. found that the qualities of spoken responses varied modestly with proficiency level and a lesser amount with task type. However, their finding of a more complex schematic structure for responses to integrated tasks was consistent with the rationale for including such tasks.

Outcomes Relevant to Extrapolation

Preliminary evidence in support of the extrapolation warrant, that performance in the test domain is consistent with performance in the academic domain, was sought by investigating the relationship of performance on the prototype measures to other criteria of language proficiency. The criteria of language proficiency we used were the students' own judgments of their English abilities in the academic domain, actual class placements, and instructors' ratings of students' English language skills. Relationships between each of these criteria with the corresponding prototype measures were examined to provide evidence for extrapolation of scores. Relationships between these criteria and the TOEFL PBT and PhonePass were also examined to provide a point of comparison.

Because the domain of extrapolation was English-medium institutions of higher education, data about students' own judgments of their English abilities in academic situations, their academic placements, and instructors' ratings of students' English language skills were collected only at North American and Australian sites. The sample sizes for the latter two types of data varied considerably depending on instructors' willingness to participate. The scores on the prototype measures used in these analyses were the unscaled scores presented in Table 5.5. Given the exploratory and formative nature of these analyses, tests of statistical significance were not routinely conducted on the data.

Measures of Language Proficiency and Test Takers' Self-Assessments

Self-assessments as indicators of learners' language ability were used based on the assumption that learners have a much more extensive database to evaluate than do external observers. People may be biased observers of their own behavior, but as Shrauger and Osberg (1981) noted, "There seems to be substantial support for the notion that self-assessors frequently have the appropriate information and motivation to make as effective judgments about their own behavior as can be made by other means" (p. 347). Others who have noted the potential value of self-assessments are Bachman and Palmer (1989), who argued that second language learners can provide valid self-ratings of their communicative language ability.

TABLE 5.10
Means and SDs for Self-Assessment Questions and Factor Loadings
from Confirmatory Factor Analysis

Item	M	SD	Factor			
			1	2	3	4
Listening to lectures and discussions to						
understand facts and details	1.9	1.0	.85			
understand what the instructor tells you to do for homework	1.5	0.7	.80			
understand main ideas	1.8	0.9	.70			
understand words and expressions that you do not know	2.2	1.1	.76			
Reading for classes to						
identify the main idea of a reading passage	1.7	0.9		.91		
read and understand directions for assignments and exams	1.5	0.8		.95		
remember the major ideas in the books and papers you read	1.8	0.9		.85		
make notes about important ideas	1.9	1.0		.79		
Speaking in class to						
get the instructor to understand you	1.9	1.0			.81	
participate in discussions	2.1	1.1			.92	
make presentations	2.2	1.1			.91	
summarize information, give and support opinions	2.1	1.0			.86	
Writing for class to						
respond to an assigned topic	2.0	0.9				.91
organize and discuss major ideas	2.0	0.9				.94
support a position or idea	2.1	1.0				.88
use correct grammar, sentence structure, spelling, and punctuation	2.5	1.1				.55

Note. Loadings less than .40 have been omitted.

Before correlations were calculated, the construct validity of the self-assessment results was investigated through a confirmatory factor analysis that verified four well-defined factors could be created from the four questions on each modality. The factor loadings, along with the means and standard deviations for each question on each scale, are shown in Table 5.10. The response scale ranged from 1 (not difficult) to 5 (extremely difficult). Means for most tasks were around 2.0, suggesting that on average this sample perceived relatively little difficulty in accomplishing these tasks, but the standard deviations of about 1.0 suggested that there was also a fair amount of variability in the perceived difficulty of these tasks. For each modality, the four questions were summed to form a total self-rating for each individual on that modality.

The correlations of self-assessments with the TOEFL PBT and the prototype measures are summarized in Table 5.11.

These correlations can be characterized as high and are similar in magnitude to other test-criterion relationships, such as the typical correlation of .5 often found between scores from aptitude batteries and school grades (Cohen, 1988). When compared with the correlations between two tests of the same ability, test-criterion correlations are usually lower because they are constrained by factors such as range restriction and the reliability of the criterion measure (Messick, 1989). Another factor contributing to lower correlations is that measures of perceptions of ability are more distinct from tests of abilities than are two tests. An important point to note in this table, though, is that there is no apparent difference between the correlations of self-assessments with the TOEFL PBT and the prototype measures.

Measures of Language Proficiency and Class Placements

Placement into ESL courses reflects a judgment by an institution that a nonnative speaker of English requires additional training in English to handle the standard curriculum. This judgment is typically made from multiple sources of information including previous coursework and test scores. If initial place-

TABLE 5.11
Correlations between Self-Assessments and Test Performances on the TOEFL PBT and Prototype Measures (n = 220–250)

Self-assessment	TOEFL PBT			Prototype Measures			
	L	R	SWE	L	R	S	W
Listening	.62	.54	.56	.55	.50	.57	.59
Reading	.55	.53	.53	.51	.53	.56	.53
Speaking	.30	.25	.30	.23	.25	.45	.44
Writing	.36	.33	.40	.35	.31	.50	.50

Note. L = listening, R = Reading, SWE = structure and written expression, S = speaking, W = writing. Cell contents in boldface indicate correlation between the same language skills measured by different instruments.

TABLE 5.12
Number of Students in Each Classification at Three Universities

University	Student Classification		
	ESL support	ESL no support	Native speaker
A	23	24	4
B	15	12	19
C	19	20	21

Note. University A = a Midwestern state university, University B = a Canadian university, and University C = a private Midwestern university.

ments are incorrect, students may be moved into or out of specific courses as the instructor becomes more familiar with the student's English skills. Thus, the final determination of whether a student requires ESL support can be used as one indicator of the student's academic English skills.

Information on class placements for ESL students was available at three participating institutions—a Midwestern state university, a Canadian university, and a private Midwestern university. A few native English speakers were also tested at these universities. Thus, participants at these universities could be classified with respect to levels of English language proficiency as determined by their university. The first level was students who were identified by their respective universities as requiring ESL support to succeed in the usual academic program; the second level was nonnative speakers of English who did not require support; and the third level was native speakers of English. Table 5.12 shows the number of students in each classification at each institution.

To facilitate performance comparisons, scores on both the new prototype measures and the existing measures (TOEFL PBT, PhonePass) were standardized to a mean of 0 and a standard deviation of 1.0. The mean standardized scores for students in the three classifications for the four language skills assessed by two instruments are illustrated in Figure 5.1. Because this standardization was computed on the full sample (not just the three institutions in the current analysis), the means in Figure 5.1 were typically above zero.

In general, the trends across groups are consistent with expectations for all skills and all measures. With few exceptions, native speakers score higher than ESL students not requiring support, who in turn have higher scores than ESL students requiring support. However, differences across groups are larger for the productive tasks, especially for the comparison of ESL students not needing support with native speakers. The mean listening and reading scores of these two groups were not very different, with the differences ranging from 0 to .9, or less than one standard deviation. In contrast, the differences between the speaking scores of native speakers and the ESL no support group ranged from .8 to 2.0 for both PhonePass and the prototype speaking measure. Similar differences were seen for the writing measures, especially for the new prototype measure (0.8 to 1.9), which consisted only of productive

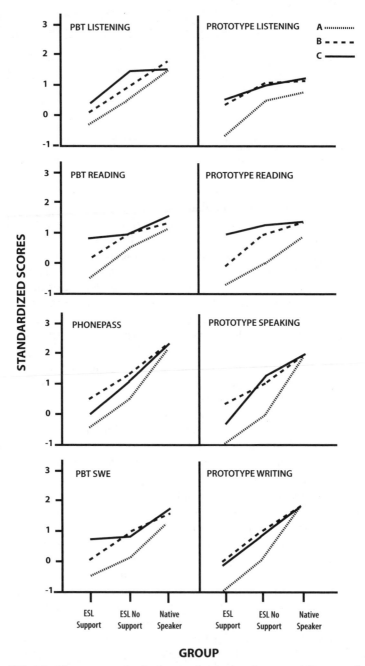

FIG. 5.1   The mean standardized scores for the four language skills assessed by existing measures (TOEFL PBT, PhonePass) and the prototypes measures for three types of students at A. a state university, B. a Canadian university, and C. a private U.S. university.

tasks. These greater differences between groups for productive skills than for receptive skills may reflect (a) the greater inherent difficulty of these tasks for nonnative speakers, (b) current selection practices that rely more heavily on the receptive tasks, or (c) instructional and test preparation activities that emphasize receptive skills.

Measures of Language Proficiency and Instructors' Ratings

For students who were enrolled in ESL courses, instructors' ratings of the students' academic English skills were obtained. Correlations between the ratings and corresponding scores on the TOEFL PBT and the prototype measures for a new TOEFL were computed in each class that had at least four students with both a rating and a test score. These correlations were weighted by the number of students evaluated, and the weighted correlations were averaged over instructors. Every average was based on ratings from at least eight different instructors. Results for the correlations of the listening, reading, speaking, and writing prototype measures with the corresponding instructors' ratings are presented in Table 5.13. The standard error of the difference between correlations was about 0.2, so the differences between existing standardized measures and the prototype measures are not statistically significant.

These correlations are somewhat lower than the correlations found between self-assessments and performance on the test measures in Table 5.11 and can be characterized as moderate (Cohen, 1988). The magnitudes of these correlations, however, are typical of criterion-related validity studies of standardized testing in the context of higher education (cf. Briel, O'Neill, & Scheuneman, 1993).

In summary, the prototype measures in all four modalities had the expected relationships with the external criteria studied. Mean scores on the prototype measures increased as the test takers' perceived need for English instruction decreased, and this was most marked for productive skills. Correlations with both instructors' ratings and test takers' self-assessments were consistent with correlations found for the TOEFL PBT.

Summary and Conclusions

As we began the second phase of test design, we were most concerned with the generalization inference for measures of speaking and writing. The generalizability issues arose because the blueprint (see Table 4.8) called for a relatively small number of tasks due to constraints of both administration time and rating costs, and because the blueprint called for performance on these tasks to be combined into a single score that was to be generalized to a single universe of tasks. The study addressed these concerns through G-studies and D-studies and also allowed us to gather evidence relative to other inferences in the emerging validity argument and to identify issues that would need fur-

TABLE 5.13
Average Correlations of Instructors' Ratings with Measures of English Language Proficiency

Instructors' Ratings of	*Measures*	
	TOEFL PBT listening	Listening prototype
Listening	.37	.46
	TOEFL PBT reading	Reading prototype
Reading	.42	.27
	PhonePass	Speaking prototype
Speaking about personal experience and opinions	.38	.51
Speaking about academic topics	.26	.36
	TOEFL PBT SWE	Writing prototype
Writing about personal experience and opinions	.27	.34
Writing about academic topics	.40	.28

ther exploration. The outcomes of this study are summarized in Table 5.14, with respect to the inferences they address and their implication for design and further investigation.

Issues relevant to the evaluation inference included (a) how complex multiple selected-response items should be scored, (b) the appropriateness of the rating scales for integrated speaking and writing tasks, and (c) the statistical characteristics of tasks and measures. After a number of alternatives were reviewed, a rationale for a threshold scoring procedure for complex selected-response items was proposed and accepted. Overall, the rating scales for scoring speaking and writing tasks were found to be appropriate, but some areas needing improvement were noted. Raters experienced difficulties in scoring integrated speaking and writing samples because many test takers copied material directly from the texts. Methods that would reduce the impact of copying, such as rater training or clearer directions to test takers, would need to be devised. The features of speaking samples noted by ESL specialists were consistent with those mentioned in the rating scales and included attention to content as well as other features. But along with attention to content came some confusion about what was appropriate content. This indicated the need for task-specific support for evaluating content. In general, the statistical characteristics appeared to be appropriate for supporting norm-referenced decisions, but the integrated writing tasks were found to be somewhat difficult in this study.

Reliability and generalizability analyses were important sources of information that would influence future test design. We found that the different configurations of task types had little impact on reliability and generalizability

TABLE 5.14

Summary of Outcomes Relevant to the Inferences in the TOEFL Interpretative Argument and Implications for Further Development

Outcomes	Implication
Evaluation	
A threshold procedure was developed for scoring complex selected-response items polytomously.	This procedure should be used for scoring the reading-to-learn tasks and also should be useful for some listening tasks.
ESL specialists attended to features of spoken responses that were consistent with those in the scoring rubrics.	Rubrics for scoring speaking were appropriate, but raters need some support in deciding key content.
Copying from reading passages posed problems for the evaluation of some integrated tasks.	Ways to minimize the effects of copying needed to be devised, or advice to raters about this issue needed to be improved.
There was a reasonable distribution of scores on the four measures although some of the integrated writing tasks were relatively difficult	Overall, the measures appeared appropriate for norm-referenced decisions, but the difficulty of integrated writing tasks would need further evaluation.
Generalization	
When the number of tasks or items is held constant, alternative configurations of text types or task types had little impact on reliability for listening, speaking, or writing.	Other factors, such as domain representation or cost of task development, should be taken into consideration in deciding on final configuration of measures.
The universe (true) score correlations between sections composed of different task types were high for both speaking and writing tasks.	Including both independent and integrated tasks on the speaking and writing measures was justified.
For writing and speaking, the test taker ability accounted for the most variability in scores, followed by interactions of test takers with tasks, and the rating and rater effects were relatively modest.	The writing and speaking tasks should be used, but efforts should be made to reduce test taker x task interactions in a manner that would not lessen domain representation.
For writing and for speaking, increasing the number tasks improved reliability more than increasing the number of raters when the total number of ratings was held constant.	If costs associated with task development are lower than costs associated with scoring, then the number of tasks should be maximized within the amount of time available.
For speaking, large gains in reliability were observed as the number of tasks increased from 1 to 5, but there was comparatively little further increase as the number of tasks increased to 12.	The speaking measure should consist of 5 or 6 tasks.

(continued)

TABLE 5.14
Continued

Outcomes	Implication
For writing, large gains in reliability were observed as the number of tasks increased from 1 to 2 to 3, but reliability per unit of testing time was low compared with a multiple-choice measure of written expression.	If time allowed, the writing test should include three writing tasks.

Explanation

The prototype writing measure assessed writing in a different manner than multiple-choice structure and written expression items	Although a writing measure composed of constructed-response items would be less reliable than one composed of multiple-choice items, it would be more reflective of the important writing skills.
The correlations among the prototype measures of the four skills were very high.	More powerful analytical techniques should be applied to understanding the structure of the assessment and whether the structure reflected method or ability factors.
While the qualities of speech samples varied modestly with proficiency level, they varied less with task type	Theoretical assumptions that integrated tasks assessed different aspects of language proficiency than those assessed by independent tasks were only weakly supported.

Extrapolation

The prototype measures and existing measures of the four skills had positive relationships with external criteria such as course placements, instructors' ratings, and self-assessments	Self-assessment information and instructors' ratings might provide meaningful descriptors for scores bands.
Differences between native speakers and ESL students were greatest on productive measures of speaking and writing	ESL students may need more support and instruction in these skills.

over and above considerations of the number of tasks. Thus, other factors such as domain coverage would be more important in determining the configuration of measures. Related to this was the finding of high universe (i.e., true) score correlations among task types that justified creating composite scores for measures composed of both integrated and independent tasks. Another important result concerned rating designs: When the total number of ratings was held constant, single rating designs—in which each response was rated only once, but each response from a test taker was rated by a different rater—proved to be at least as reliable as double rating designs. Nevertheless, given that only a few extended constructed responses were envisioned for writing, the generalizability of the writing measure was likely to be substantially lower than a measure that also included some selected-response items.

With respect to the explanation inference, there was a certain irony in the finding that the four prototype measures were highly correlated with each other. As noted earlier, we began this phase of development with a major psychometric concern that integrated and independent tasks would not be homogeneous enough to support a composite writing score or a composite speaking score. The results of the various analyses not only supported the homogeneity of the writing and speaking measures, but also revealed very strong relationships among the four measures. Apparently, the psychometric issue was whether the four measures would be distinct enough to provide unique information about the four skills for individual test takers.[7] However, the finding of high correlations among measures of the four skills was consistent with current theories of language proficiency. In the analysis of the features of the speech samples, only minor differences were found between independent and integrated speaking tasks.

Evidence that supported extrapolation inferences—the relationship between performance on the prototype measures and other criteria of language proficiency—was found, although these relationships were no stronger than those found for existing measures such as TOEFL PBT or PhonePass.

Overall, the outcomes of this phase encouraged us to think that the tasks proposed to assess communicative aspects of language proficiency in an integrated manner could be combined into measures of the four skills and administered within a reasonable test period. The next stage of development, described in the next chapter, would be a field study of a prototype test. The results of field study would be used to refine the item and task specifications and the evolving test blueprint.

NOTES

1. This issue was inconsequential for reading because different types of input—lectures, conversations, reading passages—were not associated with different tasks, as they were for listening, speaking, and writing.
2. At the time of the study, PhonePass was available from Ordinate Corporation in Menlo Park, CA. Ordinate Corporation was purchased by Harcourt in 2004.
3. We are indebted to Diana Marr for this analysis.
4. In the right/wrong scoring described here, a right answer could either be all correct or at least N correct.
5. To minimize the overestimation of reliabilities for the listening and reading measures due to dependency of items within each set associated with a reading passage or listening text, the scores on items within each set were summed, and the set-based scores were used in the calculation of coefficient alpha.
6. In practice, there would be a detection mechanism to flag unusual ratings for adjudication, as is currently the case for single writing samples.
7. The rationale for reporting scores on separate but highly correlated measures should take into consideration other factors, such as usefulness in an instructional context.

REFERENCES

Bachman, L. F., & Palmer, A. (1989). The construct validation of self-ratings of communicative language ability. *Language Testing, 6,* 14–29.

Biber, D., Conrad, S. M., Reppen, R., Byrd, P., Helt, M., Clark, V., et al. (2004). *Representing language use in the university: Analysis of the TOEFL 2000 spoken and written academic language corpus* (TOEFL Monograph No. 25). Princeton, NJ: Educational Testing Service.

Breland, H., Bridgeman, B., & Fowles, M. E. (1999). *Writing assessment in admission to higher education: Review and framework* (ETS Research Rep. No. RR-99-03). Princeton, NJ: Educational Testing Service.

Brennan, R. L. (2001). *Generalizability theory.* New York: Springer.

Brennan, R. L., & Johnson, E. G. (1995). Generalizability of performance assessments. *Educational Measurement: Issues and Practice, 14*(4), 9–12.

Briel, J. B., O'Neill, K. A., & Scheuneman, J. D. (Eds.). (1993). *Graduate Record Examinations technical manual.* Princeton, NJ: Educational Testing Service.

Brown, A., Iwashita, N., & McNamara, T. (2005). *An examination of rater orientations and test-taker performance on English for academic purposes speaking tasks* (TOEFL Monograph No. 29). Princeton, NJ: Educational Testing Service.

Campbell, D. T., & Fiske, D. W. (1959). Convergent and discriminant validation by the multi-trait-multimethod matrix. *Psychological Bulletin, 56,* 81–105.

Cohen, J. (1988). *Statistical power analysis for the behavioral sciences* (2nd ed.). Hillsdale, NJ: Erlbaum.

Cronbach, L. J., Gleser, G. C., Nanda, H., & Rajaratnam, N. (1972). *The dependability of behavioral measurements: Theory of generalizability.* New York: John Wiley.

Gao, X., Shavelson, R. J., & Baxter, G. P. (1994). Generalizability of large-scale performance assessments in science: Promises and Problems. *Applied Measurement in Education, 7*(4), 323–342.

Lee, Y.-W. (2005). *Dependability of scores for a new ESL speaking test: Evaluating prototype tasks* (TOEFL Monograph No. 28). Princeton, NJ: Educational Testing Service.

Lee, Y.-W., & Kantor, R. (2005). *Dependability of new ESL writing test scores: Evaluating prototype tasks and alternative rating schemes* (TOEFL Monograph No. 31). Princeton, NJ: Educational Testing Service.

Linn, R. L., Burton, E., DeStefano, L., & Hanson, M. (1996). Generalizability of new standards project 1993 pilot study tasks in mathematics. *Applied Measurement in Education, 9*(3), 201–214.

Messick, S. (1989). Validity. In R.L. Linn (Ed.), *Educational measurement* (3rd ed.; pp. 13–103). New York: Macmillan.

Miller, M. D., & Linn, R. L. (2000). Validation of performance-based assessments. *Applied Psychological Measurement, 24,* 367–378.

Rosenfeld, M., Leung, S., & Oltman, P. K. (2001). *The reading, writing, speaking, and listening tasks important for academic success at the undergraduate and graduate levels* (TOEFL Monograph No. 21). Princeton, NJ: Educational Testing Service.

Sasaki, M. (1999). *Second language proficiency. Foreign language aptitude, and intelligence: Quantitative and qualitative analyses.* New York: Lang.

Shavelson, R. J., Baxter, G. P., & Gao, X. (1993). Sampling variability of performance-based assessments. *Journal of Educational Measurement, 30,* 215–232.

Shrauger, J. S., & Osberg, T. M. (1981). The relative accuracy of self-predictions and judgments by others of psychological assessment. *Psychological Bulletin, 90,* 322–351.

6

Prototyping a New Test

Kristen Huff
Donald E. Powers
Robert N. Kantor
Pamela Mollaun
Susan Nissan
Mary Schedl

The period from 2001 to 2002 was a crucial one in the new TOEFL® project. If the new test was to become a reality, Educational Testing Service® (ETS®) needed to begin operational planning for the production, delivery, and scoring of test forms to be administered worldwide to 700,000 or more candidates per year. To facilitate this planning, a concrete example of the new test was needed to demonstrate feasibility of such a test on a larger scale, to determine operational requirements, and to inform test users about impending changes. This called for a field study of the proposed new test. In this chapter, we discuss the empirical evaluation of two prototype test forms in a field study.

GUIDING QUESTIONS FOR THE THIRD PROTOTYPING PHASE

Central issues during this phase concerned the generalization inference, but questions relevant to many of the inferences in the interpretative argument were investigated, as summarized in Table 6.1. The evaluation inference is based on the warrant that performances on the TOEFL tasks are evaluated to provide scores reflective of language abilities. We therefore examined the statistical characteristics of the measures to determine if they would support norm-referenced decisions. Whether the integrated writing tasks were too

TABLE 6.1
Questions Investigated in the Third Prototyping Phase Relevant to Assumptions Underlying
Inferences and Warrants in the TOEFL Interpretative Argument

Assumptions Underlying Warrant	*Related Questions*
Evaluation	
The statistical characteristics of items, measures, and test forms are appropriate for norm-referenced decisions	What are the statistical characteristics of the proposed measures? Are the integrated writing tasks too difficult?
Generalization	
Appropriate equating and scaling procedures for test scores are used.	What equating and scaling procedures would be appropriate for the four measures?
A sufficient number of tasks are included on the test to provide stable estimates of test takers' performances.	How reliable are scores on the four skill measures?
Task and test specifications are well defined so that parallel tasks and test forms are created.	Are the speaking and writing tasks comparable in difficulty across forms? Are the task specifications satisfactory?
Explanation	
Performance on new test measures relates to performance on other test-based measures of language proficiency as expected theoretically.	Do the prototype measures assess language skills in a manner that is similar or different from other standardized language tests?
The internal structure of the test scores is consistent with a theoretical view of language proficiency as a number of highly interrelated components.	What was the internal structure of the prototype for a new TOEFL?
The linguistic knowledge, processes, and strategies required to successfully complete tasks are in keeping with theoretical expectations.	Do the qualities of writing vary with proficiency level and task type as hypothesized? Were the strategies engaged by reading tasks in accord with theoretical expectations?
Extrapolation	
Performance on the test is related to other criteria of language proficiency in the academic context.	How did performance on the prototype of a new TOEFL relate to test takers' self-assessments and instructors' ratings of students' English language skills?
Utilization	
The meaning of test scores is clearly interpretable by admissions officers, test takers, and teachers.	Can performance at different score levels be linked to descriptions of students' English language skills?
The test will have a positive influence on how English is taught.	How can teachers help students learn the academic language skills required by the new test?

difficult to provide evidence of differences in test takers' abilities remained a concern.

The generalization inference is based on the warrant that observed test scores are estimates of expected scores over parallel versions of tasks, test forms, and across raters. Analyses of reliability and generalizability were reported in Chapter 5 in support of this inference. In this third phase, issues of equating and scaling, psychometric procedures that would ensure comparability of scores across forms, were considered for the first time. We also examined reliability of the measures across forms as well as within forms, and we compared scores of the speaking and writing tasks across forms. The results of these analyses allow us to determine whether the task and test specifications were satisfactory.

Three questions pertained to the explanation inference based on the warrant that test scores could be attributed to a construct of language proficiency. The relationships of the four measures on the prototype test with other test-based measures of English language proficiency were explored. Confirmatory factor analyses of the field study data were carried out to examine the internal structure of the test and the invariance of its factors for three different first language groups. Ancillary studies were conducted, seeking support for theory-based hypotheses that the qualities of writing would vary with proficiency level and task type and that appropriate strategies would be engaged by reading tasks.

The extrapolation inference is based on the warrant that the construct of language proficiency assessed by the test accounts for linguistic performance in the target domain. As in Chapter 5, the relationship between performance on the test and two other criteria—test takers' self-assessments and instructors' ratings of students' English language skills—were examined to support the extrapolation inference.

The utilization inference rests on the warrant that test scores are useful for making decisions about admissions and appropriate curriculum for test takers. This assumes that the test scores are meaningful to test users. As described in previous chapters, preliminary attempts to link scores to substantively meaningful descriptors through difficulty modeling of test tasks had not been fruitful. Consequently, we explored an alternative approach to developing score descriptors by linking test score levels to criteria external to the test itself—test takers' self-assessments and instructors' evaluations of students' language skills. The utilization inference also rests on the assumption that the new test would have a positive effect on language learning. Although empirical evidence to support this assumption could not be collected until after the test was operational, the publication of the test tasks and preliminary test forms would help teachers prepare students for a new TOEFL in a way that was more consistent with communicative language learning.

FIELD STUDY METHODOLOGY

The field study design called for the administration of two prototype test forms for a new TOEFL to randomly equivalent samples of participants. Two new parallel computer-based test forms were constructed. Because generalization inferences required an examination of the consistency of test scores over forms, the field study required a sample of participants who would be both representative of the TOEFL population and of sufficient number so that appropriate analyses could be conducted. A small subsample of the participants was asked to take both prototype test forms, and these forms were administered in a counterbalanced order to these participants.

In addition to new TOEFL prototype test forms, participants completed a background questionnaire, a TOEFL paper-based test (PBT), and a self-assessment questionnaire. Participants in English-speaking countries were asked to request instructors to complete a questionnaire evaluating the student's English language proficiency.

PARTICIPANTS

More than 3,000 participants were recruited both domestically (18 sites throughout the United States and Canada) and internationally (12 sites). Potential test sites were contacted, and recruiters at those test sites were given guidance on the number of participants to recruit and the level of English language ability that the sample of recruits should demonstrate. Participants were paid $50 for each test they completed. Because the study involved a number of measures, the number of participants who were included in the final data analysis was somewhat less than the total number of actual participants.

MATERIALS

Prototype Test Forms for a New TOEFL

Two test forms were created. The composition of each field study form is presented in Table 6.2.

The first section of the prototype test forms included six listening texts: two conversations and four lectures with accompanying multiple-choice items to assess listening comprehension. One of the lectures was also followed by a speaking question, and another of the lectures was followed by a writing question. A total of 75 minutes was allotted to this listening/speaking/writing section. Each of the six listening texts was from 4 to 6 minutes long, and a total of 25 minutes was allowed for answering the listening comprehension

TABLE 6.2
Composition of Sections on the 2002 Field Study Test Forms

Section	Stimulus	Items per Form
Section 1: Listening/speaking/writing		
Section time – 75 minutes	2 conversations	5–6 basic understanding items
		2–3 pragmatic understanding items
		2 connecting information items
	4 lectures	10–11 basic understanding items
		5–6 pragmatic understanding items
		7–8 connecting information items
		1 listening/speaking task
		1 listening/writing task
Section 2: Independent speaking		
Section time – 4 ½ minutes	3 brief prompts	3 independent speaking tasks
Section 3: Reading/speaking/writing		
Section time – 103 minutes	3 passages	35–36 basic comprehension items
		3 reading-to-learn items
		1 reading/speaking task
		1 reading/writing task
Section 4. Independent writing		
Section time –30 minutes	1 brief prompt	1 independent writing task

questions. The speaking task took 90 seconds (30 seconds preparation, 60 seconds for speaking), and 15 minutes was allowed for the writing task. The second section was composed of three independent speaking tasks; it took only 4 ½ minutes. Test takers were allowed 103 minutes to complete the third section: reading/speaking/writing. A maximum of 25 minutes was allowed for each of three reading comprehension sets that consisted of a reading passage and either 12 or 13 items. One of the reading comprehension sets was followed by a speaking task (30 seconds preparation, 60 seconds for speaking), and another set was followed by a writing task (25 minutes). The final 30-minute section consisted of a single independent writing task. The total testing time for the four measures was approximately 3 1/2 hours.

Note that because the integrated speaking and writing tasks were based on texts that were also used to assess either listening or speaking, multiple skills were assessed within test sections. This contrasts with the more traditional organization of language tests where each section assesses a separate skill. Nevertheless, separate scores were to be computed for each of the four skills by aggregating scores on related tasks across sections. For example, the writing score would be based on the scores for the listening/writing task in section 1, the reading/writing task in section 3, and the independent writing task in section 4.

Task Specifications for the Measures of the Four Skills

The specifications for the four measures of the prototype test forms used for the 2001 field study defined the types of texts to be presented, the abilities to be assessed, and the types of questions that would serve as indicators of specific abilities. The specifications also provided detail about the number and format of questions and the scoring information for individual questions and for the four measures. These specifications for the measures of the four skills had evolved from the original conceptions put forth in the frameworks to practical guidelines for creating test tasks, based on the refinement of the task specifications and draft test blueprint (first presented at the end of Chapter 4) and in light of the outcomes described in Chapters 4 and 5.

The listening measure   Based on the reliability analysis described in Chapter 5 (see Table 5.8), considerations of the time needed to administer various configurations of text types, and the relative difficulty of creating conversations and lectures, it was decided to include six listening sets on each form. A listening comprehension set consisted of listening (audio) text accompanied by visuals and a set of questions that targeted different aspects of listening abilities. The listening texts on each form included two conversations and four lectures, as shown in Table 6.3.

There were 4 to 6 questions associated with each text, for a total of 32 to 34 questions that could provide a maximum raw score of 34 points. About one-half of the questions measured basic understanding, one-quarter measured pragmatic understanding, and one-quarter measured the ability to connect information. There were 6 to 10 connecting information questions in each form; at least one of these questions in each form asked about the organization of the text. These questions could be either simple dichotomously scored selected response formats or more complex partial credit formats that would be scored according to the rationale described for the reading-to-learn item type in Chapter 5.

The reading measure   The test specifications for the reading measure described in Table 6.4 were based on the results of the pilot tests described in Chapters 4 and 5.

The goal of including longer passages (600–700 words) with more complex organization and sufficient topic variation was judged to be feasible although this meant using fewer texts (three instead of five) than in previous versions of TOEFL. Each reading passage was accompanied by 10 to 12 basic comprehension questions and one reading-to-learn item. The reading-to-learn items included prose summary items and a schematic table item. The response format for both of these item types was complex selected response (i.e., the test taker had to select more than one correct response). Partial credit was awarded for these tasks, based on the scoring rules described in Chapter 5. The maximum

TABLE 6.3
Specifications for the Prototype Listening Measure

Types of Input Texts	Language Abilities	Types of Questions	Number of Questions	Response Types	Rubric	Total Points
4 lectures: (approximately 5 minutes) at least 1 (but no more than 2) is interactive rather than monologic	Basic comprehension—ability to understand important information based on the lexical, syntactic, and semantic content of an aural text.	Questions about main ideas and supporting details	16–21; at least 6 are main idea questions	Simple selected response	Dichotomous Right/wrong 0–1	0–34
2 conversations: 1 office hour between professor and student and either 1 service encounter or 1 student-student interaction	Pragmatic understanding—ability to understand the communicative functions of utterances	Questions about a speaker's purpose and attitude	6–10	Simple selected response	Dichotomous right/wrong 0–1	
All texts have a lead-in by a narrator and visuals	Connecting information—ability to infer relationships among ideas in an aural text or to integrate textual information with own ideas.	Questions about the relationships among ideas and about the organization of a text	6–10	Simple and complex selected response	Dichotomous right/wrong 0–1 Partial credit 0–2	

TABLE 6.4
Specifications for the Prototype Reading Measure

Types of Input Texts	Language Abilities	Types of Questions	Number of Questions	Response Types	Rubric	Total Points
3 passages on different topics selected from exposition, argumentation, or historical background/ autobiographical narrative around 600–700 words	Basic understanding – ability to understand important information based on the lexical, syntactic, and semantic content of a written text.	Questions about main ideas and supporting details based on individual propositions in a text	30–36	Simple selected response	Dichotomous right/wrong 0–1	0–42
All texts categorized as having one major focus of development or more than one focus	Reading to learn—ability to recognize the organization and purpose of the text; conceptualize and organize text information into a mental framework; distinguish major from minor ideas and essential from nonessential information; understand rhetorical functions such as cause-effect, compare-contrast, arguments, etc.	Questions about the relationships among ideas and about the organization of a text	3	Complex selected response-prose summary, schematic table	Partial credit 0–3	

number of points for this measure was 42; the number of points could vary because the reading-to-learn items were worth 2 or 3 points.

The speaking measure   The specifications for the speaking measure are presented in Table 6.5.

Two results from the generalizability analyses reported in Chapter 5 influenced the design of the measure. One was that a total of five tasks was considered sufficient for a reasonable level of generalizability. The other was that the composition of the measure in terms of task type did not affect generalizability. Therefore, the composition of the measure was based on other considerations. For example, given that the conversations on the listening measure were shorter than the lectures, it was more difficult to develop speaking questions for conversations that did not overlap with points also tested by the listening questions than it was to develop the questions for lectures, so conversation-based speaking tasks were not included. The tasks were scored using 5-point holistic rubrics, and the total score for the measure was the average of the scores on the five tasks.

The three different task types on the speaking measure were designed to assess slightly different aspects of speaking ability, and each required a different type of input text. Different 5-point holistic rubrics were used to evaluate the responses to the independent and to the integrated tasks. In addition, brief outlines of the relevant key ideas from the lecture and reading were provided for raters to assist them in determining the content accuracy and completeness of the responses to integrated tasks.

The writing measure   Table 6.6 summarizes the specifications for the writing measure, which was composed of three writing tasks—one independent and two integrated (listening/writing and reading/writing).

While the test takers could not listen to a lecture again as they prepared their written response, their notes from the lecture were available. The reading passage remained available to the test takers as they wrote their answers. Each writing task was scored using the 5-point rubrics and scoring criteria that had been developed as described in Chapter 4. In addition to two of the criteria used to evaluate independent writing—organization and language use—a third criterion, content accuracy, was included in the rubric for the integrated tasks. Content accuracy referred to the degree to which relevant points from the lecture or reading, which were outlined for the raters, were stated correctly.

Background Questionnaire

The background questionnaire surveyed participants on their native language, gender, and whether they planned to study for a degree in the United States or Canada.

TABLE 6.5
Specifications for the Prototype Speaking Measure

Types of Input Texts	Language Abilities	Types of Tasks	Number of Questions	Response Types	Rubrics	Total Points
Brief questions about general topics	Ability to formulate and communicate ideas orally on a variety of general topics	Independent—questions that draw on a variety of rhetorical and pragmatic functions	3	Constructed response	Partial credit holistic scale of 1–5 Criteria: appropriate content, intelligibility, fluency, coherence, language use	1–5 average score across all tasks
One of the lectures in the listening section	Ability to understand and convey orally key ideas from academic lectures	Listening/speaking—A question based on a lecture that draws on a rhetorical and pragmatic function	1	Constructed response	Partial credit holistic scale of 1–5 Criteria: Accurate and ample content, intelligibility, fluency, coherence, language use	
One of the passages in the reading section	Ability to understand and convey orally key ideas from academic texts	Reading/speaking—A question based on a reading passage that draws on a rhetorical and pragmatic function	1	Constructed response	Partial credit holistic scale of 1–5 Criteria: Accurate and ample content, intelligibility, fluency, coherence, language use	

TABLE 6.6

Specifications for the Prototype Writing Measure

Types of Input Texts	Language Abilities	Types of Tasks	Number of Questions	Response Types	Rubrics	Total Points
Brief questions about general topics	Ability to formulate and communicate ideas in writing on a variety of general topics	Independent—Questions about personal opinions or preferences	1	Constructed response	Partial credit holistic scale of 1–5 Criteria: topic responsiveness, organization, coherence, and language use	1–5 average score across all tasks
One of the lectures in the listening section	Ability to understand and convey in writing key ideas from academic lectures	Listening/writing—A question about information presented in a lecture	1	Constructed response	Partial credit holistic scale of 1–5 Criteria: organization, language use, and content accuracy	
One of the passages in the reading section	Ability to understand and convey in writing key ideas from academic texts	Reading/writing—A question about information presented in a reading passage	1	Constructed response	Partial credit holistic scale of 1–5 Criteria: organization, language use, and content accuracy	

Paper-Based TOEFL

A TOEFL PBT, described in Chapter 5, was administered to the participants. The TOEFL PBT provided measures of listening, structure and written expression (SWE), and reading.

Self-Assessment Questionnaire

Before they tested, participants were asked to complete a number of questions about their English language skills. Five kinds of self-assessment questions were used to probe the relationships between scores on the prototype test forms and self-assessment more deeply than had been reported in Chapter 5.

Two sets of "can-do" type statements were devised with regard to the claims being made for a new TOEFL. Only statements that concerned academically related language competencies, not more general language skills, were written. One set (19 items) asked test takers to rate (on a 5-point scale ranging from "extremely well" to "not at all") their ability to perform each of several language tasks. The other set (20 items) asked test takers to indicate the extent to which they agreed or disagreed (on a 5-point scale ranging from "completely agree" to "completely disagree") with each of several other can-do statements. For each set, approximately equal numbers of questions addressed each of the four language modalities. A third type of question asked test takers to provide a rating (on a 5-point scale from "extremely good" to "poor") of their overall English language ability. Test takers were asked to answer a fourth type of question comparing (on a 5-point scale from "a lot higher" to "a lot lower") their English language ability in each of the four language modalities with those of other students—both in classes they were taking to learn English and also, if applicable, in subject classes (biology or business, for example) in which the instruction was in English. Finally, test takers who had taken some or all of their classes in English were asked to indicate (on a 5-point scale ranging from "not at all difficult" to "extremely difficult") how difficult it was for them to learn from these courses because of problems with *reading English* or with *understanding spoken English*. They were also asked to indicate how much difficulty they had encountered when attempting to *demonstrate* what they had learned because of problems with *speaking English* or with *writing English*.

Instructors' Ratings of Students' Language Skills

In addition to completing self-assessment questions about their language skills, study participants who tested at U.S. sites (but not international sites) were asked to contact two people who had taught them during the past year and who had had some opportunity to observe their English language skills and to give each one an instructor rating form.

The instructor rating form asked instructors to indicate (on a 5-point scale ranging from "not successful at all" to "extremely successful") how successful the student had been at the following:

1. Understanding lectures, discussions, and oral instructions
2. Understanding (a) the main ideas in reading assignments and (b) written instructions for exams/assignments
3. Making him/herself understood by the instructor and other students during classroom and other discussions
4. Expressing ideas in writing and responding to assigned topics

Instructors were also asked to compare (on a 7-point scale ranging "well *below* average" to "well *above* average") the student's *overall* command of English with that of other nonnative English students he/she had taught.

PROCEDURES

Each participant took at least one computer-based prototype form of a new TOEFL as well as a TOEFL PBT. The two prototype test forms were administered to randomly equivalent samples of volunteer test takers. Participants at some sites were also asked to take both prototype test forms, which were administered in a counterbalanced order. Site administrators were asked to administer the prototype test forms prior to the administration of the TOEFL PBT if resources and scheduling permitted. The computer-based testing session, which included the administration of background and self-assessment questions and a tutorial prior to the start of the test, lasted approximately 4 hours. The TOEFL PBT took approximately 2½ hours. Both the TOEFL PBT and one prototype test form could be administered on the same day, provided that there was a break of at least 2 hours between tests. However, no one was permitted to take three tests on the same day.

Speaking and writing responses were scored on 5-point scales by experienced raters, trained by ETS staff. Initially, responses received only a single rating that was used in most of the analyses. The single rating scenario, in which each response from a test taker was rated by a different rater, was justified by the results of the generalizability studies summarized in the previous chapter. The average score on the five speaking tasks and the average score on the three writing tasks were rounded up and used as the total scores for the speaking and writing measures, respectively. Due to the limited purposes of this field study, it was not necessary to score all the speaking and writing responses. A small percentage of randomly chosen tasks were scored by two raters to assess interrater reliability.

PRELIMINARY DATA ANALYSES

The initial review of the data from the field study focused on two issues: the identification of usable data records and the representativeness of the samples who took the two prototype test forms.

Identification of Usable Data Records

Once all data were collected, there were 1,327 participants with Form 1 data and 1,306 participants with Form 2 data. In addition, there were 316 participants who took both prototype test forms. Together, this represents data from 2,949 participants. (Although more than 3,000 participants actually participated, some data were lost due to technical difficulties.) A potential negative consequence of using volunteers is that the performance on the prototype test forms might not accurately reflect how they would perform under real testing conditions. An initial analysis was conducted using three criteria to exclude any test taker's field test record that was reasoned to show evidence of unmotivated testing behavior. Overall, the data records for 246 test takers were removed for one or more of the following reasons. First, participants who did not take the TOEFL PBT were excluded. Second, based on an examination of the timing data from the study reported in the previous chapter, we determined that the minimum time in which a motivated nonnative speaker of English could complete a reading section was 10 minutes. Data from the reading sets in the forms used in this study were examined first. Participants who had spent less than 2 minutes each on at least two of the three passages were excluded. Once these participants were removed based on the reading time data, no remaining participants in the listening section were flagged as spending less than a reasonable amount of time on at least three of the six listening sets. Third, participants' performance on the listening and reading measures on the prototype test forms was compared to their performance on corresponding measures on the TOEFL PBT. Participants who performed differently on the two measures were excluded from further analyses, as the disparate performance was taken as a sign of unmotivated behavior. To compare performance on the two measures, test taker scores were standardized, and the differences between the standardized scores on the corresponding measures were calculated for each test taker. Participants for whom the difference in the standardized scores exceeded +/− 3 were excluded.

An examination of the mean scores on all four measures for the small subsample that took the two prototype test forms in counterbalanced order revealed no effects due to order. Therefore the data from the two counterbalanced orders were combined in subsequent analyses.

Sample Demographics

After usable data records were identified, the final sample sizes were 1,372 and 1,331 for Form 1 and Form 2, respectively. (The data for participants who had taken both forms in counterbalanced order were included in the analyses of the first form they took.) The first language background and other characteristics of the participants who took the two prototype test forms were compared with each other and with those of the TOEFL population to determine how representative the samples were. As might be expected given the random assignment of test forms to participants, the field study samples were quite similar to each other. However, they did differ in some ways from the TOEFL population.

As illustrated in Table 6.7, the first language distributions of the field test test takers mirrored those of the operational TOEFL population fairly well. Note that the top five native languages represented in the TOEFL population—Chinese, Spanish, Arabic, Korean, and Japanese—were also the top five native languages represented in the field study samples. However, Spanish speakers were somewhat overrepresented while Korean and Japanese

TABLE 6.7
Native Language Distribution for 2002 Field Study Participants and the 2000–2001 TOEFL Population

| Native language | Field Study Participants | | TOEFL Population[a] (2000–2001) |
	Form 1 (N = 1,372)	Form 2 (N = 1,331)	(N = 703,021)
Chinese	17.6%	18.0%	23.3%
Spanish	12.0%	3.5%	5.5%
Arabic	7.0%	7.4%	4.6%
Korean	7.1%	7.3%	12.2%
Japanese	4.7%	4.7%	13.5%
French	3.9%	3.5%	2.1%
Indonesian	3.5%	3.0%	1.2%
Latvian	2.6%	2.6%	0.0%
Thai	2.3%	2.1%	2.3%
Hindi	2.0%	1.8%	2.1%
German	1.8%	1.7%	2.0%
Other	16.4%	14.7%	24.6%
No response/missing	19.1%	19.7%	6.5%

[a] Based on test takers who took TOEFL CBT or TOEFL PBT between July 2000 and June 2001

speakers were underrepresented. Of the 17 other native languages represented in the field study, the percentage ranged from 1% to 3% of the total field study sample, which also reflects the typical incidence of these first language backgrounds in the TOEFL population. The frequency of test takers who did not report their native language in the field study (19%) was greatly inflated due to a technical difficulty with collecting information on this variable.

Other background characteristics of the study samples and the TOEFL population are found in Table 6.8. Both similarities and differences between the field study samples and the TOEFL population are evident in Table 6.8. The similarities include the percentages of females and males and performance on the listening and reading sections of the TOEFL PBT. One difference between the field study participants and the TOEFL population was their reason for taking the TOEFL. Field study participants were volunteers, many of whom were taking the TOEFL because they had been asked to take part in the study, and so they responded "other" or did not respond to a question about their reason for taking the TOEFL. Finally, the field study sample scored a half of standard deviation lower than the TOEFL population on structure and written expression.

TABLE 6.8
Background Characteristics of 2002 Field Study Participants
and 2000–2001 TOEFL Population

	Field Study Participants		TOEFL Population (2000–2001)
	Form 1 (N = 1,372)	Form 2 (N = 1,331)	
Gender			
Female	48.1%	48.0%	47.0%[a]
Male	50.8%	50.4%	52.2%[a]
No response	1.1%	1.6%	0.8%[a]
Objective			
Bachelors degree	14.1%	13.2%	30.0%[a]
Graduate degree	21.2%	21.3%	52.4%[a]
Other degree	0.6%	1.0%	2.3%[a]
Professional certification or work	13.2%	12.4%	4.5%[a]
Other/No response	50.9 %	52.1%	10.8%[a]
TOEFL PBT scaled scores			
Listening—M (SD)	53.6 (6.9)	53.8 (7.0)	52.1 (6.4)[b]
Structure—M (SD)	51.5 (8.0)	52.0 (8.0)	55.6 (7.2)[b]
Reading—M (SD)	52.8 (7.6)	53.0 (7.3)	54.4 (6.7)[b]
Total—M (SD)	526.6 (67.5)	529.3 (67.4)	540.0 (61.0)[b]

[a] Data for 703, 021 TOEFL CBT and TOEFL PBT test takers (combined) tested between July 2000 and June 2001.

[b] Based on 230,877 test takers who took the TOEFL PBT between July 2000 and June 2001.

FINDINGS

Outcomes Relevant to Evaluation

Raw scores for the four measures were inspected to gauge whether the measures would support norm-referenced decisions. Then the mean ratings for each of the speaking and writing tasks were inspected because some of the integrated tasks had appeared to be relatively difficult for participants in the previous pilot study reported in Chapter 5.

Raw score totals for listening and reading were calculated by summing the number of points awarded for each item answered correctly.[1] Partial credit items, included on Listening Form 2 and Reading Form 1 and 2, were scored based on the rationale described in Chapter 5. Listening and reading scores were on untransformed scales that ranged from 0–34 and 0–41 (or 42), respectively. In Listening Form 1, there were 34 items worth a total of 34 points; in Reading Form 1, there were 38 items worth a total of 41 points. Similarly, for Listening Form 2, there were 33 items worth a total of 34 points, and for Reading Form 2, there were 39 items worth a total of 42 points.

The means and standard deviations, by form, on each of the four measures are presented in Table 6.9. For all four measures, the mean scores for both forms were similar. However, differences in the difficulty of different measures are evident. It appears that participants scored somewhat higher on the listening measure, where the mean scores on the two forms represented 66% to 68 % of the total possible score, than on the reading measure, where the mean scores on the two forms represented 60% to 61 % of the total possible score. A similar difference is evident between the speaking and writing sections, both of which were scored on a scale of 1 to 5. The mean scores for the speaking measure were higher than those for the writing measures.

Performance on each of the five speaking tasks and the three writing tasks on Form 1 and Form 2 is illustrated in Table 6.10. Overall, the speaking tasks do not appear to be very difficult as the mean scores are close to the midpoint of the 5-point rating scale. The independent speaking tasks appear to have

TABLE 6.9
Descriptive Statistics for Four Measures for Two New TOEFL Prototype Test Forms

	Form 1				Form 2[a]			
Task	Range	n	Mean	SD	Range	n	Mean	SD
Listening	5–34	1,372	22.6	6.8	4–34	1,331	23.2	6.7
Reading	4–41	1,372	25.1	8.7	5–41	1,331	24.7	7.8
Speaking	1.4–5	841	3.4	0.8	1.8–5	68	3.7	0.7
Writing	1–5	841	2.7	0.9	1–4.8	242	2.7	0.8

[a] Given the purposes of Field Study 1 and the limited resources available, it was deemed unnecessary to score all the Form 2 spoken and written responses.

TABLE 6.10
Descriptive Statistics for Speaking and Writing Tasks

Task	Form 1			Form 2		
	n	Mean	SD	n	Mean	SD
Speaking						
Listening/speaking	1049	2.81	1.26	145	3.33	0.93
Reading/speaking	1053	3.14	1.20	135	3.14	1.06
Independent Speaking 1	1110	3.26	0.99	162	3.75	0.85
Independent Speaking 2	1089	3.56	0.94	139	3.66	0.88
Independent Speaking 3	1057	3.48	0.94	135	3.47	0.91
Writing						
Listening/writing	1366	2.53	1.03	256	2.31	0.94
Reading/writing	1357	2.04	1.01	256	2.15	0.92
Independent writing	1366	3.24	1.12	257	3.21	1.06

been easier than the integrated speaking tasks. (Comparing the difficulty of the tasks on the two forms is not appropriate based on the data in Table 6.10 because of the large differences in the number of speaking samples that were scored for Form 1 and Form 2. However, data on task difficulty for a matched sample are presented later when we discuss generalization.)

In contrast with speaking, the integrated writing tasks do appear to be somewhat difficult, with mean scores ranging from 2 to 2.5 on a 5-point scale. Performance on the three writing tasks indicated that the independent tasks were considerably easier than the integrated tasks, as shown in Table 6.10.

Overall, the statistics for the listening, reading, and speaking measures supported their use for norm-referenced decisions, but concern remained about the difficulty of the writing measure. The writing tasks were more difficult than the speaking tasks, and the integrated tasks were more difficult than the independent tasks. Although the participants in the field study had scored somewhat lower on the TOEFL PBT than the TOEFL population, these results continued to raise a question: Are the integrated writing tasks, as designed, too difficult for this population, or is the difficulty of the tasks due to other factors, such as novelty or test taker motivation? At the very least, the difficulty of these tasks suggests that test takers needed to be better prepared to complete these tasks.

OUTCOMES RELEVANT TO GENERALIZATION

A central purpose for conducting the 2002 field study was to decide how the comparability of the scores on alternate test forms could be ensured. The first consideration was what equating and scaling procedures would be appropriate for the four measures on the test. As described below, the outcome of the discussions on this issue was an initial proposal that the listening and reading measures should be equated and scaled, but the speaking and writing measures should not. Next, the equating and scaling of the listening and reading measures on these prototype test forms are described. The reliability of the four measures, both within and across forms, is reported. Since no plans were made to equate the speaking and writing measures, the form-to-form comparability of these measures was investigated by inspecting the difficulty of parallel task types between forms. In summary, the implications of these analyses for the adequacy of the task specifications are reviewed.

Considerations of Equating and Scaling

Initial thinking about these issues was influenced by past practice and experience with multiple-choice tests (TOEFL PBT), and constructed-response tests such as the Test of Written English™ (TWE®), which consisted of a single writing task, and the Test of Spoken English™ (TSE®), which consisted of 12 speaking tasks. The raw scores for the listening, reading, and structure and written expression measures on the TOEFL PBT were both equated and scaled. When parallel test forms are administered to different groups of test takers, group differences in test scores can be due to differences in the difficulty of the test forms or to differences in the abilities of the different groups. For selected response tests that contain many items, the most common way in which measures on different forms of a test are equated is to embed common material in the two measures under consideration. The form to be equated is typically called the *new* form to contrast it with the *old* form for which raw scores have already been transformed onto the scale. Performance on the common material is used to assess the ability differences between the groups. This allows an equating of the scores on the two measures to take into account differences in the difficulty of the measures. The equated scores on the new form are then transformed onto the same scale that exists for the old form.

However, TWE and TSE scores were neither equated nor scaled. A common task equating model was considered impractical for such tests because it is impossible to ensure the security of tasks to be used as common material that have been already administered. The common material in the case of speaking and writing must be made up of extended or performance tasks. Such tasks are highly memorable and may have to be considered to have been completely exposed prior to consideration for use the second time. Such tasks would not provide pure measures of differences in group ability.

Based on these past practices, a number of preliminary proposals were made about equating and scaling the scores on the four measures for the new TOEFL. First, it was proposed that a total score would not be reported in order to emphasize the addition of a measure of a fourth skill, speaking. One implication of this proposal was that a similar scale would not be required for all four skills if there was no intention to combine the scores from the four measures into a total score. Therefore, it was proposed that raw scores for the listening and reading measures would be equated over forms and then scaled, but those for speaking and writing would not. The comparability of scores on alternate forms of the speaking and writing measures would have to be assured through other practices, such as detailed task specifications and controlling task difficulty across forms.

Decisions about how to scale the scores for the listening and reading measures were informed by previous practice with TOEFL and by what might be called good testing practice. Previous practice with the TOEFL PBT and the TOEFL computer-based test (CBT) suggested score scales for the all measures should have approximately the same number of units. Good practice calls for a sufficient number of scaled score points to map the section raw scores onto the associated scale adequately without causing different raw scores to map into the same scaled score and without causing scaled scores with no associated raw score. This is usually accomplished by having the number of scaled score points closely approximate the number of raw score points. Since the listening and reading measures had different maximum raw scores (34 and 41–42, respectively), the mapping could not be exactly one-to-one for each of the sections. Given this constraint, a decision was made that an appropriate scale for each of the sections would be 1–25.

Another decision was to use an arbitrary scale transformation rather than a distributive scale transformation for the listening and reading measures. An arbitrary scale transformation is characterized by mapping two values on the raw score scale to two specified scaled score points, and, thus, the means and standard deviations of the scale are allowed to vary. An arbitrary scale transformation is distinct from a distributive scale transformation, in which the mean and standard deviation are fixed to specified values. An arbitrary scale transformation was chosen as more appropriate than a distributive scale transformation because there was no specified requirement at this time to make the scale amenable to summing (e.g., adding listening total to reading total to form a composite), nor were we interested in developing a scale with a fixed mean and standard deviation.

The scores for the prototype listening and reading measures were equated for the two forms. That is, the scores for the listening measures on Form 1 and 2 were equated to each other, and the scores for the reading measures on Form 1 and 2 were equated to each other. Although the corresponding measures on the two forms did not have overlapping items to allow for equating based on common items, it was possible to equate the measures using a randomly-equivalent-groups equating design and a classical equipercentile equating method. As noted earlier the two test forms had been randomly assigned to participants within each test center, and inspection of participants' background characteristics and scores on the TOEFL PBT confirmed that the random assignment had been effective. One reason for equating these prototype test forms was that a decision, discussed below, was made to publish the prototype test forms so that teachers and learners would be better able to prepare for forthcoming changes in the TOEFL. The teachers and learners would need to be able to use the scores on the two forms interchangeably.

After the score distributions for each listening and reading measure on the two forms were transformed to a scale of 1–25, the scales were inspected and were found to have the desired psychometric properties. These desirable psychometric properties included (a) score ranges at every value on the scale, (b) no "bunching" at any point in the scale (e.g., where several raw score points convert to one scale score point, or vice-versa), and (c) a scale that will allow for minor adjustments in difficulty across alternate forms. A linear transformation of scale is meant to preserve to some degree the shape of the raw score distribution. All desirable psychometric characteristics were observed for the 1–25 linear scale for each of the listening and reading measures on the two prototype test forms.

Reliability Analyses

Basic analyses of test and rater reliability were also carried out to evaluate whether the proposed task and test specifications would be likely to provide support for the generalization inference. Because a subsample had taken both prototype test forms, we were able to estimate alternate forms reliability as well as the internal consistency reliability. We also estimated the standard error of the four measures. Finally, we inspected the interrater reliability for the small set of speaking and writing tasks on Form 1 that had been rated by two raters.

Internal consistency and alternate forms reliability estimates   For the listening and reading measures, the estimates of internal consistency and the standard error of measurement (SEM) for both forms were acceptable. As shown in Table 6.11, the estimates of internal consistency were consistent with those for TOEFL PBT—.90 for listening and .89 for reading (Educational Testing Service, 1997).

TABLE 6.11
Reliability Estimates for Four Measures on the Prototype Test Forms

| | Internal Consistency and SEM[a] | | | | | | | |
| | Form 1 | | | Form 2 | | | Alternate forms | |
Measure	n	α	SEM	n	α	SEM	n	r
Listening	1372	.88[b]	2.02	1331	.88[b]	2.00	283	.82
Reading	1372	.89[b]	1.96	1331	.87[b]	2.14	283	.81
Speaking	841	.80	0.34	68	.89	0.24	68	.79
Writing	841	.76	0.43	242	.74	0.40	242	.71

[a] SEM based on 1–25 scale for listening and reading; on 1–5 scale for speaking and writing.
[b] Reliability estimates are slight overestimates as passage-based effects were not taken into account in order to remain consistent with other TOEFL publications.

The alternate forms reliabilities were lower than the estimates of internal consistency. While this difference could reflect, in part, the difference in the samples, alternate form reliabilities are typically lower because they include additional sources of variation (forms or time of administration).

The internal consistency reliabilities for writing were consistent with expectations based on the generalizability studies in Chapter 5. However, the internal consistency reliabilities for speaking were somewhat lower than expected based on the analyses in Chapter 5.

Interrater reliability estimates   As mentioned previously, a small sample of speaking and writing tasks was selected and scored by a second rater. The correlation coefficient between the scores from the two raters on a given task provides an estimate of the interrater reliability. These estimates for Form 1 speaking and writing tasks are presented in Table 6.12. Ranging between .53 and .74, these correlations were lower than expected. For comparison, typical interrater reliabilities for scoring TWE essays ranged from .77 to .81 (Educational Testing Service, 1996).

Comparability of Parallel Speaking and Writing Tasks

Given that it was unlikely that the speaking and writing measures could be equated, we asked whether tasks on alternate forms of these measures received similar scores. Table 6.13 presents the mean scores and standard deviations for a matched sample of participants who had speaking and writing scores on both Form 1 and Form 2 tasks.

Although the matched sample received very comparable total scores for speaking, the differences in the mean scores for parallel versions of the speaking tasks across the two forms ranged from .11 to .43 of a standard deviation. The largest differences observed were for the first independent speaking task and the reading/speaking task.

TABLE 6.12
Interrater Reliability Estimates for Form 1—Speaking and Writing

Task	n	Interrater Reliability
Speaking		
Independent Speaking 1	99	.64
Independent Speaking 2	95	.61
Independent Speaking 3	96	.53
Listening/speaking	99	.74
Reading/speaking	97	.69
Writing		
Independent writing	141	.68
Listening/writing	131	.72
Reading/writing	142	.66

TABLE 6.13
Descriptive Statistics for Speaking and Writing Tasks on Two Forms for Matched Sample

Task	n	Form 1		Form 2	
		Mean	SD	Mean	SD
Speaking					
Listening/speaking	87	3.33	1.07	3.43	.83
Reading/speaking	81	3.49	1.09	3.25	1.06
Independent speaking 1	107	3.45	.94	3.83	.82
Independent speaking 2	80	3.93	.83	3.77	.83
Independent speaking 3	83	3.73	.82	3.58	.93
Total score	68	3.64	.74	3.65	.72
Writing					
Listening/writing	256	2.62	.90	2.31	.94
Reading/writing	254	2.14	.99	2.15	.92
Independent writing	248	3.31	.97	3.12	1.06
Total score	242	2.68	.74	2.56	.79

For writing, differences across forms in the difficulty of the independent writing task and the listening/writing task represented .19 and .34 of a standard deviation, respectively. (Because the easier versions of these two types of writing tasks were both on Form 1, the total scores for the matched sample on the writing measure on the two forms differed somewhat on the order of .16 of a standard deviation.)

Summary and Appraisal of Task Specifications

Taken as a whole, the outcomes described in this section support the generalization inference for the listening and reading measures. The scores on the listening and reading measures were reliable, and minor differences in the difficulty of measures between forms could be controlled through the score equating process. Although the equating procedure used for this field study was appropriate for the way the test forms had been administered, a complex linking plan to allow for equating based on common items would be needed for an operational test.

In contrast with listening and reading, supporting the generalization inference for the speaking and writing measures would be more challenging. Methods of equating that relied on previously exposed items were considered unacceptable; parallel task types varied more in difficulty than was desirable; scores on speaking and writing measures were only moderately reliable; and interrater reliability was less than expected. These results indicated that the task specifications for speaking and writing needed to be improved. More detailed task specifications would be necessary to support the development of parallel tasks. Furthermore, better training and monitoring of raters would be required to improve rater reliability. And finally, the novelty of certain of the speaking and writing tasks meant that test takers needed to be better prepared to complete these tasks.

OUTCOMES RELEVANT TO EXPLANATION

Both correlational and qualitative methods were used to address theoretical issues about the nature of language proficiency and what aspects of language proficiency were being assessed. The correlational approaches were used to evaluate whether the new measures assessed language abilities in a manner that was different from a previous version of TOEFL and to examine the structure of the prototype test for a new TOEFL. Two qualitative studies were conducted to determine if performance on tasks was consistent with theoretical expectations. One study examined the linguistic and discourse qualities of responses for the writing tasks, while the other investigated strategies used on the reading measure.

Relationships among Measures on the Paper-Based TOEFL and the New TOEFL Prototype Test

As in Chapter 5, we examined the correlations among the skills as measured by two different instruments, the TOEFL PBT and Form 1 of the prototype for a new TOEFL (eee Table 6.14). The correlations in Table 6.14 have been corrected for attenuation to take into account measurement error and to provide a better estimate of the true relationship among the skills. This table was inspected for evidence as to whether the measures on the prototype test assessed different aspects of language ability than did the measures on the TOEFL PBT. This was an especially pertinent question for the writing measure on the prototype test because of the response format differences between the new writing measure and the TOEFL PBT measures.

Table 6.14 was examined to see if there was evidence that the prototype measures of writing, which included three writing samples, and the selected-response SWE measure on the TOEFL PBT assessed different aspects of writing ability. In contrast with most analyses of construct and method effects, in this case a method effect, response format, was viewed as construct-relevant—that is, writing as assessed by productive tasks signifies a different aspect of ability than that assessed by selected-response tasks. (The same would apply to speaking if anyone ever developed a multiple-choice test of speaking.)

The evidence relevant to this question was mixed. On the one hand, the new writing measure showed only a moderate convergent relationship with the SWE measure (.80). Moreover, the new writing measure was less correlated than was the SWE measure with scores on the TOEFL PBT measures of reading (.77 vs. .87) and listening (.61 vs. .75), suggesting that the new writ-

TABLE 6.14
Disattenuated Correlations among Four Language Skills Measured
by Different Instruments (n = 894)

		TOEFL PBT			Prototype measures			
		Read	Listen	SWE	Read	Listen	Write	Speak
TOEFL PBT	Reading							
	Listening	.66						
	SWE	.87	.75					
Prototype	Reading	.89	.62	.78				
measures	Listening	.84	.82	.82	.87			
	Writing	.77	.61	.80	.83	.81		
	Speaking	.68	.80	.79	.69	.84	.80	

Note. These correlations have been corrected for attenuation (i.e., these correlations represent the relationship between the pairs of measures after correcting for reliability). SWE = structure and written expression.

ing measure was assessing writing in a way that was different than the SWE measure. However, the prototype writing measure was more highly correlated with the prototype reading (.83) and listening measures (.81) than it was with the TOEFL PBT reading (.77) and listening (.61) measures. One possible explanation for these differences was the use of the reading comprehension and listening comprehension texts as the input for the writing tasks. Another was simply an occasion effect in that the two instruments were administered at different, albeit closely related, times. However, this effect was less evident for the prototype speaking measure, where the correlations between the selected-response measures on the TOEFL PBT and the prototype measures were very similar (see the last row of Table 6.14).

The results for listening were also somewhat difficult to interpret. The TOEFL PBT measure of listening exhibited discriminate validity in that it correlated more highly with the new listening measure than with both the TOEFL PBT and the new measures of the other skills. However, the new listening measure correlated more highly with measures of reading (.87) than it did with TOEFL PBT listening (.82). One possible explanation for this is that the longer length of the lectures and conversations on the new listening measure as compared to the TOEFL PBT drew on language abilities in a way that was similar to those required for reading.

Finally, a comparison of the correlations in the upper left corner of Table 6.14 and the lower right corner provided some preliminary evidence about the structure of a test that included integrated tasks. For the TOEFL PBT, listening appeared to be a distinctive skill, while reading and SWE were closely related. In contrast, for the prototype of a new TOEFL, listening and reading were most closely related and speaking appeared to be the most distinctive skill. As described in the next section, the issue of the structure of the prototype for a new TOEFL was investigated using more powerful factor analytic techniques.

Factor Analyses of the Prototype of a New TOEFL

In Chapter 5, we noted that there was considerable theoretical debate about the structure of language proficiencies. Given that the sample size for Form A in this field study was large enough to support factor analyses, Stricker, Rock, and Lee (2005) examined whether the structure of the prototype for a new TOEFL was consistent with any of these theoretical views and the results of similar studies in the field. These analyses were carried out separately for test takers from three first language backgrounds (Arabic-, Chinese-, and Spanish-speaking) to determine if the test structure was invariant across language groups.

The researchers conducted confirmatory factor analyses of a number of proposed models—a one-factor model consistent with a unitary competence view, and a model with four correlated factors (a prerequisite to building a hierarchical model with four first order factors and one general factor). Based on the findings of previous studies, Stricker et al. (2005) also examined a model with three correlated factors—listening, speaking, and a combination of reading and writing. Because they were not impressed with the plausibility or fit of these three models, Stricker et al. conducted an exploratory analysis of data from a sample of 436 test takers with varied language backgrounds who were not a part of the samples of Arabic, Chinese, and Spanish speakers. This analysis indicated that an appropriate model had two factors—a speaking factor and a factor combining listening, reading, and writing. This two-factor model, illustrated in Figure 6.1, provided satisfactory fit in the confirmatory factor analyses of the first language subgroups.

Stricker et al. (2005) noted that the finding of the invariance of factor structure across different first language groups was generally consistent with the findings from many other studies. However, the factor structure they found to be most plausible was not consistent with the results in many other studies. In speculating on the reasons for this difference, they dismissed an explanation based on the inclusion of integrated tasks. They noted that listening and reading loaded on the same factors even though no tasks integrated these two skills to a significant extent. Instead, they suggested that this organization of language skills may reflect the impact of the previous versions of TOEFL on teaching and learning. In the absence of a speaking measure, teachers and students may have emphasized the acquisition of those skills (listening, reading, and writing) but not speaking.

Linguistic and Discourse Features of the Writing Tasks

The rationale for including both independent and integrated tasks on the writing measure for a new TOEFL was that the different tasks types would differ in the nature of discourse produced, thereby broadening representation of the domain of academic writing on the test. Independent tasks required

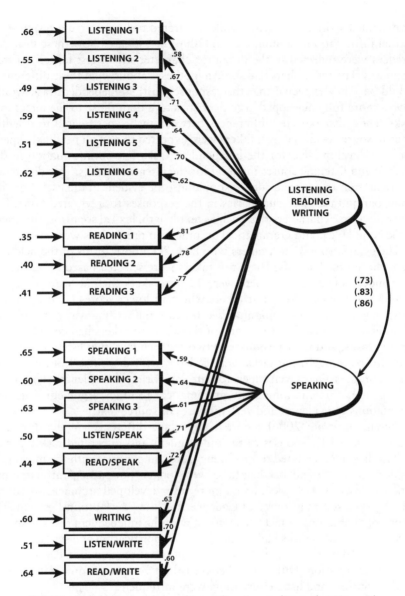

FIG. 6.1 Two factor model—speaking vs. listening, reading, and writing, with common metric, completely standardized factor loadings and error variances shown. From *Factor Structure of the LanguEdge Test Across Language Groups* (TOEFL Monograph No. 32) by L. J. Stricker, D. A. Rock, and Y.-W. Lee, 2005, Princeton, NJ: Educational Testing Service. Copyright 2005 by Educational Testing Service. Adapted with permission.

an extended written argument, while integrated tasks required a response to textual information. Cumming et al. (2006) investigated how these task differences were reflected in the discourse characteristic of test takers' written responses. The researchers had some hypotheses about what these differences would be. They expected that the responses to the independent task would have a more fully developed argument structure than those to the integrated tasks. They also expected differences between task types related to orientations to source evidence. Test takers were expected to rely on personal experiences to develop ideas for the independent tasks but on information in the reading and listening source material for the integrated tasks. This difference in orientation to source evidence should also be evident in the use of quotations, paraphrases, and summaries in the responses to integrated tasks. For other discourse characteristics, such as text length, lexical sophistication, syntactic complexity, and grammatical accuracy, no predictions were made.

The essays from 36 test takers who had taken both forms of the field test were chosen for analysis. These test takers were selected based on scores on their independent essays. There were 12 test takers each at Score Levels 3, 4, and 5. Responses from test takers who had lower scores (1 or 2) on the independent essays were not analyzed because the writing was not sufficient to observe discourse features. Each of these 36 test takers had completed six writing tasks, and their responses to two independent, two listening/writing, and two reading/writing tasks were coded for 22 discourse features. These features represented seven superordinate categories of text length, lexical sophistication, syntactic complexity, grammatical accuracy, argument structure, orientations to evidence, and verbatim uses of source text.

Cumming et al. (2006) reported important differences in the discourse characteristics of responses to the independent and integrated task types as well as differences related to proficiency level. In contrast with the integrated tasks, responses to independent tasks were longer (but participants had more time to answer these tasks), had a more fully developed argument structure, relied on the self as a source of evidence, and used declarations—statements of personal opinions or facts. In contrast with the independent tasks, responses to the integrated tasks had greater lexical sophistication and syntactic complexity, relied on the source materials for information, and used paraphrasing and summarization. Differences between the two types of integrated tasks, reading/writing and listening/writing, were infrequent.

Greater writing proficiency (as determined by test takers' scores on the independent writing tasks) was associated with longer responses, greater lexical sophistication, syntactic complexity, and grammatical accuracy. Furthermore, these differences tended to be consistent for task types.

Overall, Cumming et al. (2006) stated that their findings provided evidence and support for the claims put forth in the original writing framework (Cumming, Kantor, Powers, Santos, & Taylor, 2000). The tasks had been designed so that test takers would produce extended written arguments for the independent essay and would write and respond to textual information in the integrated essays.

Strategy Use on Reading Tasks

Using protocol analysis, Cohen and Upton (2006) probed the strategies that proficient readers used to answer questions on the reading comprehension measure of the field study test forms. The researchers identified strategies used for basic comprehension, inferencing,[2] and reading-to-learn questions and sought to determine if strategies differed for different question types. They also asked whether reading-to-learn questions were more difficult than basic comprehension questions, as question type had originally been hypothesized as one of the variables that might affect task difficulty (see Chapters 3 and 4). Thirty-two participants from four language groups (Chinese, Japanese, Korean, and other) were pretested with one field study test form and then, in a subsequent session, the participants provided verbal protocols as they completed two of the reading sets from the other form. The forms used for pretesting and for protocol collection were counterbalanced over participants. Students with low English proficiency (scoring at or below the 25th percentile on the pretest form) were not included in the study because pilot testing established that such students found the test-taking demands beyond their language abilities. The mean scaled score for reading of the participants who did participate in the study was 18.9 on the pretest, which placed them near the 75th percentile of those who participated in the field study.

Cohen and Upton (2006) analyzed the participants' protocols with respect to three categories of strategies. Reading strategies describe how readers go about making sense of or comprehending what they read (e.g., reading the text, paraphrasing parts of the text, looking for main ideas). Test-management strategies describe how students approach answering questions (e.g., rereading the questions, evaluating options). Test-wiseness strategies represent shortcuts to answering questions that do not reflect comprehension, such as a surface matching of words in options and the passage.

Cohen and Upton (2006) maintained that the primary goal of the students was to answer the questions correctly and not to understand or learn from the text. Nevertheless, in summarizing the reading and test-taking strategies that were used for the full range of questions types, the authors noted that

> All these strategies reflect the fact that respondents were in actuality engaged with the reading test tasks in the manner desired by the test designers...respondents were actively working to understand the text, to understand the expectations of the questions, to understand the meaning and implications of the different options in light of the text, and to select and discard options based on what they understood about the text. (p. 105)

Cohen and Upton (2006) concluded that different strategies were not used for different question types and that the reading-to-learn questions were not more difficult than basic comprehension or inferencing questions for this group of proficient readers. Nevertheless, the authors report some interesting observations about the way the students responded to the reading-to-learn questions. The strategy of reading the question and considering options before going back to the passage occurred at a higher rate for reading-to-learn questions than for the other question types. In contrast, the strategy of reading the question and then going back to the passage to look for clues to the answer occurred at a high rate for other question types but not for reading-to-learn questions. Cohen and Upton suggested that this was because the students had a "good handle on the main ideas in the passage from working through the previous items on the test" (p. 99). This interpretation seems consistent with the proposal by Enright and Schedl (2000) that these tasks would assess aspects of reading to learn that are not currently assessed on the TOEFL including "… remembering information from a text … and reconstructing information from a text" (Enright & Schedl, p. 20) based on an organized mental representation of the text. This may explain why the questions were easy for high proficiency students and why, as reported in Chapter 4, performance on these questions was not worse when the passage was not available.

OUTCOMES RELEVANT TO EXTRAPOLATION

As in Chapter 5, the relationships between two criterion measures of language ability—test takers' self-assessments and instructors' ratings of students' language skills—and the scores on the prototype test forms were inspected to determine if they would support the extrapolation inference.

Measures of Language Proficiency and Test Takers' Self-Assessments

The responses to the self-assessment questions that the test takers had answered at the outset of the field study were summed to create a number of scales (Powers, Roever, Huff, & Trapani, 2003). Scales were formed by summing responses to individual items having the same response format (e.g., "how well" or "agree") for each of the four language modalities and for a composite of the four modalities.

Each of the various scales exhibited reasonably high internal consistency, ranging from a low of .81 (for a four-item scale asking students to compare their English language skills with those of other students in English language classes) to a high of .95 (for a 5-item scale asking students to rate how well they could perform various reading tasks).

TABLE 6.15
Mean and Standard Deviations for Self-Assessment Scales and Their Correlations
with the Prototype Measures

Self-Assessment Scale	M	SD	Prototype Measures			
			Listening	Reading	Speaking	Writing
How-well scales						
Listening	12.8	4.1	.47	.31	.49	.29
Reading	12.4	4.0	.46	.41	.42	.31
Speaking	14.0	4.1	.33	.18	.43	.19
Writing	11.4	3.1	.36	.26	.41	.26
Composite	51.0	13.5	.46	.32	.48	.29
Agreement scales						
Listening	8.4	2.9	.48	.34	.46	.28
Reading	12.9	4.3	.51	.43	.44	.32
Speaking	11.0	3.7	.41	.28	.44	.26
Writing	11.4	3.7	.40	.31	.40	.28
Composite	43.8	13.3	.49	.37	.48	.31
Comparison scales						
Students in ESL classes	10.5	2.7	.25	.14	.33	16
Students in subject courses	11.1	3.1	.16	.07	.21	.04
Overall English ability	11.2	3.0	.36	.22	.44	.21
Difficulty with English	8.1	2.9	.40	.29	.40	.24

Note. Ns range from 2,235 to 2,616 for reading and listening, from 818 to 952 for speaking and from 1,117 to 1,303 for writing.

Table 6.15 shows the correlations of each of the various test taker self-assessment scales with performance on each measure in the prototype test form.

Though not as high as the typical correlation of .5 often found between school grades and aptitude batteries (Cohen, 1988), these correlations can be categorized as moderate. However, there is little evidence of convergent or discriminant relationships in the table. For example, the self-assessment scale for reading correlated as highly with the listening measure as with the reading measure. This is really not surprising, given the results of the factor analysis of test Form 1 that failed to identify separable factors for listening, reading, and writing.

Measures of Language Proficiency and Instructors' Ratings

Powers et al. (2003) also examined the relationships between instructor ratings and scores on the prototype test forms. Instructors' ratings were returned for 819 of the study participants. For 637 participants, two ratings were available. The sample for whom instructors' ratings were returned had slightly lower scores on the prototype test form, but it was reasonably representative of the total study sample in terms of the range of test performances.

A scale consisting of all four instructor rating items (one for each language modality) was highly internally consistent, exhibiting a coefficient alpha of .91. However, agreement between instructors who rated the same student was modest, with correlations between pairs of instructor raters ranging from .47 to .52.

Table 6.16 shows the correlations of instructor ratings with each of the measures on the prototype test forms. With few exceptions, these correlations were all in the .40s, with some reaching the .50s. These correlations were somewhat higher than those reported for self-assessments and can be characterized as high (Cohen, 1988). The pattern of correlations for the instructors' ratings had certain similarities with the pattern for the test takers' self-assessments (i.e., the listening measure exhibiting the strongest relationships to the instructors' ratings, followed by the speaking measure).

All told, the four measures on the prototype test forms were associated to a reasonable degree with both test takers' self-assessments and instructors' ratings of students' language abilities. A potential application of these types of criterion measures to help test users interpret scores is described next.

TABLE 6.16
Correlation of Instructors' Ratings with Scores on the New TOEFL Prototype

	Prototype Test Score			
Instructor Rating	L	R	S	W
In general, how successful has this student been:				
in understanding lectures, discussions, and oral instructions.	.49	.42	.47	.36
at understanding (a) the main ideas in reading assignments and (b) written instructions for exams/ assignments.	.47	.45	.42	.40
at making him/ herself understood by you and other students during classroom and other discussions.	.43	.36	.42	.35
at expressing ideas in writing and responding to assigned topics.	.45	.43	.42	.42
Composite rating (sum of the four above)	.52	.47	.51	.44
Compared to other nonnative English students you have taught, how is this student's overall command of the English language.	.51	.45	.53	.41

Note. Ns range from 400 to 465 for writing, from 260 to 303 for speaking, from 716 to 819 for listening and for reading. All correlations are significant at the .001 level or beyond.

DEVELOPMENTS RELEVANT TO UTILIZATION

Two of the goals in designing a new TOEFL were to provide test users with more interpretable scores and to have a positive influence on teaching and learning. By providing test users more interpretable scores, they would be able to make better decisions. By designing a test with more academic-like tasks, test preparation would become more consistent with communicative approaches to teaching and learning. Both of these goals were seen as supportive of utilization inferences.

Linking Descriptions of Test Takers' English Language Skills to Test Score Levels

Initially there was hope that proficiency scales supported by models of task difficulty would provide more interpretable scales (see Chapter 3). However, given the challenges in implementing this internally focused approach where the description of test scores is based on the characteristics of the tasks and items on the test, we began to explore an alternative or externally focused approach.

We sought to describe relevant characteristics of test takers at various test score levels, based on the test takers' self-assessments and the instructors' ratings. As illustrated in Table 6.17, the test scores for a measure, in this case listening, were divided into five levels. Table entries indicate the percentage of test takers or instructors who gave various responses to each question. For example, in the first row in Table 6.17, we see that for students who scored at the lowest level on the listening measure, only 32% of instructors judged that the student had been more than moderately successful at understanding lectures, discussions, and oral instructions. In contrast, for students who scored at the highest level on the listening measure, fully 90% of instructors judged that the student had been more that moderately successful at understanding lectures, discussions, and oral instructions. Test takers' self-assessments are shown in a similar manner. For example, Table 6.17 reveals that only 34% of the test takers who obtained listening scores of 1-5 agreed that they could remember important points in a lecture, whereas 78% of those at the highest level (21–25) agreed that they could do this.

This approach to developing score descriptors appeared quite promising. One limitation, however, was that so few descriptive statements were included in the questionnaire. In future studies, the inclusion of a larger number of descriptive statements would allow the selection of the most discriminating items for score descriptors.

TABLE 6.17
Key Descriptors of Test Takers by Listening Score Level

Descriptor	Test Score Level				
	1–5	6–10	11–15	16–20	21–25
	Instructors (%)				
Judging that students had been more than moderately successful at understanding lectures, discussions, and oral instructions.	32	42	60	78	90
Who felt that students' overall command of English was at least somewhat above average when compared with other nonnative students they had taught.	13	22	41	68	77
	Test takers (%)				
Who agreed that they could:					
• remember the most important points in a lecture	34	37	45	63	78
• understand instructors' directions about assignments and their due dates	43	60	75	89	95
• recognize which points in a lecture are important and which are less so	33	41	57	72	84
• relate information that they hear to what they know	29	42	63	76	88
Who said they did not perform well at:					
• understanding the main ideas of lectures and conversations	31	29	14	5	2
• understanding important facts and details of lectures	36	33	19	9	5
• understanding the relationships among ideas in a lecture	36	32	18	11	5
• understanding a speaker's attitude or opinion	38	28	15	9	5
• recognizing why a speaker is saying something	43	32	16	10	4
Who felt their listening ability was lower than that of other students in ESL classes.	29	22	14	10	5
Who felt that problems understanding spoken English made learning difficult	52	41	35	22	10

Publication of LanguEdge

After this field study was completed, the texts, items, and scoring rubrics used in the study were made into a computer-based courseware package named *LanguEdge* (Educational Testing Service, 2002). The purpose of the course-ware was to give students and teachers experience with materials that would be similar to the new TOEFL before the test became operational. Much of the information contained in this chapter was included in the manuals that accompanied the courseware. In addition, detailed information on scoring speaking and writing tasks was provided in a separate handbook. The courseware itself had a student mode and a teacher mode. The teacher mode let teachers assign students to the courseware and grade spoken and written responses; training for scoring speaking and writing was part of the teacher mode. Ideas for classroom activities connecting instruction and assessment were also provided. The publication of *LanguEdge* was the first large scale effort to promote positive washback among teachers and learners (Alderson & Wall, 1993) from a new TOEFL. *LanguEdge* provided instructional materials that would support English instruction anchored in the construct of communicative competence as it was operationalized at this stage of the project.

SUMMARY AND CONCLUSIONS

On the whole, the outcomes of this phase of test design, summarized in Table 6.18, were very encouraging. The international delivery of two computer-based test forms that included complex speaking and writing tasks was successful. Although there was clearly a need to improve the specifications and rating procedures for the speaking and writing tasks, the results of the field study and subsequent analyses offered much support for the inferences in the TOEFL interpretative argument.

The outcomes relevant to the evaluation inference were that the listening, reading, and speaking measures were appropriate for norm-referenced decisions, but the difficulty of the integrated writing tasks was of concern. From a theoretical perspective, differences in the difficulty of independent and integrated writing tasks were not unreasonable, as the integrated writing tasks can certainly be viewed as linguistically and cognitively more demanding. However, there were questions about how difficult such tasks could be and still support norm-referenced decisions. Also it wasn't clear if the apparent difficulty of these tasks was due to language proficiency or to the novelty of the task.

During this phase, a central concern was how generalization inferences were to be supported when many test forms would be required each year. Issues of equating and scaling were explored. It was recommended that the listening scores should be equated across forms and the reading scores should be equated across forms. A next step would be to develop a plan for equating many different versions of the listening and reading measures over time, using common items.

As discussed earlier in this chapter, it was proposed that scores on the listening and reading measures be reported on a scale of 1 to 25 while the scores for the speaking and writing measures would be unscaled and reported as the mean score for the tasks on each measure. At this juncture, no thought was

TABLE 6.18

Summary of Outcomes Relevant to the Inferences in the TOEFL Interpretative Argument and Implications for Further Development

Outcomes	Implications
Evaluation	
Statistical characteristics of the listening, reading, and speaking measures would support norm-referenced decisions. However, the integrated writing tasks were relatively difficult for this group of test takers.	Questions remain as to whether the integrated writing tasks are too difficult or if performance will improve as test takers become more familiar with the new task types.
Generalization	
Equating—listening and reading measures should be equated, but it would be difficult to equate speaking and writing measures.	A linking plan needs to be developed to equate listening and reading based on common items.
A scale of 1 to 25 was used for listening and reading; no plans were made for placing speaking and writing scores on similar scales or for reporting a total score.	Feedback on these plans should be sought from test users.
The reliability of the listening and reading measures was acceptable, but problems with interrater reliability for speaking and writing were evident.	Rating processes need to be improved for speaking and writing. Raters need to be better trained and monitored.
Parallel versions of some speaking task types and some writing task types varied in difficulty more than is desirable.	Given that the speaking and writing measures would not be equated, better control of task difficulty would be necessary to develop parallel forms.
Task specifications for listening and reading were satisfactory, but those for speaking and writing were not.	Task specifications for speaking and writing need improvement.
Explanation	
The new writing measure appeared to assess writing in a way that was different than the SWE measure.	Results support the rationale for assessing writing skills with constructed responses rather than multiple-choice items that assess grammatical knowledge.
The discriminant validity of the new measures of listening and reading was weaker than that observed for the TOEFL PBT.	The reason for differences was not clear. Possibly the greater complexity of the listening and reading texts contributed to greater convergence in the skills assessed on the new listening and reading measures.
A two-factor model (listening, reading, writing versus speaking) best fit the field study data.	Results are more consistent with a unitary than divisible view of language abilities. Alternatively, the structure found could reflect the impact of previous versions of the test on teaching and learning.
The factor structure was invariant for three major first language groups.	Invariant factor structures for different language groups support test fairness and indicate that the same skills are being measured for different groups of test takers.

(continued)

TABLE 6.18
Continued

Outcomes	Implications
Differences in discourse characteristics of writing were related to proficiency level and tasks type (independent versus integrated).	Results were consistent with theoretical expectations.
Test takers relied on academic-like reading and test-taking strategies rather than test-wiseness strategies to complete reading tasks.	Supports the interpretation of the reading measure as an indicator of academic reading ability, but another theoretical hypothesis that basic comprehension items, inference items, and reading-to-learn tasks required different reading strategies was only weakly supported.

Extrapolation

Test performance was related to a reasonable degree to two external criteria of academic language ability, self-assessments and instructors' ratings.	The validity of the criterion measures themselves should be explored further.

Utilization

Score meaning might be enhanced by linking score levels to descriptors of abilities from self-assessments and instructors' ratings.	Self-assessment and instructor rating instruments should be improved by adding more descriptors to discriminate better among score levels.
Courseware package was published, including prototype test forms, information about how speaking and writing tasks are scored.	Efforts to inform teachers and learners about changes to the test and to provide them with materials that will promote positive washback should continue.

given to whether test users would require a total score or how such a score should be created.

A number of reliability indices for the four measures were reviewed. These indices indicated that the reliability of the listening and reading measures were satisfactory, but the reliability of the speaking and writing measures were less than expected. In particular, interrater reliabilities were lower than those observed previously. This meant that more thought needed to be given to the rater training and monitoring processes.

One concern was the finding that parallel versions of speaking and writing tasks administered to the same participants varied in difficulty. Equating speaking and writing scores was considered impractical because the tasks were too memorable to remain secure. Consequently, the comparability of speaking and writing tasks on different forms would need to be established by other means, such as task specifications that resulted in tasks of equivalent difficulty.

All in all, it was concluded that task specifications for listening and reading were satisfactory and that generalization inferences for these measures could be supported. However, for the speaking and writing measures, the task specifications and rating processes needed to be improved to support generalization inferences.

A number of findings were relevant to explanation inferences. Analyses based on correlations among the four measures on the prototype for a new TOEFL and with the three measures on the TOEFL PBT indicated support for two distinctions between the TOEFL PBT and the prototype for a new TOEFL. One was that the writing measure, as intended, assessed a different aspect of ability than did the SWE measure. The other was that the structure of the new test was more unified than that of the previous test. The reasons for the more unified structure of the new test are in need of further investigation. Understanding what factors influence correlational structures would help to refine theories of language proficiency.

Two qualitative studies examined some hypotheses about the linguistic knowledge and strategies that were involved in completing test tasks. The discourse qualities of writing varied with ability level and task type in accord with the rationale for creating a writing measure that included complex tasks. An investigation of how test takers completed items on the reading measure revealed that test takers used academic-like reading strategies rather than test-wiseness strategies to answer items. However, only a little support was found for hypotheses about the use of different strategies for different item types.

In support of extrapolation inferences, the relationship between performance on the test measures and test takers' self-assessments and instructors' ratings of students' language abilities were found to be moderate and comparable to the magnitude of correlations usually found for these kinds of measures. These data were then used to support the utilization inference by creating score descriptors to improve the interpretability of test scores for test users. This approach was thought to have promise, and recommendations for improvements in the kinds of descriptive data used for this purpose were made. Finally, it was thought that publishing the field study test forms and information about how to prepare for a test that would include integrated tasks would be another way to support the utilization inference. Providing test users with appropriate test preparation material would be an important way to encourage a positive impact on teaching and learning.

Overall the field study was very successful as a proof of concept. The kind of operational planning that would be needed to scale up the production, delivery, and scoring of this new test now had specific information on which to base requirements. At the same time, the field study also provided evidence supporting many of the inferences in the interpretative argument and identified some areas of weakness. In the next phase of development, the few remaining areas of concern would be addressed through refinement of the task specifications.

NOTES

1. Item 9 of Passage 2 in Reading Form 1 did not contribute to the test taker's raw score point total that was used to calculate the test taker's final reading score.
2. A decision was made in 2003 to specify inferencing as a third task type for reading by reclassifying some of the basic comprehension items and reading to learn items.

REFERENCES

Alderson, J. C., & Wall, D. (1993). Does washback exist? *Applied Linguistics, 14*, 115–129.

Cohen, J. (1988). *Statistical power analysis for the behavioral sciences* (2nd ed.). Hillsdale, NJ: Erlbaum.

Cohen, A., & Upton, T. (2006). *Strategies in responding to the New TOEFL reading tasks* (TOEFL Monograph No. 33). Princeton, NJ: Educational Testing Service.

Cumming, A., Kantor, R., Baba, K., Eouanzoui, K., Erdosy, U., & James, M. (2006). *Analysis of discourse features and verification of scoring levels for independent and integrated prototype writing tasks for new TOEFL* (TOEFL Monograph No. 30). Princeton, NJ: Educational Testing Service.

Cumming, A., Kantor, R., Powers, D., Santos, T., & Taylor, C. (2000). *TOEFL 2000 writing framework: A working paper* (TOEFL Monograph No. 18). Princeton, NJ: Educational Testing Service.

Educational Testing Service. (1996). *TOEFL Test of Written English guide*. Princeton, NJ: Author.

Educational Testing Service. (1997). *TOEFL test & score manual, 1997 edition*. Princeton, NJ: Author.

Educational Testing Service. (2002). *LanguEdge*. Princeton, NJ: Author.

Enright, M. K., & Schedl, M. (2000). *Reading for a reason: Using reader purpose to guide test design* (internal report). Princeton, NJ: Educational testing Service.

Powers, D. E., Roever, C., Huff, K. L., & Trapani, C. S. (2003). *Validating new TOEFL courseware scores against faculty ratings and student self-assessments* (ETS Research Rep. No. RR-03-11). Princeton, NJ: Educational Testing Service.

Stricker, L. J., Rock, D. A., & Lee, Y.-W. (2005). *Factor structure of the LanguEdge test across language groups* (TOEFL Monograph No. 32). Princeton, NJ: Educational Testing Service.

7

Finalizing the Test Blueprint

Mari Pearlman

The 2002 field study demonstrated that a computer-based test of communicative academic language proficiency could be successfully delivered on a small scale (3,000 test takers) in a low-stakes environment. The next step in the developmental process was to finalize the test blueprint. This required an evaluation of whether the proposed test design was robust enough to be sustained on a much larger scale (700,000 to 900,000 test takers per year) in a high-stakes environment. A review of the proposed test design and the results of the 2002 field study raised a number of issues that needed resolution.

Major issues were related to test security. In an age where nearly instant electronic communication around the world was becoming the norm, the security of a testing model that relied on a small number of paper-based test forms (12–17 per year) or repeated use of test items (computer-adaptive testing) could not be assured. These concerns about test security led to a decision that many linear test forms (50–70 per year), with minimal reuse of items, would be needed to maintain security. The development of multiple parallel test forms, in turn, would require detailed task specifications that could be communicated to many item writers.

Another issue arose from a decision to use an item response theory common item equating with the common item equating to a calibrated pool design (Kolen & Brennan, 2004). When considered in conjunction with the decision to allow some reuse of old final form items, new items would need to be calibrated prior to operational administration and placed in the pool so that they could then serve as common items in new final forms to be equated. This would require pretesting of some listening and reading item sets so that they could appear later in final forms as common item sets to link final form parameters to the pool for equating purposes.

Test developers also raised issues concerning the feasibility of finding or creating texts that would support the assessment of both a receptive skill as well as a productive skill. For example, after 12 to 14 reading questions had been developed for a 700 word reading passage, there would be little untested content that could provide material for an extended writing task. This led to reconsideration of prior decisions that the same stimulus material should be used to assess more than one skill.

Still other issues that emerged as test developers reviewed the earlier results included the relatively low interrater reliability for speaking and writing scores for the tasks included in the 2002 field study and the tendency of test takers to use verbatim material from reading passages for reading/speaking and reading/writing tasks.

In light of these issues, a final design process was needed to produce task specifications and a test blueprint that would ultimately support the generalization of test scores from any individual set of test tasks to those that might be obtained on other test tasks. This chapter describes task design analysis as practical processes for confronting these issues and task shells as documents for design decisions for the final blueprint. Although the construction of the operational delivery system is not discussed in detail in this volume, two technological solutions required for delivery and scoring of the new test are mentioned at the end of the chapter because of the significant role they played in making the operational test a reality.

EVIDENCE-CENTERED DESIGN AS THE BASIS
FOR TASK DESIGN ANALYSIS

The processes and concepts drawn from discussions of evidence-centered design (ECD; Mislevy, Steinberg, & Almond, 2002, 2003) served as the foundation for task design analysis although ECD, in all its complexity,[1] was not fully implemented. Examples of how task design analysis was used to create task specifications for speaking tasks are provided. The task specifications are formalized into a framework called a task shell, which I describe and illustrate with an example of a speaking task that was considered, but not adopted, for use on the test.

Evidence-Centered Design

One can view ECD as a family of test development best practices designed to clarify what is being measured by a test and to support inferences made on the basis of evidence derived from the test. ECD was useful for the new TOEFL® because it helped test designers to attend to competencies, tasks, and the relationship between them during test design. ECD, as described by Mislevy et al. (2002, 2003) and summarized in Table 7.1, systematizes test design by

TABLE 7.1
Mislevy's Four Stage ECD Process for Test Design

Stage	Process	Component	Definition of Component
1. Domain analysis	Preliminary synthesis of what is known about what is to be assessed	No specific components specified although useful categories enumerated	NA
2. Domain modeling	Incorporation of information from stage one into three components; sketch of potential variables and substantive relationships	Proficiency paradigm	Substantive construct expressed as claims
		Evidence paradigm	Observations required to support claims
		Task paradigm	Types of situations that provide opportunities for test takers to show evidence of their proficiencies
3. Construction of conceptual assessment framework	Development of a final blueprint; provision of technical detail required for implementation including statistical models, rubrics, specifications, and operational requirements	Student model	Statistical characterization of the abilities to be assessed
		Evidence model	1. Rules for scoring test tasks 2. Rules for updating variables in the student model
		Task model	Detailed description of assessment tasks
		Presentation model	Specification of how the assessment elements will look during testing
		Assembly model	Specification of the mix of tasks on a test for a particular student
4. Deployment of operational assessment	Construction of the operational delivery system	Presentation	Presentation, interaction, and response capture
		Response scoring	Evaluation of response; task level scoring
		Summary scoring	Computation of test score; test level scoring
		Activity selection	Determination of what to do next

specifying a four-stage process consisting of domain analysis, domain modeling, construction of a conceptual assessment framework, and deployment of an operational assessment. These building blocks describe what we want to be able to say about test takers based on observations we make on the test.

The first stage of test design, domain analysis, consists of a preliminary synthesis of what is known about the proficiency in the field to be assessed. Domain analysis focuses on questions such as the following: What are the skills, knowledge, and abilities important for successful performance in the field? What are the real world situations in which we can see people using the kinds of knowledge we care about? What are the important features of these situations? What theoretical perspectives have been proposed to explain performance? While this information was not originally created or organized for the purposes of an assessment, it provides a foundation for further development.

In the second stage, domain modeling, the information collected in the first stage is refined as it is incorporated into three interrelated components or structures that will guide the development of the assessment:

1. Proficiency Paradigm—What substantive claims will be made about test takers' abilities or competencies?
2. Evidence Paradigm—What observable features in test takers' performances would provide data to support these claims?
3. Task Paradigm—What kinds of tasks provide an opportunity for test takers to demonstrate evidence of their proficiencies?

In the third stage, the conceptual assessment framework (CAF) for the assessment adds a great deal of technical detail to the sketch obtained in the domain modeling stage. The CAF has five components or models. The student model is a statistical characterization of test takers such as their locations on a continuous or unidimensional scale or at a specific level on an ordered categorical scale. The evidence model has two subcomponents: The evaluation component prescribes the rules for scoring test tasks, and the measurement component contains the statistical machinery to be used to accumulate data across tasks to update the student model. The task model provides a detailed description of the characteristics of test tasks. The task model, in many ways akin to task specifications, provides guidance to generate multiple exemplars of a particular task type. For linear tests, the assembly model, which stipulates the mix of tasks to be presented to test takers, corresponds to the test blueprint. The test blueprint provides a template that details requirements that must be met for each test form, such as the number tasks of each type to be presented, the content to be covered, and the order of presentation of tasks. Finally, the presentation model lays out the formatting specifications for a test.

The final stage of ECD, an operational assessment, consists of a four-process delivery system. This includes (a) presentation of information, interaction between the information and the test taker, and the capture of the test takers' response; (b) scoring of the response; (c) summarization of the scores across several responses; and (d) determination of what might be useful to do next.

ECD provides a framework to formalize and document traditional test design processes in greater detail and to articulate the connections between elements of the test design more clearly. Although ECD terminology was not used earlier in the test design process for new TOEFL, parallels to the iterative stages of ECD are evident in the previous chapters: domain analysis (Chapters 2 and 3), domain modeling (Chapters 4 and 5), and development of a conceptual assessment framework (Chapter 6). Deployment of an operational assessment would be extremely challenging for the new TOEFL because of the need for worldwide Internet-based test delivery as well as a computer-based system to collect and score speech samples. These are briefly described at the end of this chapter.

ECD was implemented in this final stage of test design in the form of task design analysis and task shells. These were procedures for evaluating what had been learned in the previous prototyping efforts and for finalizing task specifications and the test blueprint. At the outset of this process, certain practical considerations were rearticulated as constraints on the final design, which served as parameters for the test design team as they finalized the blueprint. These considerations included the challenge of security for an international test used for high-stakes decisions, the resolve to make the new TOEFL solely a computer-based test, the determination to keep total test time to no more than 4 hours, and the commitment to maintain consistently high standards of technical quality across all editions of the new test.

Task Design Analysis

Task design analysis (TDA) was conducted by following six steps that were formulated based upon the general principles of ECD as just described. In particular, the six steps of TDA drew upon the first two stages of ECD, domain analysis and domain modeling. The correspondences between the components of domain analysis and domain modeling that were relevant to each step of TDA are outlined in Table 7.2.

The first step in TDA is reviewing prior theory and research pertaining to the testing issues. The TOEFL design team accomplished the first step by reviewing the framework papers that were described in Chapter 3 (Bejar, Douglas, Jamieson, Nissan, & Turner, 2000; Butler, Eignor, Jones, McNamara, & Suomi, 2000; Cumming, Kantor, Powers, Santos, & Taylor, 2000; Enright, Grabe, Koda, Mosenthal, Mulcahy-Ernt, & Schedl, 2000; Jamieson, Jones, Kirsch, Mosenthal, & Taylor, 2000). The design team, consisting primarily of assessment specialists at Educational Testing Service® (ETS®), read and discussed these papers in addition to the other materials about design and research that had been produced in the new TOEFL project. This review of prior work provided them ideas about language proficiency and potential test tasks that would be useful for the subsequent five steps.

TABLE 7.2
Steps Carried Out in TDA Guided by Aspects of ECD

Six Steps in Task Design Analysis	Component from Evidence-Centered Design	Stage of Evidence-Centered Design
1. Reviewing prior theory and research pertaining to testing issues	No specific components defined	Stage 1—Domain analysis: preliminary synthesis of what is known about what is to be assessed
2. Articulating claims about test takers' language proficiency in all modalities and stating more detailed claims as subclaims	Proficiency paradigm	Stage 2—Domain modeling: incorporation of information from stage 1 into three components; sketch of potential variables and substantive relationships
3. Listing sources of evidence for each claim	Evidence paradigm	
4. Listing real world tasks for which test takers can provide relevant evidence	Task paradigm	
5. Identifying characteristics that could affect task difficulty	Task paradigm	
6. Identifying criteria for evaluating performance on the tasks	Task paradigm	

The second step of TDA, articulating claims, is a means of specifying the proficiency paradigm for the test. The proficiency paradigm is specified as the substantive ability construct that the test is intended to measure. Following Mislevy et al. (2002, 2003), such constructs are expressed as claims that one would like to make about test takers. Using the speaking measure as an example, the construct of ability to communicate successfully in an academic context would be expressed as a claim, such as: The test taker can communicate effectively by speaking in English-speaking academic environments. Such a general claim can be specified further through development of subclaims as well. A subclaim for speaking, therefore, provides a means of articulating a more specific construct, such as ability to speak about something in a particular context: The test taker can speak intelligibly about familiar low risk subjects, based on personal preferences and experiences.

The third step, listing sources of evidence for claims, refers to the process of defining an evidence paradigm. The evidence paradigm characterizes the observations that are required to support claims by listing as many sources of evidence as possible for each of the claims. Continuing with the example of the speaking measure, the following aspects of the test takers' responses were identified as the relevant evidence in the spoken response: intelligibility, fluency, vocabulary, grammatical correctness, appropriateness, coherence, and content relevance.

Steps 4–6 of TDA define a task paradigm by listing real world tasks in which test takers can provide relevant evidence, identifying task characteristics that might affect difficulty, and establishing criteria for evaluating performance. For example, real world tasks for the speaking test consisted of those requiring test takers to ask and respond to questions in class; participate in in-class and out-of-class academic group discussions; and exchange information one-on-one with professors, classmates, and other campus staff such as the librarian or financial aid officer. Task characteristics potentially affecting difficulty included the characteristics of reading and listening material and the nature of their connections with each other. Important features for evaluating speaking performance on these types of tasks include the range and complexity of vocabulary and structures, clarity and pace of speech, coherence and cohesion, progression of ideas in response, and relevance and thoroughness of the content of the response. Table 7.3 summarizes the outcomes from the six-step TDA conducted for the speaking measure.

The outcome of TDA brings the test design team closer to specification of test tasks by compiling the necessary information. This information, which is exemplified for the speaking test in Table 7.3, is used to construct the task shells, which in turn are used to generate test tasks.

Task Shells

A task shell is a template for generating parallel items or test tasks. Task shells are composed of two primary parts: a summary of what the task is intended to measure and a task model.

The summary of what is being measured is shown in Table 7.4, which contains two entries in the first column, What is Being Measured? The first entry states the claim that the test design team intends to make about the test taker on the basis of performance on the task. This claim comes directly from Step 2 of the TDA. The second entry includes the observable behaviors of the test taker that are to be used to indicate a degree of support for the claim. This comes from Step 3 of the TDA.

The task model in the task shell comes from Steps 4–6 in the TDA, as shown in Table 7.4. The task model consists of four parts: fixed elements, variable elements, the rubric, and variants. The fixed elements refer to the aspects of a class of tasks that remain constant across different instances of that task. The features specified are what the students are asked to do to complete the task and the sequence and timing of the task components. Examples of fixed features for the TOEFL speaking section include exact length of stimulus materials; exact timing for stimulus, preparation, and response; and exact specification of the nature of the prompt. The variable elements refer to the

TABLE 7.3
Example Test Design Analysis for Speaking

Step in TDA	Outcome for the Speaking Test
1. Reviewing previous research	Ideas about language proficiency and potential test tasks
2. Articulating claims and subclaims	Claim: Test taker can communicate effectively by speaking in English-speaking academic environments. Subclaims: 1. The test taker can speak intelligibly about common, everyday topics based on personal experience/ knowledge. 2. The test taker can appropriately and intelligibly state and support preference for a certain behavior or course of action from a given choice. 3. The test taker can appropriately and intelligibly combine and convey key information from reading and listening texts based on a situation typically occurring in a campus environment. 4. The test taker can appropriately and intelligibly combine and convey key information from reading and listening texts representative of academic course content. 5. The test taker can appropriately and intelligibly convey key ideas from a conversation about a problem typically occurring in a campus environment and can use personal knowledge to expand on information provided. 6. The test taker can appropriately and intelligibly convey key ideas from a lecture segment representative of academic course content.
3. Listing sources of evidence	Intelligibility, fluency, vocabulary, grammatical correctness, appropriateness, coherence, and content relevance
4. Listing real world tasks in which test takers can provide relevant evidence	Asking and responding to questions in class; participating in in-class and out-of-class academic group discussions; exchanging information one-on-one with professors, classmates, and other campus staff such as the librarian
5. Identifying aspects of situations that would affect their difficulty	Characteristics of reading and listening material; the nature of their connections to each other (referring to Subclaim 4)
6. Identifying criteria for evaluating performance on the tasks	Range and complexity of vocabulary and structures; clarity and pace of speech; coherence and cohesion; progression of ideas in response; relevance and thoroughness of content of response

TABLE 7.4
Components of a Task Shell

What is Being Measured?	Task Model			
	Fixed elements	Variable elements	Rubric	Variants
Claim: Statement that one would like to make about the test taker on the basis of test results	Aspects of this class of task that remain constant across tasks	Aspects of this class of task that can be changed across tasks	Procedures and criteria for evaluation of learners' responses	Descriptions of example tasks
Measurement: Aspects of the test taker's response that are the focus of evaluation	• Nature of the task: Description of what students are asked to do and materials that they are given			
	• Order of item elements: Sequence and timing of task components			

aspects of the class of tasks that can be changed across different instances of that task, such as the topic. The set of possible varieties of these elements is also included. The rubric specifies the procedures and criteria for evaluation of the test takers' responses. The variants define the range of tasks that are specified by the task shell.

ECD's influence in the formulation of the framework for task shells is illustrated in Table 7.5. In providing technical detail required for implementation, task shells reflect many aspects of ECD's conceptual assessment framework (CAF). Measurement and the rubric used for scoring reflect the evidence model in the CAF, and the fixed elements, variable elements, and variants are contained in ECD's task model. The only exception is that the task shell's claim parallels domain modeling's proficiency paradigm as it is a substantively meaningful statement about students (rather than the statistical characterization of the student model).

An example of a task shell for a speaking task is shown in Table 7.6. In the first column, a claim is specified based on those claims identified for speaking during Step 2 of the TDA (shown in Table 7.2). The claim in this example, test takers can apply understanding of written texts to orally communicate a reasonable summary and conclusion, reflects an early version of Subclaim 4 in Table 7.3, in which two reading texts were considered instead of one reading text and one listening text. The phrase above the claim in Table 7.6,

TABLE 7.5
Elements in the Task Shell Guided by ECD

Task Shell Element	ECD Component	ECD Stage
Claim	Proficiency paradigm Evidence paradigm Task paradigm	2. Domain modeling
	Student model	3. Construction of conceptual assessment framework (CAF)
Measurement Rubric	Evidence model	
Fixed elements Variable elements Variants	Task model	
	Presentation model Assembly model	

spoken ability in a pedagogic context based on reading material, is shorthand for the construct that tasks developed from this shell are intended to measure. Under the claim, the aspects of the test takers' responses that are the focus of measurement are listed. The task model is completed with the specifications for the fixed elements, variable elements, rubric, and list of variants. While the rubric is part of the task model, it was described in a separate document because of its size.

The task shell shown in Table 7.6 was used to develop the task shown in Figure 7.1. The task requires the test taker to read two passages whose characteristics are specified under the fixed elements in the task model.

As the task model indicates, the topic and the precise relationship between the two passages can vary; therefore, the example about malaria is only one possible topic that could appear in such a task. The list of variants for each task, however, further specifies the topics that can appear in these tasks. They must be academic subject areas. The list of variants also gives the possible relationships that can hold among the texts. In the malaria example, as specified by Variant 2b of the task model, the first passage presents a description of a problem, in this case, the problem of the spread of malaria. The second passage presents an attempt to solve the problem. The question that the test taker must address is about the attempt to solve the problem, which can only be adequately explained through the use of information in the first passage.

Once a shell and some sample tasks were created, the shell was evaluated by item writers according to certain criteria. A proposed task shell had to provide evidence for a subclaim, sustain the production of many task variants, contribute to content representation of the domain, and not be easily undermined by inappropriate test-taking strategies. The task shell illustrated in Table 7.6 was, in fact, rejected because item writers did not believe that they could generate a sufficient number of variants for this task type.

TABLE 7.6
An Example of a Task Shell for a Read-Read-Speak Task

What is Being Measured?	Task Model			
	Fixed elements	Variable elements	Rubric	List of variants for each
Spoken ability in a pedagogic context based on reading material	1. Nature of the task: Demonstrate understanding of the relationships among ideas from two sources.	1. The topic, which will vary over academic areas	See Table 7.12	1. Academic subject areas: life science, arts, humanities, physical science, and social science
Claim: Test takers can apply understanding of written texts to orally communicate a reasonable summary and conclusion	Reading text A of approximately 100–150 words briefly describing a theory, concept, condition, term, or other subject of academic relevance; 40–60 seconds for the test taker to read the passage	2. The precise relationship between the two reading passages, according to which the stem will vary		2a. Reading text A that presents a definition of a general principle or process. Reading text B that presents a specific instantiation of the principle or process. A stem that asks the test taker to explain how the content of Reading B instantiates the content of Reading A.
Measurement: Linguistic resources (especially range and complexity of structures and vocabulary; clarity and pace of speech)	Reading text B of approximately 100–150 words providing further elaboration on topic of Reading text A; 40–60 seconds for the test taker to read the passage			2b. Reading text A that presents a description of a problem Reading text B that presents the success, failure, partial success, or unintended consequences of an attempt to solve the problem. A stem that asks the test taker to explain the attempt to solve the problem and its results.
Discourse competence (especially cohesion and progression of ideas in sustained speech)	Both texts should avoid technical vocabulary that is difficult to pronounce and/or easily glossed. Prompt directly asks about the opinions/ideas expressed in Reading text B, indirectly requesting information from the reading text A.			

(continued)

TABLE 7.6
Continued

What is Being Measured?	Task Model			
	Fixed elements	Variable elements	Rubric	List of variants for each
	The question should not allow for portions of a response to be taken directly from either reading text. Prompt should elicit a response that demonstrates understanding of the relationship between the two reading texts.			
Content (especially relevance, accuracy, and completeness)	2. Order of item elements: Item directions (audio) stated simply. They explain what test taker will be required to do to complete the task. Reading A directions (audio) stated simply. They provide context for the reading text. They will include specific reference to the title/heading of the reading text. Reading text A Reading B directions (audio) stated simply. They provide the setting and general topic of the text. Reading text B Prompt is written and spoken. Preparation time: 30 seconds Response time: 60 seconds			

(Narrator) Read passage A about malaria. You will have 45 seconds to read the passage. Begin reading now.

Reading time: 45 seconds

Passage A

Efforts to control the spread of malaria have been much more successful since it was discovered that the disease is spread by the bite of certain kinds of mosquito. It is common near swamps in warm climates, since many mosquitoes lay their eggs in still water. Malaria cannot be spread directly from one person to another; instead, a mosquito bites an infected person and then passes the infection to the next person it bites. Protecting people from being bitten by mosquitoes and reducing mosquito populations are therefore central to modern efforts at malaria prevention.

(Narrator) Now read passage B on the same topic. You will have 50 seconds to read the passage.

Passage B

People have been getting malaria since prehistoric times, yet the cause of the disease was not known until relatively recently. For a long time, its cause was attributed to *air*. In the summer in the swampy areas around Rome, for example, the disease was so common that people began to associate the disease with swamps, and the bad-smelling air around swamps. In fact, the name malaria means "bad air" in Italian.
In the 1830s, a doctor in Florida working with malaria patients attempted to stop its spread. He recommended draining the swampy ground around the town in order to make the climate healthier. He was very close to the correct cause of malaria when he recommended that people put gauze or other light fabric over their windows. He believed the fabric would filter the air coming in, preventing the bad air from entering the home. His recommendations were effective, of course.

(Narrator) Explain what the doctor believed to be the cause of malaria, and what he recommended to prevent its spread. Explain why his recommendations worked.

Prep time: 30 seconds
Response time: 60 seconds

FIG. 7.1   Example task developed from the task shell shown in Table 7.6.

Task shells were developed for each of the subclaims shown in Table 7.3 that define the aspects of speaking to be measured on the speaking section. Similarly, TDA was conducted for the listening, reading, and writing tests and task shells were developed for each of these parts based on the claims and subclaims for each of these. These analyses resulted in the final test blueprint and the specifications for each of the four measures that are summarized in the next section.

THE FINAL BLUEPRINT AND SPECIFICATIONS FOR THE FOUR MEASURES

The TDA process resulted in significant changes to the speaking and writing measures and minor changes to the listening and reading measures. These changes are evident in the contrasts between the 2002 field study blueprint with the final blueprint described below. Then the specifications for each of the four measures are summarized.

Modifications to the Test Blueprint

Table 7.7 compares the 2002 field study blueprint described in Chapter 6 with the final blueprint. One major difference is that evidence of proficiency for up to three measures (e.g., listening, speaking, and writing) would be gathered in one test section in the 2002 blueprint while evidence of proficiency for only one measure would be gathered in each test section in the final blueprint. This reflected the decision that the same stimulus would not be used to provide evidence relevant to two measures in the final blueprint. That is, a listening set that included a lecture and listening comprehension questions would not also include a speaking task as in the 2002 blueprint. Instead, in the final blueprint, a unique listening stimulus would be used for a listening/speaking task. This change reflected assessment specialists' concerns about finding a sufficient number of listening and reading stimuli that could support the assessment of more than one skill.

A second major modification was that the final blueprint allowed for pretesting a certain number of listening and reading sets to serve as common items to appear in later final forms for IRT equating purposes. As discussed earlier, these common item sets are needed to employ the common item equating to a calibrated pool design.

Procedures Planned for the Listening and Reading Measures

The range of stimuli and items for the listening and reading sets in Table 7.7 reflects the inclusion of items for the purpose of pretesting. The additional time required for pretesting had to be offset by a reduction in test time in some other way. This was one factor that contributed to a third change—to include only two writing tasks instead of three on the writing measure. Other reasons for this change are discussed below when the task specifications for the writing measure are described.

TABLE 7.7
Comparison of 2002 Blueprint and the Final Blueprint for TOEFL iBT

2002 Field Study Blueprint		Final Blueprint—TOEFL iBT	
Stimulus	*Items per form*	*Stimulus*	*Items per form*
Section 1. Listening/speaking/writing—75 minutes		Section 1. Reading—60 to 100 minutes	
2 conversations	5–6 basic understanding items 2–3 pragmatic understanding items 2 connecting information items	3–5 passages	30–40 basic comprehension items 15–30 inferencing items 3–5 reading to learn items
4 lectures	10–11 basic understanding items 5–6 pragmatic understanding items 7–8 connecting information items 1 listening/speaking task 1 listening/writing task		
Section 2. Independent speaking—6 minutes		Section 2. Listening—50 to 90 minutes	
3 brief prompts	3 independent speaking tasks	2–3 conversations 4–6 lectures	16–31 basic understanding items 6–15 pragmatic understanding items 6–15 connecting information items
10 minute break		10 minute break	
Section 3. Reading/speaking /writing—103 minutes		Section 3. Speaking—20 minutes	
3 passages	35–36 basic comprehension items 3 reading to learn items 1 reading/speaking task 1 reading/writing task	brief prompt brief listening and reading texts brief conversation or lecture	2 independent tasks 2 listening/reading/ speaking tasks 2 listening/speaking tasks
Section 4. Independent writing—30 minutes		Section 4. Writing—60 minutes	
1 brief prompt	1 independent task	brief listening and reading texts brief prompt	1 reading/listening/ writing task 1 independent task
Total test time ~ 3 hours, 45 minutes		Total test time ~ 4 hours	
		3 hours 20 minutes + 30–40 minute pretest section	

Summary of Specifications for the Four Measures

The outcome of ECD was a set of specifications for each of the four measures. These specifications included an overall claim and subclaims about what each measure is intended to assess. Linked to each of the subclaims are task model components that describe the nature of the task, response type, scoring rubrics, number of questions, the nature of the stimulus information, and task or section timing. The summary that follows these specifications for each measure describes the total number of questions and stimulus materials that would contribute to a test taker's score and excludes a count of pretest sets that might be included on an operational form.

Listening   The specifications for the listening measure (see Table 7.8) were little changed from those in the previous field study. The overall claim that a test taker can understand spoken English in an academic environment was supported by three subclaims that reflected basic comprehension, pragmatic understanding, and connecting information. Linked to each of these subclaims were question types that had been evaluated in previous studies. The number of questions, the nature of the stimulus materials (two conversations and four lectures), and the scoring rubrics also remained unchanged. The total testing time for the listening measure, excluding pretest items, was approximately 50 minutes.

Reading   The overall claim for the reading measure is that a test taker can understand English language texts in an academic environment. One change to the specifications for the reading measure (see Table 7.9) was that three subclaims were identified rather than two. As assessment specialists gained more experience authoring the reading items, it was generally believed that the ability to comprehend ideas or connections between propositions that are not explicitly stated in the text or to understand an author's rhetorical purpose could be distinguished from abilities involved in basic comprehension. The assessment specialists referred to this ability as *inferencing* and distinguished it from reading to learn because it did not require connecting information across a large portion of the text. This change did not require the development of new question types but simply reflected a reclassification of some question types that had been previously considered as providing evidence for basic understanding. The total testing time for the reading measure, excluding pretest items, was approximately 60 minutes.

Speaking   A number of issues considered during the TDA process led to significant changes to the speaking measure. First and foremost, the existing specifications were not detailed enough to support the development of multiple parallel speaking measures, especially since no equating of these measures across forms was planned. Second, interrater reliability for individual tasks

TABLE 7.8
Summary of Specifications for Listening Measure of TOEFL iBT

Listening Claim	Test Taker Can Understand Spoken English in an Academic Environment		
Subclaims	Basic understanding: can understand the overall gist, important points and supporting details of lectures and conversations	Pragmatic understanding: can understand the speaker's purpose for making a statement in a lecture or conversation; understand the speaker's stance, either the attitude expressed or the degree of certainty	Connecting information: can understand connections between or among pieces of information in a single stimulus; can integrate information, draw inferences and conclusions, form generalizations, and make predictions on the basis of information heard in lectures and campus-based conversations
Nature of listening task	Questions about main ideas and important supporting details	Questions about a speaker's attitude or purpose, a speaker's degree of certainty, or a speaker's source of information	Questions about the relationships among ideas or about the organization of the aural text
Response types	Simple selected response	Simple or complex selected response[a]	Simple and complex selected response
Scoring rubric	Dichotomous right/wrong 0-1	Dichotomous right/wrong 0-1; partial credit 0-2	Dichotomous right/wrong 0-1; partial credit 0-2
Number of questions (34 per form)	16–21; at least 6 main ideas	6–10	6–10
Nature of stimulus material	4 lectures: The content of the lectures is representative of an introductory level academic lecture; they present a variety of academic subject matter. Lectures may be monologic or interactive. In the interactive lectures, a student may ask the professor a question; the professor may ask the students a question and someone responds; and a student may comment on what the professor has said. Typically, half of the lectures in a form are interactive. (3–5 minutes)	2 conversations: One conversation in each form is in the office setting and includes interaction between a professor and a student (may include academic content); the other conversation is a service encounter (interactions between a student and a nonstudent that take place in university-related setting and have nonacademic content). (2-3 minutes)	
All texts have a lead-in by a narrator and at least one. context visual. Some have content visuals as well.			
Total time	Approximately 50 minutes for 34 questions		

[a] In principle, pragmatic understanding (PU) items can be multiple selection, multiple-choice (MSMC); order/match, etc., though in practice they are SSMC (single selection, multiple-choice). Similarly, in principle there can be a PU 2-point item, though none may have been written to date.

TABLE 7.9
Summary of Specifications for the Reading Measure of TOEFL iBT

Reading Claim	Test Taker Can Understand English Language Texts in an Academic Environment		
Subclaims	Basic comprehension: can understand the lexical, syntactic, and semantic content of the text and the major ideas; can understand important sentence-level information; can connect information locally.	Inferencing;[a] can comprehend an argument or an idea that is strongly implied but not explicitly stated in the text, identify the nature of the link between specific features of exposition and the author's rhetorical purpose, and understand the lexical, grammatical, and logical links between successive sentences in a passage.	Reading to learn: can connect information across the entire text; can recognize the organization and purpose of a text, understand the relative importance/scope of ideas in a text; can understand rhetorical functions and purposes and organize (categorize/classify) important information into an appropriate mental framework representative of the organization and interrelationship of ideas in a text.
Nature of reading task	Questions about main ideas and supporting details based on individual propositions in a text, including vocabulary, reference, sentence simplification, factual information, or negative fact	Questions about information or an idea that is implied but not stated, about the author's purpose in employing an expository feature, or about where in a text a new sentence should be inserted	Questions that require test takers to create a summary of the main ideas and questions that require test takers to classify/ categorize information into a schematic table
Response types	Simple selected response	Simple selected response	Complex selected response—prose summary, schematic table
Scoring rubric	Dichotomous right/wrong 0-1	Dichotomous right/wrong 0-1	Dichotomous right/wrong 0-1; partial credit 0–4
Number of questions	9–28	9–18	3
Nature of stimulus material	Three passages on different topics selected from exposition, argumentation, or historical background/ autobiographical narrative; all texts categorized as having one major focus of development or more than one focus (approximately 700 words)		
Total time	Approximately 60 minutes for 39 to 45 questions		

[a] Added later; not in framework.

observed in the 2002 field study was considered too low. This suggested the rubrics and/or tasks needed to be refined. Third, the decision not to use the same texts on the listening or reading measures and the speaking measures meant that the characteristics of stimulus materials for integrated speaking tasks needed to be defined. The results of the TDA for the speaking measure are summarized in Table 7.10.

As described earlier, six subclaims were identified that underlay the overall claim that a test taker can communicate effectively by speaking in English-speaking academic environments. Task types that would provide evidence related to each of the six subclaims were defined, including two independent speaking tasks, two integrated listening/speaking tasks, and two integrated reading/listening/speaking tasks. Note that, to avoid the problem observed in previous prototyping studies of test takers simply reading portions of the text aloud, no task that relied on only reading passages was developed. The stimulus materials for the integrated speaking tasks represented either a campus context or an academic context and consisted of brief reading passages (75-100 words) and/or listening stimuli (60–120 seconds).

During the TDA discussions and the development of the task shells, assessment specialists also revisited the 5-point rubric that had been previously developed (see Chapter 4). They recommended that a 4-point rubric be considered because it was difficult to clearly distinguish five levels of proficiency.

Because these proposed speaking tasks differed considerably from those that had trialed in previous prototyping studies, a pilot study was carried out to refine the rubrics and to evaluate these tasks. A six-item speaking test was developed according to the specifications in Table 7.10 and administered to 180 test takers at seven institutions in the United States. In the first phase of this study, the rubrics were refined. Four groups of four individuals each listened to batches of randomly selected responses to each of the six items, ranked them impressionistically from 1 to 4, and discussed salient features of the responses. The results of the group discussions were then synthesized to create performance profiles at the various levels to identify salient boundary features and relevant evaluative criteria at each level. The information was used to formulate descriptors for the four scoring levels. In addition, a score of 0 was assigned if the test taker failed to respond or the response was off-topic. Two rubrics were developed, one for the stand-alone or independent tasks (Table 7.11) and one for the integrated tasks (Table 7.12).

Raters are directed to use the four categories—general description, delivery, language use, and topic development—across the top of the rubric to direct their attention to aspects of the test taker's response that should affect their rating. Characteristics of responses at each of the four scoring levels are described in the cells under each of the category headings. These response characteristics were developed beginning with the areas of measurement specified in the task shell: Linguistic resources (especially range and complexity of

TABLE 7.10
Summary of Specifications for Speaking Measure of TOEFL iBT

Examinee Can Communicate Effectively by Speaking in English-Speaking Academic Environments

Speaking Claim						
Subclaims	Can speak intelligibly about common everyday topics based on personal experience/knowledge	Can appropriately and intelligibly state and support preference for certain behavior or course of action from a given choice	Can appropriately and intelligibly combine and convey key information from reading and listening texts based on a situation typically occurring in a campus environment	Can appropriately and intelligibly combine and convey key information from reading and listening texts representative of academic course content	Can appropriately and intelligibly convey key ideas from a conversation about a problem typically occurring in a campus environment; can use personal knowledge to expand on info provided	Can appropriately and intelligibly convey key ideas from a lecture segment representative of academic course content
Nature of speaking task	Personal; describe and explain reason for a personal opinion about familiar persons, places, objects, events, activities, etc.	Personal; describe and support personal preference with respect to a given pair of behaviors or courses of action	Campus situation; recount the stance taken by a speaker in the listening stimulus and explain the relationship to the issues/position presented in the reading passage	Academic content; explain how examples/specific information/etc. provided in a listening stimulus support a broader process/concept/etc. presented in the reading passage	Campus situation; describe problem and solution(s) and propose an alternative solution or evaluate given solutions	Academic content; summarize a short lecture segment that explains meaning of term or concept

Response type	Constructed response	Constructed response	Constructed response	Constructed response	Constructed response	Constructed response
Scoring rubric	Independent 0–4	Independent 0–4	Integrated 0–4	Integrated 0–4	Integrated 0–4	Integrated 0–4
Number of questions	1	1	1	1	1	1
Nature of stimulus material	None	None	Reading passage: logically structured description of a position taken on some campus-related topic (75–100 wds.) Listening stimulus: logically structured response to position in reading passage (60–80 sec.)	Reading passage: broad description of theory, concept, term or other subject of academic relevance (75–100 wds.) Listening stimulus: detailed information about topic, or concrete example (60–80 sec.)	Listening passage: conversation about a problem and one or two possible solutions (75–90 sec.)	Listening passage: lecture on academic topic presenting two aspects or perspectives on a concept with concrete illustrations (60–120 sec.)
Prep time	15 sec.	15 sec.	30 sec.	30 sec.	20 sec.	20 sec.
Response time	45 sec.	45 sec.	60 sec.	60 sec.	60 sec.	60 sec.
Total time	Approximately 20 minutes for 6 questions					

TABLE 7.11
TOEFL Scoring Rubric for Independent Speaking Tasks

Score	General Description	Delivery	Language Use	Topic Development
4	The response fulfills the demands of the task, with at most minor lapses in completeness. It is highly intelligible and exhibits sustained, coherent discourse. A response at this level is characterized by all of the following:	Generally well-paced flow (fluid expression). Speech is clear. It may include minor lapses, or minor difficulties with pronunciation or intonation patterns, which do not affect overall intelligibility.	The response demonstrates effective use of grammar and vocabulary. It exhibits a fairly high degree of automaticity with good control of basic and complex structures (as appropriate). Some minor (or systematic) errors are noticeable but do not obscure meaning.	Response is sustained and sufficient to the task. It is generally well developed and coherent; relationships between ideas are clear (or clear progression of ideas).
3	The response addresses the task appropriately, but may fall short of being fully developed. It is generally intelligible and coherent, with some fluidity of expression though it exhibits some noticeable lapses in the expression of ideas. A response at this level is characterized by at least two of the following:	Speech is generally clear, with some fluidity of expression, though minor difficulties with pronunciation, intonation, or pacing are noticeable and may require listener effort at times (though overall intelligibility is not significantly affected).	The response demonstrates fairly automatic and effective use of grammar and vocabulary, and fairly coherent expression of relevant ideas. Response may exhibit some imprecise or inaccurate use of vocabulary or grammatical structures or be somewhat limited in the range of structures used. This may affect overall fluency, but it does not seriously interfere with the communication of the message.	Response is mostly coherent and sustained and conveys relevant ideas/information. Overall development is somewhat limited, usually lacks elaboration or specificity. Relationship between ideas may at times not be immediately clear.

2	The response addresses the task, but development of the topic is limited. It contains intelligible speech, although problems with delivery and/or overall coherence occur; meaning may be obscured in places. A response at this level is characterized by at least two of the following:	Speech is basically intelligible, though listener effort is needed because of unclear articulation, awkward intonation, or choppy rhythm/pace; meaning may be obscured in places.	The response demonstrates limited range and control of grammar and vocabulary. These limitations often prevent full expression of ideas. For the most part, only basic sentence structures are used successfully and spoken with fluidity. Structures and vocabulary may express mainly simple (short) and/or general propositions, with simple or unclear connections made among them (serial listing, conjunction, juxtaposition).	The response is connected to the task, though the number of ideas presented or the development of ideas is limited. Mostly basic ideas are expressed with limited elaboration (details and support). At times relevant substance may be vaguely expressed or repetitious. Connections of ideas may be unclear.
1	The response is very limited in content and/or coherence or is only minimally connected to the task, or speech is largely unintelligible. A response at this level is characterized by at least two of the following:	Consistent pronunciation, stress, and intonation difficulties cause considerable listener effort; delivery is choppy, fragmented, or telegraphic; frequent pauses and hesitations.	Range and control of grammar and vocabulary severely limit (or prevent) expression of ideas and connections among ideas. Some low-level responses may rely heavily on practiced or formulaic expressions.	Limited relevant content is expressed. The response generally lacks substance beyond expression of very basic ideas. Speaker may be unable to sustain speech to complete the task and may rely heavily on repetition of the prompt.
0	Speaker makes no attempt to respond OR response is unrelated to the topic.			

TABLE 7.12
TOEFL Scoring Rubric for Integrated Speaking Tasks

Score	General Description	Delivery	Language Use	Topic Development
4	The response fulfills the demands of the task, with at most minor lapses in completeness. It is highly intelligible and exhibits sustained, coherent discourse. A response at this level is characterized by the following:	Speech is generally clear, fluid, and sustained. It may include minor lapses or minor difficulties with pronunciation or intonation. Pace may vary at times as the speaker attempts to recall information. Overall intelligibility remains high.	The response demonstrates good control of basic and complex grammatical structures that allow for coherent, efficient (automatic) expression of relevant ideas. Contains generally effective word choice. Though some minor (or systematic) errors or imprecise use may be noticeable, they do not require listener effort (or obscure meaning).	The response presents a clear progression of ideas and conveys the relevant information required by the task. It includes appropriate detail, though it may have minor errors or minor omissions.
3	The response addresses the task appropriately, but may fall short of being fully developed. It is generally intelligible and coherent, with some fluidity of expression, though it exhibits some noticeable lapses in the expression of ideas. A response at this level is characterized by at least two of the following:	Speech is generally clear, with some fluidity of expression, but it exhibits minor difficulties with pronunciation, intonation, or pacing and may require some listener effort at times. Overall intelligibility remains good, however.	The response demonstrates fairly automatic and effective use of grammar and vocabulary, and fairly coherent expression of relevant ideas. Response may exhibit some imprecise or inaccurate use of vocabulary or grammatical structures or be somewhat limited in the range of structures used. Such limitations do not seriously interfere with the communication of the message.	Response is sustained and conveys relevant information required by the task. However, it exhibits some incompleteness, inaccuracy, lack of specificity with respect to content, or choppiness in the progression of ideas.

2	The response is connected to the task, though it may be missing some relevant information or contain inaccuracies. It contains some intelligible speech, but at times problems with intelligibility and/or overall coherence may obscure meaning. A response at this level is characterized by at least two of the following:	Speech is clear at times, though it exhibits problems with pronunciation, intonation, or pacing and so may require significant listener effort. Speech may not be sustained at a consistent level throughout. Problems with intelligibility may obscure meaning in places (but not throughout).	The response is limited in the range and control of vocabulary and grammar demonstrated (some complex structures may be used, but typically contain errors). This results in limited or vague expression of relevant ideas and imprecise or vague expression of relevant ideas and imprecise or inaccurate connections. Automaticity of expression may only be evident at the phrasal level.	The response conveys some relevant information but is clearly incomplete or inaccurate. It is incomplete if it omits key ideas, makes vague reference to key ideas, or demonstrates limited development of important information. An inaccurate response demonstrates misunderstanding of key ideas from the stimulus. Typically, ideas expressed may not be well connected or cohesive so that familiarity with the stimulus is necessary to follow what is being discussed.
1	The response is very limited in content or coherence or is only minimally connected to the task. Speech may be largely unintelligible. A response at this level is characterized by at least two of the following:	Consistent pronunciation and intonation problems cause considerable listener effort and frequently obscure meaning. Delivery is choppy, fragmented, or telegraphic. Speech contains frequent pauses and hesitations.	Range and control of grammar and vocabulary severely limit (or prevent) expression of ideas and connections among ideas. Some very low-level responses may rely heavily on isolated words or short utterances to communicate ideas.	The response fails to provide much relevant content. Ideas that are expressed are often inaccurate, limited to vague utterances, or repetitions (including repetition of prompt).
0	Speaker makes no attempt to respond OR response is unrelated to the topic.		

Note. From *TOEFL iBT/Next Generation TOEFL Test Integrated Speaking Rubrics*, 2004, Princeton, NJ: Educational Testing Service. Copyright 2004 by Educational Testing Service. Reprinted with permission.

structures and vocabulary, clarity and pace of speech), discourse competence (especially cohesion and progression of ideas in sustained speech), and content (especially relevance, accuracy, and completeness). The details for each level were filled in based on the analysis of the piloted sample tasks. A major difference between the rubrics for the independent and integrated tasks is the description of evidence for topic development. While the independent rubric mentions the quality, number, and relationships among ideas, the integrated rubric mentions the relevance, completeness, accuracy, and progression of information and content drawn from the stimulus material.

In the second phase of the study, 16 raters scored 180 sets of test taker responses using the revised rubrics. A portion of the responses was double-scored. The analyses of these data indicated that this version of the speaking measure was an improvement over the version used in the 2002 field study. The new rubrics were found to distinguish well at all four levels; the internal consistency as assessed by Cronbach's alpha coefficient was .91; and inter-rater reliability for each of the six tasks ranged from .73 to .92.

Writing   The general claim for the writing measure, that test takers can communicate effectively in writing in English-language academic environments, was consistent with the original writing framework and subsequent development of the measure. One of the two subclaims, however, reflected a different emphasis than previous descriptions of the abilities to be tested. The second subclaim in Table 7.13 places more emphasis on synthesizing or relating ideas from two different academic sources rather than summarizing ideas from one source. The revision of the writing measure had to take into account two factors. One concerned test takers copying verbatim material from the text for integrated tasks based solely on reading passages. The second concerned the time-consuming nature of writing tasks. In the original test blueprint, the stimuli from the listening and reading measures served the dual purpose—assessing comprehension and providing content for the integrated writing tasks. But the decision to use unique listening and reading texts for the writing measure meant that additional time would be needed for the test takers to listen to or read the new material.

These factors led to a decision to trial an integrated listening/reading/writing (L/R/W) task that required test takers to summarize a short lecture and to explain how these points were related to points in the reading passage. A small-scale pilot study of types of integrated writing tasks (L/W, R/W, and L/R/W) convinced the assessment specialists that the L/R/W task provided better evidence of writing ability than did the L/W and R/W tasks. As a result of the TDA process, the writing measure had two subclaims, each assessed by a single task. Both tasks were scored using a 5-point scale with the addition of a 0 for off-topic essays. Other than this, the rubric for the independent task (see Table 7.14) was unchanged from the rubric used in the previous field study. However, based on the responses to the L/R/W task, a new rubric was

TABLE 7.13
Summary of Specifications for Writing Measure of TOEFL iBT

Writing Claim	Test Taker Can Communicate Effectively in Writing in English-Language Academic Environments	
Subclaims	Can formulate and communicate ideas in writing on a variety of general topics, producing extended, organized written text expressing and supporting his/her own opinions based on own knowledge and experience, taking into account the knowledge of the intended audience	Can coherently organize and accurately express in writing the content and structure of academic discourse, demonstrating an understanding of key ideas on an academic topic as presented in reading and lecture formats and the rhetorical relationships such as claim/rebuttal, problem/solution, and proposal/counter proposal that link the information in these texts
Nature of writing task	Independent: state, explain, and support an opinion on an issue	Integrated: summarize the points made in the lecture and describe how these points respond to points made in the reading passage
Response type	Constructed response	Constructed response
Scoring rubric	Independent 0–5	Integrated 0–5
Number of questions	1	1
Nature of stimulus material	Brief prompt	A reading passage, 230–300 words long, that conveys a position, problem, or explanation. A 2-minute lecture that provides a detailed response to the position, problem, or explanation presented in the reading passage. Reading passage is available during response time.
Response time	30 minutes	20 minutes
Total time	Approximately 60 minutes for 2 questions	

developed (see Table 7.15) that required some inclusion of information from both the lecture and the reading to receive a score of 2 or greater.

TECHNOLOGICAL INNOVATIONS

The design of this new test presented challenges for test delivery and scoring that would be resolved, in part, through technology. First, the decision to commit to worldwide computer-based test administration created the need for an enormous expansion of the test delivery system. Second, the number

TABLE 7.14
TOEFL Scoring Rubric for Independent Writing Tasks

Score	Task Description
5	An essay at this level largely accomplishes all of the following: • effectively addresses the topic and task • is well organized and well developed, using clearly appropriate explanations, exemplifications, and/or details • displays unity, progression, and coherence • displays consistent facility in the use of language, demonstrating syntactic variety, appropriate word choice, and idiomaticity, though it may have minor lexical or grammatical errors.
4	An essay at this level largely accomplishes all of the following: • addresses the topic and task well, though some points may not be fully elaborated • is generally well organized and well developed, using appropriate and sufficient explanations, exemplifications, and/or details • displays unity, progression, and coherence, though it may contain occasional redundancy, digression, or unclear connections • displays facility in the use of language, demonstrating syntactic variety and range of vocabulary, though it will probably have occasional noticeable minor errors in structure, word form, or use of idiomatic language that do not interfere with meaning.
3	An essay at this level is marked by one or more of the following: • addresses the topic and task using somewhat developed explanations, exemplifications, and/or details • displays unity, progression, and coherence, though connection of ideas may be occasionally obscured • may demonstrate inconsistent facility in sentence formation and word choice that may result in lack of clarity and occasionally obscure meaning • may display accurate but limited range of syntactic structures and vocabulary.
2	An essay at this level may reveal one or more of the following weaknesses: • limited development in response to the topic and task • inadequate organization or connection of ideas • inappropriate or insufficient exemplifications, explanations, or details to support or illustrate generalizations in response to the task • a noticeably inappropriate choice of words or word forms • an accumulation of errors in sentence structure and/or usage.
1	An essay at this level is seriously flawed by one or more of the following weaknesses: • serious disorganization or underdevelopment • little or no detail, or irrelevant specifics, or questionable responsiveness to the task • serious and frequent errors in sentence structure or usage.
0	A essay at this level merely copies words from the topic, rejects the topic, or is otherwise not connected to the topic, is written in a foreign language, consists of keystroke characters, or is blank.

Note. From *TOEFL iBT/Next Generation TOEFL Test Independent Writing Rubrics* (Scoring Standards), 2004, Princeton, NJ: Educational Testing Service. Copyright 2004 by Educational Testing Service. Reprinted with permission.

TABLE 7.15
TOEFL Scoring Rubric for Integrated Writing Tasks

Score	Task Description
5	A response at this level successfully selects the important information from the lecture and coherently and accurately presents this information in relation to the relevant information presented in the reading. The response is well organized, and occasional language errors that are present do not result in inaccurate or imprecise presentation of content or connections.
4	A response at this level is generally good in selecting the important information from the lecture and in coherently and accurately presenting this information in relation to the relevant information in the reading, but it may have minor omission, inaccuracy, vagueness, or imprecision of some content from the lecture or in connection to points made in the reading. A response is also scored at this level if it has more frequent or noticeable minor language errors, as long as such usage and grammatical structures do not result in anything more than an occasional lapse of clarity or in the connection of ideas.
3	A response at this level contains some important information from the lecture and conveys some relevant connection to the reading, but it is marked by one or more of the following: • Although the overall response is definitely oriented to the task, it conveys only vague, global, unclear, or somewhat imprecise connection of the points made in the lecture to points made in the reading. • The response may omit one major key point made in the lecture. • Some key points made in the lecture or the reading, or connections between the two, may be incomplete, inaccurate, or imprecise. • Errors of usage and/or grammar may be more frequent or may result in noticeably vague expressions or obscured meanings in conveying ideas connections.
2	A response at this level contains some relevant information from the lecture but is marked by significant language difficulties or by significant omission or inaccuracy of important ideas from the lecture or in the connections between the lecture and the reading; a response at this level is marked by one or more of the following: • The response significantly misrepresents or completely omits the overall connection between the lecture and the reading. • The response significantly omits or significantly misrepresents important points made in the lecture. • The response contains language errors or expressions that largely obscure connections or meaning at key junctures, or that would likely obscure understanding of key ideas for a reader not already familiar with the reading and the lecture.
1	A response at this level is marked by one or more of the following: • The response provides little or no meaningful or relevant coherent content from the lecture. • The language level of the response is so low that it is difficult to derive meaning.
0	A response at this level merely copies sentences from the reading, rejects the topic or is otherwise not connected to the topic, is written in a foreign language, consists of keystroke characters, or is blank.

Note. From *TOEFL iBT/Next Generation TOEFL Test Integrated Writing Rubrics* (Scoring Standards), 2004, Princeton, NJ: Educational Testing Service. Copyright 2004 by Educational Testing Service. Reprinted with permission.

of constructed responses to be scored would increase by a factor of 10, from 600,000 to 5 to 6 million. To meet these challenges, the development of an Internet-based test delivery system and the expansion of an online scoring network were planned.

An Internet-Based Test (iBT) Delivery System

The decision to create and deliver 50 or more linear forms per year via computer worldwide required expanding the test delivery network from 600 test centers to more than 2,000. The technology supporting the TOEFL computer-based test (CBT) had entailed local area networks that delivered tests at a few hundred test centers. The TOEFL CBT required continuous, automated test assembly of test forms from a pool of reusable test items that resided on servers at the test centers. Experience with the TOEFL CBT revealed shortcomings in this operational model related to test security and access. The security of the test was compromised because some test takers memorized and then published items in various venues. The number and locations of the test centers limited access to the TOEFL CBT for test takers.

The worldwide expansion of Internet connectivity during the 1990s presented an opportunity to increase the number of test administration sites that could deliver a computer-based test. An Internet-based test (iBT) delivery system would increase access to test centers for test takers worldwide. An iBT would not require dedicated test centers. Instead, a variety of institutions with the necessary hardware, a broadband Internet connection, and qualified staff could be certified to administer the new TOEFL on a fixed schedule. The development of this iBT network proceeded as the test specifications were finalized. As a result, the new test became known as the TOEFL iBT, to distinguish it from previous versions that had been also identified by the delivery method (the TOEFL PBT and the TOEFL CBT).

An Online Scoring Network

One of the practices ETS has always used to assure reliability of constructed-response scoring has been continuous monitoring of raters as they score. For the tests that were administered on an intermittent schedule, the Test of Written English™ (TWE®; ~5 times per year) and the Test of Spoken English™ (TSE®; ~12 times per year), this was accomplished by having raters meet at central locations for scoring sessions. Raters read the handwritten essays or listened to TSE audio tapes and recorded their ratings on paper. At these meetings, scoring leaders constantly monitored rater consistency and agreement.

With the introduction of the TOEFL CBT, the essays needed to be scored on a continuous basis. To meet the challenge, ETS began to use the patented

Online Scoring Network (OSN) for TOEFL essay scoring. OSN is a computer-based system used to distribute essays to raters, to record ratings, and to monitor rating quality constantly. When the OSN system was first implemented, raters came to one of four central locations very nearly on a daily basis and scored essays on workstations connected to a client/server network. In 1999, the OSN system was redesigned from client-server architecture to a Web-based system wherein ratings are performed via the Internet over a secure connection to ETS. Scoring leaders and raters thus began to work from home. A Web site for self-training was created for prospective raters to learn about the TOEFL CBT essay scoring guide and see how it is applied to sample papers. Potential raters could then take a certification test remotely from home in the secure OSN setting.

Under the OSN Web-based rating system for scoring essays, raters submit their availability to work and are then notified when they have been scheduled to work. When they log into OSN, they are told who their scoring leader is, and they are presented with a calibration test. They must pass this test in order to proceed to operational scoring. Throughout the day, raters and scoring leaders can talk via a toll-free phone arrangement, and scoring leaders continue to have the same real-time capabilities to monitor raters under their supervision. Assessment specialists at ETS monitor the quality of the ratings and communicate with scoring leaders during rating sessions. Above all this, the quality of the daily reports on raters received from scoring leaders is reviewed at ETS.

The existing Web-based system for scoring TOEFL CBT writing was well-suited to scoring TOEFL iBT writing. The major innovation to the Web-based OSN system for TOEFL iBT was to support the delivery of sound files to raters. The procedures for training and monitoring raters developed for writing were adapted for speaking. As with writing, raters for speaking are trained before they are certified to rate. When scheduled to score, raters must calibrate for each prompt they are assigned to rate.

CONCLUSION

As a result of the ECD process described in this chapter, modifications were made to tasks to solve the problems that had appeared in piloting. The TDA process required careful rethinking and further specification of all of the tasks in the draft blueprint, which in turn resulted in a revision of the draft blueprint itself. The outcome from this process was the detailed task specifications required for developing and giving the operational test. The next phase in test design was a large scale field study of the final test blueprint intended to establish the psychometric properties of TOEFL iBT and provide test users with information about the new test.

NOTE

1. One ultimate goal of ECD, to embody in the test specifications a formal statistical model of a complex theoretical construct, is difficult to achieve at present in many domains.

REFERENCES

Bejar, I., Douglas, D., Jamieson, J., Nissan, S., & Turner, J. (2000). *TOEFL 2000 listening framework: A working paper* (TOEFL Monograph No. 19). Princeton, NJ: Educational Testing Service.

Butler, F. A., Eignor, D., Jones, S., McNamara, T., & Suomi, B. K. (2000). *TOEFL 2000 speaking framework: A working paper* (TOEFL Monograph No. 20). Princeton, NJ: Educational Testing Service.

Cumming, A., Kantor, R., Powers, D., Santos, T., & Taylor, C. (2000). *TOEFL 2000 writing framework: A working paper* (TOEFL Monograph No. 18). Princeton, NJ: Educational Testing Service.

Enright, M. K., Grabe, W., Koda, K., Mosenthal, P., Mulcahy-Ernt, P., & Schedl, M. (2000). *TOEFL 2000 reading framework: A working paper* (TOEFL Monograph No. 17). Princeton, NJ: Educational Testing Service.

Jamieson, J., Jones, S., Kirsch, I., Mosenthal, P., & Taylor, C. (2000). *TOEFL 2000 framework: A working paper* (TOEFL Monograph No. 16). Princeton, NJ: Educational Testing Service.

Kolen, M. J., & Brennan, R. L. (2004). *Test equating: Methods and practices* (2nd ed.). New York: Springer-Verlag.

Mislevy, R. J., Steinberg, L. S., & Almond, R. G. (2002). Design and analysis in task-based language assessment. *Language Testing, 19*, 477–496.

Mislevy, R. J., Steinberg, L. S., & Almond, R. G. (2003). On the structure of educational assessment. *Measurement: Interdisciplinary Research and Perspectives, 1*, 3–62.

8

A Final Analysis

Lin Wang
Daniel Eignor
Mary K. Enright

The revisions in the test specifications described in the previous chapter and the needs of test users set the stage for the final phase of test design. Attention now focused on two goals—verifying that the new test met psychometric requirements and making the transition from current versions of the TOEFL® to the TOEFL Internet-based test (iBT) as seamless and easy as possible for test users.

Psychometric issues centered on establishing the measurement properties of the items and measures, given the revised test specifications, and planning for scaling and equating. The evidence-centered design process, described in the previous chapter, resulted in modifications to the proposed speaking and writing tasks and measures. Chief among these modifications were decisions to (a) use separate listening and reading texts for integrated tasks rather than the same texts that were used for listening and reading comprehension questions, (b) include some speaking and writing tasks that required the integration of information from both reading and listening texts, (c) include only two writing tasks, and (d) use a 4-point scale for scoring speaking tasks. The intent of these changes was to improve score comparability across forms, but their effects had to be assessed.

Critical score user needs were identified by TOEFL program management in discussions with admissions officers about the new test. One was the desire for a total score, and the other was for information linking scores on the new test to scores on previous versions of the TOEFL. Additionally, the needs of teachers and students for information about the content of the new test and how to prepare for it had long been recognized by the TOEFL program.

Plans were made to address these three user needs. First, a preliminary proposal to scale the listening and reading scores, but not the speaking and writing scores, (see Chapter 6) was revisited in light of users' requirements for a total score. Second, linking relationships between the scores on the TOEFL iBT and scores on the TOEFL computer-based test (CBT) would have to be established. And third, materials to help score users, teachers, and students prepare for the transition to a new test were to be made available.

Psychometric requirements and users' needs created certain tensions about how to best address all these issues. Ideally, the psychometric issues would be addressed best under operational conditions with a representative and highly motivated sample of the test taker population. However, test users needed information about the test well in advance of its release to plan for score use and to prepare for the test. The resolution of these conflicting needs was a plan for a final field study to evaluate the revised test specifications and to provide test users with information about the content of the new test, the new score scales, and how to interpret scores.

GUIDING QUESTIONS FOR THE FINAL PHASE OF TEST DESIGN

With these needs in mind, a final field study was designed to answer critical questions related to evaluation, generalization, and utilization inferences. The field study also served as an opportunity to address questions related to explanation and extrapolation inferences in the interpretative argument as well. Table 8.1 lists these questions as they pertain to assumptions underlying the warrants associated with five of the inferences in the interpretative argument.

Three questions were relevant to the evaluation inference based on the warrant that performance on the TOEFL is evaluated to provide scores reflective of targeted language abilities. The statistical characteristics of the test tasks were examined with two questions in mind. To provide a basis for norm-referenced decisions, tasks had to be of an appropriate level of difficulty for the population and to differentiate levels of ability among test takers. The difficulty level was a particular concern for the integrated writing tasks that were found to be quite difficult in the previous field study. The fit of item response theory (IRT) models to listening and reading items needed to be established because IRT true score equating would be used for the listening and reading measures. This meant that calibrated items were needed to equate future operational forms. A third question, concerning the relationship between test takers' familiarity with English language computers and test performance, was examined as computer familiarity was one factor that could interfere with the assessment of language ability on an Internet-based test.

The generalization inference entails the warrant that observed scores are estimates of expected scores from form to form. Psychometric procedures for

TABLE 8.1

Questions Investigated in the Final Analysis that Are Relevant to the Assumptions Underlying the Inferences and Warrants in the TOEFL Interpretative Argument

Assumptions Underlying Warrant	*Related Questions*
Evaluation	
The statistical characteristics of items, measures, and test forms are appropriate for norm-referenced decisions.	Were the test tasks psychometrically sound? How well did IRT models fit the listening and reading items?
Task administration conditions are appropriate for providing evidence of targeted language abilities.	Is performance affected by computer familiarity?
Generalization	
Appropriate equating and scaling procedures for test scores are used.	What equating procedures and score scales would be appropriate for the four skill measures?
A sufficient number of tasks are included on the test to provide stable estimates of test takers' performances.	How reliable are scores on the four skill measures?
Task and test specifications are well defined so that parallel tasks and test forms are created.	Are the speaking and writing tasks comparable in difficulty across forms?
Explanation	
The internal structure of the test scores is consistent with a theoretical view of language proficiency as a number of highly interrelated components.	What factor model best fit the test scores?
Test performance varies according to amount and quality of experience in learning English.	Is performance on the test related to the number of years of English instruction?
Extrapolation	
Performance on the test is related to other criteria of language proficiency in the academic context.	How does performance on the test relate to • students' academic placement? • test takers' self-assessments of their English language proficiency?
Utilization	
The meaning of test scores is clearly interpretable by admissions officers, test takers, and teachers.	How do scores on the new test correspond to scores on previous versions of the TOEFL? How should institutions set standards for score use? Can performance at different score levels be linked to descriptions of students' linguistic abilities?
The test will have a positive influence on how English is taught.	How did teachers and learners prepare for TOEFL before the introduction of TOEFL iBT? How can teachers and students prepare for the new test?

scaling and equating test forms are one way to support this inference. The issue of what scales would be appropriate for the test measures, first discussed in Chapter 6, needed to be revisited in view of users' desire for a total score. In previous studies, we had investigated the reliability and generalizability for test measures of varying configurations, using a variety of indices that needed to be estimated again as a result of the modifications in the design of the speaking and writing measures.

Given that there were no plans to equate the speaking and writing scores, an alternative type of evidence, the comparability of scores for parallel versions of speaking and writing tasks, was examined. If parallel tasks did not vary in difficulty when administered to the same group of test takers, confidence in the ability to control form-to-form variation in difficulty through test development and scoring practices would be increased.

The explanation inference is based on the warrant that test scores are accounted for by the construct of academic language proficiency. One related research question was whether the internal structure of the test was consistent with theoretical expectations of a hierarchical model. A confirmatory factor analysis was carried out to investigate the fit of such a model to the field study data. Another question concerned the associations between test performance and the number of years test takers reported that they had studied English.

The extrapolation inference is based on the warrant that the construct of academic language proficiency accounts for the quality of linguistic performance in English-medium institutions of higher education. As in previous studies, evidence to support this inference was sought by examining the relationships between performance on the field study test and two other criterion measures of language proficiency—test takers' academic placement and their own assessments of their English language abilities and test performance.

Prior to the operational release of a test, there are limited opportunities to collect empirical data to support the utilization inference based on the warrant that test scores are useful for making decisions about admissions and appropriate curriculum for test takers. However, there is much a testing organization can do to inform test users about the new test prior to its release that will encourage appropriate test score interpretation and use. To help test users understand the meaning of TOEFL iBT test scores, the field study data was used to link TOEFL iBT scores to TOEFL CBT scores, to develop a standard-setting manual for institutions, and to describe performance at different score levels in terms of score levels of what students know and can do. To monitor the impact of TOFL iBT on instruction, an investigation of test preparation practices prior to the introduction of the TOEFL iBT was undertaken to provide a baseline against which changes in test preparation practices could be measured. Information and materials to support instruction were developed for teachers and students to foster positive test impact on teaching and learning.

The field study described in this chapter provided an opportunity to collect evidence relevant to many of the assumptions underlying the inferences and warrants in the TOEFL interpretative argument.

TOEFL IBT FIELD STUDY METHODOLOGY

The TOEFL iBT field study was designed to provide data relevant to both test user needs and psychometric issues. Test users' desire for information to link scores on the TOEFL CBT with scores on the TOEFL iBT meant that both tests would have to be administered to a representative sample of TOEFL test takers. A sample of 2,500 to 3,000 would be large enough for IRT analyses of listening and reading items on a TOEFL iBT form for use in equating future test forms. A second TOEFL iBT form was to be administered to a subsample of field study participants to provide evidence of score consistency across forms. This second TOEFL iBT form, which did not include items secured for future equating, also would provide teachers and students with opportunities for test familiarization. Study participants also completed a background questionnaire and a self-assessment instrument.

Participants

A two-stage sampling and recruiting procedure was adopted. First, Educational Testing Service® (ETS®) recruited test sites with local test supervisors serving as contact persons. Then the local test supervisors recruited individuals according to ETS requirements for participation. The sampling plan to recruit 3,000 participants was based on the 2001–2002 testing year volumes for both the current TOEFL CBT and the TOEFL paper-based test (PBT). Thirty-one countries were identified for the study based on these countries' TOEFL testing volumes and their geographic locations. The number of participants per country was chosen in proportion to the country's TOEFL testing volume, with some modifications. The 31 countries contributed to about 80% of the 2001–2002 TOEFL testing volume. It was assumed that the geographic representation of the sample also implied adequate representation of the sample with respect to native languages.

In addition to the geographic representation of the desired sample, level of English proficiency of the participants was also an important element of the sampling plan. Local test supervisors were asked to recruit participants whose levels of English proficiency varied from low to high according to TOEFL scores or some other criterion or criteria that were used in local English instructional programs. Each participant was paid $50 U.S. for each test he or she took.

MATERIALS

Test Instruments

Both the TOEFL iBT and the TOEFL CBT were administered to participants to obtain data for score linking. Two TOEFL iBT forms, Form A and Form B, were assembled according to the TOEFL iBT test form specifications described in the previous chapter. Form A, which was to provide items to equate the initial operational test forms, was taken by every participant. Form B was administered to a subset of about 500 participants. The tests were administered in computer labs at a number of institutions rather than existing CBT test centers. Therefore, a TOEFL CBT version that could be installed on local computers for administration was needed. A stand-alone item pool was created for each measure of the TOEFL CBT following the same standards that are used in creating the operational TOEFL CBT item pools. TOEFL CBT test forms were then created and administered from these pools. The two TOEFL iBT test forms were delivered via the Internet.

Table 8.2 presents a comparison of TOEFL CBT and TOEFL iBT test forms.

Listening As is evident in Table 8.2, there were fewer and longer listening stimuli on the TOEFL iBT than on the TOEFL CBT. For the TOEFL CBT, all items were dichotomously scored. The listening measures on TOEFL iBT Forms A and B each consisted of six sets of items. Each form had two conversation stimuli and four lecture stimuli. There were about five to six items associated with each stimulus. TOEFL iBT Form A had 31 dichotomously scored items and two polytomously scored items. TOEFL iBT Form B had 34 dichotomously scored items.

Reading A major difference between the TOEFL CBT and TOEFL iBT was the number and length of the reading passages, with fewer and longer passages on the TOEFL iBT. Also, the TOEFL iBT included both dichotomously scored and polytomously scored items; the TOEFL CBT included only dichotomously scored items. The reading measures on TOEFL iBT Forms A and Form B each consisted of three sets of passage-based items. In each set, there were 12 to 14 items based on a passage of about 600 to 700 words on a certain academic topic. All except one item in each set were dichotomously scored. The one complex selected-response item per set was scored according the rules developed in Chapter 5, and the maximum points awarded varied from 2 to 4, depending on the complexity of the item.

Speaking The TOEFL CBT did not have a speaking measure, whereas the TOEFL iBT speaking measure includes six tasks: Two independent tasks require test takers to express an opinion on a familiar topic. Another two

TABLE 8.2
A Comparison of TOEFL CBT and TOEFL iBT

TOEFL CBT	*TOEFL iBT*
Listening	
11–17 dialogues 1 question each 2–3 short conversations, up to 1 minute long 2–3 questions each 4–6 mini-lectures and discussions, up to 2 minutes long, 3–6 questions each Time: 40–60 minutes	4–6 lectures, some with classroom discussion, 3 to 5 minutes long 6 questions each 2–3 conversations, up to 3 minutes long 5 questions each Time: 40–60 minutes
Reading	
4–5 passages from academic texts, 250–350 words long, 11 questions per passage Time: 70–90 minutes	3–5 passages from academic texts, 600–700 words long, 12–14 questions per passage Time: 60–100 minutes
Speaking	
Not assessed	6 tasks 2 independent tasks–express an opinion on a familiar topic 4 integrated tasks–speak based on what is heard and read Up to 30 seconds to prepare a response Up to 1 minute to respond Each task rated on a 0–4 scale Time: 20 minutes
Writing	
1 independent task–support an opinion on a topic Rated on a 0–6 scale Combined with structure score Typing optional Time: 30 minutes	2 tasks 1 independent task–support an opinion on a topic (30 minutes) 1 integrated tasks–write based on what is heard and read (20 minutes) Each task rated on a 0–5 scale Typing required Time: 50 minutes
Structure	
20–25 questions Combined with writing score Time: 15–20 minutes	No separate grammar measure although grammar is evaluated in speaking and writing responses
Other differences	
Notetaking not allowed Adaptive forms (listening, structure), Linear-on-the-fly forms (reading)[a]	Notetaking allowed Linear forms for all measures

[a] Linear-on-the-fly (LOFT) is the method that is used in TOEFL CBT reading to assemble unique test forms in real time from a pool of test items. An assembled test form is then administered to a candidate as an intact form without any adaptive procedures that are used in TOEFL CBT listening and structure sections.

tasks require the integration of skills by asking the examinees to read and listen to a topic first and then respond orally by referring to what was presented in the reading and listening materials. The final two tasks also required the integration of skills by asking examinees to listen to some materials and then talk about the topic with reference to the listening materials.

Writing The TOEFL CBT structure and writing (SW) measure included both single-selection multiple-choice structure items and one independent writing (IW) task. There were no structure items on the TOEFL iBT writing measure, which consisted of two writing tasks. One was an integrated reading/listening/writing task (R/L/W) that required test takers to read a passage, listen to a discussion on the reading topic, and then write a response. The other task, similar to the TOEFL CBT writing task, was an IW task that required writing on a general topic.

Other Instruments

Participants were presented with a series of computer-based background and self-assessment questions at the start of their first test session. The background questions concerned test takers' characteristics, such as gender, native country, educational status, interests, and future plans, computer familiarity, and English-learning experiences. The self-assessment questionnaire described in Chapter 6 was modified by including more "can-do" statements (14 to 19 per modality for a total of 65 can-do items). All the can-do items were worded so that test takers could indicate the degree to which they agreed with each statement on a 5-point scale ranging from completely agree to completely disagree.

PROCEDURES

Study Design and Data Collection

To provide data for score linking, each participant took Form A of the TOEFL iBT and TOEFL CBT. A subgroup of participants was also asked to take Form B of the TOEFL iBT to provide data for analysis of alternate forms (Forms A and B). Because of the length of each test and the fact that a participant might be required to take up to three tests (Form A, Form B, and the TOEFL CBT), a counterbalanced design was necessary to control for the effects of fatigue and practice on any one of the tests. For the participants who took only two tests, the order of administration of the TOEFL iBT Form A and the TOEFL CBT was counterbalanced. For the subgroup who also took Form B, the TOEFL CBT was always administered second in the series; either Form A or B was administered first, and the remaining form was administered third.

The guidelines to the local test supervisors stipulated that no one was to take two tests consecutively without a break of at least 2 hours, and no one was to be allowed to take three tests on a single day. The actual test administrations spanned the time period from December 7, 2003 to February 4, 2004, in 31[1] countries or regions across five continents.

Scoring Speaking and Writing

Speaking   The responses for the six speaking tasks on the TOEFL iBT forms were captured as audio samples and scored by trained raters at ETS. Each response was scored on a 1 to 4 scale, with 0 given to an off-topic or unscorable response. Each speaking response for the main group of participants, who took Form A and the TOEFL CBT, was rated once (single scoring). This one score was the final score for that task. The total speaking raw score was the sum of the final scores on the six tasks, ranging from 0 to 24.

The speaking responses for the subgroup of participants who took Form B as well as Form A and the TOEFL CBT were rated twice (double-scoring) for use in the analyses of reliability and generalizability. When there was a discrepancy of more than 1 point between the first and second ratings, the final score was provided by a chief rater.

Writing   Each participant's response to each writing task was scored by two raters (double-scoring) using a rating scale of 1 to 5, and a 0 was assigned to off-topic and unscorable responses. If two raters' scores on the same response differed by more than one point, an adjudication process was invoked whereby a third rater would score the response. The final score for this task was either the average of the three scores if they were adjacent to each other (e.g., 3–5–4) or the average of the two closest scores in a sequence. For example, if the three scores were in a sequence like 3–5–2, then 2 and 3 were the closest scores. Therefore, the final score was the average of the two adjacent scores, or 2.5.

A participant's total writing raw score was the sum of the averaged scores on the two writing tasks. Therefore, task scores range from 0 to 5 in increments of 0.5, and the total score ranged from 0 to 10 in increments of 0.5.

PRELIMINARY ANALYSES

Preliminary analyses addressed three concerns. First, given that test sessions were long and occurred over a number of days and that the motivation of study participants was uncertain, criteria for including data records in further analyses needed to be established. Second, before combining the data from different groups for analyses, it was necessary to determine if either practice or fatigue affected performance on the test forms. Third, because the field study was conducted on a convenience sample of volunteer participants, their characteristics were examined to assess ways in which they were similar to or different from TOEFL test takers.

Identification of Usable Data Records

During the 2-month period of administration, 3,284 participants were administered TOEFL iBT Form A and the TOEFL CBT. In addition, 519 of the 3,284 participants were also administered TOEFL iBT Form B. Data cleansing was performed, using a number of criteria, to remove unusable records from further analysis. First, there were some known system-test cases in the returned data, and these records were removed. Second, due to various technical problems, some participants could not complete the tests and returned incomplete data; other records were corrupted beyond recovery. These records were also removed. Third, candidates who provided responses to fewer than ten test questions in the listening or reading measures or spent less than 5 minutes responding to a measure were considered as not having really attempted to take the tests for lack of motivation. These candidates' records were also removed. In addition, some records had incorrect or missing candidate ID numbers so it was not possible to merge their data from the TOEFL iBT and TOEFL CBT. As a result of such data-cleansing and data-merging requirements, and depending on the specific measures and analysis requirements involved, the achieved sample sizes for the Form A /TOEFL CBT combination varied from 2,194 to 2,937, and the sample size for TOEFL iBT Form B varied between 290 and 465. For most analyses on the overall sample, the sample size was 2,720.

PERFORMANCE OF THE COUNTERBALANCED GROUPS ON TOEFL IBT MEASURES

As noted previously, because of the amount of time and effort required of the participants in completing the tests, a counterbalanced design was implemented to deal with practice and fatigue effects. In a preliminary data analysis step, the performance of the counterbalanced groups was compared. Large performance differences across the counterbalanced groups would indicate undesired effects associated with the order of administration of the tests due to fatigue, practice, or both. If such large differences are ignored and the data from the counterbalanced groups are pooled to form one overall group, subsequent analyses may not provide valid results (Kolen & Brennan, 1995).

The means and standard deviations (SDs) of the unscaled or raw scores of the counterbalanced groups for TOEFL iBT Form A and Form B were examined. The differences in the mean raw scores on Form A between the participants who took Form A and the TOEFL CBT in a counterbalanced order were trivial, representing effect sizes of 0.01, 0.08, 0.02, and 0.00 for listening, reading, speaking, and writing, respectively. The order differences for Form B were also very small, representing effect sizes ranging from 0.05 to 0.18, showing little evidence of any order effect.

Overall, the performances of the counterbalanced groups did not exhibit differences that would preclude pooling the data for subsequent analyses on all the measures and the tests. Hence, the data from counterbalanced administrations of Form A, of the TOEFL CBT, and of Form B were pooled for analysis purposes.

Sample Demographics

In general, the overall study sample was reasonably representative of the operational population in terms of reported native countries or regions, although there were a few exceptions. Table 8.3 displays the 22 reported native

TABLE 8.3
Native Country of Field Study Sample and 2002-2003 TOEFL Test Takers

Reported native country	Field Study Sample N = 2720 Percentage	TOEFL Population[a] N = 672,341 Percentage
China	13.6	14.6
India	13.1	9.3
Korea (South)	8.8	12.9
Japan	5.8	12.5
Taiwan	4.6	4.0
Thailand	2.8	1.6
Malaysia	2.7	0.4
West Bank	2.5	1.3
Colombia	2.5	1.0
Mexico	2.4	1.3
Brazil	2.3	1.0
Ethiopia	2.2	0.1
France	2.2	1.6
Argentina	1.9	0.4
Norway	1.8	0.1
Egypt	1.8	0.5
Hong Kong	1.7	1.3
Philippines	1.7	2.6
Russian Federation	1.5	0.7
Turkey	1.5	1.7
Romania	1.1	0.5
Germany	1.0	1.9
Subtotal	79.7	76.8
No response	10.1	8.6
Other countries	10.2	14.5
Total	100.0	100.0

[a] Data for TOEFL CBT and PBT test takers (combined) tested between July 2002 and June 2003.

countries or regions with 30 or more participants in the study sample in descending order according to their percentages in the sample. The 22 reported countries made up 79.7% of the analysis sample of 2,720. About 76.8% of the 2002–2003 TOEFL population was also from these 22 countries or regions. The exceptions shown for individual countries were due either to sample size considerations in the sampling design (i.e., to obtain the required size) or to changes in recruiting when it became clear that more people were available at one place but fewer at others.

Table 8.4 describes other characteristics of the study sample and, if available, corresponding characteristics of TOEFL test takers in 2002–2003. Over half of the study participants did not respond to a question about gender. Among those who responded to the gender question, there were 1.2% more females than males. The reverse was true for the TOEFL population, where there were about 4% more males than females. When asked about their highest educational objective, more study participants reported a graduate degree than did TOEFL test takers, and fewer study participants reported a bachelor's degree than did TOEFL test takers.

Compared with the 2002–2003 testing year data, the sample's mean scores were lower on all three measures and on the total score of the TOEFL CBT. The differences in the mean CBT scores between the field study sample and the 2002–2003 population were larger than half of an SD of the 2002–2003 scores on all but the SW measure. These differences suggested that the field

TABLE 8.4
Background Characteristics of the TOEFL iBT Field Study Participants and the 2002–2003
TOEFL Population

	Field Study Sample	TOEFL Population (2002–2003)
	(N = 2,720)	(N = 672,341)[a]
Gender		
Female	24.8%	47.4%
Male	23.6%	51.2%
No response	51.5%	1.5%
Educational objective		
Bachelors degree	12.5%	29.6%
Graduate degree	64.9%	50.1%
Other degree	7.2%	2.7%
Professional certification	2.3%	6.5%
No degree/undecided/no response	13.2%	11.2%
TOEFL CBT scaled scores-M (SD)		N = 577,038[b]
Listening	17.7 (6.0)	20.9 (5.3)
Reading	18.3 (6.0)	21.8 (4.9)
SW	19.5 (6.5)	21.7 (5.0)
Total	185 (55)	215 (46)

[a] Data for TOEFL CBT and PBT test takers (combined) tested between July 2002 and June 2003.
[b] Data for TOEFL CBT test takers only tested between July 2002 and June 2003.

study sample appeared to be a lower performing group compared with the 2002–2003 population. This lower performance could have resulted from such factors as lower motivation, lower ability levels, or both. This characteristic of lower performance on the TOEFL CBT needs to be kept in mind when analyzing the sample's performance on the new test for scaling and linking purposes.

FINDINGS

Outcomes Relevant to Evaluation

To assess if the psychometric characteristics of the test items and tasks were appropriate, both classical and IRT item analyses were conducted on the listening and reading measures. The IRT item parameters were estimated for the Form A listening and reading items because an IRT true score equating method was planned for use for the operational TOEFL iBT. Form A items' IRT parameters, calibrated using the field study data, were to be used to equate the initial listening and reading measures on operational forms back to Form A. IRT calibrations were not conducted on Form B: As fewer than 500 participants took this form, the sample size was too small for the IRT calibration models used.

For speaking and writing, only the descriptive statistics for the tasks on Form A and Form B were examined, and no IRT analyses were conducted on these constructed-response tasks.[2]

Listening

Both classical and IRT item analyses were carried out on the listening items. The three-parameter logistic (3PL) and generalized partial credit models were used to calibrate concurrently the dichotomously and polytomously scored items on Form A, using an internal ETS version of the computer program PARSCALE (Muraki & Bock, 1999). One flawed dichotomously scored item was removed from Form A during the stage of preliminary item analysis.

The item statistics are summarized in Table 8.5. As previously mentioned, most items were dichotomously scored, and a few items were polytomously scored. The average item difficulty, expressed as proportion correct, is not applicable to the polytomously scored items because these items had multiple score ranges and were not scored as simply correct or incorrect.

Table 8.5 shows that the average item difficulty or mean proportion correct of the 31 dichotomous items for Form A was 0.66, and the individual item difficulties ranged from 0.32 to 0.88, showing a relatively wide range spread of item difficulty. Item discrimination was calculated as an item-test correlation coefficient or r biserial correlation for the dichotomous items. For

TABLE 8.5
Listening Item Statistics

	Form A (N = 2,937)		Form B (N = 465)	
	Dichotomously scored items	Polytomously scored items	Dichotomously scored items	Polytomously scored items
Number of items	31[a]	2	34	0
Average item difficulty and range	0.66 (0.32–0.88)	—	0.68 (0.32–0.92)	—
Average item discrimination and range	0.60 (0.36–0.76)	0.65 (0.57–0.72)	0.55 (0.29–0.71)	—

[a] This was the number of scorable items and did not include the one item that was removed.

these items, the average item-test correlation was 0.60 with a range from 0.36 to 0.76. The item-test polyserial correlation coefficients (an index of item discrimination for polytomously scored items, corresponding to the biserial correlation for the dichotomously scored items) for the two polytomously scored items were 0.57 and 0.72, respectively. The score ranges and the percentage of the sample receiving various scores are given in Table 8.6 for the two polytomously scored items on Form A. Both of these items were difficult as over one half of those who attempted the items did not receive any credit.

For the subsample who took Form B, the average item difficulty of the dichotomous items was 0.68 (see Table 8.5). The individual item difficulties ranged from 0.32 to 0.92. The average item discrimination for Form B listening was 0.55 with a range from 0.29 to 0.71.

The set-specific mean IRT item statistics are presented in Table 8.7. For the IRT calibration results, the model-to-data fit analyses did not show any particular problems for these items; the evaluation of fit was done using both item-fit statistics and item-ability regression plots. Of the 31 dichotomously scored items, only one showed a misfit problem. The two polytomously scored items both showed acceptable model fit. Tables 8.7 shows that the average IRT item parameter estimates are within the typical ranges of values that are seen for four-option multiple-choice items calibrated using the 3PL IRT model. The average a-parameter of all the Form A listening items was

TABLE 8.6
Score Distributions on the Listening Polytomously Scored Items

Score	Item 1	Item 2
2	12.1%	20.7%
1	33.5%	23.2%
0	54.5%	56.1%
N	2,720	2,717

Note. Differences in N were due to differing omission rates for each item.

TABLE 8.7
Mean IRT Parameter Estimates for the Six Form A Listening Sets

Item Parameter	Set 1[a]	Set 2	Set 3	Set 4	Set 5	Set 6	Average of All 6 Sets
a	1.162	0.911	1.069	0.915	1.267	0.799	1.027
b	−0.688	−0.529	0.217	−0.535	−0.964	0.301	−0.357
c	0.212	0.136	0.181	0.153	0.194	0.143	0.169

[a] Polytomous items are excluded as they were included only in some sets.

1.027 and ranged from an average of 0.799 in Set 6 to an average of 1.267 in Set 5. This average a-parameter value of 1.027 indicated a good average discriminatory power for the items. The average b-parameter value for the Form A listening items was −0.357, with a range from −0.688 (easier) in Set 1 to 0.217 (harder) in Set 3. The c-parameter values were also within the expected range, varying from 0.136 to 0.212, and showed no extreme values.

Reading

Both classical and IRT item analyses were also carried out on the reading items. The 3PL and generalized partial credit models were used to calibrate concurrently the dichotomously and polytomously scored items in Form A. One item in Form A was removed during the initial item analysis phase because it did not perform as intended.

Averages of classical item statistics are summarized in Table 8.8. Form A polytomously scored items' score distributions are provided in Table 8.9.

Table 8.8 shows that the average item difficulty value of the 35 dichotomously scored items on Form A was 0.67 and ranged from 0.41 to 0.94, showing a relatively wide spread of difficulties. The average item-test correlation coefficient was 0.56 for dichotomously scored items, suggesting that these 35 items were homogeneous and had good discrimination power. The

TABLE 8.8
Reading Item Statistics

	Form A (N = 2,937)		Form B (N = 465)	
	Dichotomously scored items	Polytomously scored items	Dichotomously scored items	Polytomously scored items
Number of items	35[a]	3	36[a]	3
Average item difficulty and range	0.67 (0.41–0.94)	—	0.63 (0.25–0.92)	—
Average item discrimination and range	0.56 (0.33–0.73)	0.67 (0.59–0.74)	0.55 (0.13–0.74)	0.51 (0.31–0.79)

[a] This was the number of scorable items and did not include the one item that was removed.

TABLE 8.9
Score Distributions on the Reading Polytomously Scored Items

Score	Item 1	Item 2	Item 3
4	21.2%	—	—
3	16.4%	—	15.4%
2	31.3%	32.7%	21.5%
1	16.1%	51.0%	27.1%
0	15.0	16.2%	36.1%
N[a]	2882	2877	2650

[a] Differences in N were due to differing omission rates for each item.

average item-test polyserial correlation coefficient of the three polytomously scored items was 0.67.

For the three polytomously scored items on Form A, the score ranges and the percentage of the sample receiving various scores are given in Table 8.9.[3] It appears that Item 3 was a difficult item as over one third of those who tried the item did not receive any credit.

Table 8.8 also shows that the Form B items performed in much the same way as the Form A items. There was also one item that was removed from Form B during the initial item analysis phase because it did not perform as intended. The average item difficulty was 0.63, and the average item discrimination was 0.55. There were also three polytomously scored items in Form B. The item-test polyserial correlation coefficients for the three items were 0.79, 0.44, and 0.31, respectively. The mean correlation coefficient of the three items was 0.51 a little lower than the average of the 33 dichotomously scored items, which was 0.55.

Set-specific IRT item statistic averages for Form A are given in Table 8.10. All items provided acceptable model fit. The item-parameter estimates in Table 8.10 were within the typical ranges of values that are seen for four-option multiple-choice items calibrated with the 3PL IRT model. The average a-parameter of all the Form A reading items was 0.961. The average a-parameter values for the three reading sets on Form A ranged from 0.893 (Set 3) to 1.044 (Set 2). These average a-parameter values indicated good average discriminatory power for the items. The average b-parameter value for all the

TABLE 8.10
Mean IRT Parameter Estimates for the Three Form A Reading Item Sets

Item Parameter	Set 1	Set 2	Set 3	Average of All Three Sets
a	0.935	1.044	0.893	0.961
b	-0.409	-0.658	-0.137	-0.408
c	0.188	0.174	0.204	0.188

[a] Polytomous items are excluded as there was only one per set; no average was calculated.

TABLE 8.11
Descriptive Statistics for Task Scores: Speaking Form A and Form B

Task	Form A			Form B		
	N	Mean	SD	N	Mean	SD
1. Independent speaking	2,608	2.21	0.91	403	2.44	0.93
2. Independent speaking	2,683	2.42	0.91	409	2.55	0.88
3. Reading/listening/ speaking	2,505	2.27	0.94	393	2.41	0.91
4. Reading/listening/ speaking	2,430	2.39	0.99	376	2.49	1.00
5. Listening/speaking	2,557	2.65	0.94	396	2.76	0.85
6. Listening/speaking	2,508	2.37	0.92	392	2.53	0.84
Average	2,698	2.25	0.87	414	2.41	0.88

Note. Tasks scored on a scale of 1 to 4; "0" scores are excluded.

reading items is -0.408. For the three sets, the average b values ranged from -0.658 (Set 2) to -0.137 (Set 3). The c-parameter values for the sets were also within the expected range of about 0.15 to 0.25 and show no particular abnormal values.

Speaking

The task means and SDs for the six speaking tasks on the two forms are provided in Table 8.11. On Form A, the easiest task was Task 5, whereas the most difficult was Task 1, with a mean difference of 0.44 of a raw score point between the two tasks. The SDs were similar for all tasks. On Form B, the easiest task was Task 5, whereas the hardest task was Task 3. Task 4 had the largest variation in scores, and Task 5 and Task 6 had the smallest variation in scores. Although the tasks on Form B appeared to be slightly easier on the average then those on Form A, these differences are not meaningful in any practical sense because of differences in the sample sizes. (A comparison of task difficulty for the test takers who took both Form A and Form B is discussed in the Generalizability section of this chapter.)

Writing

Table 8.12 displays the task means and SDs for both forms. For Form A, the R/L/W task mean of 2.14 was lower than the IW task mean of 2.90 and had

TABLE 8.12
Descriptive Statistics for Task Scores: Writing Forms A and B

Task	Form A			Form B		
	N	Mean	SD	N	Mean	SD
1. Independent writing	2687	2.90	1.14	436	2.76	1.16
2. Reading/listening/ writing	2687	2.14	1.26	436	2.38	1.18

Note. Tasks scored on a scale of 1 to 5; "0" scores are excluded.

a slightly higher SD. A very plausible reason for this difference is that R/L/W was a new task type that no test taker had an opportunity to see or to practice before the field study. About 39.6% of the Form A test takers received a score of 1 on this task. According to staff in charge of the scoring work, many test takers wrote on this task without making reference to the reading and listening materials that were part of the task, and these responses received a score of 1 according to the scoring rules. On the other hand, IW was similar to the operational TOEFL CBT essay, and only about 14% of the Form A examinees received a score of 1 on this task. On Form B, the mean scores on the R/L/W and the IW tasks were 2.38 and 2.76, respectively. The difference again showed that the mean score on the familiar independent task was higher than on the new integrated task.

Computer Familiarity

When the TOEFL CBT was introduced in 1998, test takers were offered the option of either handwriting or typing their independent essay in the writing measure. Initially 50% of test takers chose to handwrite their essays, but, by 2004, 82% were choosing to type their essays. Surprisingly, research on scores for handwritten versus typed essays for other tests as well as for the TOEFL indicated that handwritten essays received higher scores than word-processed essays, introducing unexpected bias associated with mode of writing (Breland, Lee, & Muraki, 2004; Powers, Fowles, Farnum, & Ramsey, 1994; Wolfe & Manalo, 2004). The increase in the number of test takers choosing to type their essays, the rater bias in favor of handwritten essays, and the logistic difficulties of handling handwritten essays for scoring purposes all contributed to a decision to require typing for the TOEFL iBT writing measure.

The impact of computer skills on test performance was investigated prior to the introduction of the TOEFL CBT and found to have no practical effect on most computer-based TOEFL test tasks, after adjusting for language ability (Taylor, Jamieson, Eignor, & Kirsch, 1998). However, the study by Taylor et al. did not include a writing task. Thus, the impact of computer familiarity on test performance, especially for writing, remains a potential threat to test interpretation.

In the current field study, one background question concerned the frequency with which study participants used English language computers. As shown in Table 8.13, the more frequently test takers used an English language computer, the higher their scaled scores[4] on the measures of the TOEFL iBT field study were. However, the impact of computer familiarity does not appear to be any stronger for writing, which places the greatest demands on keyboard skills, than for the other skills.

One cannot infer from this data that weak computer skills are the reason that some study participants did poorly on this test. As documented by Taylor

TABLE 8.13
Mean Scaled Scores for Form A Test Takers Who Varied in Familiarity
with English Language Computers

Frequency of English Language Computer Use	Measure										
		Listening		Reading		Speaking		Writing		Total	
	N	Mean	SD	Mean	SD	Mean	SD	Mean	SD	Mean	SD
Daily	1,412	18.9	6.3	18.6	6.3	18.8	6.5	17.8	6.6	74.1	22.9
Weekly	646	15.7	6.9	16.1	6.8	16.2	6.7	15.0	6.2	63.0	23.7
Monthly	297	13.7	6.7	14.4	6.4	13.5	6.5	13.2	5.6	54.8	22.2
Never	190	14.4	7.0	14.9	7.1	13.7	7.1	13.2	6.0	56.2	24.1

et al., other variables, such as English language proficiency, must be taken into account before any conclusions about the impact of computer skills on test performance can be drawn. Nevertheless, this issue should be explored further in a more systematic study of the impact of computer skills on TOEFL iBT writing.

Summary

Evaluation of item performance focused on Form A items because the data from this form was used to accomplish the main measurement objectives of the field study. The average item difficulties and discrimination values for listening and reading items were within the typical ranges for such indices and were appropriate for making norm-referenced decisions. The IRT item calibration results were found to be better than expected. All the items in the study were new items that had not been pretested. It was anticipated that certain items might have problems that could cause the 3PL IRT model not to work well. However, the 3PL model fit the data reasonably well for the majority of the items when model fit was evaluated using both fit statistics and item/estimated ability regression plots. With respect to IRT calibration results, model-to-data fit for the listening and reading items was good for all items used in the calibration. This result was encouraging because it lessened the concern about the potential for model fit problems for new items on future operational forms that will not be pretested.

The six speaking tasks showed small variations in performance across different task types. Of the two writing tasks, the new integrated task appeared to be difficult for many candidates. Nearly 40% of the test takers appeared not to understand the task requirements. This finding underscored the need for test preparation materials to familiarize test takers with new task types.

One issue that suggested the need for further research had to do with the relationship between test scores and computer familiarity. Infrequent users of English language computers had lower scores on the TOEFL iBT test measures than frequent users. However, this relationship did not appear to be stronger for writing, which places the greatest demands on keyboarding skills, than for the other three skills. Nevertheless, a more systematic study of the relationship between computer usage and test performance is needed.

Outcomes Relevant to Generalization

When many alternative forms of a test are to be administered, the warrant underlying the generalization inference is supported by the psychometric procedures of scaling and equating. As discussed below, the desire of admissions officers for a total score led to a decision to scale all four measures on the test, and the data from the field study was used to create these scales. Given that there were no plans to equate speaking and writing, the comparability of scores for parallel speaking and writing tasks across forms for the participants who took both forms was inspected to determine if parallel tasks were equivalent in difficulty. Further evidence relevant to the generalization inference was obtained through classical analyses of reliability for all four measures as well as through generalizability studies for speaking and writing. These results allowed us to verify whether the revision of the task specifications described in Chapter 7 resulted in improvements in the comparability of speaking and writing tasks.

Scaling

Although the TOEFL program has continuously attempted to persuade score users to make use of scores for measures of the individual skills instead of the total score, many test users expressed a need for a total score to be reported. Therefore, the scaling plan explored in Chapter 6 was revisited. Based on guidance from the measurement literature (Angoff, 1971; Dorans, 2002; Petersen, Kolen, & Hoover, 1989), scale requirements, the scaling sample, scale score ranges, and the scaling method to be used were reconsidered. The following sections describe the role these considerations played in setting scales for the TOEFL iBT.

Scale requirements and the scaling sample   The initial proposal in Chapter 6 was to use a scale of 1-25 for listening and reading but not to scale speaking and writing scores. Instead, the mean raw score, ranging from 1 to 5, would be reported for the speaking and writing measures. However, if the scores for the four skill measures were to be summed to create a total score, one sensible requirement was that all reporting scales have the same score range so that it would not be possible for less informed score users to attempt to judge the importance of a particular measure versus another by comparing the maximum score values of the two measures. For example, if the measure for reading were to be scaled from 0–30 while the measure for speaking was scaled from 0–15, the resulting difference in the maximum score values could mislead some users into believing that reading would be twice as important as speaking. It was deemed to be appropriate to use the same score range for all four measures' reporting score scales to avoid confusion.

Another requirement was that all four measures contribute equally in creating the total reported score. Having all measures contribute equally to the total score could be achieved by setting the four measure scales to have the same range and the same mean and SD, provided that all of the measures had similar distributions and reliabilities. The total scale score could then be the simple arithmetic sum of the four measure scores. Under this scenario, no differential weights would be needed in deriving the total score. The rationale behind this is that the four skill measures of the TOEFL iBT gauge the four equally important language skills of English that are required for studying in English-medium educational institutions. Hence, this equal weighting should also be reflected in the scales that will be used to report examinees' level of performance on the TOEFL iBT.

Still another requirement was to have the scales established before the first official administration of the TOEFL iBT, which was scheduled for September 2005, because one of the business requirements was to report TOEFL iBT test scores within 15 days. This requirement meant that it would not be possible to use operational data from the first administration of the new test to construct the new TOEFL iBT scales. Thus, the current field study was designed to provide data for the scalings of the four skill measures of the TOEFL iBT. Nevertheless, there remained legitimate concerns about the sample limitations in terms of representativeness, motivation, and actual sample size. The samples and data were closely scrutinized with this in mind, particularly with respect to the issue of representativeness as described earlier. However, other limitations of the sample, particularly issues surrounding the level of motivation of the test takers, must be fully recognized and kept in mind with the understanding that some adjustments to the scales may need to be considered when sufficient operational data has been accumulated after September 2005.

Scale score ranges   Given the decision to use scales for the four measures that had the same ranges, another issue had to be considered. This issue had to do with exactly what scale range to use for the measures, which differed in their maximum raw scores. For example, Form A for reading yielded a maximum of 44 raw score points, while Form A for listening had a maximum of 35 raw score points. Both forms of speaking had a maximum raw score of 24, and both forms of writing could reach a maximum raw score of 10 in increments of 0.5 (or a 20-point scale in increments of 1.0.) Therefore, the maximum number of raw score points on the four measures ranged from 20 to 44 on Form A.

To reach a reasonable balance among the maximum raw scores of the four measures, it was deemed that a score of 30 would be appropriate for the maximum scaled score point as it was close to the middle of the two extremes (20 and 44). It was fully recognized that this 0–30 scale range would compress the reading and listening raw score scales by mapping 45 and 36 raw score points to 31 scaled score points, respectively. On the other hand, the speaking and writing raw scales would be stretched by mapping the 21 possible writing raw scores and the 25 possible speaking raw scores into 31 scaled score points.

Scaling method With the decision to use 0–30 for scaled or reported scores for the four skill measures and 0–120 for the total scaled or reported score, the next decision was how to actually bring about the scalings. If each of the skill measures were to count equally in creating the total, this required that the raw score means and SDs for each of the measures be mapped to have a common scaled-score mean and SD. Such a transformation would be linear in nature and hence would allow the scaled score distributions for the measures to retain the same distributional characteristics as the raw score scales for each of these measures.

Two issues regarding choice of the scaled-score mean and SD required attention and careful consideration. One issue was where to set the mean for the scales. The ideal method would be to set the mean at the middle score point or center of the scale, that is, at 15 (Dorans, 2002). This would work fine if the raw score distributions closely resembled symmetrically centered distributions like a normal distribution. With a skewed raw score distribution, centering the mean at 15 would result in too many out-of-range scaled score points (scaled scores falling below 0 or beyond 30). Because out-of-range scaled score would not be reported, truncation would be needed in determining the scaled scores for reporting purposes. If too many out-of-range scaled scores needed to be truncated, the resulting scaled-score distribution's mean and SD would change from what was desired due to the truncation of the out-of-range scores.

The second issue was an outcome of dealing with the first issue. While it might be possible to work out a best solution that set the mean and SD of the scale for a measure such that out-of-range scores were kept at a minimum, the resulting means and SDs might end up not being the same for the four measures. Because it was required that the four measures have the same scaled-score means and SDs, it was necessary to find a compromise for the mean and SD that would allow both issues to be dealt with in a satisfactory fashion.

So, in making decisions about scales and carrying out the scaling work, these two issues had to be handled together because the first issue would impact the second one. While the raw score distributions varied in shape for the four measures, priority was given to the reading and listening measures in selecting the scaled-score mean and SD because the scores on these two measures will be equated when the test is introduced operationally. The speaking and writing measures will not be equated, at least in the formal sense, as rough score comparability for these constructed response measures was expected to be maintained through test development efforts and rating quality control measures. After balancing the specific requirements for the raw-to-scale conversion results for each of the four measures, the final scale mean was set at 17 and the SD was set at 7. Therefore, the mean scaled score was slightly higher than the center of the scale to accommodate the score distributions for reading and listening. The SD was relatively larger than might be expected due to a relatively large proportion of low scores from the field study sample.

The means and SDs for the raw and scaled scores for the four measures of Form A are presented in Table 8.14. The scale score mean and the SD are 17.0 and 7.0 for the reading, listening, and speaking measures for the sample of 2,720 examinees. The writing measure scale score mean is 16.0 and SD is 6.8. This is because a different sample ($N = 2,194$) was used for setting the writing scale; this sample did not include candidates who had a large discrepancy in scores (2.5 points on the 5-point scale) between the IW task and the new integrated task. Specifically, examinees receiving a score of 1 on the new integrated writing task but a score of 3.5 or higher on the IW task were excluded from the writing sample. A score of 1 was given on the new integrated writing task if the writing response failed to refer to the reading and listening materials embedded in this task how well the response was written. Many examinees did well (received a score of 3.5 or higher) on the IW task, which was familiar to TOEFL test takers, but received a score of 1 on the new integrated task. Such a difference was assumed to be related to these examinees' lack of familiarity with the new integrated task, not to their writing ability,

TABLE 8.14
Raw and Scaled Score Descriptive Statistics for Four TOEFL iBT Measures: Form A

	N	Raw Score			Scaled Score		
		Range	Mean[a]	SD[b]	Range	Mean	SD
Reading	2,720	4–44	27.6 (62.7)	9.0 (20.5)	0–30	17.0	7.0
Listening	2,720	2–35	21.7 (62.0)	7.4 (21.1)	0–30	17.0	7.0
Speaking	2,720	6–24	13.3 (55.4)	5.5 (22.9)	0–30	17.0	7.0
Writing	2,720	0–10	4.8 (48.0)	2.3 (23.0)	0–30	16.0	6.8
Total	2,720	16–112	67.0	22.0	6–119	67.0	25.0

[a] The numbers in parentheses in this column are means as percentages of the maximum score.
[b] The numbers in parentheses in this column are SDs as percentages of the maximum score.

which should be somewhat consistent across the two tasks. Therefore, it was reasoned that these examinees should be excluded from the writing analysis sample to minimize the impact of such lack of familiarity with the new task on the evaluation of the writing ability as a whole. As a consequence, the sample of 2,720 had slightly lower writing scale score mean and SD than the sample of 2,194.

In sum, setting the TOEFL iBT scales was a complex endeavor involving the balancing of test user requirements with psychometric standards and best practices. The characteristics of the field study data resulted in the decision to set the scales for the four skill measures to have a mean of 17 and SD of 7. Because the scales were set on the field study sample, which clearly had limitations (e.g., assumed level of motivation, ability level) and may not fully represent the future TOEFL iBT population, it is important to keep in mind that the scales may be subject to adjustment using future operational data and will be reviewed regularly to see if important scale properties are being retained.

Internal Consistency and Alternate Form Reliabilities

The internal consistency reliabilities of the scores for the four measures on Form A and Form B were estimated using the Cronbach alpha coefficient. Because a small group of participants took both Form A and Form B, it was also possible to estimate the alternate-forms reliability. The alternate-forms reliability was the correlation between the raw scores on the two forms for the sample of participants who took both forms. The results of these analyses are presented in Table 8.15. Different sample sizes in the table were due to varying amounts of missing data for each measure.

The estimates of internal consistency reliability for listening, reading, and speaking were all 0.88 on Form A and ranged from 0.87 to 0.92 on Form B. These estimates are all in the typical range for reliability values for tests used to make high-stakes decisions. The values for listening and reading are comparable to the reliability estimates for the TOEFL CBT listening (.89) and reading measures (.88) (Educational Testing Service [ETS], 2001). For writing,

TABLE 8.15
Reliability Estimates for the Four Measures

| | Internal Consistency Reliability | | | | Alternate Forms Reliability | |
| | Form A | | Form B | | | |
Measure	N	α	N	α	N	R_{AB}
Listening	2,937	.88	465	.87	374	.80
Reading	2,937	.88	467	.88	374	.83
Speaking	2,434	.88	407	.92	374	.87
Writing	2,704	.77	432	.83	339	.82

coefficient alpha for Form A and Form B were .77 and .83, respectively. This is a typical result for writing measures composed of only two tasks (Breland, Bridgeman, & Fowles, 1999) and reflects one well-documented limitation of performance testing—measures composed of a small number of time-consuming tasks result in less reliable assessment than measures composed of many shorter, less time-consuming tasks (see Chapter 5 for more detailed discussion).

The alternate-form reliability estimates for the four measures, based on the Pearson correlation coefficient between the raw scores on the two forms for the subgroup of participants who took both forms, are reported in Table 8.15. These alternate-forms reliabilities range from 0.80 to 0.87. An alternate-form reliability estimate is an estimate of the reliability of either one of the alternate forms and reflects how reliable the test scores are as well as how parallel the two forms are (Allen & Yen, 1979). Estimates of alternate-form reliability are lower than estimates of internal consistency because they take into account an additional source of variance, test form. The apparent exception to this rule in Table 8.15, where internal consistency for writing on Form A is lower than the alternate form reliability, reflects the differences in the samples used for the two estimates.

Interrater Reliability Estimation

The interrater reliability for the speaking and writing measures was calculated using the coefficient alpha method.

Speaking Two raters scored the speaking responses to the six tasks on Form A and Form B from the field study participants who took both forms. The usable sample sizes were 377 and 373 on Form A and Form B, respectively. Table 8.16 shows that the interrater reliabilities for the six tasks on Form A varied from .68 (Task 2) to .83 (Task 4), and were in the moderate to high reliability ranges. On Form A, the interrater reliability estimates also appeared to differ by the type of task. For example, the estimates of the two independent tasks were alike and somewhat different from those of the two R/L/S tasks. The same was also true for the two L/S tasks. However, such patterns were not observed on the tasks on Form B. Form B had slightly higher estimates than Form A on all the tasks except Task 3. These results show an improvement over those found in the first field study (see Table 6.17) where the interrater reliabilities for the speaking tasks ranged from .53 to .74.

Writing All writing tasks on both forms were scored by two raters. The interrater reliability estimates for the two writing tasks on each of the test forms are presented in the lower part of Table 8.16. The interrater reliability estimates were .92 and .89 for the IW and R/L/W tasks, respectively, on Form

TABLE 8.16
Interrater Reliabilities for TOEFL iBT Speaking and Writing Tasks

Task	Interrater Reliability	
	Form A	Form B
	Speaking	
	(N = 377)	(N = 373)
1. Independent speaking	.69	.81
2. Independent speaking	.68	.74
3. R/L/S	.81	.77
4. R/L/S	.83	.88
5. L/S	.77	.78
6. L/S	.74	.78
	Writing	
	(N = 2677)	(N = 432)
1. Independent writing	.92	.87
2. R/L/W	.89	.91

A, and were .87 and .91 on the two tasks on Form B. Since Form A results were based on a much large number of participants, these results should be more stable than those on Form B. The difference in interrater reliability between the two tasks on Form A was small. Again, the interrater reliability for these writing tasks was better than that found for the writing tasks in the first field study (range .66–.72).

Generalizability

Generalizability theory (G-theory) (Brennan, 1992; Cronbach, Gleser, Nanda, & Rajaratnam, 1972) provides a framework for investigating the degree to which performance assessment results can be generalized. This theory provides a conceptual and statistical framework to examine the impact of multiple sources of error on the generalizability or reliability of assessment scores. By using an ANOVA approach to decompose score variance into various sources, the generalizability method separates multiple sources of error that cannot be differentiated by classical methods. Not only does G-theory model the major sources of variation that might affect scores, such as raters, tasks, and occasions, it also provides statistical estimates of the magnitudes of the these different sources of variation and their interaction effects.

Two steps are typically involved in a generalizability study. The first step is a generalizability study (G-study), in which a universe of admissible observations is defined and all possible sources of variation that may influence measurement results are identified and estimated. The second step is a decision study (D-study), in which the universe of generalization is defined and reliability indices are estimated for specific applications by manipulating such factors as number of raters, number of tasks, etc. The results of a D-study provide information for designing tests to maximize reliability within practical constraints. The results of fairly extensive D-study analysis by Lee (2005) and Lee & Kantor (2005) were reported in Chapter 5 for prototype speaking and writing measures. That analysis involved both univariate and multivariate methods to explore rating scenarios for various configurations of number of raters and number and types of tasks. The findings from those D-studies were used to set the scoring procedures that were implemented for the speaking and writing measures in the current field study. Therefore, the generalizability analysis done on the field study data did not involve manipulation of factors such as different number of raters per task or different number of tasks per candidate. The following sections on the generalizability analyses report only the univariate analysis results that were based on the chosen models for speaking and writing as will be described below.

Speaking   Form A speaking data were analyzed first using a person by rating (p × r′) random effects ANOVA design, where the rater effect and task effect was replaced by the rating effect, r′. There were two reasons for this exclusion of the task and rater factors. First, the majority of Form A speaking responses were scored only once (single scoring), and, because no rater could score more than two samples from the same participant, each score on a participants' six speaking samples could be from a different rater. This was a confounded design as the rater effect was entangled with the task effect and could not be estimated from this design. Second, the rigorous rater quality control measures could effectively minimize rater effect to the extent that all raters could be considered as exchangeable (Lee & Kantor, 2005). This was the same design for the G-study as well as the D-study because no manipulation of factors was done. This design was applicable to the main sample that contained scorable speaking responses from 2,305 participants. The computer program GENOVA (Crick & Brennan, 1983) was used to estimate the variance components and the score generalizability coefficient ($E\rho^2$) for a univariate G-theory analysis.

Table 8.17 presents the estimated G-study variance components and the percentage of each variance component contributing to the total raw score variance. The estimates were based on all   six speaking items on Form A. The person (p) variance was the largest variance component and accounted for about 85.8% of the total variance. This means that most score variation can be attributed to differences in candidates' performances on the Form A speaking measure. The rating (r′) variance accounted for only 0.8% of the total variance. Because this rating is a combination of rater and task effects, when the rater effect was assumed to be minimal, this rating then suggested that the six speaking tasks on Form A were not very different in their levels of difficulty. This result is consistent with the task level means in Table 8.11. The person by rating (pr′) interaction and the undifferentiated error variance

TABLE 8.17
Variance Component Estimates for the Generalizability Analysis (p × r′) of
TOEFL iBT Form A Speaking Data

Effects	Variance	Percentage
Person (p)	0.44	85.8
Rating (r′)	0.00	0.8
Person-by-rating (pr′, undifferentiated)	0.07	13.4
Total	0.51	—
$E\rho^2$	0.87	—

Note. (n_p = 2,305, n_t = 6).

components together accounted for 13.4% of the total variance. This is not a trivial amount and indicates that not all examinees were ranked consistently across the six tasks.

The Form B speaking data were all scored by two raters (double-scored). The raters were divided into two groups. The first group scored only Tasks 1 and 2 (the independent tasks) while the second group scored Tasks 3 to 6 (the integrated tasks). Because the scoring rule was that a rater could not score more than two tasks from the same participant, a participant's six responses could be scored by at least three pairs of raters. In addition, the same pair of raters did not score all the speaking samples on each type of task, so raters are actually also nested within persons. However, if the raters in each of the two task-based groups were treated as interchangeable, as was discussed earlier, then, within a task, the rater effect can be replaced by rating, r′. This means that a partially nested design (p × (r′: t)) was applicable for the G-study analysis. Since all the participants (p) took the same six tasks (t), participants were crossed with tasks (p × t). Ratings (r′) were partially nested within tasks. The variance component estimates from this design are presented in the columns under $p \times (r' : t)$ design in Table 8.18. The empty cells indicate conditions not applicable to this design.

Furthermore, if this definition of *ratings* is extended to all six speaking tasks without considering the two task-specific groups for the raters, then all the raters could be assumed to be interchangeable, and ratings could be used in place of raters on all six tasks. Since each response received two ratings (r′) regardless of which raters gave these two ratings, the rating effect (r′) could be treated as being crossed with both person (p) and task (t). As a result, the G-study on the Form B speaking data was also analyzed using a person-by-task-by-rating (p × t × r′) random effects group design. The variance components from this design are presented in the columns under $p \times t \times r'$ design in Table 8.18. Again, the empty cells indicate conditions not applicable to this design.

The variance component estimates were almost identical for both designs. In both cases, where the six tasks were double scored, the person (p) variance component accounted for approximately 91% of the total variance, indicat-

TABLE 8.18

Variance Component Estimates for Two Generalizability Analyses of TOEFL iBT Form B
Speaking Data

Effects	$p \times (r' : t)$ Design		$p \times t \times r'$ Design	
	Variance	Percentage	Variance	Percentage
Person (p)	0.46	91.2	0.46	91.1
Task (t)	0.00	0.4	0.00	0.4
Rating (r')			0.00	0.1
Rating task (r':t)	0.00	0.1		
Person-by-task (pt)	0.02	4.9	0.02	4.9
Person-by-rating (pr')			0.00	0.0
Task-by-rating (tr')			0.00	0.1
Person-by-rating (nested within task) (pr':t, undifferentiated)	0.02	3.4		
Person-by-task-by-rating (ptr', undifferentiated)			0.02	3.4
Total	0.51		0.51	
$E\rho^2$	0.92		0.92	

Note. For the p × (r' : t) design, n_p = 373, n_t = 6, n_r = 2. For the p × t × r' design, n_p = 373, n_t = 6, and $n_{r'}$ = 2.

ing that the largest portion of the speaking score variation was attributable to differences in the participants' levels of speaking ability. The task variance accounted for only 0.4% of the total variance, suggesting that the tasks (t) differed very little in difficulty. The person-by-task variance accounted for the next largest amount of total variance (about 4.9% in both designs), indicating that a certain number of participants were not ranked consistently across the six tasks. The generalizability coefficient $E\rho^2$ was 0.92 in both designs.

Writing Both the integrated writing and IW tasks on Form A and Form B were scored by two raters. Since Form A had a much larger sample size than Form B, the focus was placed on Form A in this analysis, and only Form A results are discussed in this section. GENOVA was used to estimate the variance components and the score reliability coefficient. The available sample size for this analysis was 2,677. Adjudicated scores were included in calculating the average scores on this analysis, but 0s were excluded.

The raters on Form A were divided into two groups, and each group was responsible for scoring only one type of task (integrated or independent); therefore the same pair of raters did not score all the participants' writing samples. For example, one group of raters (say, Rater A, Rater B, ..., Rater F) scored the integrated writing task only, and different pairs of raters (say, Raters A and B, or Raters A and C, or Raters C and F, etc.) scored each task. As a result, raters nested within not only tasks but also persons. There was no easy way to analyze the data of such a structure, and rater effect was replaced with rating effect to simplify the analysis. Again, rating was used first within each type of task to indicate that the raters were treated as interchangeable

TABLE 8.19
Variance Component Estimates for Two Generalizability Analyses of TOEFL iBT Form A Writing Data

Effects	$p \times (r' : t)$ Design		$p \times t \times r'$ Design	
	Variance	Percentage	Variance	Percentage
Person (p)	0.89	67.9	0.89	67.8
Task (t)	0.14	11.0	0.14	11.0
Rating (r')			0.00	0.0
Rating: task (r':t)	0.00	0.01		
Person-by-task (pt)	0.24	17.9	0.24	17.9
Person-by-rating (pr')			0.00	0.1
Task-by-rating (tr')			0.00	0.0
Person-by-rating (nested within task)(pr':t, undifferentiated)	0.04	3.2		
Person-by-task-by-rating (ptr', undifferentiated)			0.04	3.2
Total variance	1.32		1.32	
Eρ2	0.76		0.76	

Note. For the p × (r' : t) design, $n_p = 2,677$, $n_t = 2$, $n_r = 2$. For the p × t × r' design, $n_p = 2,677$, $n_t = 2$, and $n_{r'} = 2$.

within each task type, but were not interchangeable across the two tasks. The variance component estimates of this analysis are presented under $p \times (r': t)$ design in Table 8.19. As was done with speaking, rating was then extended to all the ratings on the two tasks by four raters, and this changed the nested design to a fully crossed design, $p \times t \times r'$. The variance component estimates for this design are under $p \times t \times r'$ design in Table 8.19.

Both designs show similar results: the person variances were the largest components of the total variance of all sources (67.9% for the nested design and 67.8% for the crossed one). This indicates the largest portion of the writing score variation can be attributed to differences among the participants' level of writing ability. The task variance accounted for 11% for both designs, suggesting that the two writing tasks varied in difficulty. The raters or the ratings appeared to be consistent as the variances associated with (r':t) in the nested design and r' in the crossed design were both very small (both accounting for 0.0% of their total variances, respectively). The person-by-task (pt) effect accounted for the second largest proportion of the total variance, 17.9%, in both designs. It is apparent that the participants did not perform consistently on the two tasks. The reliability coefficient ($E\rho^2$) estimates were 0.76 for both designs.

Comparability of Parallel Speaking and Writing Task Types

The generalizability analyses described above did not provide information about the comparability of alternate forms. As discussed in Chapter 6, com-

TABLE 8.20
Mean Scores on Six Parallel Speaking Tasks and Two Parallel Writing Tasks for Test Takers
Who Took Both TOEFL IBT Forms

	Form 1		Form 2		
Task	Mean	SD	Mean	SD	Difference
Speaking tasks[a] (n = 290)					
1. Independent speaking	2.48	0.80	2.61	0.89	−0.13
2. Independent speaking	2.72	0.81	2.73	0.82	−0.01
3. R/L/S	2.44	0.89	2.57	0.87	−0.13
4. R/L/S	2.73	0.87	2.62	0.96	0.10
5. L/S	2.92	0.78	2.94	0.78	−0.01
6. L/S	2.52	0.83	2.66	0.82	−0.14
Writing tasks[b] (n = 339)					
1. Independent writing	2.91	1.2	2.86	1.16	0.05
2. R/L/W	2.24	1.3	2.51	1.20	−0.28

[a] Tasks scored on a scale of 1 to 4.
[b] Tasks scored on a scale of 1 to 5.

parability of alternate forms for test measures composed of a few highly memorable tasks is seldom established by equating because the security of these tasks cannot be guaranteed. Instead efforts are made to insure that parallel tasks have similar content and statistical characteristics across forms. The content characteristics are controlled by the task and test specifications. One statistic characteristic important in this context is task difficulty. Therefore we inspected the mean difficulties of the parallel speaking task types and the parallel writing task types (see Table 8.20) for the sample of test takers who completed both test forms.

For speaking, the differences in mean scores between parallel task types were rather small. The largest difference, −0.14, represented 0.17 of the SD. This is an improvement over the largest difference observed for parallel speaking tasks, 0.43 of the SD, in the previous field study. Although the integrated writing task in this study (listening/reading/writing) was not the same as the two integrated writing tasks in the previous field study, the difference in the mean scores for the task in this field study, 0.22 of the SD, was slightly smaller than the largest difference, 0.34 of the SD, found for the writing tasks in the previous field study.

Summary

All in all, the results of these analyses provided strong preliminary support for generalization inference in the TOEFL iBT interpretative argument. This support is preliminary because it was based on a convenience sample of volunteer test takers rather than on operational data. Nevertheless, the data from this sample was useful in setting scales that score users could use as soon as scores from operational administrations of the TOEFL iBT became available. The data from this field study also indicated that the internal consistency reliabilities of the listening, reading, and speaking measures were all within the typical range for tests that are used to make high-stakes decisions. As expected, the internal consistency reliability for the writing measure was lower because it included only two tasks. The alternate form reliability of the four measures also was acceptable. The generalizability coefficient for speaking for the single-rating-per-task design was also reasonable, and only a relatively small degree of improvement was found if the tasks were double-rated. And the generalizability coefficient for writing was as high as can be expected for a measure composed of two tasks. In one of the two generalizability analyses for speaking and both of the generalizability analyses for writing, the person-by-task interactions were nontrivial. A possible explanation for this is the novelty of the integrated tasks. It will be interesting to see if this effect is reduced for operational administrations with test takers who are more motivated and better prepared.

Inspection of the differences in difficulty of parallel versions of speaking and writing found small differences overall, with the integrated writing task showing the largest difference. The revised task specifications for speaking and writing appeared to be an improvement over the earlier version in two ways. First, the interrater reliabilities for speaking and writing were better than those found in the previous field study. And secondly, the differences in difficulty for parallel versions of tasks were reduced when compared with those in Chapter 6. Nevertheless, efforts to monitor and reduce these differences need to continue to insure the comparability of speaking and writing scores across forms.

OUTCOMES RELEVANT TO EXPLANATION

Two questions relevant to the explanatory inference were examined using the field study data. The first concerned the structure of the test. As discussed in Chapter 5, the theoretical debate about the structure of language abilities has evolved from opposing views that contrasted "unitary competence" and "divisible competence" models to a consensus view that language proficiency is multicomponential, with a general factor as well as smaller group factors (Carroll, 1983; Oller, 1983). A confirmatory factor analysis of the first field study, summarized in Chapter 6, found that a two-factor model, speaking versus a composite listening-reading-writing factor, fit the data best. Given changes in the test design between the 2002 and the 2003 field studies, this issue of test structure was revisited. The second question concerned the relationship between length of language study and test performance.

Test Structure

Sawaki, Stricker, and Oranje (in press) investigated the factor structure of the 2004 TOEFL iBT field study test Form A. They analyzed the field study data with three particular goals in mind: (a) to investigate the factor structure of the entire test, (b) to investigate the factor structure of the reading and listening measures, which now incorporate items designed to assess a broader range of language skills, and (c) to investigate the relationships between the integrated speaking and writing tasks, which require language processing in more than one modality, and the four TOEFL iBT measures.

The data analyzed were scored item responses of 2,720 test takers who completed Form A. A polychoric correlation matrix for the 79 items in the test form was obtained and used as the input data for testing a series of confirmatory factor analysis (CFA) models. First, the reading and listening measures were analyzed separately to provide an in-depth investigation of the interrelationships among multiple skills defined in the test specifications for each of the two measures. For listening, the skills were basic understanding, pragmatic understanding, and connecting information; for reading the skills were basic comprehension, inferencing, and reading to learn. Different CFA models about the relationships among the skills were tested. A model that specified a single trait factor was the best representation of the data for each measure. This result suggested that the traits assessed in each of these measures were essentially unidimensional, although they may be psychologically distinct skills and processes (Henning, 1992). Set effects, due to the dependencies of items based on a common text, were negligible.

Next, the reading and listening data analyzed above were combined with data for the speaking and writing measures to develop a CFA model for the entire TOEFL iBT. Several models about the relationships among the constructs assessed by the entire TOEFL iBT were tested. Both a higher-order factor model and a correlated trait model fit the data well. However, the higher-order factor model consisting of a general language proficiency factor and four group factors corresponding to the four language modalities (reading, listening, speaking, and writing) was selected as the best representation of the data for the entire test because it was more parsimonious than the CT model and allowed analysis of the relationship among the four subscores and the total score. The factor loadings of the integrated speaking and writing tasks on the speaking and writing factors were uniformly substantial, whereas their loadings on the factors associated with the task input (listening and reading) were negligible. The model is portrayed in Figure 8.1

Sawaki et al. (in press) concluded that the identification of the four distinct factors corresponding to the four measures in the final CFA model broadly supported the current policy of reporting the separate scores for the four skill measures and a single composite score (i.e., TOEFL total score) encompassing the four measures. Moreover, the pattern of loadings for the integrated

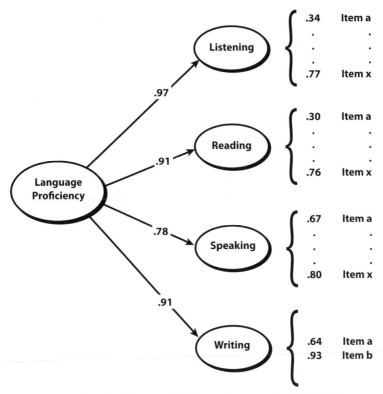

FIG. 8.1   Higher-order factor model. The numbers on the right in the figure represent the range of the completely standardized loadings of the individual items to the factors corresponding to the four measures (first-order factor loadings). The numbers in the center represent the completely standardized loadings of the four measures to the higher order factor (second-order factor loadings).

speaking and writing tasks supported the TOEFL iBT test design where performance on these tasks contributes only to the scores for the target modalities, (i.e., scores on the speaking or writing measure).

Sawaki et al. (in press) discussed their findings about a higher order factor model in the context of previous results. One notable difference between these and previous results has to do with the number of factors identified. The authors suggested that the larger number of factors identified in this study than in the previous studies may be attributable to the wider range of language abilities assessed in the TOEFL iBT. However, this did not explain the difference between the findings of this study and those of Stricker, Rock, and Lee (2005), summarized in Chapter 6, who analyzed a new TOEFL prototype test, which also had reading, listening, speaking, and writing measures. In their study, Stricker et al. found only two correlated factors—one for speaking and the other for a combination of reading, listening, and writing.

One explanation they offered for this difference concerns the samples studied. Stricker et al. conducted analyses only for Arabic, Chinese, and Spanish speakers. In contrast, Sawaki et al. analyzed a composite sample with diverse language and instructional backgrounds.

Relationship of Test Scores to Language Learning Experience

As a measure of language proficiency, we expect that TOEFL iBT scores will be related to the language learning experiences of test takers. Time spent learning a language is an important factor among the many that affect the acquisition of language proficiency. One of the field study background questions asked test takers how many years of classroom English instruction (at least 4 hours per week) they had had so far. Participants were grouped by their selection of one of the following six response options: less than 2 years, 3 to 4 years, 5 to 6 years, 7 to 8 years, 9 to 10 years, and more than 11 years. Five 1-way ANOVAs with years of English instruction as the independent variable and TOEFL iBT scores as the dependent variable were conducted.

The results for the total score and for the measures of the four skills are illustrated in Figure 8.2. For the total score, the effect of years of English instruction was significant, $F(5, 2523) = 53.9$, $p < .0001$. The Eta square for years of English instruction was .10, which represents a medium effect size according to Cohen (1988). Post hoc comparisons revealed significant differences between each interval from 5–6 years through more than 11 years.

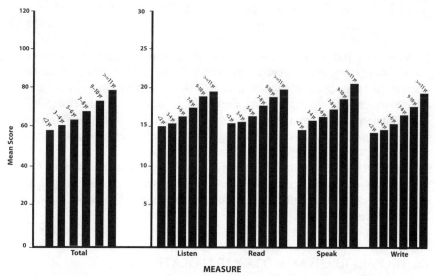

FIG. 8.2   Mean total test scores and mean scaled scores for measures of four skills for test takers who had studied English at least 4 hours a week for $< = 2$ years ($n = 332$), 3–4 years ($n = 384$), 5–6 years ($n = 415$), 7–8 years ($n = 425$), 9–10 years ($n = 302$), or $> = 11$ years ($n = 671$).

Significant differences between the intervals from less than 2 years up to 5 to 6 years were not observed.

Significant effects for years of English instruction were also found for each of the four skill measures: listening, $F (5, 2523) = 36.9, p < .0001$, reading, $F (5, 2523) = 34.5, p < .0001$, speaking, $F (5, 2523) = 52.1, p < .0001$, and writing, $F (5, 2523) = 45.9, p < .0001$. Eta squares ranged from .06 to .09, a medium effect size according to Cohen (1988). As illustrated in Figure 8.2, only small differences in test scores for the four skills were apparent in the first few years of instruction. This is followed by fairly steady increases thereafter, although post hoc comparisons indicate that significant increases tend to occur across 4-year intervals. For listening and reading, post hoc comparisons were significant between more than 11 years and 7 to 8 years or less, between 9 to 10 years and 5 to 6 years or less, and 7 to 8 years and 3 to 4 years or less for listening and 5 to 6 years or less for reading. The pattern was slightly different for speaking and writing in that significant increases occurred in a narrower band between 9 to 10 years and more than 11 years. For earlier development, the 4 years = significant increases pattern held, although for slightly different intervals. The increase between 9 to 10 years and 5 to 6 years or less was significant for both speaking and writing. However, speaking showed significant improvement between 5 to 6 years and less than 2 years while for writing significant improvement was evident between 7 to 8 years and 3 to 4 years.

To put these results into perspective, we first note that there is an orderly progression in the development of academic English language skills as assessed by TOEFL iBT that is associated with amount of instruction. The fact that differences in the first 5 to 6 years of instruction are not very evident is to be expected. It reflects the fact that the test is designed to assess a high level of proficiency required for study at English-medium colleges and universities rather being designed to assess proficiency in the earlier stages in the development of language proficiency. It is also worth noting that although these effects are statistically significant, they only account for a moderate amount of the variation in language proficiency. Many other factors, such as motivation and type of instruction, also contribute to the development of language proficiency.

Overall, the analyses of test structure and the influence of length of language study on performance provided evidence that is consistent with theoretical expectations about the internal structure of the test and the effects of English instruction.

OUTCOMES RELEVANT TO EXTRAPOLATION

For the TOEFL, one assumption underlying the extrapolation inference is that performance on the test corresponds to performance in the real world contexts that the test seeks to represent. This assumption is often backed by evidence demonstrating relationships between test performance and criteria or indicators of performance in the target contexts. Indicators of real world performance that were obtained in the field study included information about the test takers' academic placements and their self-assessments of their English language ability.

Academic Placements

One concurrent indicator of some test takers' English language proficiency is the course placement when they are in English-speaking countries. International students who are studying in English-speaking counties may or may not require additional English language instruction to succeed at English-medium colleges and universities. This additional instruction may be delivered in English as a second language (ESL) support courses at colleges and universities or in intensive English programs (IEPs). Placement into ESL courses reflects a judgment by an institution that a nonnative speaker of English requires additional training in English to cope with the standard curriculum. This judgment is typically made from multiple sources of information, including previous coursework and test scores. If the initial placement is incorrect, the student may be moved into or out of specific courses as the teacher becomes more familiar with the student's English skills. For students intending to attend English-medium colleges and universities, enrollment in IEPs also reflects a judgment, either their own or an academic adviser's, that their academic English language skills need further development. In the 2004 field study, participants who were studying in English-speaking countries were asked to indicate whether they were enrolled in (a) an IEP but not courses in subjects (for example, biology or business), (b) ESL courses and courses in other subjects (for example, biology or business), or (c) courses in subjects (for example, biology or business) but not ESL courses.

Five one-way ANOVAs with academic placement as the independent variable and TOEFL iBT scores as the dependent variable were conducted. The results for the total score and the scores on the measures of the four skills are illustrated in Figure 8.3.

For the total score the effect of academic placement was large ($\eta^2 = .17$) and significant, $F(2, 978) = 101.8$, $p < .0001$. Effects for academic placement, illustrated in Figure 8.3, were also significant for each of the four skill measures: listening, $F = 83.9$, $df = 2, 978$, $p < .0001$, reading, $F = 86.3$, $df = 2, 978$, $p < .0001$, speaking, $F = 59.6$, $df = 2, 978$, $p < .0001$, and writing, $F = 75.3$, $df = 2, 978$, $p < .0001$.

According to conventional standards (Cohen, 1988), large effect sizes were observed for listening ($\eta^2 = .15$), reading ($\eta^2 = .15$), and writing ($\eta^2 = .13$), and a medium effect size was observed for speaking ($\eta^2 = .11$). These differences between students who are enrolled in subject matter courses only and

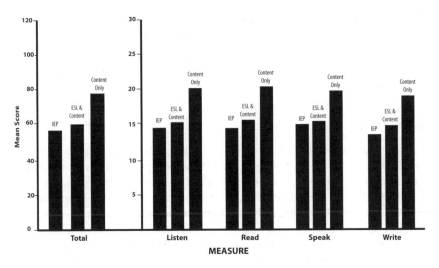

FIG. 8.3   Mean total test scores and mean scaled scores for measures of four skills for test takers studying in English-speaking countries who were enrolled in institutional English programs ($n = 208$), taking both ESL courses and content courses ($n = 285$) or only content courses ($n = 488$).

students who are taking some ESL courses or are enrolled in IEPs are evident in these figures and were confirmed by post hoc comparisons. In contrast, differences between students enrolled in IEPs and students taking both ESL support courses and subject matter courses were significant only for the writing measure.

Self-Assessments of Academic Language Skills

Another measure of English language proficiency is test takers' self-assessment of their own academic language skills. During the development of the new TOEFL, Powers and his associates developed and evaluated a self-assessment questionnaire (Powers, Roever, Huff, & Trapani, 2003). The items in this questionnaire were recast as can-do statements and administered as part of the 2003 field study. For each of the language modalities, self-assessment scales were formed by summing the responses to the individual items. The four scales showed high internal consistency, ranging from .91 to .94. The observed correlations among the self-assessment scales are presented in Table 8.21.

The correlations among the test taker self-assessments in Table 8.21 are high and suggest that the test takers did not differentiate their levels of proficiency with respect to the four skills. The correlations between these test takers' test scores on Form A and the self-assessment scales are presented in Table 8.22.

TABLE 8.21
Correlations among Self-Assessment Scales (n = 2,224–2,309)

Self-Assessments	M	SD	Correlations Among Self-Assessment Scales		
			Listening	Reading	Speaking
Listening	44.0	6.7			
Reading	64.2	11.2	.83		
Speaking	51.4	8.9	.81	.80	
Writing	38.9	6.5	.82	.81	.82

These results indicate a relationship between self-assessments of language proficiency and performance on the test overall. While the correlations between the self-assessment scales and the test measures can be characterized as moderate in magnitude, they are similar to other test-criterion relationships, such as the typical correlation of .5 often found between scores from aptitude batteries and school grades (Cohen, 1988). When compared with the correlations between two tests of the same ability, test-criterion correlations are usually lower because they are constrained by factors such as range restriction and the reliability of the criterion measure (Messick, 1989). As noted in Chapter 5, the different methods of assessing ability (perceptions versus tests) also would be expected to result in lower correlations than when the similar methods are compared.

However, given that the test takers did not differentiate their proficiency as regards the four skills, it is not surprising that the relationships between self-assessments and the four test measures do not provide evidence of discriminant validity. For example, scores on the listening measure are associated as strongly with self-assessments of reading ability as with listening ability. A similar pattern is evident for writing. Overall, self-assessments of all four skills correlated most highly with performance on the speaking measure.

To conclude, test scores clearly distinguished between test takers who required additional instruction in English and those who did not as demonstrated by academic placement. The moderate relationship between test takers' self-assessments of their language abilities and test performance also provided some support for extrapolation.

TABLE 8.22
Correlations of Self-Assessment Scales With Scores on Test Measures (n = 2,365–2,427)

Self-Assessment Scales (Criteria)	Test Measures				
	Listening	Reading	Speaking	Writing	Total
Listening	.47	.37	.53	.46	.52
Reading	.50	.45	.53	.49	.55
Speaking	.42	.36	.55	.45	.49
Writing	.42	.36	.52	.46	.50

DEVELOPMENTS RELEVANT TO UTILIZATION

The warrant authorizing the utilization inference is that test scores are useful for making decisions about test takers. These decisions might be judgments about the readiness of international students to study at English-medium colleges and universities, about placement in ESL classes, or about best practices for teaching and learning English for academic purposes. Empirical evidence to support assumptions that the TOEFL test scores are useful for admissions or placement decisions or that the test will have a positive impact on teaching and learning cannot be obtained until the test has been operational for some period of time. However, ETS has undertaken a number of activities to support appropriate test score use and English language learning based on the data obtained in the final field study. These activities include:

- Conducting analyses to support TOEFL iBT score interpretation for the purposes of admissions
- Funding long-term research to assess the impact of TOEFL iBT on teaching and learning
- Using the field test materials and research results to help teachers and students prepare for the TOEFL iBT in a manner that is more consistent with communicative approaches to learning English

Over time, experience with the scaled scores on a test allows faculty and admissions officers to develop selection criteria appropriate for their institution. In light of the changes in the test content and the score scale, and the fact that scores on different test versions would be in use for a certain period of time after the TOEFL iBT became operational, institutions would need information to ease the transition from previous score scales to the new score scales. Therefore, ETS decided to provide institutions with a variety of supporting materials to aid in the interpretation of the TOEFL iBT scores. These materials included links between TOEFL CBT and TOEFL iBT scores, and a standard setting manual. As these materials were made available, institutional score users were informed of the preliminary nature of this interpretative material that was based on the results of the field study rather than on operational data

As noted in Chapter 2, the revision of the TOEFL was motivated in part by language teachers' desires for a test that would reinforce a communicative-language curriculum. Many educators believed that multiple-choice tests had negative effects (i.e., negative washback) on language instruction. Early in the development of the new TOEFL, Bailey (1999) was commissioned to review the literature and research on TOEFL washback. She recommended that studies using both qualitative and quantitative methodologies be conducted as a new TOEFL became a reality. In 2002, as the design of the new TOEFL was being finalized, two baseline studies of teaching and learning practices for the

TOEFL were initiated. These studies were to examine teaching and learning practices in TOEFL preparation courses as well as general English for academic purposes (EAP) courses prior to the release of the new TOEFL. One study, carried out by Wall and Horák (2006), focused on TOEFL test preparation in eastern Europe. This geographic region was selected by TOEFL program management for study because it is an area undergoing rapid social, economic, and political changes. Assuming that communication with American educational institutions, such as ETS, had been limited until recently, this region presents a test case for the extent of and barriers to the diffusion of knowledge about innovations in the test and implications for teaching. The other study[5] (Hamp-Lyons & Brown, 2006) was to be carried out at selected institutions in other areas of the world.

The needs of teachers and students are different from those of institutional decision makers. While institutional decision makers often need numeric scaled scores to help them make decisions, teachers and students need to understand what the scores indicate about test takers' abilities and how they should prepare for the test and improve their academic English skills. To meet these needs, qualitative score descriptors were developed and information about the new test disseminated so that teachers, students, and publishers of instructional materials could prepare for it.

Linking CBT Scores to TOEFL iBT Scores

While the TOEFL iBT will eventually replace both the CBT and PBT versions of the TOEFL,[6] a phased rollout of the TOEFL iBT was planned to ensure the quality of the new test and associated service to test users. As a consequence, the TOEFL iBT, the TOEFL CBT, and the TOEFL PBT will all be administered for a period of time, but in different regions of the world. In addition, even after the CBT and PBT versions of the TOEFL are phased out, the TOEFL CBT and TOEFL PBT scores will still be reportable for two years after the test is taken, according to the TOEFL score reporting policy. Therefore, for a few years after September 2005, an admissions office can expect to receive three types of TOEFL scores. Many college and university admissions officers have requested that ETS provide some score-linking information between TOEFL iBT and TOEFL CBT scores, just as ETS provided such information for the TOEFL CBT and the TOEFL PBT (ETS, 2001) when the TOEFL CBT was launched in 1998. Hence, a decision was made to provide TOEFL CBT–TOEFL iBT score-linking information to institutional score users.

The results of the linking of test scores from different tests have been used for various purposes in educational measurement and research. Interpretation or use of score-linking results depends mainly on the similarities between the two tests that are to be linked. When two tests are developed from the same content and statistical specifications (i.e., alternate or parallel test forms), the process of relating scores on the two forms is the most statistically rigorous type of linking and is called *equating*. This is typically conducted for different test forms of the same testing program, and the outcome is that scores on the forms can be used interchangeably. On the other hand, what is often needed is the ability to link scores from two tests that may measure a similar skill but are developed from different specifications, as is the case with the TOEFL CBT and the TOEFL iBT. Although the same statistical procedures that are used in equating may be applied to linking scores on the two tests, the linked scores are not interchangeable, nor do they have the same interpretation. This is a weaker form of linking than an equating (Pommerich, Hanson, Harris, & Sconing, 2000) and is often called *concordance*, or forming a concordance relationship between scores on the two tests. In other words, this concordance differs from the equating not so much in the statistical procedures employed as in the level of score exchangeability and resulting score interpretation. Linking via the establishment of concordance relationships was employed for relating the scores on the TOEFL CBT and the TOEFL iBT.

Scores to link   Table 8.23 lists the scores on the TOEFL iBT and the TOEFL CBT that might be linked in the first columns and their correlations in the second column. The reading and listening measures on the two tests have similar content specifications even though new item types have been added to TOEFL iBT. The TOEFL CBT structure measure, which is part of the TOEFL CBT SW measure, is not included in TOEFL iBT. In TOEFL CBT, the structure scores and writing scores are used to form a composite score that is reported as the SW score. The justification for this composite score is that the structure items measure English grammar knowledge, which is closely related to writing skills. The TOEFL iBT writing measure has a new integrated-skill writing task in addition to the IW task that is also in the TOEFL CBT writing measure, but there are no structure items in the TOEFL iBT. Hence, the TOEFL iBT writing and TOEFL CBT SW measures are a good deal less parallel than is the case for reading or listening. However, a linking can be justified in that both tests measure English writing skills, albeit in different ways. Finally, the TOEFL iBT speaking measure is totally new,

TABLE 8.23
Correlations between Scores on the TOEFL iBT Form A and CBT Measures

Scores to be Linked	Correlation Coefficients (N = 2,720)
TOEFL iBT reading and TOEFL CBT reading	0.81
TOEFL iBT listening and TOEFL CBT listening	0.81
TOEFL iBT writing and TOEFL CBT SW	0.75
TOEFL iBT R/L/W and TOEFL CBT total	0.90
TOEFL iBT total and TOEFL CBT total	0.89

and no speaking measure appears in the TOEFL CBT, so no linking could be performed.

When considering the linking of total scores, the most obvious link would be between a TOEFL iBT R/L/W artificially created total score and the TOEFL CBT total score because in this case both totals would be based on similar measures. In addition, the actual TOEFL iBT total scaled scores, created from the R/L/W/S measure scaled scores, were linked to TOEFL CBT total scaled scores, created from the R/L/SW measure scaled scores. Such a link can be considered weak at best, given that TOEFL iBT contains speaking and the TOEFL CBT does not. Clearly, linked total scaled scores do not measure the same constructs.

Table 8.23 presents the correlations between the scale scores to be linked. These correlations range from moderate (0.75 for writing scores) to high (0.90 for TOEFL iBT R/L/W scores and TOEFL CBT total scores) and provide some basis for justifying the linking of scores to be done. These correlations between the scores to be linked show consistency with the correlations between the TOEFL CBT scores and the TOEFL PBT scores derived in a concordance study conducted in 1997–1998 (Jiang, 1999, Table 8). In interpreting the relatively high correlation between the two total scaled scores, it should be kept in mind that the TOEFL iBT total, which includes speaking, cannot be considered in any way to be parallel to the TOEFL CBT total, which does not include speaking.

Establishing the linkages   A single-group data collection design (all the participants took both TOEFL iBT Form A and the TOEFL CBT) was used in the field study for the purpose of linking scores. Before the scores could be linked, it was necessary to smooth the score distributions on the two tests. Data smoothing was needed because the scores could only be discrete values, and the distributions of these discrete values had many spikes, particularly the TOEFL iBT writing scores. In performing score linking, observed score distributions are typically smoothed to remove score spikes, and smoothing can be implemented either before linking (presmoothing), using the original score distributions, or after linking (postsmoothing), using the resulting conversions (Dorans, 2002; Kolen & Brennan, 1995). Past research has reported little difference in the outcomes of these two smoothing methods when applied in the equating context (Hanson, Zeng, & Colton, 1994).

Presmoothing was used for the score linkings to be performed in this study. A log-linear smoothing procedure (Holland & Thayer, 1987) was used to produce smoothed frequency distributions of the TOEFL iBT and TOEFL CBT scores to be linked. This log-linear smoothing procedure creates a smoothed distribution that approximates the unsmoothed distribution by matching an optimal number of moments of both distributions. For each score distribution, several smoothings were explored by matching three to eight unsmoothed and smoothed moments. In most cases, the fit between the distributions from six matched moments appeared to be the best. The smoothing results were evaluated using fit indices as well as by visually inspecting how closely the smoothed distribution approximated the unsmoothed one.

Both equipercentile and linear methods were applied in linking the scores, using the smoothed score frequency distributions. The relationships between TOEFL CBT and TOEFL iBT scores appeared to be nonlinear in all cases, and since the equipercentile procedure can reflect these nonlinearities while the linear procedure cannot, the equipercentile results were chosen for all linkings.

Understanding linked scores   Interpretation of the linking results for the reading and listening measure scaled scores should present relatively little difficulty as the changes in these two measures from the TOEFL CBT and the TOEFL iBT are minor, and hence these measures assess similar constructs. For other linked scores (e.g., the TOEFL CBT SW to the TOEFL iBT writing, the TOEFL CBT total to the TOEFL iBT total, and the TOEFL CBT total to the TOEFL iBT RLW, respectively), the interpretation of the linking results is less straightforward. This is because these measures and totals do not measure the same constructs in the TOEFL iBT and the TOEFL CBT, and consequently, the linked scores cannot be considered to be strictly interchangeable.

Test score users were informed about the meaningfulness of score comparisons made in light of the differences in the content, and therefore the underlying constructs, of the tests. For instance, a TOEFL CBT total score contains no information about speaking ability, whereas a TOEFL iBT total score does. Similarly, a TOEFL CBT SW score is based on a combination of the score on multiple-choice grammatical knowledge items and the score on a written essay. The underlying construct for such a combination is likely to differ from that of the TOEFL iBT writing measure that contains an independent writing task and an integrated writing task. It is also useful to remember that another factor that complicates the interpretation of the linked scores is related to the limitations of the 2003 field study sample. As was noted before, the sample was relatively small and possibly did not constitute a truly representative sample of the TOEFL iBT population. Also, because the TOEFL iBT tests given in this study were not used in reporting scores, there may have been motivational problems.

Because of the aforementioned issues, score users need to be cognizant of the following constraints surrounding the appropriate interpretation of the linked scores:

1. The linking relationships should not be used to directly translate scaled scores on one test onto the scaled scores for another test. For the total score, this is because the TOEFL iBT contains a speaking measure while

the TOEFL CBT does not. Similarly, the TOEFL iBT writing measure and the TOEFL CBT SW measure assess different constructs.

2. Use of the linking relationships to translate old TOEFL CBT cut-off scores onto the new TOEFL iBT measure and total score scales can yield useful preliminary information, but this must be followed up by studies that establish that the new cut-off scores provide results that make sense to the users. In other words, the linking can be used to establish initial tentative cut-points on the TOEFL iBT, but subsequent data must then be collected to establish the validity of these tentative cut-points.

3. The existing relationships—based on data from a small, possibly unmotivated, sample—may not be the same as the relationships that would be derived were the full population available for linking purposes under motivated conditions.

In sum, the main purpose for conducting a score-linking study of the TOEFL iBT to the TOEFL CBT was to provide college and university admissions staff with linkages between TOELF CBT and TOEFL iBT scores that can be used for the period of time when both TOEFL CBT and TOEFL iBT scores will be available for decision-making purposes. A decision was made to link all reported measure scores that could be linked as well as the total scores. The field study sample was used for the linking study, and the equipercentile method was applied to establish linking relationships. The linked scores should provide relatively comparable rank-orderings of examinees on the two tests. The substantive meaning that can be attributed to the linked scores depends on the degree of comparability of the content on the measures or totals for which scores are linked. Because of content differences, great caution must be exercised in using the linking results for the total scores on the TOEFL iBT and the TOEFL CBT. Cautionary statements were provided to test score users in an effort to guard against inappropriate uses of the linked scores in practice.

Standard Setting

As noted above, the interpretation of score-linking information was constrained by a number of factors, and, most importantly, by the differences in the constructs assessed by the TOEFL iBT and previous versions of TOEFL. One method of establishing admissions criteria that circumvents this limitation is standard setting. Standard setting is a judgmental process by which staff at institutions review a test form, responses, and test scores to decide systematically on a cut-score band for admissions or placement purposes.

In 2004, a standard-setting kit was developed, pilot tested at a number of institutions, and published in an electronic format so that institutions could conduct their own standard-setting meetings (ETS, 2004a). The manual laid out procedures for standard setting and provided the necessary materials, such as sound files for speaking responses at different score levels. The manual recommended that a panel of 15 to 20 academic staff who were familiar with international students,—including content course faculty, English language specialists, and admissions office staff—be convened. Because standards need to be set for all four test measures, such a panel meeting requires 2 days, the first day focused on standard setting for speaking and writing, and the second day focused on listening and reading.

Different standard-setting methods were used for the constructed-response (speaking and writing) and the selected-response (listening and reading) test measures. For the constructed-response measures, panelists reviewed a profile of actual responses produced by examinees at different score levels and determined what score level corresponded to a minimally acceptable level of language ability for admissions purposes. For the listening and reading measures, the panelists reviewed the items and determined for each item whether a student with a minimally acceptable level language ability would answer correctly.

The manual also describes the wide variety of factors, in addition to language ability, that should be considered in making admissions decisions. Furthermore, a number of factors beyond the panel's recommendations should be considered in setting final cut scores. These factors include the needs of different departments and the implications of setting lower or higher cut scores. Additional information that would help the institution set final cut scores, such as the percentile ranks of scores from the field study and tables linking TOEFL CBT scores and the field study scores, were included in the manual.

A number of institutions used the standard-setting manual to set their admissions standards. Other institutions based their admissions standards on the other information provided by ETS, such as the percentile score ranks and score linking tables. As institutions reviewed the available information, many of them provided ETS with the score standards that they would use during the first year of operational testing. These initial standards were published on the TOEFL iBT Web site. It is worth noting how admissions criteria varied across institutions. For instance, seven to nine institutions reported graduate admission cut-off scores for some of the four test measures. A wider range of cut-off scores was reported for listening (14–21), speaking (20–27), and writing (18–25) than for reading (19–21). Factors likely to affect variation in standards among institutions include the availability of ESL instructional support, the disciplinary concentrations of international students, institutional selectivity, and instructional roles of the graduate student. This variation in standards reinforces the importance for institutions to evaluate their own needs when setting admission standards.

A Study of TOEFL Preparation in Eastern Europe

In 2003, Wall and Horák began a long-term qualitative study of test wash-back in eastern Europe. They interviewed directors of studies, teachers, and students in ten sites in Poland, Slovakia, Bulgaria, Romania, Croatia, and Lithuania. Most of these sites were private language schools and education information centers. Wall and Horák also observed TOEFL preparation classes at eight of these sites and EAP classes at five sites.

At the beginning of the study in 2003, three of the ten teachers interviewed were unaware of impending changes to the TOEFL. For the most part, stakeholders learned about the TOEFL through informal channels rather than official ones such as the TOEFL Web site. Teachers were highly dependent on test preparation course books for information about the TOEFL, and these preparation books, with their emphasis on practicing test items, greatly influenced instructional techniques. In most of the classes, students completed test exercises from the course book (either in class or as homework) and then discussed answers as a group under the guidance of the teacher.

Wall and Horák (2006) made the following observations about teaching in TOEFL preparation classes:

1. Listening—Teachers did not know how to break down listening to a set of teachable subskills. They taught in English and assumed that this and listening to TOEFL passages would improve listening skills.
2. Structure—Teachers assumed students had studied a lot of English grammar in the past and just needed to review what they knew through practice exercises and explanations in course books. Specific teaching techniques included explaining particular points of grammar, some drilling, and feedback on grammar in student-produced essays.
3. Reading—Teachers were more aware of subskills for reading, such as skimming, scanning, referencing, and inferencing, than they were for listening. The importance of recognizing question types was also emphasized. There was no evidence of prereading or reading development techniques encouraged in communicative course books.
4. Vocabulary—Although vocabulary is no longer assessed in a separate measure on the TOEFL, most teachers and students believed a rich vocabulary was very important for success on the TOEFL. Teachers encouraged students to learn lists of words, synonyms, and phrases either complied by the teachers themselves or presented in course books. Students were also encouraged to read extensively outside the classroom. It was found that many students, on their own initiative, used Internet-based resources and CDs designed to improve vocabulary.
5. Writing—Quite a bit of time was devoted to writing because it was an area where students were perceived to lack experience. Teachers

emphasized a four- or five-paragraph structure and organization rather than content; they seemed to have little understanding of the TOEFL rating scales.

6. Speaking—Many of the teachers and students felt that speaking was not an important skill to practice or learn because it was not going to be tested. Nevertheless, there was informal speaking practice because English was the medium of teaching and discussion in most classes.

This baseline study by Wall and Horák (2006) not only documented teaching practices prior to the introduction of the TOEFL iBT, but it also identified important factors that would be necessary to produce positive washback on teaching and learning. These factors included communication with teachers and students about the new test and the availability of suitable instructional materials that would promote better language learning. The efforts by ETS to provide teachers and students with information about the new test and to promote more appropriate teaching and learning practices are described next.

Score Descriptors

In the early stages of new TOEFL development, an approach to developing score descriptors supported by models of task difficulty was proposed (Jamieson, Jones, Kirsch, Mosenthal, & Taylor, 2000). This approach was put forward based on its success in establishing and communicating score interpretation information for tests of literacy (Kirsch & Mosenthal, 1988, 1990). Still, as ETS prepared for the operational release of the TOEFL iBT, the difficulty modeling approach had yet to be supported by empirical findings. As a result, test designers turned to alternative methods to create score descriptors. One method was to create competency descriptors based on test takers' self-assessments. This approach had been explored during prototyping (see Chapter 6) and was further refined using the data from the final field study. A second approach, score anchoring, which relied on expert analysis of skills required to attain certain score levels, was also used to develop descriptive information for test takers' score reports.

Competency descriptors In the previous field study, the responses to the self-assessment questions were used to develop score level descriptors. A similar process was used with the TOEFL iBT data. The can-do statements were organized in tables that illustrated the degree to which test takers at different score levels agreed that they had a variety of academically relevant English language competencies. As an example, competency descriptors for speaking are presented in Figure 8.4. These competency descriptors illustrate a hierarchy of skills. For example, test takers scoring 11 and above on the speaking measure were likely to agree that instructors could understand them when

TOEFL iBT — Speaking Competency Descriptors

Competency Descriptors	TOEFL iBT Speaking Score Levels (0–30)						
	1–5	**6–10**	**11–15**	**16–19**	**20–23**	**24–27**	**28–30**
My instructor understands me when I ask a question in English.							
When I speak in English, other people can understand me.							
I can give prepared presentations in English.							
I can talk in English for a few minutes about a topic I am familiar with.							
I can participate in conversations or discussions in English.							
I can state and support my opinion when I speak English.							
I can talk about facts or theories I know well and explain them in English.							
I can speak for about one minute in response to a question.							
I can orally summarize information I have read in English.							
I can orally summarize information from a talk I have listened to in English.							

Likelihood of Being Able to Perform Each Language Task

< 50%	50 – 65 %	66 – 80 %	81 – 95 %	>95%
Very unlikely	**Unlikely**	**Borderline**	**Likely**	**Very likely**

FIG. 8.4   Competency descriptors for score levels on the TOEFL iBT speaking measure.

they asked a question in English. In contrast, only test takers who scored 24 and above agreed that they could orally summarize information from a talk they listened to in English.

Score anchoring   Score level descriptors to be included on test takers' score reports were developed using score anchoring. The method of score anchoring (Beaton & Allen, 1992) used for listening and reading entails the following procedures. Several ability levels or ranges are selected on the overall score scales. For each of these levels, individual items are identified such that, at that given level of ability, test takers have a specified probability (e.g., 80%) of answering each of the items correctly. At lower levels of ability, however, test takers have a significantly lower probability of answering each of these items correctly, but a high probability of answering some other set of items correctly. Experts then judge the items that test takers answered correctly at each level to characterize test takers' skills at various score points. Table 8.24 provides an example of some score descriptors a test taker might receive on a score report.

A different approach to providing performance descriptors was used for speaking and writing because the substantive meaning of the score levels for individual tasks was already explicit in the rubrics used by raters.

For speaking, descriptors were developed at four performance levels (based on the four-level scoring rubric) for three general skill domains: speaking

TABLE 8.24
Examples of Performance Descriptors for Listening, Reading, Speaking, and Writing

Level	Performance Descriptors
	Listening
Intermediate (14–21)	Test takers who receive a score at the INTERMEDIATE level, as you did, typically understand conversations and lectures in English that present a wide range of listening demands. These demands can include difficult vocabulary (uncommon terms or colloquial or figurative language), complex grammatical structures, and/or abstract or complex ideas. However, lectures and conversations that require the listener to make sense of unexpected or seemingly contradictory information may present some difficulty.

When listening to conversations and lecture like these, test takers at the INTERMEDIATE level typically can

- understand explicitly stated main ideas and important details, especially if they are reinforced, but may have difficulty understanding main ideas that must be inferred or important details that are not reinforced;
- understand how information is being used (for example, to provide support or describe a step in a complex process);
- recognize how pieces of information are connected (for example, in a cause-and-effect relationship);
- understand, though perhaps not consistently, ways that speakers use language for purposes other than to give information (for example, to emphasize a point, express agreement or disagreement, or convey intentions indirectly); and
- synthesize information from adjacent parts of a lecture or conversation and make correct inferences on the basis of that information, but may have difficulty synthesizing information from separate parts of a lecture or conversation.

Reading

Level	Performance Descriptors
Intermediate (15–21)	Test takers who receive a score at the INTERMEDIATE level, as you did, typically understand academic tests in English that require a wide range of reading abilities, although their understanding of certain parts of the text is limited.

Test takers who receive a score at the INTERMEDIATE level typically

- have a good command of common academic vocabulary but still have some difficulty with high-level vocabulary;
- have a very good understanding of grammatical structure;
- can understand and connect information, make appropriate inferences, and synthesize information in a range of texts but have more difficulty when the vocabulary is high level and the text is conceptually dense;

(continued)

TABLE 8.24
Continued

Level	Performance Descriptors
	• can recognize the expository organization of a text and the role that specific information serves within a larger text but have some difficulty when these are not explicit or easy to infer from the text; and • can abstract major ideas from a text but have more difficulty doing so when the text is conceptually dense.

Speaking

Level	Performance Descriptors
Fair (2.5–3.0)	Speaking about Familiar Topics–Your responses indicate you are able to speak in English about your personal experiences and opinions in a mostly clear and coherent manner. Your speech is mostly clear with only occasional errors. Grammar and vocabulary are somewhat limited and include some errors. At times, the limitations prevent you from elaborating fully on your ideas, but they do not seriously interfere with overall communication.
Fair (2.5–3.0)	Speaking about Campus Situations -Your responses demonstrate an ability to speak in English about reading material and experiences typically encountered by university students. You are able to convey relevant information about conversations, newspaper articles, and campus bulletins; however, some details are missing or inaccurate. Limitations of grammar, vocabulary, and pronunciation at times cause difficulty for the listener. However, they do not seriously interfere with overall communication.
Limited (1.5–2.0)	Speaking about Academic Course Content–In your responses, you are able to use English to talk about the basic ideas from academic reading or lecture materials, but, in general, you include few relevant or accurate details. It is sometimes difficult for listeners to understand your responses because of problems with grammar, vocabulary, and pronunciation. Overall, you are able to respond in a general way to the questions, but the amount of information in your responses is limited and the expression of ideas is often vague and unclear.

Writing

Level	Performance Descriptors
Fair (2.5–3.5)	Writing based on Reading and Listening -You responded to the task, relating the lecture to the reading, but your response indicates weaknesses such as • an important idea or ideas may be missing, unclear, or inaccurate; • there may be unclarity in how the lecture and the reading passage are related; and/or • grammatical mistakes or vague/incorrect uses of words may make the writing difficult to understand.
Fair (2.5–3.5)	Writing based on Knowledge and Experience–You expressed ideas with reasons, examples, and details, but your response indicated weaknesses such as • you may not provide enough specific support and development for your main points; • your ideas may be difficult to follow because of how you organize your essay or because of the language you use to connect your ideas; and/or • grammatical mistakes or vague/incorrect uses of words may make the writing difficult to understand.

about familiar topics, speaking about campus situations, and speaking about academic topics. These general skill domains are inherent in the specifications for the tasks (i.e., familiar topics—Tasks 1 and 2, campus situations—Tasks 3 and 5, academic topics—Tasks 4 and 6). The four performance levels (good, fair, limited, and weak) are determined by the average rating of the two relevant tasks. The performance descriptors are primarily based on the language features defined in the rubrics (familiar topics from the independent rubric, campus situations and academic topics from the integrated rubric) at the various levels (good—average score of 3.5–4, fair 2.5–3, limited 1.5–2, weak 0–1) with specific reference to the three task domain characteristics.

While the scoring rubrics for each of the writing tasks has five levels (and 0 for off-topic or unscorable responses), it was decided to provide feedback for three performance levels (and a special report for 0). Final task scores of 4, 4.5, and 5 receive feedback labeled good; this feedback was developed from the common positive features of the rubric descriptions at the fourth and fifth levels. The rubrics, and hence the feedback, are of course different for the integrated task and the independent task. Similarly, feedback was developed and described for a limited label for task scores of 1, 1.5, and 2 (performances that are clearly flawed in various ways). The middle label, fair, reflects writing features specified for Rubric Level 3; this feedback is provided for task scores of 2.5, 3, and 3.5 (that is, writing that would have received a rating of 3 from one or both of the raters of the writing task). Feedback for a score of 0 recapitulates the rubric descriptors of the score of 0 for each task type (e.g., mere copying of the reading passage for the integrated task or rejection of the topic for the independent task).

Research on empirical approaches to developing score descriptors will continue as the test becomes operational and more data is available. Questions of interest include the consistency of the links between descriptors and score levels over forms and the usefulness of this kind of information for teachers and students.

Preparing for TOEFL iBT

Over the course of new TOEFL development, TOEFL staff kept ESL teachers and students informed of new directions for the TOEFL through a wide variety of means. Presentations were made and information sessions were held at professional conferences. Materials describing the test revision were distributed at these conferences and published on the TOEFL Web site. More importantly, practice materials and manuals were developed to help teachers and students prepare for the new test and an electronic forum, *TOEFL Practice Online*, was created.

The first release of practice and learning materials occurred in 2002 when a software product, *LanguEdge Courseware* (ETS, 2002), based on the 2002 field study (see Chapter 6), was published to acquaint teachers and students with revisions to the listening and reading test measures and examples of integrated speaking and writing tasks. Once the test specifications were finalized in 2003, a sample test and animated tour of the TOEFL iBT was made available for viewing. Furthermore, a free publication, *TOEFL iBT Tips* (ETS, 2005), was prepared to help test takers and their instructors understand the new test and prepare for it.

Through *TOEFL Practice Online*, teachers and students had access to speaking samples, listening and reading questions, test-taking tips, and discussion boards where students and teachers could exchange study tips. For a fee, Internet-based practice tests were made available that could be scored automatically.[7]

To help curriculum coordinators, academic directors, and teachers prepare their students for the TOEFL iBT, a manual, *Helping Your Students Communicate With Confidence* (ETS, 2004b), was published. This manual discusses the relationship between TOEFL iBT and communicative approaches to teaching and learning, with sample tasks and suggestions for classroom activities. Workshops using this manual were held throughout the world to support ESL specialists in the use of communicative language teaching practices when preparing students to take the TOEFL iBT.

In May 2005, a conference at ETS was attended by 28 English language training and test preparation publishers from the United States and Europe. Publishers learned about the new test's content, scoring, delivery, and administration. The goal of this conference was to encourage publishers to create high-quality study materials that reflected the communicative constructs and task characteristics of the TOEFL iBT.

Summary

Throughout the course of the development of a new TOEFL, project staff sought to keep stakeholders apprised about plans for the new test. The 2003 field study represented the culmination of these efforts. The results of the field study and the final test design provided a basis for the dissemination of information to aid admissions staff, teachers, and students. Information that would help institutions plan how to use the new score scales for admissions purposes included score linking tables and a standard-setting manual. Long-term investigations of the assumption that the new TOEFL would have a positive impact on teaching and learning were launched. Descriptive information about test takers at different score levels was developed. To promote a positive impact on teaching and learning, efforts were made to inform teachers and students about the content of the new test and to make available quality materials to support learning. Among the many routes for ESL specialists, teachers, and students to learn about and prepare for the TOEFL iBT were an electronic forum, computer-based test familiarization and practice materials, and a teacher manual.

CONCLUSIONS

The long-term commitment by ETS to create a new TOEFL that embodied communicative views of language proficiency and that met high standards of educational measurement was realized in the 2003 field study for the TOEFL iBT.

In this final stage of test design, the primary motivation for a field study of two new test forms was the need for data and practices to support generalization and utilization inferences. The field study was designed to provide stakeholders with information that would help them bridge the transition to the new test. The generalization inference would be supported by setting scales for the new test, planning for equating future test forms, and providing evidence of the reliability and generalizability of the new test. It was recognized that much of this information would be provisional because the field study was conducted on a sample whose motivation was suboptimal and because, as test takers became more familiar with and better prepared for the new test, performance would improve.

The utilization inference would be supported by providing admissions staff with the means to set admission standards for the new test. Because one assumption underlying the test redesign was that it would have a positive influence on teaching and learning, long-term research to examine the impact of the new test on test preparation was initiated. To promote positive washback, a number of opportunities to learn about and prepare for the introduction of the new test were provided for teachers, students, and textbook publishers.

The field study also provided an opportunity to collect evidence relevant to evaluation, extrapolation, and explanatory inferences. Table 8.25 summarizes the outcomes and implications of the field study in relation to the inferences addressed.

Two issues relevant to evaluation inferences were the psychometric quality of test items and tasks and the impact of computer familiarity on test performance. Clear evidence in support of psychometric quality of listening, reading, and speaking items was found. Speaking tasks were of a reasonable level of difficulty. However, the integrated writing task turned out to be difficult for many test takers. Whether this outcome reflected the novelty of the task, the test takers' motivation, or an integral characteristic of such tasks would need further study. The fit of IRT models to new listening and reading item data was quite good and provided some indication that all items for these measures would not need to be pretested before use in operational forms. This result was important because it would reduce security risks related to item exposure, maintain reasonable testing time, and still provide items to be used for true score equating.

One factor that has the potential to undermine the assessment of language proficiency is computer familiarity, and there was some indication that familiarity with English language computers affected test performance. The impact

TABLE 8.25
Summary of Outcomes Relevant to the Inferences in the TOEFL Interpretative Argument and
Implications for Further Development and Research

Outcomes	Implications
Evaluation	
Range of item difficulties and discrimination indices for listening and reading items were within typical ranges. Speaking tasks were of an appropriate level of difficulty.	Listening, reading, and speaking measures would support norm-referenced decision-making.
The independent writing tasks were of an appropriate level of difficulty. However, many test takers found the new integrated writing tasks difficult.	The novelty of the new integrated writing tasks may influence their difficulty. Test takers need opportunities to learn about and practice these tasks before taking the test. The impact of practice on task performance should be studied.
IRT calibrations for listening and reading items were satisfactory. Only one item in each measure was removed due to poor model fit.	Good model/data fit for the listening and reading items could be expected. Plans for IRT true score equating of the listening and reading measures appeared to be feasible. All listening and reading items might not need to be pretested if the pretesting was being done to identify items for which the IRT model did not fit the data.
Computer familiarity	Importance of familiarity with English language computers should be noted in test preparation materials. Impact of computer skills on test performance should be studied more systematically.
Generalizability	
Scaling—A scaled score range of 1–30 would be used for all four test measures.	Given the limitations of the field study sample the scales would be reevaluated on operational data.
Equating—IRT true score equating method was planned for the listening and reading measures of operational TOEFL iBT. The speaking and writing measures would not be equated. Reuse of speaking and writing tasks for equating purposes was not feasible because these tasks were highly memorable and were likely to be compromised through exposure.	Alternative methods for monitoring the comparability of speaking and writing measures across test forms need to be developed.
Reliability and generalizability—estimates of internal consistency and alternate forms reliability were satisfactory for listening, reading, and speaking but less satisfactory for writing. Generalizability coefficient for the speaking measure was high. It was somewhat lower than desirable for writing due to the task effect and the person by task interaction.	Generalizability of the writing measure should be monitored for operational data to determine if task effects and person by task interactions decrease as test takers become more familiar with the novel integrated writing task. All the same, the generalizability of the writing measure is likely to be lower than the other measures because it consists of only two tasks.

(continued)

TABLE 8.25
Continued

Outcomes	Implications
Interrater reliability was very high for writing (.87–.92) and somewhat lower for speaking (.69–.88).	The interrater reliability for some speaking tasks was lower than desirable but was offset by sufficient number of tasks to provide highly generalizable speaking scores. Nevertheless, as the pool of raters is expanded for operational scoring, raters should be closely monitored.

Explanation

Structure—The structure of the test was best represented by a higher order factor model consisting of a general factor and four group factors, corresponding to the four language modalities (reading, listening, speaking, and writing.)	Results are consistent with theoretical expectations and support reporting four separate skill scores, as well as a total score. The results also support the inclusion of the scores on the integrated speaking and writing tasks in the respective speaking and writing measures.
Integrated speaking and writing tasks loaded on the speaking and writing factors, respectively, and minimally on listening and reading factors.	Because results differed from the factor analyses of the previous field study, further research on how test structure varies with test takers' background characteristics and learning experiences should be conducted with operational data.
Language learning experience—performance on the field test related to number of years test takers had studied English.	Results were consistent with theoretical assumptions that language proficiency should improve with practice and exposure. Further studies of how different learning experiences and other individual characteristics impact language acquisition would improve our knowledge about language acquisition processes.

Extrapolation

Test scores distinguished between students who did or did not need further English language instruction for study in English medium academic institutions.	Supports assumption that test scores are indicative of English language abilities needed in academic contexts.
Students' self-assessments of their English language proficiency were moderately associated with performance on the test.	Results were consistent with many other studies of test-criterion relationship. Future research should develop better alternative criteria of English language proficiency.

Utilization

Information for institutional score users included score linking tables illustrating the relationships between TOEFL PBT, TOEFL CBT, and TOEFL iBT, a standard-setting manual, and the percentile ranks associated with the new scaled scores.	This information should help institutional score users interpret the meaning of the new scaled scores. However, given the limitations of the field study sample, score users were advised of the provisional nature of this information. As operational data become available, some of this information will be reevaluated.

(continued)

TABLE 8.25
Continued

Outcomes	Implications
Impact on teaching and learning—two studies that would monitor the long term impact of TOEFL iBT on English language teaching and learning worldwide were launched.	These baseline studies of TOEFL test preparation practices will allow an evaluation of whether TOEFL test preparation practices become more aligned with communicative language teaching practices after the release of TOEFL iBT. These studies will also help to identify barriers to the implementation of good teaching practices.
Information for teachers and learners–Score descriptors based on students' self assessments were developed to help teachers and learners understand the meaning of test scores. A variety of avenues to help teachers and learners prepare for TOEFL iBT and to improve their communicative English language skills were provided. These included paper-based and computer-based familiarization materials, practice materials, and learning materials. Information about TOEFL iBT was shared with text publishers to encourage the development of high quality test preparation materials.	These activities served one of the major goals of this test revision project—to have a positive impact on English language teaching and learning.

of this factor on test performance needs to be investigated on larger and more representative samples.

The practices and evidence relevant to the generalization inferences were very promising. The scores for each of the four skill measures would be reported on a scale of 1 to 30, and a total score that was the sum of the scores on the four skill measures would also be reported. Given the limitations of the field study sample, however, plans were made to reevaluate the scales with operational data. Generalization inferences would be supported further by equating the listening and reading measures across forms. Using previously exposed speaking and writing tasks for equating was deemed a threat to test security, so alternative approaches to monitoring the comparability of speaking and writing measures across forms would need to be implemented. Indices of reliability for listening, reading, and speaking were all satisfactory, as were generalizability coefficients for speaking. The reliability and generalizability indices for writing were somewhat lower but typical for writing measures composed of only two tasks. For writing, psychometric ideals had to be balanced with educators' beliefs about the positive impact of extended writing tasks and the negative impact of short, discrete writing-related tasks on teaching and learning.

Support for explanations of test performance in terms of a construct of academic language proficiency was found. The factor structure of the test was consistent with the current theoretical consensus that language proficiency is best described as a hierarchy with a general factor presiding over more specific factors. The higher-order factor model that best fit the results of the field study also supported decisions to include integrated skills tasks on the speaking and writing measures and to report separate scores for the four skills as well as a total score. Another finding that was consistent with theoretical expectations was the ordered relationship between years of English language instruction and test scores.

Academic language proficiency as assessed by the TOEFL iBT field test was related to two other measures of language proficiency in academic contexts. These measures included test takers' self-assessments of their English language skills and their current academic placements. Test takers who were enrolled in institutional English programs or who were taking English language support classes scored lower on all test measures than did students who did not need additional English language courses. Both of these findings support extrapolation inferences.

Finally, a number of activities were undertaken to support utilization inferences. The activities were undertaken so that (a) score users would interpret and use test scores appropriately, (b) the impact of TOEFL iBT on teaching and learning could be evaluated, and (c) test preparation practices would have a positive impact on teaching and learning. Materials developed for institutional score users included a standard-setting manual, information to link cut scores on previous versions of TOEFL to tentative cut scores on TOEFL iBT, and percentile information for the new score scales. The provisional nature of this information, based on field study and not operational data, was emphasized for institutional score users. Long-term studies to monitor the impact of TOEFL iBT on teaching and learning practices were initiated. And teachers and students were provided with a variety of opportunities to learn how to prepare for the test in ways that were consistent with communicative teaching practices.

All in all, throughout the development of the new TOEFL, evidence to support the assumptions and warrants underlying multiple inferences in the TOEFL interpretative argument was gathered. In the next chapter, the status of the TOEFL validity argument will be reviewed by synthesizing the evidence supporting each inference.

NOTES

1. Some technology issues prevented China from participating in the 2003 field study. Instead, some alternative sites in North America, Australia, and New Zealand were selected to recruit newly arrived students from China for the study.
2. As discussed in Chapter 6, equating of the speaking and writing measures based on the reuse of previously exposed tasks was not deemed feasible because these tasks are highly memorable and likely to be compromised by exposure.

3. These results contrast with those reported by Cohen & Upton (2006) in their verbal protocol study of very able students, reported in Chapter 6.
4. The derivation of the scaled scores for the test measures is discussed in a subsequent section of this chapter.
5. The results of this study were not yet available when this chapter was written.
6. Administration of the TOEFL PBT continued in some areas of the world after the introduction of the TOEFL CBT due to technological limitations.
7. The e-rater® essay scoring system was used to score the practice writing tasks and in 2006 SpeechRater™ was introduced to score speaking samples.

REFERENCES

Allen, M. J., & Yen, W. M. (1979). *Introduction to measurement theory*. Monterey, CA: Brooks/ Cole Publishing Company.

Angoff, W. H. (1971). Scales, norms, and equivalent scores. In R. L. Thorndike (Ed.), *Educational measurement* (2nd ed., pp. 508–600). Washington, DC: American Council on Education.

Bailey, K. M. (1999). *Washback in language testing* (TOEFL Monograph No. 15). Princeton, NJ: Educational Testing Service.

Beaton, A. E., & Allen, N. L. (1992). Interpreting scales through scale anchoring. *Journal of Educational Statistics, 17*, 191–204.

Breland, H., Bridgeman, B., & Fowles, M. E. (1999). *Writing assessment in admission to higher education: Review and framework* (ETS Research Rep. No. 99-3). Princeton, NJ: ETS.

Breland, H., Lee, Y.-W., & Muraki, E. (2004). *Comparability of TOEFL CBT writing prompts: Response mode analysis* (TOEFL Research Rep. No. RR-75). Princeton, NJ: Educational Testing Service.

Carroll, J. B. (1983). Psychometric theory and language testing. In J.W. Oller, Jr. (Ed.), *Issues in language testing research* (pp. 80–107). Rowley, MA: Newbury House.

Cohen, A., & Upton, T. (2006). *Strategies in responding to the New TOEFL reading tasks* (TOEFL Monograph No. 33). Princeton, NJ: Educational Testing Service.

Cohen, J. (1988). *Statistical power analysis for the behavioral sciences* (2nd ed.). Hillsdale, NJ: Erlbaum.

Dorans, N. J. (2002). *The recentering of SAT scales and its effects on score distributions and score interpretations* (College Board Research Rep. No. 2002-11). New York: College Entrance Examination Board.

Educational Testing Service. (2001). *Computer-based TOEFL score user guide* (2000–2001 ed.). Princeton, NJ: Author.

Educational Testing Service. (2002). *LanguEdge courseware*. Princeton, NJ: Author.

Educational Testing Service. (2004a). *Standard-setting materials for the Internet-based TOEFL test* (CD), Princeton, NJ: Author.

Educational Testing Service. (2004b). *Helping your students communicate with confidence*. Princeton, NJ: Author.

Educational Testing Service. (2005). *TOEFL iBT Tips: How to prepare for the next generation TOEFL test and communicate with confidence*. Princeton, NJ: Author.

Hamp-Lyons, L. & Brown, A., (2006). The effect of changes in the new TOEFL format on the teaching and learning of ESL/EFL: Report of the development and conduct of the baseline study (2002-2005). Unpublished manuscript.

Hanson, B. A., Zeng, L., & Colton, D. (1994). *A comparison of presmoothing and postsmoothing methods in equipercentile equating* (ACT Research Rep. No. 94-4). Iowa City, IA: ACT.

Henning, G. (1992). Dimensionality and construct validity of language tests. *Language Testing, 9*, 1–11.

Holland, P. W., & Thayer, D. R. (1987). *Notes on the use of log-linear models for fitting discrete probability distributions* (ETS Research Rep. No. RR-87-31). Princeton, NJ: Educational Testing Service.

Jamieson, J., Jones, S., Kirsch, I., Mosenthal, P., & Taylor, C. (2000). *TOEFL 2000 framework: A working paper* (TOEFL Monograph No. 16). Princeton, NJ: Educational Testing Service.

Jiang, H. (1999, April). *Estimation of score distributions for TOEFL concordance tables.* Paper presented at the annual meeting of the National Council on Educational Measurement, Montreal, Canada.

Kirsch, I. S., & Mosenthal, P. B. (1988). *Understanding document literacy: Variables underlying the performance of young adults* (ETS Research Rep. No. RR-88-62). Princeton, NJ: Educational Testing Service.

Kirsch, I. S., & Mosenthal, P. B. (1990). Exploring document literacy: Variables underlying performance of young adults. *Research Quarterly, 25*(1), 5–30.

Kolen, M. J., & Brennan, R. L. (1995). *Test equating: Methods and practices.* New York: Springer-Verlag.

Lee, Y.-W. (2005). *Dependability of scores for a new ESL speaking test: Evaluating prototype tasks* (TOEFL Monograph No. 28). Princeton, NJ: Educational Testing Service.

Lee, Y.-W., & Kantor, R. (2005). *Dependability of new ESL writing test scores: Evaluating prototype tasks and alternative rating schemes* (TOEFL Monograph No. 31). Princeton, NJ: Educational Testing Service.

Messick, S. (1989). Validity. In R.L. Linn (Ed.), *Educational measurement* (3rd ed.; pp. 13–103). New York: Macmillan Publishing Co.

Muraki, E., & Bock, R. (1999). PARSCALE: IRT item analysis and test scoring for rating-scale data [Computer software]. Chicago, IL: Scientific Software, Inc.

Oller, J. W. (1983). A consensus for the eighties? In J. W. Oller, Jr. (Ed.), *Issues in language testing research* (pp. 351–356). Rowley, MA: Newbury House.

Petersen, N. S., Kolen, M. J., & Hoover, H. D. (1989). Scaling, norming, and equating. In R. L. Linn (Ed.), *Educational measurement* (3rd. ed., pp. 221–262). New York: Macmillan.

Pommerich, M., Hanson, B. A., Harris, D. J., & Sconing, J. A. (2000). *Issues in creating and reporting concordance results based on equipercentile methods* (ACT Research Rep. No. 2000-1). Iowa City, IA: ACT.

Powers, D. E., Fowles, M. E., Farnum, M., & Ramsey, P. (1994). Will they think less of my handwritten essay if others word process theirs? Effects on essay scores of intermingling handwritten and word-processed essays. *Journal of Educational Measurement, 31*(3), 220–233.

Powers, D. E., Roever, C., Huff, K. L., & Trapani, C. S. (2003). *Validating New TOEFL courseware scores against faculty ratings and student self-assessments* (ETS Research Rep. No. 03-11). Princeton, NJ: Educational Testing Service.

Sawaki, Y., Stricker, L., & Oranje, A. (in press). *Factor structure of the TOEFL Internet-based test (iBT): Exploration in a field trial sample.* Princeton, NJ: Educational Testing Service.

Stricker, L., Rock, D., & Lee, Y.-W. (2005). *Factor structure of the LanguEdge test across language groups* (TOEFL Monograph No. 32). Princeton, NJ: Educational Testing Service.

Taylor, C., Jamieson, J., Eignor, D., & Kirsch, I. (1998). *The relationship between computer familiarity and performance on computer-based TOEFL test tasks* (TOEFL Research Rep. No. 61). Princeton, NJ: Educational Testing Service.

Wall, D., & Horák, T. (2006). *The impact of changes in the TOEFL examination on teaching and learning in central and eastern Europe: Phase 1, the baseline study* (TOEFL Monograph No. 34). Princeton, NJ: Educational Testing Service.

Wolfe, E. W., & Manalo, J. R. (2004). Composition medium comparability in a direct writing assessment of non-native English speakers. Language *Learning & Technology, 8*(1), 1–13.

9

The TOEFL Validity Argument

Carol A. Chapelle

In the first chapter of this volume, we echoed Mislevy's perspective that the backing for warrants in an interpretive argument for a test would become comprehensible by constructing a narrative that points to a plausible conclusion (Mislevy, 2004). As the previous chapters show, however, the data that help to construct the TOEFL® narrative are generated from a variety of diverse scenarios, and therefore they need to be woven into a single account of the TOEFL interpretive argument. The purpose of this chapter is to develop this single narrative, which is the validity argument for TOEFL score interpretation and use.

An argument assumes an audience, and like the rest of the volume, this chapter is written primarily for the audience consisting of professionals in applied linguistics and measurement, who in turn will communicate it to other test users. The argument, therefore, draws upon the values and practices of educational measurement as reflected in the current standards for educational testing (American Educational Research Association, American Psychological Association, & National Council on Measurement in Education, 1999) and *The ETS Standards for Quality and Fairness* (Educational Testing Service, 2002). These formal standards and their predecessors are the results of ongoing input from the profession about the *evolving* or *shifting* concept of validation, as some have put it (Anastasi, 1986; Angoff, 1988; Messick, 1989; Moss, 1992). The evolving concepts of validation from educational measurement have been taken up and further developed in language assessment (Bachman, 1990; Bachman & Palmer, 1996; Brown, 1996; Chapelle, 1999; Cumming, 1996; Kunnan, 1998; Oller, 1979; Weir, 2005).

These perspectives on validation have been reflected throughout this volume: The theoretical and empirical work pertaining to the TOEFL revision has been discussed in view of the evidence it provides for TOEFL interpretation and use. However, the approach taken in this volume also contributes toward the evolving conception of validation by presenting the research in terms of its role in an interpretive argument (Kane, 1992, 2001, 2004, 2006). The point of organizing research around an interpretive argument is to make clear the intended interpretations and uses of test scores. In other words, the interpretive argument defines what the validity argument is about. Before synthesizing the research, however, the role of the validity argument at this stage of the TOEFL's design needs to be clarified.

A VALIDITY ARGUMENT FROM TEST DESIGN

The validity argument presented in this chapter is the first of two stages in validation (Kane, 2004). The first stage, which Briggs (2004) called *design validity*, results from the test development process when each of the inferences of the interpretive argument has been investigated to the extent possible in view of the fact that the test has not yet been used. The validation work and the resulting validity argument at this stage are confirmationist: The research seeks evidence that helps to support intended interpretations and uses with the aim of developing a test whose interpretations and uses can be justified. The results from research are the data used in this chapter as backing for the inferences in the interpretative argument. The second phase of validation takes place after the test is operational, when additional data are brought to bear on the inferences and the extent to which the conclusions of the original TOEFL validity argument remain supported.

The basis for the design validity argument, referred to in this chapter as the validity argument, consists of theoretical analysis and empirical data that serve as backing for the inferences of the interpretive argument. The conclusion for this argument is that TOEFL scores are valid for making decisions about the test takers' language readiness for academic study at English-medium universities. This conclusion about TOEFL score use is supported with backing for the warrants in the chain of inferences leading to this conclusion. To begin, the grounds include selected features of test takers' performance and the tasks used to elicit that performance. These grounds serve as the intermediate conclusion for the domain definition inference, and at the same time they are the grounds for the subsequent part of the argument, evaluation. The grounds, inferences, and conclusion comprising the chain in the TOEFL interpretive argument are outlined in Figure 9.1.

Each of the six inferences in the TOEFL interpretive argument prompted particular investigations throughout the process of research and development of the TOEFL iBT. This organization of the research evidence represents a different approach to validation than the accumulation-of-evidence approach

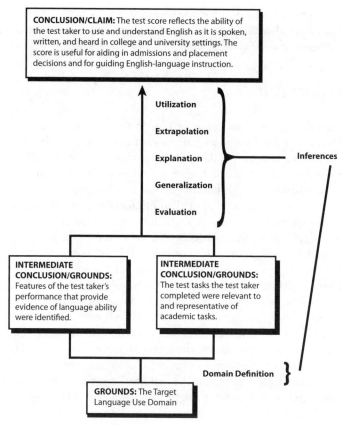

FIG. 9.1   Inferences in the TOEFL interpretive argument in need of backing for the TOEFL validity argument.

that derives from the past work in educational measurement (Cronbach & Meehl, 1955; Messick, 1989) and language assessment (Bachman, 1990; Weir, 2005). The accumulation-of-evidence approach can be problematic because of the difficulty in deciding what kind of evidence to gather and how much evidence is enough (Shepard, 1993). An interpretive argument consisting of different types of inferences provides guidance as to the types of research needed. Research produces the backing required to support assumptions associated with each inference. The backing is expressed through statements that summarize findings that support inferences, and the design validity argument is composed of these statements within an overall argument leading to the intended conclusion. Such an argument might ultimately include rebuttals, which would weaken the strength of the inferences, but at this stage of design validity, the emphasis is on the warrants supporting the inferences and their backing. This chapter, therefore, takes each inference in turn, beginning at the bottom of Figure 9.1, and summarizes research results as support for assumptions; this chapter also demonstrates how such statements are structured into a validity argument for TOEFL iBT.

DOMAIN DEFINITION

The domain definition inference is based on the warrant that observations of performance on the TOEFL reveal relevant knowledge, skills, and abilities in situations representative of those in the target domain of language use in English-medium institutions of higher education. This warrant, in turn, is based on the assumptions (a) that assessment tasks representing the academic domain can be identified, (b) that critical English language skills, knowledge, and processes needed for study in English-medium colleges and universities can be identified, and (c) that assessment tasks requiring important skills and representing the academic domain can be simulated as test tasks. Figure 9.2 illustrates how the backing supports the part of the validity argument that rests on domain definition, which moves the argument from the language use domain to specific performance on the test tasks. Making this inference requires the interpreter to accept the warrant that observations of performance on the TOEFL are representative of performances in the target domain of language use in English-medium institutions of higher education. The validity of the warrant rests on the support that can be found for the assumptions that underlie it, as illustrated in Figure 9.2. Support for these three assumptions was obtained and documented through processes that took place during test development, as described in Chapters 2, 3, and 7.

Domain Analysis

The backing for the assumptions that representative tasks and relevant abilities can be identified comes from domain analysis, which Mislevy, Steinberg, and Almond (2003) defined as the process of gathering information about "the nature of knowledge in [the relevant] arena, how people acquire it, and how they use it" and of recognizing "within those bits of information, patterns, structures, and relations from which [the test designer] will begin to organize assessment arguments and sketch assessment objects" (p. 18). From the days of the early TOEFL, a mechanism was in place for the TOEFL program to gather professional judgment about test content through the regular meetings of the TOEFL Committee of Examiners, as described in Chapter 2. For the new TOEFL, however, domain analysis activities, described in Chapters 2 and 3, are documented in a series of reports that (a) examines the nature of professional knowledge about academic language proficiency, (b) surveys language tasks in an academic context, and (c) reports empirical investigations of students' and teachers' views about academic language tasks.

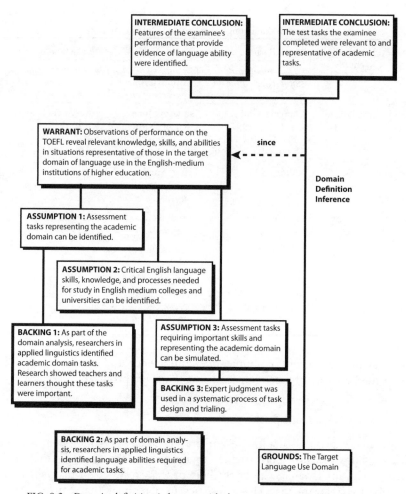

FIG. 9.2   Domain definition inference with three assumptions and backing.

References for reports commissioned by the TOEFL program to gather professional knowledge about academic language proficiency and tasks for the new TOEFL are listed in the second column in Table 9.1. The papers referred to in the third column, the framework papers, built upon this first set of papers by organizing the information in a way that was intended to inform language assessment for the TOEFL. The papers in the fourth column analyzed academic tasks through empirical investigation of perceived task importance by teachers and students (Rosenfeld, Leung, & Oltman, 2001), professional judgment (Enright & Schedl, 1999), or documentation of actual task use (Hale et al., 1996). As Chapter 2 explains, all of this work was a continuation of an ongoing discussion that the TOEFL program engaged

TABLE 9.1
Reports Documenting the Results of Domain Analysis

Area of the Domain Covered	Purpose of Paper Documenting Professional Knowledge		
	Documents initial knowledge gathering	Organizes knowledge for assessment argument	Analyzes important academic tasks
Academic language proficiency and tasks	Chapelle, Grabe, & Berns, 1997; Ginther & Grant, 1996; Waters, 1996	Jamieson, Jones, Kirsch, Mosenthal, & Taylor, 2000	Rosenfeld et al., 2001
Listening	Rubin, 1993	Bejar, Douglas, Jamieson, Nissan, & Turner, 2000	
Reading	Hudson, 1996	Enright et al., 2000	Enright & Schedl, 1999
Speaking	Douglas, 1997	Butler, Eignor, Jones, McNamara, & Suomi, 2000	
Writing	Hamp-Lyons & Kroll, 1996	Cumming, Kantor, Powers, Santos, & Taylor, 2000	Hale et al., 1996

in about the nature of communicative competence and academic tasks and about the best way of assessing academic language proficiency.

Simulation of Academic Tasks

A systematic process of task design drew upon expert judgment and empirical analysis of task performance to simulate academic tasks that would engage relevant language abilities. This process resulted in task shells that describe the relevant task characteristics in a manner that can be used to produce comparable tasks. Chapter 3 explains how the framework papers organized the information about the domain in a way that suggested initial task designs, and Chapter 4 describes how the initial possibilities were pared down to create a set of test tasks that would allow test takers to demonstrate relevant language performance in a manner that would provide evidence of their proficiency.

For each of the four measures, expert judgment as reflected in the framework was used as a basis for task design, and questions specific to each were raised. For example, designing academic listening test tasks raised the question about the extent to which listening texts could be modeled on the corpus. Overall, the listening texts presented in the test could not be drawn directly from the corpus of academic English; instead, the corpus was found useful as a check on the authenticity of the texts. Moreover, nonnative varieties could not be used despite their regular occurrence in the academic domain, and tasks requiring integration of information across two texts could not be used.

In response to questions raised about the reading measure, research helped to determine that texts needed to be in a range of 550–700 words and that they should be chosen on the basis of complexity of rhetorical organization rather than type of organization (e.g., comparison or chronology). On speaking, it was decided to include two types of monologic speaking tasks, one requiring test takers to speak based on their own knowledge, and the other requiring test takers to speak about something they had heard or read. On the writing tasks, independent and integrated tasks were also planned, and the use of short responses or multiple-choice questions was rejected as not appropriate for eliciting the language relevant to the framework. These and other insights that came from attempts to develop trial tasks based on the framework papers guided the design of measures used in the research reported in Chapter 5 and in the first field study.

This research identified additional task design issues, which were addressed by an evidence-centered design (ECD) process called task design analysis (TDA). TDA was used to review prior work systematically to distill implications for test design. This process, which is described in Chapter 7, resulted in task shells. TDA built upon the professional expertise that had been documented during the domain analysis, the expert judgment applied in task design, and the results of the task trials. One example of a task design decision resulting from TDA was the decision to alter the rating scale for the speaking measure, which had been found to produce scores that were not as reliable as desired in the first field study (Chapter 6). Most importantly, TDA resulted in task shells, which serve as the formal test specifications for developing multiple parallel tasks that measure designated aspects of academic language proficiency.

How can this complex process of domain analysis and task construction be summed up to serve as backing for the inference of domain definition in the interpretive argument? Kane (2006) suggested that a warrant can be viewed as a ticket allowing the score interpreter to traverse an inferential bridge; this ticket has to be valid for the crossing to be made, and it is the backing that validates the ticket. Figure 9.3 shows the backing for the warrant about observations of performance on the TOEFL (see Figure 9.2). The combination of the domain analysis, expert judgment, task trials, and task shells serves as a ticket allowing the inference from the target-language-use domain to relevant, observable performance. In other words, because of these four aspects of the task design process, test users can be confident that the performance test takers display as they take the test reflects their academic language ability and use in the academic domain. However, a series of bridges remains between that performance and the test use; the next bridge is evaluation.

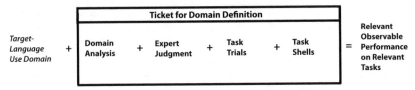

FIG. 9.3   Backing that licenses traversal of the domain definition inference in the TOEFL interpretive argument.

EVALUATION

The evaluation inference is based on the warrant that observations of performance on TOEFL are evaluated to provide observed scores that reflect targeted language abilities. As shown in Figure 9.4, this warrant is based on three assumptions about scoring and conditions of task administration: (a) rubrics for scoring responses are appropriate for providing evidence of targeted language abilities, (b) task administration conditions are appropriate for providing evidence of targeted language abilities, and (c) the statistical characteristics of items, measures, and test forms are appropriate for norm-referenced decisions. Backing for these assumptions was obtained from research reported in Chapters 4 through 8.

Appropriate Scoring Rubrics

The backing for the assumption that scoring rubrics are appropriate comes from rubric development that was reported in Chapters 4, 5, and 6, as well as the finalization of the scoring rubrics reported in Chapter 7. For example, Chapter 4 describes the decision that the scoring of writing should consist of holistic ratings that include consideration of language use, discourse organization, and content. Scoring rubrics for writing were developed on the basis of research examining the factors affecting both analytic and holistic ratings that experienced raters awarded to test takers' performance on the writing tasks (Cumming, Kantor, & Powers, 2001, 2002). Subsequent trialing of the holistic rubric revealed problems posed to raters by responses composed of large segments of text copied from what the test takers had read. The resolution for this problem is described in Chapter 7. The integrated task was modified to require synthesis of information from a listening and reading text. Furthermore, a low score was to be given for using only one text, and therefore, a response that is largely copied is disadvantaged.

Appropriate scoring rubrics were determined for the speaking measure on the basis of an iterative process of rubric development, trialing, and revision. The first attempt at a scoring rubric was made on the basis of a series of meetings of experts followed by trialing of the rating scheme they proposed. The outcome of this process was a 5-point holistic rubric, which was subsequently

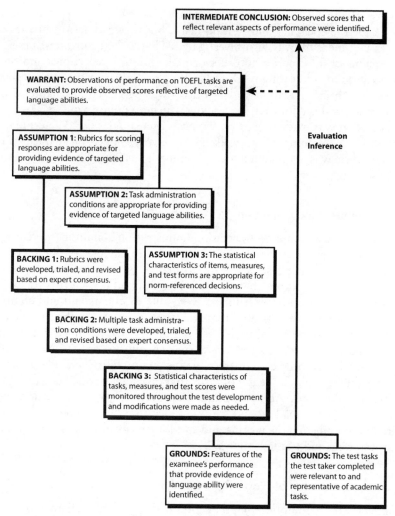

FIG. 9.4 Evaluation inference with three assumptions and backing.

investigated in a study examining raters' use of the rubric (Brown, Iwashita, & McNamara, 2005), as described in Chapter 5. One problem identified in the research was raters' uncertainty about how to evaluate the content of the test takers' responses. Chapter 6 describes how the rubric was modified to include content guidance for the raters, but in the first field study the inter-rater reliability for the 5-point speaking scale was not sufficient. This problem was addressed during the ECD process described in Chapter 7, during which it was decided that the rubric should distinguish among only four levels of performance. The 4-point scale was implemented in the second field study (Chapter 8), with a finding of better interrater reliability.

Most of the backing about appropriate scoring rubrics pertains to the rubrics for the speaking and writing tasks, but the reading-to-learn task in the reading measure was also investigated. That task requires test takers to place pieces of information in order or make multiple selections, and therefore a rubric for indicating relevant levels of partial correctness was needed. A scoring rubric for reading-to-learn tasks was described in Chapter 5 that specified a threshold for each item below which no points would be awarded. This decision was made in part on the basis of a simulation to determine the likelihood of obtaining a nonzero score purely by chance. Subsequently, this scoring rubric was adopted for some listening items that also required partial credit scoring.

Task Administration Conditions

Backing for the assumption that task administration conditions were appropriate comes from prototyping studies reported in Chapter 4. These task trials demonstrated that test takers' performance for selected task types was obtained under conditions that allowed them to exhibit what they knew. The trials focused on whether test takers were able to understand and complete proposed test tasks in a manner that was appropriate given their proficiency levels. Through these initial trials, task parameters were defined in a manner that would eliminate tasks that were unclear and those that failed to elicit the expected performance. For example, listening ability was determined to be elicited best through the use of tasks that provided test takers with opportunities to take notes. An appropriate interface and set of instructions were determined for the reading and speaking measures. The amount of time required for completing the writing and speaking measures was set on the basis of prototyping and trialing studies.

Psychometric Quality of Norm-Referenced Scores

Backing for the assumption that the scores had appropriate characteristics for norm-referenced decisions is found in the item analyses reported in Chapters 5 and 6. The psychometric quality of a norm-referenced test is supported by evidence that tasks are of an appropriate level of difficulty and differentiate among test takers' levels of ability. Therefore, task performance was examined on proposed task types to verify that they produced the appropriate difficulties and discriminations.

In the TOEFL iBT field study reported in Chapter 8 the items on the reading and listening measures exhibited a wide range of item difficulty and an appropriate level of discrimination as indicated by both classical and item response theory (IRT) item analyses. Based on the results for the IRT analyses, plans for IRT true score equating were put into place for operational testing. The TOEFL iBT field study found that the speaking tasks were at an appropriate

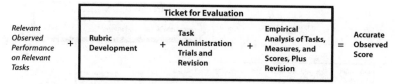

FIG. 9.5 Starting point (in italics) and backing that licenses traversal of the evaluation inference in the TOEFL interpretive argument.

level of difficulty for the test takers who participated in the study, but that the integrated writing tasks were difficult for many test takers. Nevertheless, it was decided to retain this task type for the purpose of domain representation and in the expectation that test takers would be more motivated and better prepared to complete these tasks under operational conditions. Test preparation materials would need to be made available to help test takers become familiar with the integrated writing task. Overall, the psychometric results from the TOEFL iBT field study provide good backing for the psychometric quality of the scores.

Figure 9.5 depicts the summation of backing that supports the movement across the evaluation inference in the TOEFL interpretive argument. The evaluation inference starts with relevant observed performance on relevant tasks, which was the intermediate conclusion from the domain definition inference. The ticket for the evaluation inference becomes valid through a combination of rubric development, task administration trials and revision, and empirical analysis of tasks, measures, and scores, as well as revision based on those analyses. The result is an accurate observed score, which is an essential link in the chain of inferences that is to culminate in appropriate score use. However, an accurate score also needs to be representative of all the accurate scores that the test taker might receive on the relevant domain of task performance. The assumption that the score is representative requires crossing the next inferential bridge, generalization.

GENERALIZATION

Generalization is based on the warrant that observed scores are estimates of expected scores that test takers would receive on comparable tasks, test forms, administrations, and rating conditions. As Figure 9.6 illustrates, the assumptions underlying this warrant are that (a) a sufficient number of tasks are included on the test to provide stable estimates of test takers' performances, (b) the configuration of tasks on measures is appropriate for the intended interpretation, (c) appropriate scaling and equating procedures for test scores are used, and (d) task and test specifications are well-defined so that parallel tasks and test forms are created. Backing for these assumptions was obtained

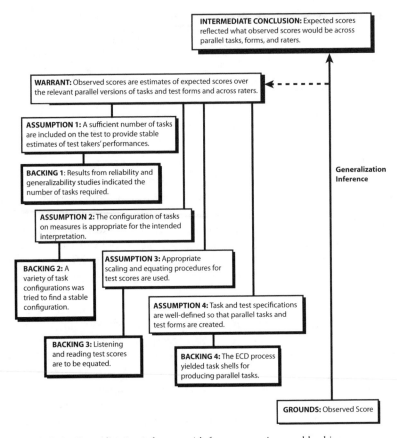

FIG. 9.6   Generalization inference with four assumptions and backing.

through studies of generalizability, reliability, scaling, and equating, which are reported in Chapters 5, 6, and 8, as well as through the task design process reported in Chapter 7.

Backing for the assumption that a sufficient number of tasks is included on the test to provide stable estimates of test takers' performances was obtained through the reliability and generalizability studies reported in Chapter 5. For all four of the measures, an ideal number of test tasks was identified which, if held constant, would maintain reliability despite changes in task configurations. For both speaking and writing, increasing the number of tasks increased reliability more than increasing the number of raters. For the speaking measure, the best number of tasks was found to be six in the first field study; increases beyond six resulted in minimal increases in reliability. Acceptable generalizability coefficients were found for the speaking measure in the TOEFL iBT field study. The inclusion of six speaking tasks resulted in a stable measure of speaking.

For the writing measure, the desired number of tasks was found to be three for obtaining adequate reliabilities. In the TOEFL iBT field study, however, only two writing tasks were included, and consequently the generalizability coefficient was lower than desired. As Chapter 7 explains, the recommended number of writing tasks was not included in the TOEFL iBT field study because of the constraints on the length of the test and the amount of time test takers need to complete the writing tasks. Therefore, two raters will evaluate each writing sample to maximize reliability given the limited number of tasks.

The number of tasks for the reading measure was set on the basis of previous experience with the TOEFL, and the number of tasks for the listening measure was explored in the research described in Chapter 5, which resulted in a recommendation for an adequate number of items. In the TOEFL iBT field study, estimates for internal consistency reliability were good on both reading and listening measures, indicating that the recommended number of items was adequate.

Configuration of Tasks

Backing for the assumption that the configuration of tasks on each of the measures is appropriate for intended interpretations comes from generalizability and reliability studies reported in Chapter 5. Researchers examined the effects of task configurations on the estimated reliability for each measure when they were composed of different combinations of task types. The result for the listening measure was that more listening texts were required than what had been indicated in the preliminary blueprint (Chapter 4). The type of text included in the measure (lecture vs. conversation), however, would not affect reliability, which would be .80 or above, provided that at least 30 test questions were included.

Chapter 5 reported the D-study scenarios of the generalizability analysis that examined effects of different configurations of listening/speaking, reading/speaking, and independent speaking tasks. When the number of speaking tasks was held constant, the types of tasks did not make any discernable difference; a reliability of above .80 could be obtained with all task configurations and a single rating for each task. The generalizability analysis of the task configuration on the writing measure indicated that the highest estimates could be obtained with two listening/writing tasks and at least one other task (reading/writing or independent writing), but in any case, time constraints limited the number of writing tasks to two, and so the task types were chosen on the basis of considerations of domain representation.

Scaling and Equating Procedures

The assumption that appropriate scaling and equating procedures for test scores are being used was backed by the TOEFL iBT scaling results reported in Chapter 8. Despite these results, the limitation of this analysis was that the sample did not reflect as closely as desired the operational TOEFL population. Therefore, scaling needs to be reevaluated on operational data. Based on the results of the second field study, IRT true score equating is planned for the listening and reading measures. This will not be feasible for the writing and speaking measures, so other means of monitoring comparability across tasks is needed; research is underway to do this.

Task and Test Specifications

The assumption that the task and test specifications are sufficiently defined to create parallel tasks and test forms was supported with two types of backing: the TDA process of formalizing task shells for creating parallel tasks and the empirical verification of reliability and generalizability. Chapter 7 documents the principled TDA approach that was taken for creating task shells through the use of fixed and variable elements defining the aspects of tasks that must remain constant to assess a particular area of competence and those aspects that can vary. Results stemming from the use of the task shells were evident in the alternate forms reliability coefficients and the empirical comparisons of difficulty across forms. All alternate forms reliabilities for measures on Forms A and B in the second field study (reported in Chapter 8) were .80 or above. In all four measures, the parallel forms reliability was slightly below the internal consistency reliability, which indicates that the variance across forms was minimal relative to the variance within a form. The differences across parallel versions of each task type were small, which suggested that the task shells had succeeded in guiding parallel test development.

In the summer of 2006, additional analyses were conducted using data from actual test takers who had taken the TOEFL twice within a 2-month period (Zhang, 2006). A sufficient number of test takers was identified in five 2-month sets: May-June (987), April-May (871), March-April (1094), February-March (809), and January-February (579). The correlations among Time 1 and Time 2 scores for these groups were all above .72, and the correlations for the Time 1 and Time 2 total scores were .90 or higher. The mean scaled score changes from Time 1 to Time 2 were less than the standard error of measurement for each of the sections and for the total score. These operational data showing the stability of different forms of the TOEFL iBT across administrations provide strong backing for the assumption that the test and task specifications result in comparable measures across forms.

Generalization entails four assumptions, and accordingly the ticket for crossing the generalization inference is obtained with a combination of four types of backing: empirical verification of the number of task performances comprising the score, empirical evidence that the configuration of tasks is appropriate, scaling and equating procedures to ensure parallel scores across forms, and task shells that yield parallel forms. As illustrated in Figure 9.7,

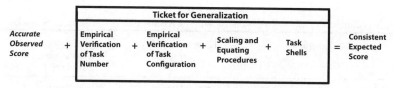

FIG. 9.7 Starting point (in italics) and backing that licenses traversal of the generalization inference in the TOEFL interpretive argument.

crossing the generalization inference begins with an accurate observed score. The destination is a consistent expected score, which can be trusted to reflect accurately not only performance on an individual occasion, but ability across a larger domain of interest to test users. Consistent performance, however, needs to be explained in terms of the construct of academic language proficiency, and therefore the next bridge in the argument is explanation.

EXPLANATION

Explanation entails the warrant that expected scores are attributed to a construct of academic language proficiency. Five assumptions about the construct of language proficiency were identified in Chapter 1 as underlying this warrant. Do this warrant and its assumptions, however, return to the issue that challenged test designers at the beginning of the project: How can language proficiency be defined in a way that helps to clarify score meaning? In the course of the TOEFL project, more than one way of explaining score meaning was attempted, drawing upon something like what validity theorists (Embretson, 1983; Messick, 1989) referred to as construct representation (a model of the knowledge, processes, and strategies underlying task performance) and nomothetic span (a theory of the network of relationships among factors associated with the construct). In addition, what one might call a concrete approach based on an analysis of task characteristics was attempted. These perspectives on explanation are not entirely distinct, but rather they might be thought of as pertaining to related planes, or strata, of explanation.

Three Planes of Explanation

The assumptions underlying explanation are based on perspectives toward construct definition, or explanations for performance consistency, each of which implies an approach to the research needed to supply backing. Table 9.2 characterizes the types of construct definition underlying each of the assumptions identified in Chapter 1. These approaches to explanation are ordered from abstract, which refers to a theoretical and the most general conception of the construct, to concrete, which refers to a construct defined

TABLE 9.2
Types of Construct Definition Associated with the Assumptions Underlying Explanation

Assumption	Type of Construct Definition	Explanatory Continuum: From Abstract to Concrete[a]
Test performance varies according to amount and quality of experience in learning English.	General language proficiency construct	Very abstract
Performance on new test measures relates to performance on other test-based measures of language proficiency as expected theoretically. The internal structure of the test scores is consistent with a theoretical view of language proficiency as a number of highly interrelated components.	General language proficiency construct divided into four language skills	Abstract, but more detailed than general language proficiency
The linguistic knowledge, processes, and strategies required to successfully complete tasks vary in keeping with theoretical expectations.	Psycholinguistic knowledge, processes, and strategies	Somewhat abstract, but small granularity and directly connected with concrete task characteristics
Task difficulty is systematically influenced by task characteristics.	Observable task characteristics	Concrete

[a] The degree of abstraction refers to the extent to which test developers and researchers can identify observable determinants of performance.

in terms of the concrete features of the test tasks. An abstract construct is an unobservable and slippery approach to explanation, whereas the concrete approach entails identification of observable task features such as the number of clauses in a sentence, the number of distractors in a multiple choice item, or the frequency of vocabulary words contained in a reading passage. The middle plane in this continuum and the link between the middle and bottom planes might be thought of as consistent with Embretson's approach to construct representation, which theorizes abstract knowledge, processes, and strategies that are linked to certain task characteristics.

The assumption that test performance varies according to test takers' language experience is based on the most abstract conception of language proficiency because it refers to all language proficiency without specifying any particular knowledge or skills as determinants of performance. Slightly more precise is the assumption that performance on each of the new measures relates to performance on other test-based measures of language proficiency as expected theoretically. This assumption refers to aspects of language ability about which one can make theoretical predictions concerning nomothetic span or relationships among related constructs. Similarly, the assumption that the internal structure of the test scores is consistent with a theoretical view of language proficiency as a number of highly interrelated components remains at a high level of abstraction. These assumptions and the explanations that underlie them suggest the need for research investigating the correlational patterns among measures of general language proficiency and of the four skills.

In contrast, the assumption about the processes, strategies, and knowledge affecting performance entails construct representation and therefore requires that the explanation for performance consistency be specified in terms of psycholinguistic processes. The assumption about the influence of task characteristics on performance requires an explanation for performance consistency based on concretely defined task features such as sentence complexity and vocabulary frequency in the input text. Ideally, these three sources of explanation—a broad construct of language proficiency, the psycholinguistic processes, and the task features—would be related to each other in a systematic way so that multiple sources of backing could be integrated into an explanation for score meaning.

The three levels of abstraction might be represented as shown in Figure 9.8, where the object of the explanation, the test score, appears at the bottom. The arrows illustrate the explanation for the test score that originates in the planes of observable task features (above arrow a), psycholinguistic knowledge, processes and strategies (above arrow b), and the abstract language proficiency constructs (above arrow c). The dotted lines represent the connections that ideally would hold the levels together. Dotted lines are used because of what is tentative and incomplete professional knowledge that would ideally provide links among the levels, allowing for an integrated construct theory. Such a theory would help to guide research that seeks backing and interpretation of research results on all these levels.

The initial interpretive argument presented in Chapter 1 included the assumption that task difficulty was systematically influenced by task characteristics that were relevant to the other aspects of the construct of academic language proficiency (as illustrated by the dotted line on the left in Figure 9.8). Backing for this assumption was sought through studies of task characteristics and item difficulty in the first round of task trialing, but as reported in Chapter 4, no backing was found. Because of the lack of backing, this assumption does not appear currently in the interpretive argument for which a validity argument is made. As the figure shows, this assumption was associated with only one level of potential explanation for the test scores, and therefore the lack of backing for this assumption does not mitigate any possibility of explanation, but rather increases the necessity for backing assumptions associated with constructs at more abstract levels. In other words, the assumptions underlying explanation in the interpretive argument are the first four in Table 9.2, which assume that explanation can be accomplished based on an abstract construct of academic language proficiency, including four language skills (listening, reading, speaking, and writing), and reflecting

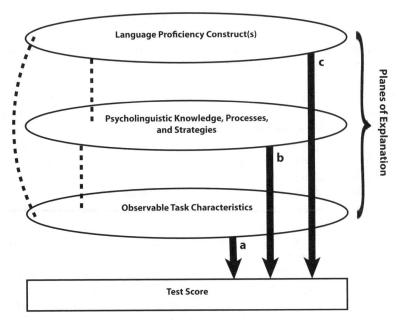

FIG. 9.8   Three planes of potential explanation for test scores.

psycholinguistic knowledge, processes, and strategies. Figure 9.9 illustrates these sources of explanation that are assumed in the TOEFL interpretive argument.

These sources of explanation are evident in the four assumptions that underlie explanation in the revised interpretive argument, which forms the basis for the validity argument. The first assumption—the linguistic knowledge, processes, and strategies required to successfully complete tasks vary in keeping with theoretical expectations—draws upon theorized knowledge and processes, depicted at the second level in Figure 9.9. The second assumption—performance on the new TOEFL measures relates to performance on other test-based measures of language proficiency as expected theoretically—assumes some distinction among the theoretical constructs for the four measures on the test, as illustrated in Figure 9.9. The third assumption—the internal structure of the test scores is consistent with a theoretical view of language proficiency as a number of highly interrelated components—also assumes constructs at the highest level of abstraction. However, in addition, it assumes that the theory specifies relationships among the constructs. The fourth assumption—test performance varies according to the amount and quality of experience in learning English—assumes a single language proficiency construct (i.e., at the highest level of abstraction) that changes with exposure to English. Backing for these assumptions appears throughout Chapters 4, 5, 6, and 8 as qualitative studies of test taking and test responses,

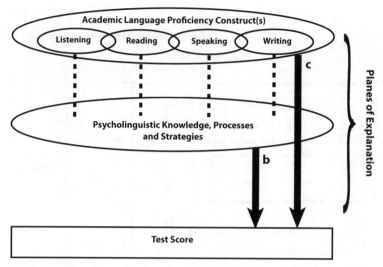

FIG. 9.9   Two planes of explanation in the TOEFL interpretive argument with the theoretical construct consisting of four components.

concurrent correlational studies, investigation of factor structure, and comparison of group differences. The assumptions and a summary of their backing appear in Figure 9.10.

Linguistic Knowledge, Processes, and Strategies for Task Performance

During initial prototyping studies (Chapter 4), performance on prototype tasks was evaluated for consistency with theoretical expectations about the knowledge, processes, and strategies that test takers should engage. Further development was continued only for tasks that met expectations. Subsequently, additional backing was obtained from discourse analysis and cognitive processing studies for the assumption that the linguistic knowledge, processes, and strategies required to complete tasks successfully varied among task types and with proficiency levels in keeping with theoretical expectations. The analysis of speaking samples by Brown, Iwashita, and McNamara, described in Chapter 5, provided evidence that the characteristics of speech samples varied with score level and, to a lesser degree, with task type. Similar qualitative research reported in Chapter 6 provided evidence that differences in writing performance were related to proficiency level and task type as expected in view of the linguistic knowledge, processes, and strategies expected to contribute to writing performance (Cumming et al., 2006). The research reported in Chapter 6 also revealed that test takers relied on academic reading and test-taking strategies rather than exclusively on test-wiseness. Cohen and Upton (2005) found evidence for such academic reading strategies as repeating, paraphrasing, and translating words as well as summarizing to improve

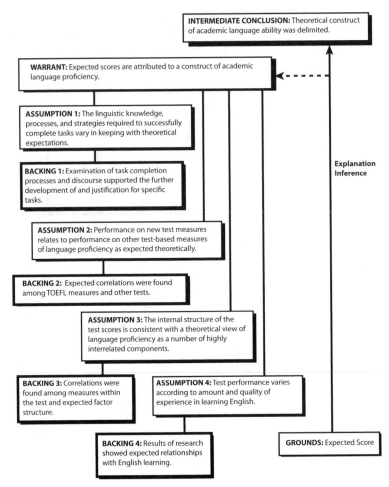

FIG. 9.10   Explanation inference with four assumptions and backing.

comprehension. These findings draw upon the second plane of explanation to show that the scores are influenced by relevant psycholinguistic knowledge, processes, and strategies.

Relationships with Other Tests

Backing was found for the assumption that performance on TOEFL measures relates as expected to performance on other test-based measures of language proficiency. The other tests used in this research consisted of earlier versions of the TOEFL in addition to a speaking test, PhonePass. One might ask why one would seek convergent correlations between the test for which improvements are sought and the new test. Such relationships are relevant to explanation inferences because other language tests for which some validity evidence exists serve as indicators of similar constructs of academic language proficiency that the new TOEFL is intended to measure. In such research, the other indicators of academic language proficiency need to produce reliable scores, and previous versions of the TOEFL do that. Table 9.3 summarizes findings concerning correlational results between the new TOEFL measures at various stages of development with previous versions of the TOEFL.

Our general finding across the three studies was that convergent relationships between measures of the same skills assessed in a similar manner were substantial. Disattenuated correlations between corresponding measures were .84 for speaking; they ranged from .89 to .95 for reading; and they ranged from .82 to .94 for listening. Correlations between prototype writing measures and the TOEFL PBT SWE measures were slightly lower, .79 and .80. We attributed these somewhat lower correlations to the differences in the skills assessed by the two types of measures, one involving productive writing tasks and the other composed of multiple-choice grammar items. The correlation between the TOEFL iBT writing measure and the TOEFL CBT structure and

TABLE 9.3
Summary of Correlational Results Pertaining to Explanation in Prototyping and Field Studies

Measures and Results	Stage of Test Design		
	Prototyping Study (Ch. 5)	Field Study 1 (Ch. 6)	Field Study 2 (Ch. 8)
Test-based measures	TOEFL PBT (Listening, reading, and SWE), and PhonePass for speaking	TOEFL PBT (Listening, reading, and SWE)	TOEFL CBT (Listening, reading, and S/W)
Correlations between corresponding existing and new measures	High correlations of TOEFL PBT measures and PhonePass with corresponding prototype measures (.79–.95)	High correlations between TOEFL PBT measures and corresponding prototype measures (.80–.89)	High correlations between corresponding measures from TOEFL CBT and TOEFL iBT (.91–.92)[a]
Convergent and discriminant relationships	Higher correlations between measures of the same skill between measures of different skills, except for SWE and the prototype writing measure	Higher correlations between measures of the same skill than between different skills for reading, except for listening and SWE with writing	(Discriminant relationships not analyzed)

[a] The observed correlations between similar measures reported in Table 8.23 have been corrected for measurement error so that they can be compared to disattenuated correlations reported in Chapters 5 and 6 (summarized in column 2 and 3).

writing measure, which included both multiple-choice grammar items and a writing sample, was much higher (.91).

The results provide little support for the expected discriminant relationships, i.e. correlations showing that different measures of the same skill are more highly related than are different measures of different skills. Such relationships were found consistently only for reading. The lack of discriminant relationships among the measures of the four skills may reflect the highly interrelated nature of all of the language skills measured, as discussed in the next section.

Internal Structure

Ideally, backing for explanation would come from results supporting a theorized factor structure of the test, and such a structure could be illustrated by hypothesized degrees of overlap among the components. Thus, the plane of explanation at the highest level would consist of not only components, but also a configuration of components relevant to explanation. However, in view of the imprecise theory of language proficiency, all that can be hypothesized is that the components of language proficiency should be related to each other somewhat and that there should also be a more general factor of language ability. Backing was found from the factor analyses for the assumption that the internal structure of the test scores is consistent with a theoretical view of language proficiency as highly interrelated components. The field study reported in Chapter 6 showed that the data for the whole group, as well as those for the three largest L1 groups, all fit a two-factor structure consisting of a listening, reading, and writing factor and a speaking factor.

The structure of the final TOEFL iBT was best represented by a higher-order factor model with a general factor and four factors, each loading most strongly on one of the four measures—listening, reading, speaking, and writing. The speaking and writing tasks loaded minimally on the listening and reading factors, respectively. These results for the factor analysis of the iBT data provided backing for the assumption that academic language proficiency as measured by the iBT consists of interrelated components, but beyond that it also provides evidence for a theoretically plausible factor structure among the sections of the test.

Relationship to English Learning

Chapter 8 reports research comparing differences in test scores among learners with varying degrees of experience with English to provide backing for the assumption that test performance varies according to amount and quality of experience in learning English. Based on responses to a background questionnaire item, examinees were placed in one of six groups, indicating length of experience in learning English. ANOVAs comparing the mean total iBT scores and those for each of the measures on the iBT indicated significantly different iBT scores among groups, and post hoc comparisons showed that the significant group differences tended to be at the upper end of the length of study groups. These findings were consistent with the differences that one would suggest based on the theoretical construct of academic language proficiency that develops with time spent learning English.

The research providing backing for explanation raises some of the same issues that were encountered by test designers at the beginning of the TOEFL revision project when they attempted to define academic language proficiency. However, at this point in the interpretive argument, we have moved some distance toward score interpretation before encountering thorny issues about construct definition. Moreover, additional light is shed on that issue because of the various research approaches that were taken to better delimit the construct during the process of test design. In short, the ticket for moving across the explanation inference is validated by four types of backing, as shown in Figure 9.11. The backing supports assumptions associated with two planes of explanation: one at the level of language knowledge, processes, and strategies, and one at the level of an abstract construct of academic language proficiency, which is composed of interrelated constructs of listening, reading, speaking, and writing. What remains is to be validated at this point in the argument is the inference suggesting that such consistencies in test performance can be extrapolated beyond the test itself to the academic domain.

EXTRAPOLATION

Extrapolation is based on the warrant that the construct of academic language proficiency as assessed by the TOEFL accounts for the quality of English language performance in English-medium institutions of higher education. Underlying this inference is the assumption that performance on the test is related to other criteria of language proficiency in academic contexts, as shown in Figure 9.12. Backing for this assumption was found in research examining relationships of the new measures with other measures of English in an academic context, including the tests described above, test takers' self-assessments, instructors' judgments about students, and course placements.

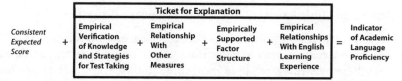

FIG. 9.11   Starting point (in italics) and backing that licenses traversal of the explanation inference in the TOEFL interpretive argument.

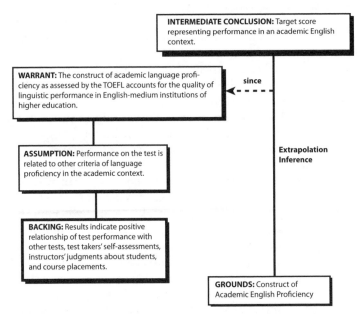

FIG. 9.12   Extrapolation inference with one assumption and backing.

Relationship to Test-Based Criteria of Academic Language Performance

Backing for the assumption that performance on the test is related to other criteria of language ability in academic contexts was obtained through criterion-related correlations that were calculated between the measures of the new test and other measures of academic language proficiency, which consisted of the previous versions of the TOEFL that were discussed above. The convergent correlational results were summarized above in support of explanation inferences. For explanation, the analysis and results focus on the extent to which test scores pattern relative to predictions from construct theory. A subset of these patterns, the convergent correlations with other measures of academic language proficiency, also serves as backing for extrapolation inferences because TOEFL scores serve as other indicators of linguistic performance in the academic domain. The relevant test results are given in the first row of Table 9.4.

Relationship to Other Criteria of Academic Language Performance

Table 9.4 summarizes the correlations between measures on the new TOEFL and the nontest criteria used as indicators of performance in the academic context. Self-assessments were used in all three studies, with findings of positive correlations between test takers' assessments of their own ability in each modality and the new TOEFL score on the corresponding modality. In the fi-

TABLE 9.4
Summary of Backing for Extrapolation Inference

Relationship of New TOEFL Measures with...	Phase of TOEFL Research		
	Prototyping Study (Ch. 5)	Field Study 1 (Ch. 6)	Field Study 2 (Ch. 8)
Test-based measures	High correlations a between prototype measures and TOEFL PBT (.79–.95)	High correlations a between prototype measures and paper-based measures (.80–.89)	High correlations a between corresponding measures of TOEFL CBT and TOEFL iBT (.91–.92)
Self-assessment	Moderate correlations between prototype measures and self-assessments (.45–.55)	Moderate correlations between prototype measures and relevant "how well" and "agreement" scales (.26–.48)	Moderate correlations between self-assessments and TOEFL iBT measures (.45–.55)
Instructor ratings	Moderate correlations with prototype measures (.27–.51)	Moderate correlations with prototype measures (.42–.49)	(Not collected)
Course placements	Differences among three groups, as predicted		Clear differences between two groups, as predicted

a Disattenuated correlations.

nal field study, the correlations across all measures were consistently between .45 and .55. Instructors' ratings of students' classroom performance on targeted language tasks were gathered in the test design research and first field study. In the first field study, the correlations were moderate, between .42 and .49. For both the test taker and instructor ratings, these moderate correlations provide backing for the assumption that the test scores are related to other criteria of language proficiency in the academic contexts. High correlations of self-assessments and instructor ratings with the TOEFL scores are not expected because of the differences in measurement methods and differences in the constructs of perceived ability and test performance.

Participants in the test design research were identified as having been placed in English as a second language (ESL) classes or not needing ESL instruction. In the first field study, one group of ESL students was taking ESL support courses and the other group was not. In addition, a group of native speakers of English was tested to comprise a third group. In general, native speakers tended to score higher than ESL students, and ESL students not needing support

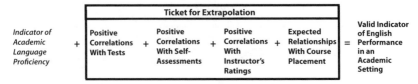

FIG. 9.13   Starting point (in italics) and backing that licenses traversal of the extrapolation inference in the TOEFL interpretive argument.

courses scored higher than those taking support classes. These differences were especially pronounced for speaking and writing. In the final field study, three groups of ESL students were identified. Two groups were taking some type of support class, either in an intensive English program or university ESL program. A third group was taking content courses at a college or university, but not ESL courses. TOEFL scores were found to differ significantly between the two groups requiring ESL support and the one that did not.

Overall, the findings from these studies supply backing for the assumption that performance on the new TOEFL is related to other criteria of language proficiency in academic contexts. The extrapolation bridge can be traversed on the basis of the relationships between TOEFL scores and other indicators of language performance in an academic context, as shown in Figure 9.13, and the result is a valid indicator of English language performance in an academic context. This intermediate conclusion provides the necessary starting point for the utilization inference.

UTILIZATION

Utilization is based on the warrant that estimates of the quality of performance in English-medium institutions of higher education are useful for making decisions about admissions and appropriate curriculum for test takers. As illustrated in Figure 9.14, this warrant is based on the assumptions that: the meaning of test scores is clearly interpretable by admissions officers, test takers, and teachers; and the test will have a positive influence on how English is taught. Some backing for both of these assumptions was provided in Chapter 8; however, this is necessarily an area of ongoing work in view of the fact that backing needs to be sought as the test is used.

The assumption that admissions officers, test takers, and teachers are able to interpret scores can be backed at this point by evidence that test users have access to materials to aid score interpretation. Backing comes from the information that Educational Testing Service has produced for admissions officers, teachers, and students. For example, information is given to test users to help them understand the relationships between the TOEFL CBT scores that the new TOEFL iBT scores will replace. Educational Testing Service cre-

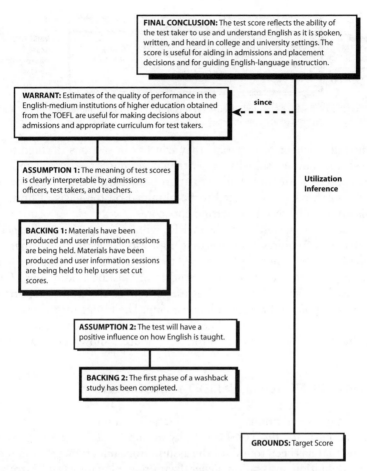

FIG. 9.14   Utilization inference with assumptions and backing.

ates these materials with the intention that test users and takers will benefit from understanding score interpretations. Additional research will be needed to provide stronger backing for the assumption that efforts in materials development lead to a better understanding and more appropriate use of test scores by stakeholders.

To help test users make appropriate decisions based on test scores, Educational Testing Service has produced materials and held information sessions to help test users set cut scores. As shown in Chapter 8, the process of cut-score setting is aided through the use of descriptors indicating the percentage of likelihood that a particular statement characterizes a test taker's capability. For example, other people are unlikely to understand a test taker who obtains a 6 on the TOEFL iBT speaking measure (i.e., with only a 50–65% probability) when he or she speaks English. Test users working to set cut

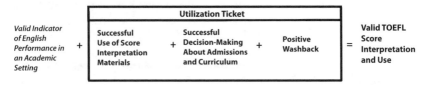

FIG. 9.15   Backing that will license traversal of the utilization inference in the TOEFL interpretive argument.

scores have the benefit of materials they can use in sessions devoted to setting cut scores that are suited to a particular setting. This type of information holds potential for contributing to appropriate, knowledgeable score use. More backing, however, will need to be obtained on the basis of how such materials are used by test users setting cut scores.

The second assumption, that the TOEFL will have a positive influence on English teaching, requires evidence that appropriate instructional materials are available and that they are being used to improve English language teaching. Backing will need to come from studies of washback after the TOEFL has been used; however, initial findings from one of the studies reported in Chapter 8 hold potential for providing backing. The bridge for the utilization inference is under construction. The assumptions have been identified, and the backing will need to come from the three sources shown in Figure 9.15.

SUMMING UP THE TOEFL VALIDITY ARGUMENT

The backing for assumptions that underlie the TOEFL interpretive argument provides the basis for the TOEFL validity argument. Table 9.5 summarizes the backing that has been found for the assumptions underlying the inferences of domain definition, evaluation, generalization, explanation, and extrapolation. The current backing for utilization is indicated as well, even though additional backing is needed through studies of score use and the consequences of TOEFL score use.

One reason the validity argument is presented in this volume is to state the justification for TOEFL score interpretation and use in a way that can be examined and critically evaluated. In presenting it, we are acting as proponents who are "stating the interpretive argument clearly, thereby demonstrating its coherence, and by providing adequate support for each of the inferences and assumptions in the interpretive argument" (Kane, 2004, p. 166). Such a presentation invites critics who can "challenge the appropriateness of the proposed goals and uses of the testing program... the adequacy of the interpretive argument, or the plausibility of the inferences and assumptions" (p. 166). Such critics are most likely to be applied linguists and educational measurement specialists, who—on the basis of additional research—might provide backing for rebuttals to the argument as it is presented in this chapter.

TABLE 9.5
The TOEFL Validity Argument Consisting of Backing for Inferences in the TOEFL
Interpretive Argument

Inference in the TOEFL Interpretive Argument	Warrant Licensing the Inference	Backing for Each Inference
Domain description	Observations of performance on the TOEFL reveal relevant knowledge, skills, and abilities in situations representative of those in the target domain of language use in the English-medium institutions of higher education.	1. Researchers in applied linguistics identified academic domain tasks. Research showed that teachers and learners thought these tasks were important. 2. Researchers in applied linguistics identified language abilities required for academic tasks. 3. A systematic process of task design and modeling was engaged by experts.
Evaluation	Observations of performance on TOEFL tasks are evaluated to provide observed scores reflective of targeted language abilities.	1. Rubrics were developed, trialed, and revised based on expert consensus. 2. Multiple task administration conditions were developed, trialed, and revised based on expert consensus. 3. Statistical characteristics of tasks and measures were monitored throughout the test development, and modifications in tasks and measures were made as needed.
Generalization	Observed scores are estimates of expected scores over the relevant parallel versions of tasks and test forms and across raters.	1. Results from reliability and generalizability studies indicated the number of tasks required. 2. A variety of task configurations was tried to find a stable configuration. 3. Various rating scenarios were examined to maximize efficiency. 4. An equating method was identified for the listening and the reading measures. 5. The ECD process yielded task shells for producing parallel tasks.
Explanation	Expected scores are attributed to a construct of academic language proficiency.	1. Examination of task completion processes and discourse supported the further development of and justification for specific tasks.

(continued)

TABLE 9.5
Continued

Inference in the TOEFL Interpretive Argument	Warrant Licensing the Inference	Backing for Each Inference
		2. Expected correlations were found among TOEFL measures and other tests.
		3. Expected correlations were found among measures within the test and expected factor structure.
		4. Results of research showed expected relationships with English learning.
Extrapolation	The construct of academic language proficiency as assessed by TOEFL accounts for the quality of linguistic performance in English-medium institutions of higher education.	Results indicate positive relationships between test performance and students' academic placement, test takers' self-assessments of their own language proficiency, and instructors' judgments of students' English language proficiency.
Utilization	Estimates of the quality of performance in the English-medium institutions of higher education obtained from the TOEFL are useful for making decisions about admissions and appropriate curriculum for test takers.	1. Educational Testing Service has produced materials and held test user information sessions. More backing is needed.
		2. Educational Testing Service has produced materials and held information sessions to help test users set cut scores. More backing is needed.
		3. The first phase of a washback study has been completed; results from this and other washback research is needed for backing.

This is the primary audience for the interpretive argument and validity argument outlined in this volume, but the messages about appropriate score interpretation and use are relevant beyond these audiences. Students, teachers, professors, and other stakeholders want to understand the TOEFL in the context of testing for English learners who are tested for admissions to English-medium universities. Ultimately, in fact, to build the backing for the utilization bridge, it is necessary for other audiences to understand the TOEFL validity argument. In this sense, the validity argument for the TOEFL can be seen from multiple perspectives (Cronbach, 1988) because it has many audiences. As Cronbach pointed out, the expression *validity argument*—rather than *validation research*—is intended to convey the fact that "validation speaks to a diverse and potentially critical audience" (p. 4). However, different audiences need differently packaged arguments (Cherryholmes, 1988).

The validity argument is presented in this volume in technical terms to an audience of specialists, but if the argument is to be made to a broader audience, it will have to be done in a more concise and transparent manner. Figure 9.16 offers a single schematic, intended to communicate to a broader audience the basis for TOEFL score use. It depicts a staircase constructed from the steps of the validity argument, each of which represents one inferential bridge. At the top of the steps is valid TOEFL score interpretation and use, consisting of decisions about readiness for academic language use. The bottom is the academic domain, the location where language proficiency is needed. At the top of each stair on the way up to valid score use is an intermediate conclusion in the argument, each one supported by the backing obtained through theoretical rationales and empirical research. One climbs the stairs one step

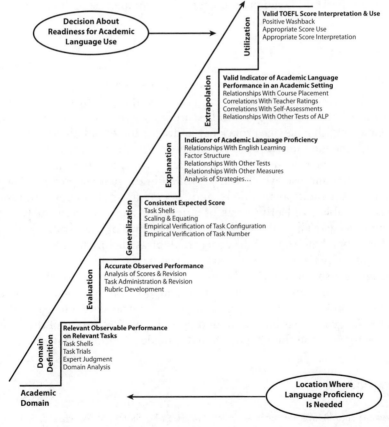

FIG. 9.16   Steps of the TOEFL validity argument, with a diagonal line showing the argument moving toward valid score interpretation and use.

at a time; one must ascend the whole structure to get to the top. The analogy is that the argument for valid score interpretation and use is a sequential one, in which each intermediate conclusion builds upon the prior one and is supported by backing specific to each inference.

The staircase is not intended to replace the validation articles presented in professional journals such as *Language Testing* or technical manuals that accompany tests. Instead, it provides a single image that includes the critical areas of support that are detailed through theory, research and data. It may be used as a basis for the story of TOEFL validation for different audiences to explain why the test tasks are constructed the way they are, why the test designers are confident that the language varieties included are appropriate, why the numbers of each type of task are acceptable, and how the test users can be confident that the score for an individual test taker is an accurate reflection of academic language proficiency. Test users raise questions about all of these issues in isolation, but the questions need to be answered in the context of the TOEFL validity argument—the complete staircase.

CONCLUSION

For the audience of applied linguists and measurement experts, the narrative of the TOEFL validity argument presented through this volume should demonstrate the validity of TOEFL score interpretation as an indicator of academic English language proficiency and score use for admissions decisions at English-medium universities. The coherence of the validity argument narrative rests in the statement of the interpretive argument that underlies score interpretation and use, which was presented in the first chapter. Because the inferences, warrants, assumptions, and backing are stated explicitly, professionals are able to identify areas of agreement and disagreement with the assumptions as well as the methods and substance of their backing. Recent developments that provided the conceptual infrastructure for defining the interpretive argument in this way have opened new possibilities to understand language assessments used in education and research. Professionals need both an integrated structure to organize test-related research results that pertain to validity and a clearly articulated argument to translate into terms that a broader range of constituents can understand. The description of the TOEFL validity argument in this chapter should provide a useful example.

REFERENCES

American Educational Research Association, American Psychological Association, & National Council on Measurement in Education. (1999). *Standards for educational and psychological testing.* Washington, DC: American Educational Research Association.

Anastasi, A. (1986). Evolving concepts of test validation. *Annual Review of Psychology, 37,* 1–15.

Angoff, W. H. (1988). Validity: An evolving concept. In H. Wainer & H. Braun (Eds.), *Test validity* (pp. 19–32). Hillsdale, NJ: Erlbaum.

Bachman, L. F. (1990). *Fundamental considerations in language testing.* Oxford: Oxford University Press.

Bachman, L. F., & Palmer, A. (1996). *Language testing in practice.* Oxford: Oxford University Press.

Bejar, I., Douglas, D., Jamieson, J., Nissan, S., & Turner, J. (2000). *TOEFL 2000 listening framework: A working paper* (TOEFL Monograph No. 19). Princeton, NJ: Educational Testing Service.

Briggs, D. C. (2004). Comment: Making an argument for design validity before interpretive validity. *Measurement, 2*(3), 171–174.

Brown, J. D. (1996). *Testing in language programs.* Upper Saddle River, NJ: Prentice Hall.

Brown, A., Iwashita, N., & McNamara, T. (2005). *An examination of rater orientations and test-taker performance on English for academic purposes speaking tasks* (TOEFL Monograph No. MS-29). Princeton, NJ: Educational Testing Service.

Butler, F. A., Eignor, D., Jones, S., McNamara, T., & Suomi, B. K. (2000). *TOEFL 2000 speaking framework: A working paper* (TOEFL Monograph No. 20). Princeton, NJ: Educational Testing Service.

Chapelle, C. A. (1999). Validation in language assessment. *Annual Review of Applied Linguistics, 19,* 254–272.

Chapelle, C., Grabe, W., & Berns, M. (1997). *Communicative language proficiency: Definition and implications for TOEFL 2000* (TOEFL Monograph No. 10). Princeton, NJ: Educational Testing Service.

Cherryholmes, C. (1988). Construct validity and the discourses of research. In C. Cherryholmes (Ed.), *Power and criticism: Poststructural investigations in education* (pp. 99–129). New York: Teachers College Press.

Cronbach, L. J. (1988). Five perspectives on validation argument. In H. Wainer & H. Braun (Eds.), *Test validity* (pp. 3–17). Hillsdale, NJ: Erlbaum.

Cronbach, L. J., & Meehl, P. E. (1955). Construct validity in psychological tests. *Psychological Bulletin, 52,* 281–302.

Cumming, A. (1996). Introduction: The concept of validation in language testing. In A. Cumming & R. Berwick (Eds.), *Validation in language testing.* Clevedon, UK: Multilingual Matters.

Cumming, A., Kantor, R., Baba, K., Eouanzoui, K., Erdosy, U., & James, M. (2006). *Analysis of discourse features and verification of scoring levels for independent and integrated prototype writing tasks for new TOEFL* (TOEFL Monograph No. MS-30). Princeton, NJ: Educational Testing Service.

Cumming, A., Kantor, R., & Powers, D. E. (2001). *Scoring TOEFL essays and TOEFL 2000 prototype tasks: An investigation into raters' decision making and development of a preliminary analytic framework* (TOEFL Monograph Series, Rep. No. 22). Princeton, NJ: Educational Testing Service.

Cumming, A., Kantor, R., & Powers, D. E. (2002). Decision making while rating ESL/EFL writing tasks: A descriptive framework. *Modern Language Journal, 86,* 67–96.

Cumming, A., Kantor, R., Powers, D., Santos, T., & Taylor, C. (2000). *TOEFL 2000 writing framework: A working paper* (TOEFL Monograph No. 18). Princeton, NJ: Educational Testing Service.

Douglas, D. (1997). *Testing speaking ability in academic contexts: Theoretical considerations* (TOEFL Monograph No. 8). Princeton, NJ: Educational Testing Service.

Educational Testing Service. (2002). *The ETS standards for quality and fairness.* Princeton, NJ: Author.

Embretson, S. (1983). Construct validity: Construct representation versus nomothetic span. *Psychological Bulletin, 93*(1), 179–197.

Enright, M. K., Grabe, W., Koda, K., Mosenthal, P., Mulcahy-Ernt, P., & Schedl, M. (2000). *TOEFL 2000 reading framework: A working paper* (TOEFL Monograph No. 17). Princeton, NJ: Educational Testing Service.

Enright, M. K., & Schedl, M. (1999). *Reading to learn and reading to integrate* (internal report). Princeton, NJ: Educational Testing Service.

Ginther, A., & Grant, L. (1996). *A review of the academic needs of native English-speaking college students in the United States* (TOEFL Monograph No. 1). Princeton, NJ: Educational Testing Service.

Hale, G. A., Taylor, C., Bridgeman, B., Carson, J., Kroll, B., & Kantor, R. (1996). *A study of writing tasks assigned in academic degree programs* (TOEFL Research Rep. No. 54). Princeton, NJ: Educational Testing Service.

Hamp-Lyons, L., & Kroll, B. (1996). *TOEFL 2000—Writing: Composition, community, and assessment* (TOEFL Monograph No. 5). Princeton, NJ: Educational Testing Service.

Hudson, T. (1996). *Assessing second language academic reading from a communicative competence perspective: Relevance for TOEFL 2000* (TOEFL Monograph No. 4). Princeton, NJ: Educational Testing Service.

Jamieson, J., Jones, S., Kirsch, I., Mosenthal, P., & Taylor, C. (2000). *TOEFL 2000 framework: A working paper* (TOEFL Monograph No. 16). Princeton, NJ: Educational Testing Service.

Kane, M. T. (1992). An argument-based approach to validity. *Psychological Bulletin, 112,* 527–535.

Kane, M. T. (2001). Current concerns in validity theory. *Journal of Educational Measurement, 38,* 319–342.

Kane, M. T. (2004). Certification testing as an illustration of argument-based validation. *Measurement, 2*(3), 135–170.

Kane, M. T. (2006). Validation. In R. Brennen, (Ed.), *Educational measurement* (4th ed.). Westport, CT: Greenwood Publishing.

Kunnan, A. J. (1998). Approaches to validation in language assessment. In A. J. Kunnan (Ed.), *Validation in language assessment* (pp. 1–16). Mahwah, NJ: Erlbaum.

Messick, S. (1989). Validity. In R. Linn (Ed.), *Educational measurement* (3rd ed., pp. 13–103). New York: Macmillan.

Mislevy, R. J. (2004). Toulmin and beyond: Commentary on Michael Kane's "Certification testing as an illustration of argument-based validation," *Measurement: Interdisciplinary Research and Perspectives, 2*(3), 185–191.

Mislevy, R. J., Steinberg, L. S., & Almond, R. G. (2003). On the structure of educational assessments. *Measurement: Interdisciplinary Research and Perspectives, 1,* 3–62.

Moss, P. A. (1992). Shifting conceptions of validity in educational measurement: Implications for performance assessment. *Review of Educational Research, 62,* 229-258.

Oller, J. (1979). *Language tests at school.* London: Longman.

Rosenfeld, M., Leung, P., & Oltman, P. K. (2001). *The reading, writing, speaking, and listening tasks important for academic success at the undergraduate and graduate levels* (TOEFL Monograph No. 21). Princeton, NJ: Educational Testing Service.

Rubin, J. (1993). *TOEFL 2000: Listening in an academic setting* (internal TOEFL 2000 report). Princeton, NJ: Educational Testing Service.

Shepard, L. (1993). Evaluating test validity. *Review of Research in Education, 19,* 405–450.

Waters, A. (1996). *A review of research into needs in English for academic purposes of relevance to the North American higher education context* (TOEFL Monograph No. 6). Princeton, NJ: Educational Testing Service.

Weir, C. J. (2005). *Language testing and validation: An evidence-based approach.* Hampshire, UK: Palgrave Macmillan.

Zhang, Y. (2006, October 13). *Statistical review of the TOEFL iBT April-June 2006 administrations.* Paper presented at the TOEFL Committee of Examiners Meeting, Philadelphia.

A

1995 Working Assumptions that Underlie an Initial TOEFL® 2000 Design Framework

From *TOEFL 2000 Design Framework: A Working Draft* by M. Schedl, 1995, Princeton, NJ: Educational Testing Service. Copyright 1995 by Educational Testing Service. Reprinted with permission.

GENERAL CONSTRAINTS/ASSUMPTIONS

1. The current target date for completion of the test design framework and construction of test(s) ready for large-scale pilot testing is the fall of 1997 with operational test delivery by or before 2000.
2. The test will be delivered to countries and regions currently served by the TOEFL® program, with the possibility of expanded delivery.
3. Research and design efforts will continue while the study of potential impact of a computer-based test (CBT) continues.
4. The test purpose will remain the same as the current TOEFL—for admissions decisions. This will drive test design and validation efforts.[1]
5. Test security will continue to be maintained through test design and test administration efforts.
6. A number of distinct or overlapping item pools will be required to minimize item exposure; thus, replicability of test items and tasks is essential.
7. A single test design will be created rather than separate undergraduate and graduate modules or discipline-specific modules because:
   - the cost of multiple designs is prohibitive
   - procedures for establishing score comparability across test based on different designs are problematic in application
   - academic levels and discipline distinctions are not consistent across the range of institutions that use TOEFL scores

8. The cost of the test will be controlled. Current feedback from score users suggests $75 as a maximum test fee for the near future.

9. Scores will be reported within the same time limits as the current program, and, ideally, cycle time for score reporting will be reduced.

10. Actual testing time will not exceed 3 hours. (The current TOEFL with TWE® is approximately 2½ hours.)

11. Assume that continuous improvement in the test beyond 2000 will be possible.

CONTENT AND CONSTRUCT ASSUMPTIONS

1. Test design efforts will be guided by the TOEFL COE model of communicative language use in an academic context.

2. TOEFL 2000 will include measures of listening and reading comprehension, direct measure(s) of writing, and, if feasible, direct measure(s) of speaking.

3. TOEFL 2000 will be a test of general English proficiency in an academic context, not English for special purposes.[2]

4. Test tasks will approximate authentic academic English tasks to the extent possible.

5. Stimulus material from a variety of topic areas will be used.[3]

6. Extended discourse will be included, to the extent possible, as stimulus material.

7. Construction of items with limited context will be guided by construct rationale. Such items will be included primarily for the purpose of improving test reliability and domain coverage.

8. Some items that integrate comprehension and production may be included. Note 5 under scoring and psychometric assumptions.

9. Study skills (e.g., note-taking and use of reference materials) will not be assessed.

10. North American English will be the form of English that is represented in the test.

11. Visuals and audio will occur wherever needed throughout test (i.e., where they occur as a natural accompaniment to the verbal or written material).

12. Both participatory and nonparticipatory language situations (e.g., lectures and classroom discussions) will be represented in the stimulus material.

13. A variety of item types will be included. Competencies will be tested multiple times in multiple ways.

14. The purpose of a test task and a general notion of how it will be evaluated (our expectations about performance) will be explicitly stated for examinees.

NOTES

1. Uses other than to inform admissions decisions may be possible. Users will be responsible for validation of test for other test purposes, perhaps with guidelines for local validity studies from the program.
2. Population too diverse in terms of special English needs. Research indicates fairness and comparability issues involved in subject-specific modules.
3. Fairness issue; variety decreases an individual's chance of being uniquely disadvantaged or advantaged by having familiarity with particular topics, vocabulary, and subject area content.

Summary of 1995 Research Recommendations

From *Research Recommendations for the TOEFL 2000 Project* by J. D. Brown, K. Perkins, and J. Upshur, 1995, Princeton, NJ: Educational Testing Service. Copyright 1995 by Educational Testing Service. Reprinted with permission.

Type	Questions
1. Construct/domain	What linguistic components belong in the test?
2. Construct/domain	What should the test tasks be? Should they be skill-based and/or integrated?
3. Construct/domain	How much additional information is gained by skill/task integration?
4. Construct/domain	What item types are proper indicators of the construct within tasks?
5. Task validity	What types of academic language tasks ought to be sampled?
6. Task validity	To what degree are the tasks that are developed for TOEFL 2000 valid?
7. Task validity	How do native speakers perform on the test tasks?
8. Task reliability	How equivalent can test tasks be made?
9. Task reliability	How long should the test tasks be to produce reliable results?
10. Task reliability	To what degree do length and type affect the way tasks function?
11. Task reliability	How short can modules be and still accommodate the TOEFL COE's model?
12. Task reliability	How many test tasks are needed for a reliable/generalizable TOEFL 2000?
13. Task reliability	How many topics are needed for a reliable/generalizable TOEFL 2000?
14. Task fairness	To what degree are test tasks unfair to undergraduate students in favor of graduate students?

Type	Questions
15. Task fairness	To what degree are test tasks unfair to EFL-trained students?
16. Task fairness	To what degree are test tasks unfair to lower proficiency examinees?
17. Delivery	To what degree are enhanced TOEFL results affected by the fact that students know that the modules being piloted are experimental?
18. Delivery	How effective[a] are TOEFL 2000 module results when administered with enhanced TOEFL?
19. Delivery	How effective[a] are TOEFL 2000 module results if incorporated in the enhanced TOEFL results?
20. Delivery	To what degree are the test results from paper-based and computer delivery comparable for both the enhanced TOEFL and TOEFL 2000 pilot modules?

Note. Enhanced TOEFL became TOEFL CBT.
[a] The term *effective* is used to encompass issues such as item discriminability, as well as test reliability and validity.

Timeline of TOEFL® Origins and the New TOEFL Project—Key Efforts and Decisions

TOEFL Origins, 1961–1992	
1961	A conference sponsored by Center for Applied Linguistics, Institute of International Education, and National Association of Foreign Student Advisors resulted in a decision to create a centralized testing program to assess international students' English proficiency. The conference outlined the test design and delivery.
1962	National Council on the Testing of English as a Foreign Language was formed and composed of representatives of more than 30 private organizations and government agencies concerned with English proficiency of foreign students in the United States and Canada.
1963	Ford and Danforth Foundations provided initial funding to launch the TOEFL test, with the program managed by the Modern Language Association.
1964	The first TOEFL test was administered at 57 test centers with 920 test candidates registered for the test.
1965	ETS and the College Board were given responsibility for operations and finances of the new testing program. The program moved to ETS in Princeton.
1966	TOEFL program began collecting evidence of validity (e.g., Angoff & Sharon, 1970; Maxell, 1965; Upshur 1966).
1967	The TOEFL COE was formed to oversee test design and content.
1973	A new agreement was reached whereby ETS was given responsibility for operations and finances and reported to the TOEFL Policy Council, composed of members of the College Board, Graduate Record Examinations Board, and other representatives of agencies and universities concerned with the admissions of international students to colleges and universities in the United States and Canada.
1974	An ad hoc committee on research was established.

1975–1976	The test was changed from a 5-section to a 3-section test, and a sample test was introduced.
1977–1978	The TOEFL program began research on a speaking proficiency test.
1978	The TOEFL Research Committee was formed to create a research agenda, review research proposals and reports, and recommend funding to the TOEFL Policy Council. The chair of the TOEFL COE served on the TOEFL Research Committee. The chair of the TOEFL Research Committee was also a member of the TOEFL Policy Council. Funds were designated within the program budget to support ongoing research.
1979	The TSE was introduced under the direction of the TOEFL COE.
1981	The TOEFL program began identifying the need for a direct measure of writing proficiency (e.g., Angelis, 1982; Bridgeman & Carlson, 1983; Hale & Hinofotis, 1981).
1984	The TOEFL program hosted an invitational conference on communicative competence in the TOEFL context.
1984–1985	The TOEFL Policy Council approved funding for the development of a writing test to be added to the TOEFL.
1985	The TWE Committee was formed to develop and approve tasks for the new writing test. The chair of the committee also served as a member of the TOEFL COE.
1986	The TWE was introduced under the direction of the TOEFL COE.
1986–1990	The TOEFL COE and Research Committee continued to elaborate research agendas, provide oversight for the TOEFL, TSE, and TWE, and discuss implications of communicative competence for TOEFL test design.
1988	The TOEFL COE held a blue-sky meeting on how to make the TSE more responsive to a communicative assessment of oral language proficiency.
1991	A group of oral language experts was invited to ETS to consider theoretical implications for a revised TSE.
1992	The TSE committee was formed to revise the TSE based on a more communicative model of oral language proficiency with a more holistic scoring model.

The New TOEFL Project, 1990–1996

1990–1996	The TOEFL COE began devoting a portion of each meeting to discuss a new test. The TOEFL COE, the TOEFL Research Committee, and the TOEFL Policy Committee provided oversight and advice for the project as they continued to meet two or more times annually.
Spring 1992	The TOEFL COE proposed a new test and presented a draft of a working model of communicative language proficiency to the TOEFL Policy Council.
Fall 1992	The TOEFL COE and TOEFL Research Committee met jointly with ETS officers. ETS committed to the project. The TOEFL Policy Council approved the launch of the TOEFL 2000 development project and provided funding support. ETS created an internal development team, the TOEFL 2000 project team, consisting of members from program direction, test development, statistical analysis, and research.

1993	A subgroup of the TOEFL COE wrote a monograph that detailed their working model (Chapelle et al., 1997).
	The TOEFL 2000 project team distributed the Chapelle et al. (1997) draft and commissioned reviews related to constructs:
	• Douglas, 1997
	• Hamp-Lyons & Kroll, 1996
	• Hudson, 1996
	• Rubin, 1993
	TOEFL program staff and an external research consultant conducted a series of score user focus groups, telephone interviews, and a written survey to determine score user needs.
1994	The TOEFL 2000 project team commissioned additional reviews:
	• Gough, 1993.
	• Powell, 2001
	• Bailey, 1999
	• Ginther & Grant, 1996
	• Hansen & Willut, 1998
	• Taylor, 1994
	• Waters, 1996
	• Burstein et al., 1999
	• Frase et al., 1997
	• Grant & Ginther, 1995
Fall 1994	The TOEFL 2000 project team met with Bachman, Alderson, and Swain to critique the commissioned reviews and plan next steps. Results of meeting and other reviews concluded that the work to date had not resulted in a test framework or clear blueprint of development work needed to create and validate a new test.
Spring 1995	The TOEFL 2000 project team with a subgroup of the TOEFL COE created several testing modules that incorporated features of the COE model and included thematically linked texts as well as integrated and performance-based tasks.
Summer 1995	ETS decided to move TOEFL to a computer-based test (TOEFL CBT) and incorporated possible test enhancements based on a release date of 2000.
	The TOEFL 2000 project team met with Brown, Perkins, and Upshur to build a research plan for the next phase of the project.
Fall 1995	ETS moved the TOEFL 2000 project to the Research division during its research and development phase.
Fall 1995–Fall 1996	Some members of the project team were charged with conducting the foundational research to inform TOEFL CBT design, and others were reassigned to develop the TOEFL CBT:
	• Kirsch, Jamieson, Taylor, & Eignor, 1998
	• Taylor, Jamieson, Eignor, & Kirsch, 1998
	• Eignor, Taylor, Jamieson, & Kirsch, 1998
	• Jamieson, Taylor, Kirsch, & Eignor, 1999
Fall 1996	A new development team was assembled to create a working framework for the new test (Jamieson et al., 2000).

Index

Page numbers in italics refer to Figures or Tables.